The Politics of Organized Crime and the Organized Crime of Politics

Critical Perspectives on Crime and Inequality

Series Editor
Walter S. DeKeseredy, University of Ontario Institute of Technology

Advisory Board
Shahid Alvi, University of Ontario Institute of Technology
Meda Chesney-Lind, University of Hawaii at Manoa
Mark Israel, Flinders University of South Australia
Barbara Perry, University of Ontario Institute of Technology
Claire Renzetti, Saint Joseph's University
Martin Schwartz, Ohio University

Critical Perspectives on Crime and Inequality presents cutting edge work informed by these schools of thought: feminism, peacemaking criminology, left realism, Marxism, cultural criminology, and postmodernism. In an age of instrumental reason and increasing state control, the need for critical and independent analysis of power and social arrangements has never been more acute. Books published in this series will be monographs for scholars and researchers, as well as texts for course use.

Titles in Series:

The Politics of Organized Crime and the Organized Crime of Politics

A Study in Criminal Power

Alfredo Schulte-Bockholt

LEXINGTON BOOKS

A division of
ROWMAN & LITTLEFIELD PUBLISHERS, INC.
Lanham • Boulder • New York • Toronto • Oxford

LEXINGTON BOOKS

A division of Rowman & Littlefield Publishers, Inc.
A wholly owned subsidary of The Rowman & Littlefield Publishing Group, Inc.
4501 Forbes Boulevard, Suite 200
Lanham, MD 20706

PO Box 317
Oxford
OX2 9RU, UK

British Library Cataloguing in Publication Information Available

Library of Congress Cataloging-in-Publication Data

Schulte-Bockholt, Alfredo, 1961–
   The politics of organized crime and the organized crime of politics : a study in criminal
power / Alfredo Schulte-Bockholt.
      p. cm. —(Critical perspectives on crime and inequality)
   Includes bibliographical references and index.
   ISBN-13 978-0-7391-0869-7 (cloth : alk. paper)
   ISBN-10 0-7391-0869-7 (cloth : alk. paper)
   ISBN-13 978-0-7391-1358-5 (pbk. : alk. paper)
   ISBN-10 0-7391-1358-5 (pbk. : alk. paper)
   1. Organized crime. 2. Organized crime—Government policy. 3. Elite (Social sciences)
4. Power (Social sciences) 5. Political corruption. 6. Transnational crime. I. Title. II.
Series.
HV6441.S38 2006
364.106—dc22   2005027902

Printed in the United States of America

⊛™ The paper used in this publication meets the minimum requirements of American
National Standard for Information Sciences—Permanence of Paper for Printed Library
Materials, ANSI/NISO Z39.48–1992.

TABLE OF CONTENTS

Preface and Acknowledgments

The work on this book began in the summer of 1992 following the completion of my master's thesis in the Department of Political Science at the University of Guelph, Ontario, Canada. After having received an invitation to live with Colombian friends whom I had met on a previous excursion to South America, I went to stay in Cali, Colombia, between August 1992 and late April 1993 with the objective to find and research a suitable topic for a doctoral dissertation. Initially, I planned to investigate the links between the country's drug traffickers and Marxist rebel organizations. I quickly realized that such links indeed existed, but they paled in comparison to the far more elaborate ties between criminal organizations and the elites of that country, the dominant political forces, the Liberal and Conservative parties, and the military.

Already during an earlier visit to Colombia in 1988, I observed the pervasive influence the so-called drug cartels had over society. Through my conversations with Colombians of many different backgrounds, it became evident that the participation of criminals in public life was an accepted fact. At the time, Pablo Escobar Gaviria, the notorious *Medellín Cartel* leader, enjoyed the reputation of a Robin Hood. Many viewed him and other traffickers as Colombian nationalists who invested their savings in the country and created jobs. Colombians were willing to overlook the cartels' deadly violence against selected targets such as judges, police officers, left-wing activists, or journalists. I encountered individuals who, although they were not involved in any illegal activities themselves, proudly extolled the traffickers to be economic success stories similar to those of the so-called American robber barons of the nineteenth century. Others excused drug trafficking as a way to get even for the perceived economic exploitation at the hands of the United States. By 1992–1993, the mood had changed considerably, because of the growing violence employed by those in the trade. The assassins of the *Medellín Cartel* had mounted a quasi-civil war against the Colombian government which involved a ruthless bombing campaign that cost the lives of hundreds of military and police personnel and innocent bystanders. Other activities included the 'social cleansing' activities in Colombia's cities, and the large-scale massacres of peasants by cartel-financed paramilitaries in the countryside.

After completing the research in Colombia I spent an additional year in Germany where I read up on much of the journalistic literature on organized crime.

In the fall of 1994, following my acceptance into the Ph.D. program at Carleton University in Ottawa, Canada, I turned my attention to the academic literature.[1] Having observed the relations between criminal and societal actors in Colombia, and having come across numerous descriptions of such links in the literature on criminal organizations in other countries, it was a surprise to discover that most of the scholars who work on organized crime–related issues in North America tended to deny that such organizations had ideological links to groups in power, or even developed such ties. It was evident that corruption alone was not a satisfactory explanation for the links between the two, although it was clearly an important factor.

My work received fresh impetus through the discovery of various papers written by Max Horkheimer and Theodor Adorno of the Frankfurt School of Critical Theory who equated Fascist practices with those of organized crime. In these writings the two scholars utilized the concept of the protection racket, a traditional mode of income for criminal organizations, and argued that societies were simultaneously protected and exploited by rackets and powerful cliques. According to Horkheimer and Adorno, the racket was a historical principle that manifested itself differently in accordance with time and place. Fascism, they argued, was merely the most evolved variant of repression. Most of their essays were written in the late 1930s and early 1940s; however, Horkheimer (1982; 1988f) returned to the topic of the racket on numerous occasions throughout his life and wrote on it as late as 1969, a few years before his death in 1973. A 1941 play by German playwright Bertolt Brecht (1965; 1987) titled *Der aufhaltsame Aufstieg des Arturo Ui* [The Resistible Rise of Arturo Ui], which transfers the takeover of Germany by the National Socialists under Adolf Hitler into an organized crime setting in the United States, also proved to be stimulating literature. While the above authors contended that Fascism and Nazism displayed some similarities to organized crime, I reversed the argument.

In 1996 and 1997, I spent a total of three months in Peru researching the drug trade, particularly the relations between that country's military and criminal organizations during the civil war against the Maoist rebels of the Shining Path. While my previous stay in Colombia had required a low profile approach and had a rather informal character, the fieldwork in Peru was more planned and co-ordinated. Not only did I interview Peruvian officials and experts, I also had the friendly assistance of the staff of the country's opposition daily *La República* as well as access to its archives. In addition, I researched at other institutes such as the Centro de Estudio y Promoción del Desarrollo (DESCO). The studies done in Peru reconfirmed many of my initial assumptions about the ideological links between criminal actors and elites in society.

The time I spent in Peru also filled me with great admiration for journalists who engaged in dangerous investigations on organized crime and government

vii

corruption, and who continued with this dangerous work, even when their lives had been threatened. My thanks go to the members of the investigative unit of *La República* to whom I dedicate this volume.

I would never have decided to start and complete a doctoral degree had it not been for the late Bill Graf, professor of political science at the University of Guelph, Ontario, to whom I dedicate this work as well. Bill supervised my honors and master's theses on German-German relations and German unification, which I completed in 1990 and 1992, respectively, and he inspired me to take the next step in my academic career. While I did not become a scholar of German and European affairs as he had hoped, he encouraged me on my new path and helped me with insightful comments on my early papers on organized crime. His untimely death in the mid-1990s not only ended a fruitful intellectual relationship but also a personal friendship.

I want to thank Sandra Bell, Diane Crocker, John McMullan, Madine VanderPlaat, Evangelia Tastsoglou, and Henry Veltmeyer from the Department of Sociology and Criminology; Jim Cameron from the Department of Psychology; Elizabeth Haigh and Bill Sewell from the Department of History; all professors at Saint Mary's University in Halifax, Nova Scotia, Canada, for their helpful commentaries during the various stages of this project. I am indebted to Prof. Walter DeKeseredy, now at the University of Ontario – Institute of Technology, who educated me on the possibilities in criminology, when none existed in political science. Many thanks go to my graduate research assistants David MacDonald and Jan Cavicchi who helped with the proofreading. A great many thanks are due to Lindia Smith whose assistance for the final manuscript was invaluable. Likewise, I would like to thank the editor at Lexington Books for the superb job done.

I am greatly indebted to my friend Peter Meisenheimer from Guelph, Ontario, Canada, who writes for the *Guelph Mercury*, a regional newspaper. Peter not only greatly refined the English usage in my honors thesis many years ago, but he again undertook the same task with my book. English is not my first language, and Peter's mastery of the idiom has once again taught me many things on its most effective application. And he did so for a mere four dinners in restaurants of his choice in the city of Guelph.

Luis Augusto Sepulveda, a human rights lawyer and political refugee from Colombia, deserves mention for the insights provided on the tormented state of his country. Thanks are also due to Alice Hum from the Saint Mary's University Library for her help in teaching me the differences between the traditional rendering of Chinese names and places into English and the *Pinyin* system that is used today. Ron Houlihan deserves mention for stocking up the Saint Mary's library with organized crime literature. Thanks to Casper, Craig, and Scott for cheering me up during those times when I felt I could not take another look at the manuscript.

My parents, Arnulf and Angela Schulte-Bockholt, who are now retired in

Germany, deserve many thanks for their patience and aid in times of need. Most of my appreciation is due to my comrade-in-life, Claire Hodge, who gave me much needed support, while burdened with work on her own career.

Endnotes

1. Organized crime is largely a men's world. While a few women may make it into leadership positions within an organized crime group, they generally occupy inferior ones. They are participants in the criminal economies from which organized crime groups profit, such as work as prostitutes or drug mules. Women also play minor roles as lovers, wives, or other female relatives of criminals. As an area of research organized crime is also largely controlled by men who write about men, a predicament from which much of criminology suffers already. Conversely, the work done by the few women researchers in this field I have come across during my research is quite superb, if not much better than what is produced by many of their male colleagues. To name two scholars whose work is impressive: Venezuelan social scientist Rosa del Olmo writes in Spanish, and only a few of her works have been translated into English. Still, she has published on a diverse number of issues related to organized crime in Latin America including international drug trafficking, the links between underdevelopment and drugs, international law enforcement, or the role of women as drug mules. Del Olmo also publishes in the general field of international development studies. Louise I. Shelley, in my judgment, has established herself as one of the leading US scholars in the field although I strongly disagree with some of her conclusions. Not only has she contributed to the literature on crime and development, her earlier publications also include many works on crime in the former Soviet Union which betray a profound knowledge of that country's system of justice and its trappings. More recently, she has published on organized crime in the former USSR. This suggests — at least to me — that female scholars from criminology and other social sciences should indeed get involved in this field, as more gender-specific research is certainly needed on issues such as the role of women in organized crime–related professions, while the field can only profit from more female scholarship in general.

Chapter 1

Foreword

Nothing's invented, nothing's new
Or made to order just for you.
The gangster play that we present
Is known to our whole continent.

(Bertolt Brecht. 1987. *The Resistible Rise of Arturo Ui*, Prologue)

This chapter provides a brief survey of the most important theoretical perspectives on organized crime, as well as some thoughts on the complex nature of the phenomenon and ensuing consequences for research and study.

Introduction

The late Cyril M. Kornbluth (1982) wrote a science fiction novel called *The Syndic*, a satirical look at a future North American society dominated by criminal fraternities. The organized crime (OC) depicted in the novel is highly unconventional and has little in common with people's general perception of the phenomenon. In *The Syndic*, mafia 'freedom fighters,' following their victory in "the Second American Revolution" against an oppressive government, establish a radical libertarian order based on the credo of a Al 'Scarface' Capone: Give the people what they want (1982: 7−15; 54).

The United States (US) is separated along a north-south divide into Syndic and Mob territories. The Syndic's territory is a comfortable place that has enjoyed peace and prosperity for a century. It has no military but relies on a citizens militia; it has social assistance and health systems maintained by voluntary contributions (*ibid.*, 200−201). The police cooperate with the mafia to control violent crime (*ibid.*, 17−18). The existing political system is undemocratic, though, because social mobility and access to positions of power depend on both 'family connections' and talent (*ibid.*, 197−198).

The American government, torn by internal squabbles, lingers in Icelandic exile; its activities on the continent largely reduced to "a little commerce-raiding and a few coastal attacks" (*ibid.*, 52). One mafia leader characterizes past government as "brutal taxation, extirpation of gambling, denial of life's simple pleasures to the poor and severe limitation of them to all but the wealthy, sexual prudery viciously enforced by penal laws of appalling barbarity, endless regulation and coercion governing every waking minute of the day. . . . " (*ibid.*, 53).

The exiled government in Iceland has an equally reviled image. One of the novel's characters observes: "The Government had degenerated into a dawn-age monster, specialized all to teeth and claws and muscles to drive them with. The Government was now, whatever it had been, a graceless, humorless incarnate ferocity" (*ibid.*, 99–100).

The Syndic is an engaging work as the author speculates about a world turned upside down. Kornbluth switches polarity and turns the state into a negative entity and organized crime into a positive one. By emphasizing the state's disagreeable aspects, it is portrayed as a coercive and murderous apparatus to which the sloppy regime imposed by criminals compares quite favorably. Kornbluth's futuristic vision of a mafia-run society belongs in the realm of science fiction. The organized crime depicted is not oppressive, and, for the most part, its rule is based on the consent of the governed. Conversely, this work aims to illustrate that organized crime groups are far more likely to be part of repressive ruling structures which do not have the approval of the governed.

The Evolution of a Project

This work developed from my doctoral dissertation entitled *Organized Crime Groups, Elites, and the State*, which I completed at the Department of Political Science at Carleton University in Ottawa, Canada, in 1999–2000. Political scientists — with few exceptions such as US scholar Peter A. Lupsha — have until recently ignored, or at least underestimated, the role of criminal organizations as actors in national and international affairs. In the words of one member of the discipline, research on organized crime is for 'cops and criminologists,' not for those of his or her own kind. If political science is the study of politics and government, this position is indeed unfortunate.[1] Consider, for example, the late Pablo Escobar's apparent ability and willingness to pay Colombia's foreign debts, or the activities of death squads who are responsible for large-scale human rights abuses and who are financed by Latin American drug lords.

Political scientists should not be averse to studying organized crime. Certainly, the research, particularly if it involves fieldwork, may expose the scholar to dangers he or she would not face with a more conventional project. But political scientists confront such challenges when researching the practices of unsavory regimes at close proximity. My own endeavors which included fieldwork in Peru and

Colombia lead me to believe that close-up inspections can indeed produce useful results if undertaken with a few precautions. These include maintaining a low profile, familiarity with local conditions, 'connections' and reliance on local protection, as well as something approaching fluency in a country's language. Language knowledge encompasses not only the ability to understand a given tongue but also the vernacular of the milieu. In addition, those researching organized crime and other potentially dangerous subjects may rely on the insights of others who 'get close' to this object of study. Journalists dedicated to exposing organized crime and government corruption can be especially great sources of information.

Another reason for the general absence of political scientists from the study of organized crime groups as political actors may be the uncertainties one encounters in the research. Organized crime is a complex phenomenon while valid information can be difficult to obtain. Even so, the problem of determining, for example, precise amounts for the drug profits repatriated to Colombia or Peru during the 1990s should not prevent scholars from coming to certain conclusions about their effects on these societies. In a similar vein, political scientists may be concerned about producing conspiracy theory merely because they discovered an uncomfortable truth. One example would be the participation of the secret service agencies of several nations in international narcotics trafficking. By doing so, they have contributed to the global drug trade as it presently exists. All the same, the scholar, not unlike the criminal investigator, is compelled to follow the technique prescribed by Arthur Conan Doyle's famous fictional hero Sherlock Holmes, namely that once one has "eliminated the impossible, whatever remains, however improbable, must be the truth" (Doyle 1987: 185).[2]

This work began in August 1992, when I arrived in Cali, Colombia, where I stayed for approximately eight months with Colombian friends. Given the generally perilous situation in that country — my arrival coincided with the hunt for Pablo Escobar who was killed in late 1993 — I engaged in what may be described as 'Colombian immersion.' For reasons of my personal safety — and that of others — I did not openly research the drug trade and those involved in it. Instead, I began by collecting data from the country's media and press and allowed the situation to develop from there. And it certainly developed. For example, I — along with my Colombian hosts — would be invited to social gatherings that were also attended by persons involved with the *Cali Cartel*. After a few months, I had encountered a good number of individuals who in some form or another were or had been, entangled in the cartel's activities. These ranged from taxi drivers who acted as lookouts, to lawyers who defended traffickers, to persons who served as armed escorts for drug transports, to retired military officers who had received bribes from members of the cartel while on active duty.

Through my hosts I met an ex-major of the Colombian army who invited me to join him and his family to attend an Andean music festival. En route, I was informed that the lodgings for the night would be in the huge villa of a retired drug trafficker. While the owner of the premises was absent, my acquaintance pointed out that he and his family had free access to the villa and could come and go whenever they pleased in repayment for a favor he had provided to the trafficker during his time as an active officer in his country's military. He did not elaborate on the nature of the services he had furnished, and I thought it was impolite to ask. Indeed, the heavily armed guards at the gate of the property allowed us to enter late at night after the aforementioned musical event with few questions asked. In the morning, I discovered that the absent landlord had invested much of his illicit income in about two dozen Arabian horses.

On another occasion, my Cali hosts and I went on a road trip that took us to another large mansion in the Andes which had formerly been inhabited by a trafficker and his family. The property also included several small cabins for the trafficker's bodyguards and servants, a full-sized soccer field, and a horse stable. I was told that this individual had 'cheated' his associates in the cartel out of several million dollars worth of cocaine. Once his theft had been discovered, cartel members allegedly sent a small army to the abovementioned location. Not only was the trafficker killed along with a dozen of his security guards, all members of his family living in the house and relatives in other locations were slain as well. On the same day, cartel leaders also sent out teams of assassins to murder all members of his wife's family. Only his spouse survived, as she was not in the country at the time of the massacre. I can neither deny nor confirm the truthfulness of this account; however, I did observe hundreds of bullet holes as well as blood stains on the walls of the property. I presumed them to be bullet holes because they looked identical to cavities I observed on buildings during visits to Berlin, Germany, and Budapest, Hungary, in 1989–1990. These markings still remained from the fighting between Soviet and German forces during World War II. In addition, I came across various instances in the literature on Colombian drug traffickers which pointed out that cartel members punished those who had betrayed them by killing not only the culprits but all of their kindred as well to avoid the possibility that a relative of the slain would take revenge on them years later.

In 1996 and 1997, I spent altogether three months in Peru researching the drug trade. I chose Peru for several reasons. First, in both Colombia and Peru exists a nexus between drug traffickers, Marxist insurgents, and coca-growing peasants. Second, having received threats in Colombia in 1993, despite the low-profile approach chosen for my research, I decided that it would be preferable to watch that country's reality from the safer distance of neighboring Peru. For this purpose, I traveled to Lima in August of 1996, to prepare a longer research stay the following year. In 1996, I made contacts with the country's experts on drug trafficking and organized crime. More important, I began a fruitful collaboration with several journalists from the country's daily newspaper, *La República*. I was provided with access to the newspaper's extensive archives and was given much useful information by the members of its special investigative unit on organized crime and government corruption.

The journeys to Peru also turned out to be more interesting than I initially anticipated because the journalists I worked with had received threats themselves for exposing government corruption and the links between the country's military and drug trafficking groups. In August 1996, I conducted close to two dozen preliminary interviews with Peruvian experts on drug trafficking, organized crime, and terrorism. Upon returning to Peru in May of 1997, I wanted to interview these and other experts in greater depth. Unfortunately, the political climate under the Fujimori regime had degenerated so much by 1997 that only three individuals agreed to be interviewed under conditions remindful of a John Le Carré spy novel. Regardless, the fieldwork I undertook in Colombia and Peru provided invaluable insights.

A Brief Introduction to Organized Crime Theory

A brief overview of the theories of organized crime, largely spawned in North America, provides some sense of the competing assumptions and perspectives driving the academic discussion of the phenomenon. Theoretical work done on organized crime not only reflects the complex and contradictory nature of the phenomenon under observation, but also the position in time and place of those who do the observing. Thus the following assertion by the Canadian political science and international relations scholar Robert Cox (1981) should also hold true for the theoretical approaches of other disciplines such as criminology where paradigms play as important a role in the attempt to explain crime and organized crime:

> Theory is always for someone and for some purpose. All theories have a perspective. Perspectives derive from a position in time and space. The world is seen from a standpoint definable in terms of nation or social class, of dominance or subordination, of rising or declining power, of a sense of immobility or of present crisis, of past experience, and of hopes and expectations for the future (1981: 128).

Scott McIllwain (1999) describes "three major paradigms used to define and comprehend organized crime" (1999: 303). The first views OC groups as organizations and institutions. This particular perspective is presented by American scholar Donald Cressey and has been in vogue until the 1960s. He maintained that organized crime in the United States was run by tightly-knit crime families who had set up a parallel criminal government that was "substituting for the state," enforcing its own rules and regulations (Cressey 1970: 579). Cressey identified organized crime in the United States as a conspiracy of ethnic Italians, and as a "lineal descendent, not a branch of the Sicilian Mafia" (*ibid.*, 595).

Another rather diverse group of criminologists has focused on the importance of client-patron relations and rejected the view that organized crime in the United States was run by a central criminal organization (McIllwain 1999: 303). Instead, these authors emphasized the informality of the relationships between those involved in OC activities. For example, Joseph Albini (1971) denied the existence of a formal organization and claimed that the *Italo-American Mafia* involved "a system of loosely structured relationships functioning primarily because each participant is interested in furthering his own welfare" (1971: 288; also see Block 1979: 94–95).

According to McIllwain (1999), the third major paradigm is influenced by economics and borrows its assumptions from the laws of demand and supply. The so-called Enterprise theory views OC groups as businesses that provide the goods and services denied to customers by the legal marketplace. Its adherents argue that economic ventures take place across a spectrum comprising both legal and illegal activities. Enterprise theorists recognize the role of lawmaking in the creation of crime. They argue that the profits of such groups derive from the provision of goods and services made illegal by law (Schelling 1967; Smith 1975).

Enterprise theory addresses why the capture of gang leaders and the suppression of crime groups often has little impact on the market because the business simply 'goes somewhere else' under new management. Howard Abadinsky (1981) claims that in the United States "the successful prosecution of a few leaders does not have a significant impact on this organization; clients will shift to other patrons and continue their operations" (1981:126). This argument is also valid beyond North America. Mario Arango and Jorge Child (1987) note in the case of Colombian drug traffickers: "If somebody falls or for whatever reason loses his [her] markets, his [her] position is immediately occupied by others" (1987: 131). Similarly, McCoy (2000) observed that successes against drug trafficking in one country lead to increased production elsewhere, thus neutralizing the initial achievements.

Social Network theory, one of the latest perspectives to emerge, combines aspects of various approaches, particularly the client-patron relations model as presented by Albini and Enterprise theory. Its usefulness lies in the fact that it takes into consideration the complexity and global extent of the relations between the various actors involved in OC activities (McIllwain 1999: 304–307, 318–320).

McIllwain did not mention Ethnic Succession theory, largely identified with the works of Daniel Bell (1953) and Francis A. Ianni (1972), as a major perspective. The theory had been a response to Cressey's identification of US organized crime with Italian groups. Ergo, American organized crime was hatched by the ventures of successive immigrant waves of various ethnic backgrounds entering the US from the late nineteenth century on. Organized crime was successively in the hands of the Irish who were supplanted by Jewish and Italian criminals, and so on. Participation in OC activities became a vehicle of social mobility for a small minority of newcomers from a given ethnic group entering the United States. Once its members, especially their offspring, had been integrated, they no longer relied on criminal activity. It should therefore be emphasized that only very small fractions of these immigrant groups were indeed involved in any criminal activities, while most were hard-working and law-abiding individuals who wanted to make a better life, if not for themselves then for their children. Ethnicity is certainly important as criminal societies in the United States and elsewhere are often organized along ethnic lines. On the one hand, members of the same ethnic origin share similar experiences in the new country and tend to be more trusting of those with related backgrounds (Lupsha 1986: 34; Kenney and Finckenauer 1995: 39). On the other hand, one aspect often overlooked is the fact that criminals of a given ethnic background are more likely to prey on their own community rather than members of other groups, although this may change as a group grows in size and acquires more 'territory.' This is generally not the impression created by the media coverage of crime or organized crime (Sifakis 1982: 599–600).

The theory's validity has been challenged by recent history, as ethnically based OC groups in the United States have not been replaced by those arriving later. For example, the *Italo-American Mafia* had not been supplanted by the 1980s but continued to be "the most formally organized, broadly established, and effective crime group" in that country, while "black, Mexican, Cuban, Colombian Asian, Middle Eastern and many WASP crime groups" appeared to be active in the United States as well (Kenney and Finckenauer 1995: 40; also see Lupsha 1986: 54).

Furthermore, while this theory discusses some aspects of the evolution of American organized crime, it is less useful when applied to groups like the *Hell's Angels* who do not have an immigrant background. Nonetheless, Ethnic Succession theory may have some explanatory capacity beyond the United States in other traditional immigrant societies, such as Australia. In fact, it may have a comeback of sorts considering that various West European nations have become de facto immigrant societies. Many countries of the European Union (EU) have received large numbers of immigrants and refugees from diverse backgrounds, some of whom are involved in ethnically based OC crime activities under conditions that differ little from those in the United States during the 1920s–1940s (See for example, *Focus*. May 6, 1996: 52–64).

Furthermore, McIllwain (1999) does not include Marxist perspectives in his list of worthy paradigms. This exclusion is reminiscent of Kelly's (1986) observation that "the atmosphere . . . . in the United States . . . . is intolerant of Marxist-oriented theory whose results might produce radically different conclusions" (1986: 15). Consequently, mainstream scholars do not conclude that organized crime does have an ideological dimension. Abadinsky (2002) claims that OC groups are "not motivated by social doctrine, political beliefs, or ideological concerns" (2002: 1–2). Indeed, many of the recognized US scholars deny that organized crime can be ideological (See for example, Alexander 1985: 89–98; Kenney and Finckenauer 1995: 3–4).

Even so, the Marxist-influenced Chambliss (1988) provides a structuralist theory which presents organized crime as a web of affiliations including people in government, state, political parties, law enforcement agencies, business, labor, and criminal groups. Although this criminologist does not concern himself with the personal motives of individuals, he argues that criminal behavior is a "response of groups and social classes to the resources and constraints that exist in the social structure" (1988: 208). Thus to explain organized crime one needs to "understand the characteristics of the social structure that create the institutionalization of criminality." (*Ibid.*). Chambliss' conclusions differ little from those drawn by the Italian Gramscian Marxist criminologist Umberto Santino (1988) who locates organized crime within a capitalist "financial-industrial complex" (1988: 203). Accordingly, organized crime is the "organic product of a social ecosystem" that is capitalist, and takes over "prominent positions within the ruling system as a whole" (*ibid.*, 204). German criminologist Henner Hess — whose studies on the *Sicilian Mafia* have earned him strong recognition among Italian OC researchers — describes its role as a system stabilizer. The so-called Sicilian men of honor practiced "repressive crime" to preserve the interests of societal elites (1986: 129; also see Hess 1988). The observations of Chambliss, Santino, and Hess suggest that the relationships between societal elites and criminal organizations may well have an ideological dimension, in the sense that ideology describes "the manner of thinking, ideas, characteristic of a person, group etc," in particular regarding "the basis of an economic or political system" (Hornby, Gatenby and Wakefield 1976: 428).

It is inconsistent to argue that the political decision making on the part of ordinary law-abiding citizens or by persons involved in legal business ventures is ideologically driven, but that criminals, who engage in the same, are merely greedy. Indeed, Merton (1957) already noted in his classic work that participation in criminal or legal business activities springs from the same desires, namely, to improve one's station in life. Arguably, the incentives behind OC decision makers to contribute to the maintenance of a government which permits them to realize unlawful profits by financing the electoral campaigns of corrupt politicians differ little from those of board members of corporations who make legal, or illegal, election donations to help keep a political party of their liking in power. It is fair to assume that those who participate in OC activities are motivated by the prospects of large illegal profits and social mobility, and that such criminals feel inclined to contribute to the establishment or maintenance of power structures wherein their activities proceed unhindered and may even be officially tolerated. Yet by doing so they act in a manner that is ideologically driven.

As I aim to demonstrate in this work, manifestations of organized crime may be generated by the contradictions of different socioeconomic formations, such as mercantilism, capitalism, or socialism. Neoliberal capitalism is the dominant form of political and economic organization of our time. Consequently, capitalist practices will inform some, albeit not all, of the conditions under which OC groups emerge and flourish. As noted by complexity theorist Uri Merry (1995):

> Each era with its different sources of energy, means of communication, bases of power, ways of government, forms of organization, scientific know-how, technological level, value systems, cultural forms, family frameworks, and individual identity coalesced around a basic mode of production (1995: 157; also

see Laszlo 1991).

Given the realities of the world in the early twenty-first century, it follows that capitalist structures are the ones to which OC groups will contribute if it is in their interest to do so. One example, that will be discussed in further detail later, are the right-wing paramilitaries in Colombia financed by drug lords who, in cooperation with the country's military, fight left-wing rebels. Doing so, I argue, was an ideologically driven decision by those in charge, as their participation in the on-going conflict against the militant left allowed drug traffickers to integrate themselves in local and regional power structures and to continue unhindered with their activities. Certainly, the potential victory of a Marxist rebel movement would represent as much of a threat to the illegal profits of Colombia's drug lords as to the legal ones of its business elites and large estate owners.

There are good examples of the affinity between mature organized criminal societies and socioeconomic elites, and it is possible to demonstrate how such groups may develop or acquire their ideological leanings. Organized criminals not only make alliances with elites or factions thereof, they may also come to their defense against counter-hegemonic groups, such as Marxist rebel groups or left-wing political parties. Indeed, OC decision makers use these struggles to further their own aim of integration into existing structures of domination. Such collaboration is most likely to take place when counter-hegemonic groups threaten elites during times of social crisis and economic upheaval. Associations between criminal organizations and socioeconomic elites also transpire for the purpose of profit sharing, consider, for example, international money laundering. Still, it is especially under the conditions of crisis and upheaval that the ideological potential of OC groups becomes apparent.

Yet when criminologists deny or ignore the possibility of organized crime's ideological proclivities, they not only reduce the phenomenon to the size of the specific theory or theories they adhere to but simultaneously limit the number of available solutions. After all, criminological theories "influence policies and practices found in criminal justice systems" (Lilly, Cullen, and Ball 1995: 10). These observations on the links between academia and political practice are mirrored by critical geographer Simon Dalby (1997) who points to "the dynamics of academic conferences where practitioners and scholars so frequently rub shoulders" (1997: 10). This predicament is apparent in the failure of the American Drug War in Latin America. Criminologists, in league with criminal justice practitioners and law makers, have either ignored or underestimated the ideological links between traffickers and elites.

Organized Crime as a Complex Phenomenon and Consequences for Research

The ideological dimension of organized crime is enhanced by its chameleon-like qualities that allow it to adapt to the specifics of a given socioeconomic formation, be it a developed, a peripheral capitalist economy, or a socialist command economy. Kelly (1986) therefore also refers to the complexity of organized crime when he writes that it grows in "many kinds of societies" that "differ politically, economically, and culturally," yet it "is intimately linked to political structures and economic infrastructures" (1986: 14).

When analyzing organized crime, an important factor to be taken into consideration is its secrecy, specifically the concealed nature of its activities and decision-making. OC groups display some likeness with secret societies and will thus share certain characteristics with other secret groups, including noncriminal ones. The study of secret societies can be helpful in the analysis of the workings of organized crime as well as the dangers one encounters combating it. Few scholars specializing on organized crime explore the notion that criminal fraternities share certain traits with secret societies. Organizations such as *Freemasons*, the Italian *Carbonari*, the Russian *Bolsheviks* (prior to the 1917 revolution), or the members of the anti-British *Mau Mau* movement in colonial Kenya, can be revolutionary, nationalistic, religious, occult, and criminal, and should be considered a universal feature, although they will differ in time and place. Historically, secret associations have forms of communications, membership rules, initiation rites, and/or other ceremonies which serve to distinguish members from the rest of society and aim to conceal their activities (Heckethorn 1966; Daraul 1969; MacKenzie 1971).

Tefft (1992) defines a secret society as "a special type of association that has a set of well-defined norms, secret rituals and oaths, or similar declarations or demonstrations of loyalty that are intended to subjectively bind members to the secrecy required by the group's affairs" (1992: 1). Serious scholars have ignored secret societies as an area of research, leaving the field to conspiracy theorists. As Roberts (1972) indicates:

> [T]he charlatan, the axe-grinder and the paranoiac long had the field to themselves . . . . The result has been the mountain of rubbish — still growing, though now more slowly — which explains everything from the collapse of the Roman Empire to the Russian Revolution in terms of secret societies (1972: 10–11).

The secrecy of the organization is part and parcel of its mythology, as the former tends to engender the latter. This is also an issue when analyzing criminal organizations. Roberts (1972) writes:

> The mythology of secret societies has many different specific embodiments, religious and non-religious, liberal and conservative, but it is always an example of the 'puppet' theory of politics. It claims that the real makers of events are not

the statesmen . . . . but secret directors who manipulate them . . . . with [or] . . . . without their knowledge. These manipulators use [them] as the instruments of great and usually sinister designs . . . . Many different versions of this . . . . force have been identified. The Freemasons, the Jesuits, the Carbonari, the Comintern have all had the blame placed on them at different times. The most ambitious theorists . . . . have identified conspiracies stretching historically in time across centuries and linking organizations as remote from one another as the Templars and Sinn Fein. But the most popular form of the myth is to identify the enduring secret societies as . . . . agents of political and social revolution. Their great aim . . . . is to sap the stabilizing certainties of society — Church, State, Morality, Property, the Family — and set up a new order (1972: 14–15).

It is important to analyze the degree to which these groups are indeed involved in political decision-making behind the scenes in order to assess their true impact. The more so as Roberts also observed that "although secret societies existed in large numbers in Western Europe between 1750 and 1830 and strove to influence events, their main importance was what people believed about them. This always mattered more than what they did and their numbers and practical effectiveness were in no way proportionate to the myth's power" (*ibid.*, 347). Mann (1986), on the other hand, still argues that the impact of secret societies on state policies has been considerable. In fact, he believes that secret societies and states share a number of similarities:

Whether [secret societies] serve the interests of the state . . . . by protecting ruling-class concerns or serving as foci of opposition to state rule, [they] employ the same power strategies as the state to neutralize opposition, guard against repression or destruction, and to maintain internal discipline. State power strategies are merely centralized versions of power found in secret society organizations or other social structures (1986: 172).

Despite these similarities, the existence of organized crime is also associated with the absence of the state. Policing and keeping the peace are functions commonly associated with the agencies of the state and its "monopoly of legitimate use of physical force within a given territory," to quote German sociologist Max Weber (Gerth and Mills 1958: 78–79).[3] Organized crime, however, evolves in the absence of the state and is a challenge to its monopoly of violence. Roth (1996), therefore, describes organized crime as the "development of zones of non-justice, virtual ghettoes in which the order of the state no longer exists; the formation of an economic system based on prohibited activities; corruption which prevents that the state guarantees public welfare and which secures the continued existence and expansion of the illicit economic system" (1996: 41).

Strong criminal organizations especially tend to emerge in times of economic crisis and transition as a fragmented social environment provides the suitable breeding ground. During such times OC groups flourish in the absence of the state which is even less able to enforce its monopoly of violence. The collaboration between organized crime and elites results from the weakness of the latter which forces them to accept the existence of and collaboration with other independent entities (Strange 1996: 116–117).

Roth emphasizes the apparent dual nature of the relationship between organized crime and the state. On one hand, the absence of the state is a necessary precondition for criminal networks to emerge and function unchecked. On the other hand, the management of the illicit economic system requires the cooperation, or rather the corruption, of state agents. Yet, Maingot (1995) laments that there is no "general theory of corruption" and points out that the issue generally refers to political corruption whereas this practice is often not covered in "private, non-governmental areas" (1995: 1). This observation is certainly significant in the light of the present-day privatization of many services originally provided by the state. Is, for example, the employee of a private prison company who takes a bribe from an inmate not as 'corrupt' as the state official who does the same in a facility run at public expense? Regardless, as noted by Lupsha (1996), the corruption of officials in government and bureaucracy "provides the air that organized crime needs for survival" (1996: 24).

Still, a definition of corruption such as the one supplied by Girling (1997) which refers to corruption as "the abuse of a public position of trust for private gain" is subject to limitations (1997: vii–viii). Such definitions treat corruption like a bad habit or an addiction, namely the personal greed of an individual. However, as observed by Lord Acton (1834–1902), 'power corrupts, while absolute power corrupts absolutely.' Put differently, a definition like Girling's has been produced from the perspective of one who views corruption as the breaking of rules in a setting which is generally not dishonest. Such a definition is not applicable in a society where corruption is the rule and results from the absence of public and democratic control. Corruption in such a context refers to a specific manifestation and management of power. It becomes an essential component of power relations, cannot be separated from power, and is a tool in the hands of the powerful. Indeed, in such a setting, power is the precondition for corruption, and corruption is the precondition for power. Power cannot be exercised unless it is corrupt (Della Porta and Vannucci 1999).

Moreover, scholars have observed considerable differences in the structure and actual organization of criminal fraternities. For example, Kenney and Finckenauer (1995) identify a structured hierarchy to be one of the characteristics of the *Italo-American Mafia*. Members function in leadership and subordinate positions and various levels of commitment and association (1995: 3–5). Similarly, they describe the Japanese *Yakuza* organizations as "sophisticated, highly structured, well-disciplined, and complex criminal" groups (*ibid.*, 262). The Colombian cartels' organizational structure is compared to an "onion like layering of organizational power, with kingpins at the center, directing operations but insulated by layer upon layer of protective subordinate operatives" (US Department of Justice 1989: 17). According to Kenney and Finckenauer (1995), the "cartels are organized into complex infrastructures" which give work to tens of thousands of people in Colombia and "with extensive networks" in the United States (1995: 263). Russian organized crime may form large informal networks at home, however, those Russian criminals operating in the United States apparently lack tight hierarchical arrangements. Meanwhile, their Albanian counterparts are organized around family units and never comprise more than twenty people (*ibid.*, 278; Mappes-Niedick 2003: 127). These very different organizational structures demonstrate the complexity of organized crime which evolves in accordance with the specifics of place and time.

Therefore I define organized crime as follows:

Organized crime refers to a group generally operating under some form of concealment with a structure reflective of the cultural and social stipulations of the societies that generate it; and which has the primary objective to obtain access to wealth and power, through the participation in economic activities prohibited by law as well as through the corruption of those engaged in enforcing it. Organized crime is a form of crude accumulation because it is based on the use or threat of physical violence which emerges — and has emerged — in different socioeconomic formations across time and place, and is generated by the specific conditions of that time and place.

Given the byzantine workings of organized crime, the late Paul Feyerabend (1993) likely would have included it in his list of phenomena that are "richer in content, more varied, more many-sided, more lively and subtle than even the best historian and the best methodologist can imagine"(1993: 9). He further wrote that

> [h]istory is full of 'accidents and conjunctures and curious juxtapositions of events' and it demonstrates to us the complexity of human change and the unpredictable character of the ultimate consequences of any given act or decision .... Are we to believe that .... simple .... rules .... are capable of accounting for such a 'maze of interactions'? (*ibid.*)

The US complexity theorist and criminologist T. R. Young (1994) points to the multi-paradigmatic nature of reality and writes that there are

> any number of coexisting paradigms none of which can encompass all of the data .... [N]ature and society are so complex and so richly interconnected that the choice of where the boundaries of theory are to be set is a matter of research interest and research capacity more than the underlying ontology at hand.

Wheatley (1992) noted that it had been the "[positivist] tradition .... to work on something and then generalize it into answers and solutions that would be widely transferred. But now this has changed. We can no longer expect to receive answers. Solutions are temporary events suited to specific conditions" (1992: 179).

Feyerabend (1993) advocated a methodological "anarchism" that would allow the scholar to employ "whatever procedure seems to fit the occasion" (1993: 10). In his words, "there is only one principle that can be defended under all circumstances and in all stages of human development. It is the principle: anything goes" (*ibid.*, 18–19).

The immense complexity of the OC phenomenon has a number of consequences for those researching it.

First, the processes which result in the emergence of organized crime are not easily ascertained. Its activities should be viewed as a set of processes of great complexity which only provide limited information about the manner in which they work. At the same time, the data available need to be treated with caution. Most of the empirical data on organized crime have been collected by law enforcement. These findings have been gathered with the needs of the police in mind, not those of the scholar. In addition, the delicate nature of police work requires that information remains classified. However, facts may also be concealed or tainted as a result of police corruption (Kelly 1986: 11–12). In addition, Kelly notes that the information released is "sometimes circumscribed by the politics" of law enforcement agencies (*ibid.*).

It appears that the unreliability of law enforcement data is mirrored by the implausibility of the information provided by organized crime figures themselves as evidenced in various biographies and various journalistic descriptions. According to Lupsha (1986), such works have to be read carefully. While he acknowledges that biographies and journalistic accounts by such criminals "provide descriptive and historical insights and information," he also claims that they are often "self-serving, exaggerated, biased, and at times full of error deliberate or accidental" (1986: 39).[4] Still, as previously noted, journalists also provide valuable information, and it is up to the researcher to determine which information is valid and which is biased.

Furthermore, the unreliability of data has consequences for building theory. If the information is flawed, then the theories stemming from it would necessarily suffer from the same predicament. Even if premised on valid information, most theoretical perspectives can at best be impermanent descriptions fixed by time and place, for they cannot necessarily be transferred elsewhere. Thus a theoretical perspective of utility for explaining certain aspects of organized crime in the United States during the 1940s and 1950s may not necessarily be useful to illustrate US or Chinese criminal organizations of the 1980s. Moreover, most theories of organized crime are of North American origin which is a reflection of the considerable academic work done in the field. Still, this state of affairs may also be indicative of a quasi-hegemony which often overwhelms and excludes material produced elsewhere.[5]

These theories may be incommensurable with each other such as Marxist and non-Marxist perspectives, nevertheless they are, or have been in the past, representative of particular parts of the reality of that phenomenon in a given location. Therefore, the exploration of organized crime requires a multi-paradigmatic understanding because no single paradigm is capable of explaining it. A given paradigm, even if it is based on reliable information, is suitable for illuminating a particular slice of the phenomenon's reality whereby the insights provided are limited by time and place. Reality, as Hein and Simonis (1973: 93) maintain, can be explained with several theories. Yet, it is also "interconnected" (Albert, Cagan, Chomsky, Hahnel, King, Sargent, and Sklar 1986: 5–21; also see Young 1994). The application of Marxist perspectives does not contradict the recognition of the complexity of the processes that generate organized crime as long as it is understood that the insights gained will help illuminate some aspects of the phenomenon's reality but not others.

The construction of a perspective that considers the complexity of a phenomenon is also compounded by the sheer quantity of knowledge available. A social scientist is primarily a specialist in a particular field. Hence, he or she is largely capable of analyzing a phenomenon only with the tools provided by that field, a predicament already lamented by Ortega y Gasset (1960), who wrote that "the specialist knows very well his own tiny corner of the universe; he is radically ignorant of all the rest" (1960: 111). The dilemma Ortega y Gasset refers to concerns the growing separation between different fields of the sciences that has increased since he originally wrote his book in 1930. The massive increase in knowledge not only resulted in divisions between different disciplines but even created boundaries within them which are maintained by academic trench lines.

However, the study of a phenomenon like organized crime not only requires a multi-paradigmatic understanding but should also be perceived as an interdisciplinary exercise. While such an approach would possibly be contested by mainstream scholars in political science, criminology, and a number of other disciplines in North America, it is nevertheless part of the European social science tradition. For example, Ernst Fraenkel and Arnold Bergstraesser, two of the most important pioneers of modern political science in West Germany after 1949, viewed the discipline as an "integrative" and "synoptic science" respectively (Bellers and Woyke 1989: 99–101; Mols 1995: 559).[6] From this perspective, criminology may be perceived as an integrative social science that considers the research results of a diverse set of disciplines. Criminologists and their colleagues in the other social sciences should attempt to understand social processes in their entirety, taking into consideration their interconnections (*ibid.*).[7]

In addition to interviews and personal experiences, I rely on a large selection of academic and journalistic literature on organized crime produced in English, German, or Spanish in this work. Included here are daily or weekly reports of the Canadian, Colombian, German, Peruvian, Spanish, Swiss, and US press. I am also utilizing publications on specific manifestations of organized crime, such as Colombian or Russian, authored by experts in their fields and published largely in English, German, or Spanish. These accounts might have been published in these languages, after being translated from the original Russian or Italian. For example, I came across a number of works on Russian organized crime written by Russian authors that were subsequently translated into German, but not into English, or rare descriptions of Italian or Bolivian organized crime translated into English, but not German.

Furthermore, to overcome the limitations imposed by the complexity of the issues, it is a necessary prerequisite to learn about the specifics of a given society where criminal organizations have emerged. To gain a sense of the *Medellín Cartel*, it is a necessary endeavor to familiarize oneself with the history, culture, and politics of Colombia. Therefore, especially as far as the case studies are concerned, I have relied on the works produced in English, German, or Spanish, by scholars from various disciplines such as anthropology, history, international relations and development studies, or political economy.

I have included material and direct quotations, translated into English by myself from German and Spanish publications, some of which may already have been published in English. All mistakes are my own, and any resemblance with existing translations elsewhere is accidental. Admittedly, I did borrow from Stirk's (1992) translations of some of Horkheimer's (1985; 1985a) and Theodor Adorno's (1990) observations on the racket.

I have also relied considerably on Internet news sources, particularly the British Broadcasting Corporation (BBC) and a few others. I found the BBC web site to be a relatively neutral source of information which I relied upon to bring the relevant chapters up to date. All web sites used were visited, or revisited, between January and April 2003, unless indicated otherwise.

Description of Chapters

In this work I aim to demonstrate the ideological dimension of crime groups and the criminal proclivities of those who hold the reigns of power. Chapter 2 provides some theoretical perspectives to illuminate the relationship between criminal organizations and elites. This analysis is largely premised on insights provided in the works of Karl Marx, the Frankfurt School's Max Horkheimer and Theodor Adorno, as well as Italian Marxist theorist Antonio Gramsci (Marx 1971; Gramsci 1971; Horkheimer 1982, 1985, 1985a, 1985b; Adorno 1990). I intend to illustrate my theoretical assumptions by employing examples from various criminal groups as geographically and culturally diverse as the *Sicilian Mafia* and the Japanese *Yakuza*.

Chapter 3 traces the emergence of the contemporary international illegal drug economy from Western practices such as the opium trade undertaken by the European colonial powers in Southeast Asia between the seventeenth and twentieth centuries, the activities of pharmaceutical companies in the late nineteenth and early twentieth century, or the involvement of secret service agencies in narcotics trafficking during the Cold War.

Chapter 4 compares the 1927 Shanghai Coup in China with a similar episode that transpired in Latin America, namely the 1980 Bolivian Cocaine Coup. Both events are prime examples of organized crime-elite cooperation as criminal organizations played pivotal roles in anti-left-wing military coups.

Chapter 5 is a comparative study of Colombia and Peru, respectively. Colombian and Peruvian elites actually established alliances with criminal groups to suppress left-wing rebels, organized labor, human rights groups, and/or the media. This chapter is the largest in volume and contains the experiences gained through research and fieldwork done in these Latin American countries.

Chapter 6, the first of two studies that analyze forms of organized crime generated in socioeconomic formations other than capitalism, provides an explanation for the emergence of organized crime in the former Soviet Union and in its most important successor state after the 1991 collapse, the Russian Federation.

Chapter 7 looks at piracy as a form of organized crime practiced in various emerging European nation-states between the sixteenth and eighteenth centuries.

Chapter 8 builds on the insights gained to explain the impact of globalization on the activities of criminal organizations. The internationalization of economic processes generates disorder, deprivation, and criminal opportunities, which are essential components for the emergence of crime and organized crime in many parts of the world.

Chapter 9 discusses the dangers of anti-crime legislation as well as solutions to the problem of organized crime. Given the transnational nature of criminal organizations in the age of globalization the most fundamental transformations required include the creation of truly international law enforcement structures and significant changes to the way the global economic system presently works.

Endnotes

1. An investigation done on political science departments that offer courses specifically dealing with organized crime, which I undertook in the late 1990s in North America and Western Europe, came up with very few results. A few Latin American Studies programs offered courses in the more limited area of cocaine production. I myself taught two well-attended graduate-level courses on organized crime while completing my doctoral degree at Carleton University in Ottawa, Canada, where I was given the opportunity to study this subject from the perspective of political science. In the fall of 1997, Professor Piotr Dutkiewicz and myself coorganized a course titled *The Political Economy of Organized Crime* (47–556). In the fall of 1999, I taught the same course at the Institute of Political Economy at Carleton university under a different designation. Most of the literature produced in the field is more concerned with the threat posed by organized crime, for example, the dangers posed by nuclear materials smuggling, rather than an evaluation of mafia groups as societal actors.

2. To quote a Peruvian journalist who researched organized crime and corruption: "Everything is probable, but nothing is provable."

3. According to German sociologist Max Weber, "a state is a human community that (successfully) claims the monopoly of the legitimate use of physical force within a given territory. The state is considered the sole source of the 'right' to use violence" (Gerth and Mills 1958: 78–79). In my argument a strong state, notwithstanding if it is a fully developed democracy or a dictatorship, is capable of imposing a monopoly of lawful armed force within its boundaries, while a weak state cannot. However, the ability of imposing such a monopoly by a strong state, even a totalitarian one, is not complete. Indeed, the notion of "the monopoly of legitimate use of physical force" should be viewed as a so-called Weberian ideal.

4. The following works have been authored or coauthored by criminals: *The Last Testament of Lucky Luciano* (1976) by Martin A. Gosch and Richard Hammer and *The Valachi Papers* (1972) by Peter Maas, both of which deal with the *Italo-American Mafia*. However, *Un narco se confiesa y acusa* (1990) was allegedly written by a Colombian drug trafficker who remained unnamed. In his autobiography, 'Lucky' Luciano strongly rejected attempts to link him personally to the drug trade, in particular the heroin trade. He admitted allowing some of his Under Bosses, such as Vito Genovese, to sell the drug while he, Luciano, did not "wanna know about it" (Gosch and Hammer 1976: 127). Other accounts also make reference to an internal prohibition within the *Italo-American Mafia* regarding drugs. However, there are various reports which differ from Luciano's recollection and which seem to indicate that he not only knew about the drugs but even organized their sale in the United States after his 1946 deportation to Italy. Jenkins (1992) concludes that "for the scholar of narcotics trafficking, however, the notion of internal prohibition remains a myth, and should not be given serious credence" (1992: 316). A British crime author, quoting a US narcotics agent sent to study Luciano's activities after his deportation to Italy, points out that the gangster "was responsible for the flow of heroin coming through the port of New York" (Short 1996: 160). The view is shared by Umberto Santino (1996), one of the most eminent Italian OC scholars (1996: 144).

Valachi's account also made reference to a massacre of mafia bosses in September of 1931 when 'Lucky' Luciano overthrew the old order by arranging for the assassination of Salvatore Maranzano, then 'capo di capi' (Maas 1972: 113). Depending on the source, between 39 and 200 mafiosi were killed all over the United States because of their past association with Maranzano. Still, Nelli (1986) maintained that a meticulous examination of newspaper articles had merely revealed the sudden and violent demise of four mafia leaders in New York and Denver (1986: 1–2). Short's (1996) thorough study of the *Italo-American Mafia* only mentioned Maranzano's demise. In fact, the author claimed that Luciano had to attend a meeting of the bosses of US crime families to 'justify' the Maranzano killing (1996: 41–42). Luciano maintained himself in his memoirs that "what writers always printed about what they called the 'Night of the Sicilian Vespers' was mostly pure imagination. Every time somebody writes about that day, the list of people who was supposed to have got bumped off gets bigger and bigger" (Gosch and Hammer 1976: 147).

Lupsha's assessment also holds true for the 1990 book *Un narco se confiesa y acusa* which was allegedly written by a Colombian drug trafficker. Still, the book is insightful. Called an "open letter to the Colombian people," the author vehemently defends the drug trade and the patriotism of those involved (Anónimo 1990: 17–25). Moreover, he/she justifies drug trafficking by pointing to the double standards of US practices. The author notes that it is the United States which has become the world's largest producer of marijuana. Likewise, he/she maintains that most of the cocaine profits are not made by

Colombians but "remain in the hands of North Americans" (*ibid.*). As well, he/she claims that large volumes of pharmaceuticals are produced for export and sold in Colombian drugstores, although prohibited in the United States because of their negative health effects (*ibid.*).

5. One encounters a similar phenomenon in other disciplines or subdisciplines. For example, the field of International Relations (IR), at least until recently, has been dominated by literature produced in Great Britain and the United States. The Scandinavian-born K. J. Holsti (1985) points out that "most of the mutually acknowledged literature has been produced by only two of more than 155 countries: the United States and Great Britain. This is, in brief, a British-American intellectual hegemony . . . . It is not so much asymmetry of production as of consumption" (1985: 4). Another observer also concluded that "only a rare foreign scholar . . . . is allowed to intrude upon thinking which carries the American trademark" (Gareau 1982: 18).

6. German scholar Reinhard Meyers (1977) also views the study of International Relations (IR) as an integrative science, "which summarizes and blends the findings of other social sciences, where these pertain to transnational, international and foreign-policy phenomena or those domestic, socio- and economic-political phenomena that condition them. Depending on the research interest and related questions, diverse conceptual and methodological devices from various social sciences can be utilized for investigation" (1977: 28–29). His Marxist colleague Ekkehart Krippendorff (1982) writes that IR "cannot be studied and taken seriously if it is not conceived within the broader framework of the social sciences in general. And if we consider ourselves social scientists, we should be aware of the fact that the science of man[/woman] and society requires at least a general knowledge or awareness of the problems and fields outside the more narrow specialization [of one's own discipline]" (1982: IX).

7. Such an analysis suggests that criminologists engage in some interdisciplinary work, for example, by looking at the aforementioned field of International Relations (IR). Officially created in the aftermath of World War I, IR may be viewed as a subdiscipline of political science, which has come into its own. The field has broadened considerably and includes several subdivisions ranging from theory of the mainstream or realist as well as Marxist and feminist varieties, international political economy, peace and/or strategic studies, or studies of international development. More recently, IR scholars have also been grappling with the realities and consequences of globalization. Within IR one also finds a subdivision that refers to itself as critical, whose members rely on philosophical foundations that do not differ fundamentally from the perspectives taken by those who describe themselves as such in the field of criminology or sociology. Several streams of critical IR are united by the questioning of positivist assumptions in the field. Accordingly, the first group are the "Neo-Gramscians," who are scholars dealing with questions concerning the global economy. A second stream within the field of IR theory is influenced by the critical theories of the Frankfurt School, and of Jürgen Habermas. A third group of authors, which includes feminist and post-colonial scholars, relies on perspectives provided by Michel Foucault and Jacques Derrida. A fourth stream of critical IR scholars includes authors who base their works on Anthony Giddens (Scherrer 1994: 306–307).

Critical social theory approaches of IR — irrespective of the label they receive — emphasize the complexity of social processes. This allows scholars to gain a new understanding of the workings of the international arena, while mainstream perspectives only superficially illuminate the interaction between diverse kinds of actors. The analysis of global processes and trends such as the growth of capitalist industrialization and bureaucratization, the internationalization of trade and finance, the increase of worldwide communications, and their consequences, can be found in the literature produced by critical IR scholars since the 1970s. Already these earlier works, mostly written by European authors, discussed the dilemmas caused by population growth, industrialization, pollution, shortage of resources, international conflicts, arms races, and so forth in a capitalist global economic system and a fragmented state system. They argued that the process of globalization was out of control and would set free enormous conflict potentials resulting in global crises. These crises, however, would not only manifest themselves as intra- or international conflicts but also as personal violence, crime, organized crime, and global anomie (Krippendorff 1972: 373; Hein and Simonis 1973: 94; also see Sörensen 1991; Passas 2000).

    While the European critical IR scholars of the 1970s and 1980s still offered an alternative vision based on a neo-Marxist paradigm, their North American colleagues of the 1990s and thereafter are less certain about solutions to global issues. Still, critical IR scholars like Andrew Linklater (1992) point to the "universality of inclusion and exclusion" because "all societies have practices and procedures which define who does or does not belong, many of which are archaic forms of inclusion and exclusion which predate the formation of class-divided societies" (1992: 82–83). He proposes to develop "a critical theory of the varieties of social and political exclusion" with the ultimate goal of overcoming these obstacles in a world that is increasingly interdependent and where exclusion is becoming anachronistic" (*ibid.*).

Chapter 2

A Neo-Marxist Interpretation of Organized Crime

.... Only death is free:
Everything else costs money. And that includes
protection, peace and quiet.

(Bertold Brecht. 1987. *The Resistible Rise of Arturo Ui.* Scene 7)

Criminal organizations acquire ideological preferences as they evolve
and integrate into elite structures. Indeed, organized crime groups may
come to the aid of elites who are threatened by counter-hegemonic
groups. This analysis is based on Marxist, Frankfurt School and
Gramscian concepts and is augmented by examples of such alliances
between elites and crime groups from Europe, Latin America and Asia.

Introduction

Most recognized scholars in mainstream North American criminology stress the
nonideological nature of organized crime, which points to corruption as the chief
explanation for the links between criminal groups and economic and political elites
(Alexander 1985: 89–98; Kenney and Finckenauer 1995: 3–4; Von Lampe 1999:
295; Abadinsky 2002: 1–2).[1] On the fringe of the discipline of criminology one
encounters authors more likely to accept the ideological nature of organized crime
(Block and Chambliss 1981; Pearce 1981; Chambliss 1988). Corruption, as noted,
is a key element of mafia-elite relations in the sense that it "provides the air that
organized crime needs for survival" (Lupsha 1996: 24). However, at the same time
such a perspective disregards the structural links between criminal groups and elites
which cannot be divorced from the specific socioeconomic context in which they
take place. Kelly (1986) noted that despite the many different societies that can
generate a mafia, the phenomenon is closely linked to political and economic power
structures (1986: 14).

It is my argument that established OC groups become ideological by adapting to the world view prevalent in the elite structures into which they integrate. Organized crime is an ideological chameleon that changes its colors in accordance with the environment in which it is generated. A useful model for this process of integration is provided by R. T. Naylor (1993). According to this Canadian economist, such organizations mature over time from a "predatory" form of illegal enrichment to a "symbiotic" one (1993: 20–22). At an early stage, a loose organization such as a street gang will largely rely on robbery or kidnaping on a local level. Once a criminal infrastructure has been set up, the group's activity will move from the "predatory" to the "parasitical" level (*ibid.*). During the "symbiotic" phase, the interests of crime groups coincide with those of society and of the formal economy, as these organizations become "an integral, functional part of the society off which they formerly preyed" (*ibid.*). Criminal societies that have entered the last stage qualify as established.

While corruption is a primary factor in the collaboration between criminal groups and elites in society, these links may actually grow further whereby corruption becomes power. First, in the course of their maturation, established criminal organizations develop ideological views resembling those of the elites. Second, criminal associations make alliances with elites, or factions thereof, and may come to their defense against counter-hegemonic groups. Evolved mafia groups, or rather their bosses, use such struggles to further their own aims of integration into existing structures of domination. Such collaboration most likely takes place when elites are, or perceive themselves to be, threatened by counter-hegemonic groups during times of social and economic upheaval. Third, the essence of the aforesaid alliances and the conditions under which they emerge differ little from arrangements that in the past have led to the emergence and maintenance of repressive regimes.

Organized Crime, Elites, and Reactionary Regimes

In 1941, while in exile in Finland, the German playwright Bertolt Brecht (1965; 1987) wrote *Der aufhaltsame Aufstieg des Arturo Ui* [The Resistible Rise of Arturo Ui]. In this play the author transfers the Nazi takeover of Germany to a criminal environment in the United States. Important stages of Adolf Hitler's political career between 1932 and 1938 — from the backroom dealings that resulted in his chancellorship to the annexation of Austria — are placed in a Chicago underworld setting. It was Brecht's intention to make the Nazis look preposterous and strip them of their demonic attributes by equating them with common gangsters who fight over control of the city's cabbage trade. At the same time, the German playwright illustrated that fascism and organized crime shared features such as the use of violence and tyrannical decision making.

This analogy was commonly reflected in the writings of other intellectuals who had fled Germany, such as Horkheimer and Adorno who wrote several essays on this subject in the 1930s and 1940s.[2] More recently, the previously mentioned Henner Hess (1988) placed OC groups together with death squads, anti-union goon squads and fascist paramilitaries (1988: vi–vii).

Organized crime is unlikely to disappear completely under any regime but can be brought to near extinction under totalitarian rule. Although ironic, it is a historic fact that the few states who successfully suppressed organized crime were Fascist Italy and National Socialist Germany as well as the Soviet Union under Stalin and other totalitarian governments. These regimes did not tolerate other organizations capable of challenging their authority and used the violence at their disposal to eliminate potential opposition. In Fascist Italy, National Socialist Germany, and the Stalinist Soviet Union, existing criminal societies lost out to the methods of the totalitarian state which itself was criminal. Given its resources, the totalitarian state could suppress organized crime efficiently and extensively (Mori 1933; Kelly, Schatzberg, and Ryan 1997: 176; also see Shelley 1991: 256).

The *Ringvereine*, Weimar Germany's most developed manifestation of organized crime, emerged in the late nineteenth century, and although it spread rapidly after World War I, it received little academic attention, and there are few published studies. *Ringvereine* translates as 'Wrestling Associations.' Supposedly, gang members practiced wrestling in order to maintain and demonstrate their physical prowess while meeting in their favorite pubs. The *Ringvereine* were hierarchically organized criminal associations that emerged in Germany's large cities, such as Berlin and Hamburg. To hide their illicit activities and to present a clean image to the public, they operated under the guise of choral societies or sports and social clubs. They were engaged in various criminal activities commonly associated with organized crime, including protection rackets, prostitution, arms smuggling, illegal lotteries, and drug trafficking, especially cocaine. Regardless, the *Ringvereine* disappeared a year after Hitler's rise to power in 1933, falling victim to the same repression to which the Nazi regime subjected its political enemies, such as the Communists and Social Democrats, as it established its dictatorship (Freiberg and Thamm 1992: 75–81; Landsberger 1994; Pohrt 2000: 199). In January 1934, the Nazis introduced laws against so-called violent habitual criminals and antisocial elements which allowed for an individual's "preventive arrest" and indefinite imprisonment without trial (Krausnick and Broszat 1968: 190–198; Broszat 1981: 338; Wagner 1996). Freiberg and Thamm (1992) write: " . . . . Sixty-two *Ringvereine* were prohibited, the Ringbrothers arrested. All went into different internment camps as parasites and professional criminals. Many died in various internment camps" (1992: 81). Surviving members sought to revive the *Ringvereine* after World War II; however, their attempts were suppressed by police in the early years of the Federal Republic of Germany (FRG) (*ibid.*).

The suppression of the *Sicilian Mafia* by the Fascist state in Italy took longer, but its members, like Communists or Socialists, became the targets of state oppression that took the form of mass arrests, unfair trials, and torture (Blok 1988: 182–189; Schneider and Zarate 1994: 58–61). Servadio (1976) pointed out:

> The 'criminal' Mafia could not work . . . . with the Fascist state. Fascism could not admit any coexistence with the Mafia, which not only gave a 'bad name' to the glittering image which Fascism wanted to give Italy . . . . but used its own methods of pseudo-legality. When elections were abolished in 1925, the Fascist party deprived the Mafia of its major instrument of alliance with the government and of control over the politicians . . . . Italy was becoming . . . . a police state, and the Fascist police could not take long in attacking the . . . . Mafia (1976: 74).

Cesare Mori, the police prefect for Sicily appointed by Italian Fascist leader Benito Mussolini, managed to suppress the *Sicilian Mafia* although he did not destroy it. Pantaleone (1966) writes that

> as an organization the Mafia disappeared . . . . Many of its more obvious activities also came to an end: cattle stealing, for instance, or the exploitation of non-Mafia criminals, racketeering on commercial deals . . . . By the beginning of the Second World War the Mafia was restricted to a few isolated and scattered groups and could have been dealt with in a resolute and radical manner, even by merely introducing a land reform (1966: 52; also see Mori 1933; Duggan 1989).

Unlike post-war Germany, the conditions of the Allied occupation in Italy provided a fertile ground which allowed the *Sicilian Mafia* to come back to its traditional role when the country turned democratic again. As an ally of rural elites, the Catholic Church, and the Christian Democrats, the *Sicilian Mafia* put a violent end to the peasants' demands for land reform. Members of the *Mafia* initiated a campaign of terror against the Italian Communist Party, the peasants' unions and their leaders, including the 1947 massacre at Portella Della Ginestra in which eleven people were killed (Servadio 1976: 74–75, 85–86; Blok 1988: 190–212; Schneider and Zarate 1994: 85–94). In Sicily, organized crime represented the continuation of Fascism by different means.[3]

Regardless, totalitarian regimes excluded criminal groups from exercising their local power because they effectively assumed the functions played by organized crime, while simultaneously relying on the very same methods of repression. OC groups also represent secret societies functioning apart from the rest of the community, yet simultaneously existing within. The secrecy of OC power is premised on the practice of clientelism which results from the absence of the state and, in fact, replaces it. The Mussolini regime in Italy reversed this process through the insertion of local representatives of the Fascist Party who supplanted the clientelist power structure in which the *Sicilian Mafia* operated, while other totalitarian regimes such as Nazi Germany did likewise. Only the *omèrta* of the totalitarian state could overcome the 'honorable society's.'

If the suppression of organized crime by an all-powerful totalitarian state represents one extreme within a broad spectrum, the control of the state by organized crime depicts the other. This corresponding alternative, the criminalized state, would describe a regime which not only permits the evolution of strong criminal societies but allows them to become part of elite structures. Although the totalitarian and the criminalized state, respectively, occupy the opposite sides of a spectrum, these extremes manifest a number of similarities. Most important, a political system that is controlled by a criminal elite bent on enriching itself with the power of the state at its disposal will likely resemble various repressive regimes, including Fascism.[4]

Introducing Adorno, Horkheimer, and Gramsci

Both Adorno and Horkheimer addressed the concept of the protection racket. Their writings reflect the pessimism of Frankfurt School scholars concerning the likelihood of progressive social change. During their US exile in the early 1940s, Horkheimer, and to a lesser extent Adorno, produced several essays comparing Nazism to American-style gangsterism. While attempting to develop a model of capitalist society that stressed "power" over "market allocation" and explained the "privatization of power" as well as the violence of Fascist practices, they had arrived at the idea of a society of rackets (Stirk 1992: 140).

To explain the emergence of Fascism in Germany and Italy, Horkheimer sought a revision of the Marxist class model by training his vision beyond classes to consider the "particularistic" interests and loyalties of groups, or what he called rackets (Stirk 1992: 143). Horkheimer's understanding of rackets encompasses the groups, cliques, councils, decision-making bodies, or committees of different epochs, cultures and subcultures, whose social function was guided by the imperative to preserve and increase their own power. Despite their constant bickering and infighting, these groups maintain internal class links for the preservation of shared fundamental interests that unite them against common foes (Horkheimer 1985a: 290; 1988: 320).[5]

Horkheimer (1988b) viewed the "clique as the central sociological concept in today's society," whereby the "clique is a subdivision of the racket or identical with it" (1988b: 317).).[6] A standard dictionary defines a racket as a "dishonest way of getting money (by deceiving or threatening people, selling worthless goods, etc.)" (Hornby et al 1976: 702). This meaning clearly denotes an affinity to the criminal milieu. Horkheimer (1997a) intimates that rackets have an inherent air of criminality about them, which is expressed by his observation that the "boundaries between respectable and illegal rackets are unclear" (1997a: 258). The legal-criminal dichotomy of the phenomenon is reinforced by the recognition that a racket indicates protection from abuse as well as the extraction of tribute, under the threat of violence. Hence, "the racketeer is both protector and exploiter" (Stirk 1992: 141). To add to Horkheimer's observations, it is my argument that the racketeer is also an agent of corruption. Corruption represents another tool in the hands of the racketeer. Moreover, like the violence used by the racketeer or racketeers, corruption represents a privatization of power.

Antonio Gramsci (1971) refers to the concepts of dominance and hegemony. He discerned between "dominance" in which a "social group dominates antagonistic groups, which it tends to 'liquidate,' or to subjugate perhaps even by armed force . . . . " and "intellectual and moral leadership" or hegemony [whereby] "it leads kindred and allied groups" (1971: 57). The Italian Marxist scholar differentiated between "political society," where a repressive apparatus is used "for the purpose of assimilating the popular masses to the type of production and economy of a given period," and "civil society," which refers to "the hegemony of a social group over the entire national society" exercised through various institutions such as the military, law enforcement agencies, church, legal and education systems, etc. This hegemonic bloc, as Gramsci called it, contributed to the continued hold of elites on power (Fontana 1993: 143–144; also see Jary and Jary 1991: 207).

Horkheimer's rackets are similar to the elites that make up Gramsci's hegemonic bloc. The difference between the two lies in the emphasis they place on different aspects of social control. While Horkheimer stressed the disunity within ruling elites and the use of violence Gramsci focused on the manner with which those in power maintained their control without coercion. Gramsci distinguished between three types of hegemony. *Integral* hegemony refers to an environment where government and citizens coexist in harmonious agreement. Such circumstances occur only during times when "well organized, widespread opposition is absent or discredited and when the ruling class performs a progressive function in the productive process" (Femia 1981: 46). *Decadent* hegemony refers to a situation where the "dominant group has exhausted its function" and "the ideological bloc tends to decay" (*ibid.*). Thus social conflicts are latent and can erupt anytime. *Minimal* hegemony describes an environment in which the major economic groups do not "accord their interests and aspirations with the interests and aspirations of other classes" (*ibid.*). The dominant groups remain in power through *trasformismo*, the practice of "incorporating the leaders . . . . of potentially hostile groups" into the élite network, the result being "the formation of an ever broader ruling class" (*ibid.*).

Proposing a merger between Frankfurt School and Gramscian concepts, I contend that a protection racket regime emerges when elites suffer a crisis of hegemony. Such crises take place during times of rapid economic change, causing social fragmentation and disruptions in society. Gramsci claimed that, once the dominant groups no longer fulfill a progressive function, the hegemonic bloc tended to introduce coercion to uphold control (Buci-Glucksmann 1980: 56–57; Fontana 1993: 143–144). Conversely, Horkheimer (1982: 35) argued that protection was the "archetype of domination" and viewed the racket as a principle that was evident irrespective of time and place, though it manifested itself in accordance with the stipulations of a given time and place. A regime becomes a protection racket when it introduces coercion and rules by dominance rather than hegemony.

Protection as Repression

The nation, Horkheimer (1988c) wrote, is an "organization that serves the rackets. That the whole is the nation is pure ideology" (1988c: 334). Protection racket regimes are states who implicitly use terrorism — or the threat thereof — to extract riches from their populations, regardless of the opposition generated. Charles Tilly (1993) compared European state-making during the sixteenth and seventeenth centuries with OC practices, particularly racketeering. He wrote that "protection rackets represent organized crime at its smoothest," while "war making and state making" represented "protection rackets with the advantage of legitimacy" (1993: 169; also see Tilly 1990: 75, 96–126). While Tilly limited the protection racket to certain historical periods, Horkheimer — as well as Adorno — viewed it as a phenomenon that manifested itself throughout history. Horkheimer (1982) wrote:

> Procurers, condottieri [referring to the leaders of mercenary troops in Renaissance Italy], manorial lords and guilds have always protected and at the same time exploited their clients. Protection is the archetype of domination. After the interlude of Liberalism, economic tendencies in Europe progressed toward a new and total protectionism [i.e., Fascism] (1982: 35).

Horkheimer emphasized rackets instead of classes to include the notion of coercion as the common denominator of history. "In the beginning of the history of the modern racket stand the inquisitioners, at its end the leaders of the Fascist racket" (Horkheimer 1997: 334). To him "history was a history of domination" (Stirk 1992: 143). Adorno (1990) shared this perspective: "The image of the most recent economic phase shows history as a history of monopolies. The image of obvious usurpation produced today . . . . [namely Fascism] shows history as a history of group struggles, gangs and rackets" (1990: 381).

Horkheimer viewed the totalitarian state of the Fascist variety as the racket in its highest form. His examination focused on important facets shared by organized crime and Fascism, in particular their criminal nature, the "parasitical" extraction of payment, "the conspiratorial distortion of language," and the "monopolization of socially necessary functions" (Horkheimer 1985a: 288–290; Stirk 1992: 142–143).

Horkheimer's (1985) position that racketeers fight each other over allotments in the "circulating surplus value" indicated some adherence to classical Marxist theory (1985: 102). He introduced the notion of the racket to modify the Marxist class model, which was incapable of explaining the lack of unity and extent of rivalry and conflict within Fascist regimes (*ibid.*, 78; Stirk 1992: 145). Therefore, the dominant class was in fact a structure of rackets rooted in a specific mode of production which "holds down and protects the lower orders" (Horkheimer 1985a: 288). Horkheimer went beyond Marx when he compared the means of production to the weapon of a criminal. While Marx had evidently viewed Liberal Capitalism as lacking, he accepted that it functioned following some tenets of justice and impartiality. Horkheimer (1985), however, came to view coercion and injustice as key attributes of the system (1985: 86,102; Stirk 1992: 142). In his words, "government in Germany was not usurped by gangsters who forced an entry from without; rather social domination led to gangster rule by virtue of its own economic principle" (Horkheimer 1982: 34).

Horkheimer noted that the Fascist takeovers in Germany and Italy resulted in increases of economic monopolies (Horkheimer 1988: 319). Social domination which in liberal-capitalist society was based on market exchange had been replaced by control through repression and by economic monopolies (*ibid.*, 319). The society of rackets, therefore, is also an incomplete theory of domination which aims to account for the fragmentation of power; the lack of unity; the extent of rivalry, conflict, and violence; as well as the indifference toward prescribed standards of law in Fascist regimes. While the liberal-capitalist state might have favored some societal interests over others, it still guaranteed certain civil and human rights which the Fascist states in Italy and Germany abolished (Horkheimer 1985: 78; Stirk 1992: 141, 145).

The theory of a society of rackets represents a fundamental break with Marxist as well as Liberal assumptions because Horkheimer insisted that rackets were *pragmatic totalities*: They were neither universal nor individual but particularistic in character and represented the ascension of the group over both the individual and society as a whole (Horkheimer 1985a: 290; Stirk 1992: 143). Thus Horkheimer (1988c) also described a racket as "a conspiring group who push for their collective interests against the interests of the whole" (1988c: 334).

Horkheimer attributed the trend toward rackets "who dominate society" to the increase in specialists including "labor leaders, politicians, highly qualified engineers, lawyers, and so forth" (*ibid.*, 335). It seems that he was familiar with the 1911 work *Political Parties* by German sociologist and elite theorist Robert Michels (1876–1936), in particular his Iron Law of Oligarchy. Michels (1966) refers to the inherent tendency of all complex organizations to develop a dominant clique of leaders with interests in the organization itself rather than in its goals. The law also applies to progressive societies, radical or socialist political parties, and labor unions. Accordingly, the day-to-day running of a large and complex organization by its membership is unworkable, and therefore, a professional full-time leadership becomes essential (1966: 61–62). In theory, the leaders of the organization are subject to control by the mass membership, through delegate conferences and membership voting, but, in reality, they are in a predominant position. They have the intimate knowledge needed to run the organization (*ibid.*, 107). They also direct the means of communication within the organization and monopolize the status of representing the organization to the public (*ibid.*, 149–152). In turn, it becomes difficult for members to effectively counter the leverage of this professional leadership which restricts the capacity for internal democracy (*ibid.*, 167–171). Michels also argued that these inherent organizational tendencies were reinforced by people's primary psychological need to be led (*ibid.*, 93–97).

Michels' work belongs in a category with elite theorists Gaetano Mosca (1939) and Vilfredo Pareto (1968) who assumed that human societies were characterized by the differences between elites and masses. Horkheimer's society of the racket, it seems, has more in common with scholars from the other side of the political spectrum who are equally pessimistic about mass democracy. The society of rackets not only is an attack on Fascist corporatism, the racket in its highest form, but also on the democratic-pluralist and neo-corporatist as well as authoritarian-corporatist models of the state. To Horkheimer these state forms, as well as Soviet-style Socialism, merely represented different versions of racket rule produced by modern industrial society.[7]

Horkheimer, nonetheless, remained within the Marxist dimensions because he maintained that rackets perform socially necessary functions. Indeed, he claimed that rackets monopolized such functions, pushing out competition as part of the protection supplied by the racketeer (Horkheimer 1985: 101; Stirk 1992: 142). This observation is of particular significance in the light of Servadio's assertion that both organized crime and Fascism in Sicily interchangeably performed the same social function, namely, becoming allies with the island's agrarian elites for the purpose of dominating the peasantry:

> The Sicilian dominant class was given by the Fascist state an effective replacement for the methods of the Mafia in matters like the repression of the organized peasants' movement . . . . In many cases the landowners provided . . . . [the Fascist authorities] with information against the Mafiosi they had so far employed, who had been their means to safeguard their interests against the peasantry (Servadio 1976: 74).

As part of its function, organized crime performs the "role of a mediator, both between social groups and between local society and the political world" which is "of central importance in . . . . [its] rise to power" (Martin 1996: 219; also see Arlacchi 1989: 49–52; Mosca 2003). The *Mafiosi* who managed "the economic relations between landlords and peasantry" in Sicily, as well as between local society and the state, differed little from their counterparts in Shanghai's *Green Gang*, who regulated the relationship between this Chinese city's economic elite and its workers during the 1920s–1940s (*ibid.*; also see Blok 1988: 7). Hess (1988) believes that it was the appropriation of the mediator function by the Fascist state in Italy which led to the *Sicilian Mafia's* decline during the 1920s and 1930s (1988: 186). Hence, OC groups and the police agencies of totalitarian regimes may perform the same social function as active participants in the establishment and maintenance of repressive rule.

The Protection Racket State

Gramsci's belief that rule by force cannot be maintained for an extended period of time is at odds with Horkheimer's understanding that coercion is the common denominator of history (Buci-Glucksmann 1980: 56–57; Stirk 1992: 143; Fontana 1993: 143–144). Yet, it is necessary to include Horkheimer's view to explain regimes whose elites have never obtained hegemony by consent. Such elites rely on coercion to maintain dominance and to assure capital extraction, while often engaged in endless struggles against counter-hegemonic forces.

Midlarsky and Roberts (1985) observed in Nicaragua and El Salvador that their respective elites had over decades ruled through the use of violence, rather than by means of a hegemonic process. The state was "an instrument of coercion to protect the perpetually threatened economic interests of the elite" (1985: 188). Similarly, Stepan (1978) discussed "corporatist regimes" established during times of crises who rely on violence to such an extent that they generate ongoing resistance and fail to secure "ideological hegemony in the Gramscian sense" (1978: 86). Such regimes are protection racket states, which implicitly use terrorism — or the threat thereof — to extract surplus, regardless of the opposition generated. State and nonstate terrorism should be understood as deliberate "coercion and violence (or the threat thereof) directed at some victim, with the intention of inducing extreme fear in some target observers who identify with that victim in such a way that they perceive themselves as potential future victims" (Mitchell, Stohl, Carleton and Lopez 1986: 5). Evidently, the purpose of terror by OC groups differs little from that of a state agency or a terrorist organization. As Servadio (1976) observes in her description of a typical *Sicilian Mafia* killing, it "must be publicized as well as untraceable. Everybody must know why it was done and on whose behalf" (1976: 27).

More recently, Stanley (1996) applied the concept of the protection racket to developing countries. Whereas Tilly (1993) emphasized that protection rackets of the elites in the European states of the sixteenth and seventeenth centuries served against external threats, Stanley writes that "Latin American states may have used analogous protection against internal enemies to increase their call on the resources of capital and strengthen the claims of militaries, rather than civilians, to control the state" (1996: 36). In the case of El Salvador he claimed that "the . . . . military state was essentially a protection racket: the military earned the concession to govern the country (and pillage the state) in exchange for its willingness to use violence against class enemies of the country's . . . . small but powerful economic elite. To put it another way, state violence was a currency of relations between state and nonstate elites" (*ibid.*, 6–7). This political economy of violence is evident in many parts of Latin America, including nominally democratic regimes where the military plays a dominating role, such as Colombia or Peru.

Marx and *The Eighteenth Brumaire of Louis Bonaparte*

Stanley argues that the nonstate and economic elites in El Salvador *gave up political power* to the military in order to *preserve their social power (ibid.)*. This idea was first described in *The Eighteenth Brumaire of Louis Bonaparte*, Karl Marx's analysis of the coup of December 2, 1852, in France, which brought about the second empire of Napoleon III. Marx described a situation where elites were divided and in fear of the left, although an attempt at a socialist revolution had only recently been defeated. He argued that French elites allied themselves to the Bonapartist party and the army and, in doing so, handed over political power to maintain social power. Ironically, after abdicating power to the Bonapartist regime to suppress the left, French elites themselves were subjected to a similar fate. As for the peasantry, the revolutionary class of 1789, they had also joined the Bonapartist camp in fear of socialist revolution (Marx 1971: 138–159).

Marx's observation that elites give up political power in order to preserve social power has since been corroborated by numerous researchers of various political orientations. It figures prominently in the literature produced by Marxist historians and social scientists who argue that the Fascist regimes of the 1920s and 1930s were established by alliances between Fascist parties and traditional elites. German Communist August Thalheimer (1930) directly applied Marx's study in his research on Fascism (1930: 14–29). The Marxist Reinhard Kühnl (1983) also observed that the establishment of National Socialism was a result of "the alliance between the Fascist party and significant parts of the social upper class. This alliance was maintained through common interest . . . . There was agreement that the socialist workers movement had to be suppressed, democracy liquidated and a dictatorial regime to be created . . . . " (1983: 130–131).

Non-Marxist scholars likewise concluded that Fascists and National Socialists could not have come to power had it not been for alliances with existing elites. For example, Hans Mommsen (1976), one of Germany's foremost historians, wrote: "Despite the organizational and electoral successes of the Nationalsozialitische Deutsche Arbeiterpartei (NSDAP), it was only able to take over political power in alliance with the traditional elites" (1976: 167).

Mommsen (1976) pointed out further that Fascist, industrial, and agrarian elites in Germany agreed "on the elimination of the Weimar Republic's constitution, the creation of strong state authority and . . . . the speedy subjugation of Marxism" (*ibid.*, 168). Martin Broszat (1981) similarly claimed that "Hitler and his conservative and nationalist allies . . . . were just as much at one in their determination to dismiss completely from Germany's political life the Communist left and . . . . Social Democracy [as they were to dispose] of the parliamentary system and [to establish] a durable authoritarian government" (1981: 57). The British historian, Alan Bullock (1961), wrote:

What the . . . . Right wanted was to regain its old position in Germany as the ruling class, to destroy the hated republic and restore the monarchy; to put the

working classes 'in their places;' to rebuild the military power of Germany; to
reverse the decision of 1918 and to restore Germany — their Germany — to a
dominant position in Europe. Blinded by interest and prejudice, the Right . . . .
made the gross mistake of supposing that in Hitler they found a man who would
enable them to achieve their ends. A large section of the German middle class,
powerfully attracted by Hitler's nationalism, and many of the . . . . officer corps
followed their lead (1961: 215).

Even Ernst Nolte (1976), who has been associated with the New Right in Germany,
acknowledged that it was proper to "strongly emphasize the inner affinities between
fascist parties and the leading strata, and to view fascism as a regime [type] which
cannot be separated from the system in which it hatched" (1976: 201). Wolfgang
Schieder (1972) observed on Italian Fascism that it would not have come to power
"if it had not found allies among [the large-estate holders class], aristocracy, the
Church, the Monarchy [and] . . . . industry. Italy's Fascist regime was a . . . .
compromise regime between the traditional elites and the Fascist state party" (1972:
168; also see Tasca 1966). This understanding is also not limited to the study of
Fascist regimes. For example, the Latin America specialist Max Cameron (1997)
employed Marx's analysis to explain the April 1992 *autogolpe*, or self-coup, by
Peruvian President Alberto Fujimori.

Organized Crime as Repression

Harold Isaacs (1962) also relied on Marx's analysis in his study of the 1927
Shanghai Coup. This coup d'état was executed by the Shanghai *Green Gang*, a
powerful criminal fraternity, and led to the establishment of the dictatorship of
Chiang Kai-shek and the *Guomindang*, or Nationalist Party (1962: 180–182). In
return for their help in the elimination of Communist party and union organizations
in Shanghai, Chiang not only gave the *Green Gang* and its most prominent leader,
Du Yue-sheng, free reign in that city's underworld and the narcotics trade, gang
members also became officers and members of the Nationalist military and police
(Martin 1996: 111; Thamm 1996: 81).

The elites of China's most industrialized city had allied themselves with Chiang
Kai-shek and funded the coup. The Nationalist party leader relied on 'troops'
provided by organized crime, who initially terrorized the left but subsequently
targeted the business groups as well. Isaacs (1962) noted:

The Chinese bankers and merchants had . . . . call[ed] in Chiang Kai-shek and the
gangsters against the workers. Now they were forced to submit themselves to the
predatory raids of their own rescuers. Like the French bourgeoisie which in 1852
"brought the slum proletariat to power" . . . . the Chinese bourgeoisie elevated
over itself the scum and riffraff . . . . of the Green Gang . . . . (1962: 180–182).

Moreover, not only did criminals perform tasks essentially similar to those of the repressive agencies in European Fascist regimes, the *Green Gang* re-organized and managed Shanghai labor for Chiang Kai-shek (Martin 1996: 216). The 1927 Shanghai Coup marked the beginning of the civil war between Nationalists and Communists which came to an end only in 1949.

Similar observations have been made about very different OC groups in other parts of the world. Hess (1986) observes that the *Sicilian Mafia* "represents a political reality, a reactionary force that is employed to resist change, to maintain privilege, and to suppress attempts to redefine property relations and political rights" (1986: 128). He described the *Sicilian Mafia* as a system stabilizer that practiced "repressive crime" with the goal of preserving the positions of elites in society (*ibid.*, 129–130). It, in effect, replaced the state, which was too weak to defend the interests of Sicily's agrarian elites. Mafia, Hess writes, is "private power employed, exercised and exploited by strong-arm men utilized in a threatening manner in all kinds of social conflicts" (*ibid.*).[8] The collaboration between socioeconomic elites and organized crime in Sicily lasted through most of the Cold War and came to an end only after the fall of Communism in Eastern Europe. Not only had the *Sicilian Mafia* outlived much of its social function, it was also increasingly viewed as a threat by Italian elites themselves (Chubb 1989: 46–54; *Time Magazine.* June 3, 1996: 21–23; Stille 1999: 493; Santino 2001).

Kawamura's (1994) study of Japanese organized crime found that the *Yakuza's* links to politics were "without exception located on the far right" (1994: 29–32). *Yakuza* leaders cooperated with right-wing officers, hunted down Communists, worked as strike breakers, and formed the economic spearhead of the Japanese invasion of China during the 1930s and 1940s (*ibid.*; also see Kaplan and Dubro 1986; Martin 1996: 228). *Yakuza* crime groups, in close cooperation with the Japanese military, profited greatly from the sale of opium and heroin to the Chinese population in occupied Manchuria. The Japanese relied on narcotics trafficking to finance their operations, earning an estimated US$300 million annually from the sale of opium and heroin. However, the practice was also part of Japan's strategy to undermine China's moral capacity to resist (Martin 1996: 260–263; 272–275; Jennings 1997: 79–81; 95; Booth 1999: 163).

As discussed in more detail in a later chapter, Peter Scholl-Latour's (1979) research on Indochina came to similar conclusions about the alliance between the French colonial authorities and the river pirates of the twin city of Saigon-Cholon, the *Binh Xuyen*, during the first Indochina War during the early 1950s. The *Binh Xuyen* profited from the opium trade, prostitution, and racketeering, sharing the proceeds with the authorities. They also participated, on the side of the French, in the anticolonial war against the Communist *Vietminh* rebels under Ho Chi Minh. The *Binh Xuyen's* leader, General Le Van Vien, was given a free reign by the colonial authorities, and his heavily armed criminals who were feared more than the *Vietminh*, succeeded in eradicating the Communist underground in and around Saigon (1979: 47, 87–88).

The connection between organized crime and right-wing politics is also evidenced in the Latin American context. As one Argentine observer wrote on the emergence and role of OC groups, "the . . . . demand for cocaine . . . . has jolted the regional economies thrusting a new and violent actor on the center of Latin American politics: the new drug trafficking right" (Collett 1989: 126).

In Bolivia, the 1980 Cocaine Coup was carried out by corrupt, reactionary military officers working with the country's leading drug traffickers and their paramilitaries. The fear of a return to democracy prompted General Luis García Meza to lead the 189th coup d'état in Bolivia's history, a so-called National Revolution to secure the country from "Communist extremists" (Hargreaves 1993: 177–178). It was financed by leading Bolivian drug dealers and coorganized by Klaus Barbie, the former Gestapo chief of Lyon, France, during the German occupation in World War II (*ibid.*).

In Colombia, drug traffickers have set up "mafia republics" (Mayer 1990: 199). These are territories where the state has little presence and thus must share control. Local police, military authorities, and agrarian elites directly collaborate with organized crime in financing and organizing right-wing paramilitaries. These groups combat local left-wing rebels but also function as death squads responsible for massive human rights abuses (*Semana.* Jan. 9, 1996: 18– 21; *Cambio 16.* Dec. 23, 1996: 14–15; *Colombia Alert.* 1997: 1–3). As Reyes (1996) so rightly observed:

> Many narcotraffickers began to invest in large haciendas in those regions where property was concentrated and where there was frequent guerilla harassment of the landowners. As a consequence, what was expected to be a way to defend the traditional social order against subversion opened a political and legal space for some narcotraffickers to join the task of counterinsurgency for their own benefit, as allies of the armed forces (1996: 126).

Finally, in Peru, the cash-starved military allied itself with drug traffickers to finance the civil war against the Maoist rebel movement *Sendero Luminoso* during the early 1990s. By participating in the cocaine economy, the military earned a considerable portion of the country's annual drug profits. These were, in turn, used to buy armaments, materials, and foodstuffs (*La República.* Feb. 29, 1992: 14–15; OGD 1993: 219–226; *Oiga.* Jan. 24, 1994: 18–22).

Criminal organizations have also participated in the suppression of left-wing politics and labor activism in the United States. For example, to prevent unionization during the 1920s and 1930s, large corporations such as Ford and General Motors kept private armies of thugs to terrorize sympathetic workers (Pearce 1981: 165–167; Block 1986: 58–77). Once unions were established, criminals played a role in running them not only to gain access to their treasuries but also to assure the acquiescence of workers and to keep them from turning to the left using tactics such as threats and murder. During the interwar years, party bosses, city officials, anti-Communist business leaders, and crime groups dominated US domestic politics (Von Lampe 1999: 284–287). For example, the Capone mob in Chicago was in league with the city's economic elite and the police to suppress organized labor. Capone recounts:

> Listen, ... don't get the idea I'm one of those goddam radicals. Don't get the idea I'm knocking the American system. My rackets are run strictly along American lines and they are going to stay that way . . . . This American system of ours, ... call it Americanism, call it Capitalism, call it what you like, gives to each and every one of us a great opportunity if we only seize it with both hands and make the most of it (Cockburn 1998: 373).

Regardless, criminal groups can become partners to elites in a manner that is remindful of Gramsci's notion of *trasformismo*, the practice of attracting counter-hegemonic groups into the ruling structures for the purpose of preserving them (Gramsci 1973: 243; Femia 1981: 47–48).

Conclusion

Organized crime can become ideological. Contrary to the claims that criminal societies do not have political designs of their own, it can be maintained that such organizations may develop or acquire ideological preferences as part of their evolution. While criminal groups may initially emerge as organizations of the excluded and exploited, established criminal societies strive to become included. The integrative tendency of organized crime is a general characteristic that plays itself out depending on the differences dictated by time and place.

The Protection Racket regime is a model of socioeconomic repression. Such a regime is formed by state and/or nonstate elites in order to preserve their domination through the often violent exclusion of large groups in societies that experience conditions of substantial social disparities. Apart from the use or threat of violence, corruption is an essential component of power relations and cannot be separated from power. Moreover, while the grounds of exclusion may differ (e.g., class, race, or gender), this condition often manifests itself in economic disadvantage, if not exploitation. Conversely, inclusion is more often than not economically rather than class based. Even if not, it bestows economic advantages to which the excluded have no access, most important the ability to take advantage of or to exploit. The specific composition and strength of groups which come to dominate a given racket regime determine its nature and conduct in internal and external affairs. Protection rackets cannot be attributed to specific types of political organization. Rather, they can be part of different regimes, ranging from formally democratic governments to totalitarian dictatorships. Nevertheless, organized crime can exist in most forms of the protection racket regime, while it is severely suppressed in its totalitarian manifestation.

Organized crime–elite alliances transpire during crises of hegemony. Elites may ally themselves with criminals as they perceive themselves threatened by counter-hegemonic groups. In the age of modern capitalism these are usually Socialist and/or Communist political parties, organized labor unions, Marxist revolutionary movements, and other organizations engendered by the excluded such as church or human rights groups. Yet, different socioeconomic formations will produce distinct hegemonic and counter-hegemonic groups as well as criminal organizations.

Elite alliances with Fascist parties, ultraconservative militaries as well as OC groups have served the same social function, namely the establishment and/or maintenance of a repressive socioeconomic order. These alliances occur when elites have been weakened by counter-hegemonic movements, forcing them to accept any partners, including criminal ones. The ability of mafia groups to integrate themselves into existing power structures depends on the need of elites for this partnership. If its services are no longer required, or if perceived as a threat, elites can and do turn against organized crime using the power of the state.[9]

Mafia groups tend to be subhegemonic because elites generally do not concede control to preserve social power but to share it. Unlike totalitarian parties or right-wing militaries, such groups are rarely equal or dominant partners. Historically, however, there have been cases of organized criminal infiltration of state, economy and society, whereby it is no longer possible to use the term 'organized crime' because the partnership has produced a new and qualitatively different phenomenon, the criminalized state.

OC practices resemble those of Fascist or other types of repressive regimes. Organized crime, in its role of oppressor, may potentially contribute to the maintenance of an unjust social order. Regime, however, not only refers to a territorial unit with defined boundaries but applies to all levels of political organization, and includes local and international power structures as well. While states are limited by their territorial boundaries, the collaboration between elites and organized crime can grow beyond the national to the international level.[10]

Finally, what the success of the totalitarian state against the mafia tells the scholar is that adherence to civil rights practices by the police favors the criminal.[11] On the other hand, the dangers posed by anticrime legislation should be apparent as policies created to combat OC groups can easily lead to abuses against individuals and groups engaged in legal opposition politics. In Colombia, policies designed to fight the country's drug cartels degenerated into mechanisms of repression of the country's legitimate opposition groups, such as organized labor and community organizations (Weiner 1996: 31–36). In the United States, the powers of law enforcement were extended considerably to combat the narcotics trade and other organized crime–related activities, causing corruption while endangering civil liberties, law, and democracy itself (Elias 1991: 45–54; *Toronto Star.* June 11, 1998: A15). A society which aims to preserve its democratic institutions and civil liberties may have to tolerate a low level of OC activity.

Endnotes

1. In this book I will also use the term 'mafia' to describe organized crime. While once used to describe Sicilian organized crime, it has been adopted to describe similar phenomena globally. The term 'mafia' has also found entry into other languages. For example, Russians refer to the *Mafiya*; Germans call it *Mafia*, and the French use *Mafie*. In this work, the term 'mafia,' when not italicized and capitalized, refers to organized crime in general. However, when used in a specific context, the term will be italicized and capitalized, such as *Sicilian Mafia*. Similarly, when discussing other criminal groups, their names will also be italicized, such as Japan's *Yakuza* groups or China's *Green Gang*. I have italicized these and other foreign terms, unless they were part of direct quotations.

2. See for example Horkheimer 1982, Horkheimer 1985, 1985a, and 1985b as well as Adorno 1990.

3. It is noteworthy that the conditions of the US occupation in Japan resulted in a similar revival of the *Yakuza* (Kawamura 1994: 29–32).

4. For a discussion of organized crime in the Soviet Union see chapter 6.

5. The disunity within Fascist regimes is an aspect often overlooked by researchers. Internal power struggles were encouraged by the respective Fascist leader, as discord had the function to maintain control by assuring that subordinates compete with each other rather than aspiring to take power themselves. Also, the disunity of the regime was caused by the 'eclectic' nature of the alliance itself, which combined elites of different and conflicting beliefs such as modernizing industrialists and reactionary large-estate holders. The leader is necessary and even accepted as such because he mediates, or rather imposes decisions which, in turn, are accepted by elites. In fact, his or her decision making is essential for keeping the elite racket united (Broszat 1981; Browder 1990; Salvemini 1971). Similar observations have been made in the case of OC groups. While gangs fight over territory, they are as likely to cooperate with other groups to avoid conflict and assure themselves continued profits. The gang leader's position greatly depends on his ability to mediate between his lieutenants and make decisions on territory, profitsharing, etc. His/her rule is not only accepted because of his/her personal power but is desired by subordinates as it is deemed essential for maintaining the peace among those involved as a precondition for continued illegal earnings. My own readings on the likes of 'Lucky' Luciano (New York 1920s–1930s), Du Yue-sheng (Shanghai 1920s–1940s) or Pablo Escobar Gaviria (Medellín 1970s–1980s) indicate that it is the leader's ability to maintain an environment for continued profits and their willingness to adapt to changes in the illegal markets they supply which keeps him (or her) in power (See for example, Gosch and Hammer 1976; Martin 1996; Strong 1996).

6. Horkheimer's colleague Friedrich Pollock with whom he collaborated referred to "a system of obtaining money fraudulently or by threat of violence, usually with the outward consent of the victims" (Horkheimer 1985c: 251).

7. Pluralists argue that state policies are a mere reflection of the influence interest groups are able to exert; or as observed by Robert Dahl (1956) "all the active and legitimate groups . . . . can make themselves heard at some crucial stage in the process of decision" (1956: 137; Nohlen 1995: 735– 736). Dahl's colleague Seymour M. Lipset (1963) wrote that the pluralist state had solved the dilemmas of modern society: "[T]he fundamental political problems of the industrial revolution have been solved: the workers have . . . . industrial and political citizenship; the conservatives . . . . accepted the welfare state; and the democratic left has recognized that an increase in overall state power carried with it more dangers to freedom than solutions for economic problems" (1963: 406). Neo-Pluralists recognized that some interests within societies were not necessarily sufficiently organized to muster adequate support to influence policy making. Neo-Pluralists argued that business interests tended to go further because of the larger resources available (Lindblom 1977). In pluralist society, numerous interest groups attempt to influence political decision making. The neo-corporatist state, prevalent in Western Europe during the 1960s and 1970s, went beyond by integrating the most powerful groups, such as labor unions, or industry associations into the actual formulation and implementation of policies. According to Lehmbruch (1977), groups in neo-corporatist society assume an intermediary position. Governments define policies in close cooperation with particular interest group partners, and policies are implemented to a large extent through these groups themselves (1977: 91–126). In the Fascist and authoritarian corporatist regimes, the ability of groups to participate in the decision-making process is severely reduced or nonexistent. Policies are imposed from above and groups merely implement them (Stepan 1978: 41; Williamson 1989: 35–36).

8. Norbert Mappes-Niediek (2003) observed that the extremist Serbian nationalist militias set up to terrorize other ethnic groups in the former Yugoslavia were largely criminals, because the Milosevic regime had to seek those with the "expertise in plundering and killing within the criminal milieu" (2003: 53).

9. Frank Pearce's (1976; 1981) excellent analysis of US organized crime reveals that its activities are tolerated by ruling elites as long as they benefit from the former's activities. Conversely, if elite interests are challenged by organized crime, elites subdue it using the repressive agencies of the state.

10. An early example of an internationalized OC group acting in support of a foreign repressive regime is the *Italo-American Mafia's* involvement with the Batista regime in Cuba prior to the 1959 Castro revolution (See Cirules 1993).

11. Aside from totalitarian regimes, revolutionary governments have also been successful in the suppression of organized crime for the following reasons. First, revolutionary governments, irrespective of their political colors, often undergo a totalitarian phase immediately after seizing power. For example, the Triads and other criminal organizations were eliminated after the 1949 Chinese revolution, while American-Italian and domestic organized crime disappeared in Cuba after the Castro revolution in 1959. Second, revolutionary regimes may also contribute to the demise of organized crime by addressing the conditions of social disorganization that contribute to crime. Third, similar to Fascist regimes, socialist ones also eliminate the local power structures on which mafia clientelism thrives by inserting their own representatives.

Chapter 3

Historical Observations on 'Clear[ly] and Present[ly] Danger'[ous] Plant Life

It would not be right to pass over the herb
the Indians call cuca and the Spaniards coca,
which was and still is the chief source of wealth of Peru
for those engaged in the trade.

(Sixteenth-century Peruvian historian Garcilaso de la Vega (1966: 509).

The coca and opium plants provide the raw materials for the two most important products on the illegal global narcotics market. The history and the political economy of these plants and their derivatives relate directly to the existing dilemma of international drug trafficking. Most important, today's developed countries have in their past relied on the cultivation, production, and sale of narcotics to increase their treasuries, to balance their budgets, to finance colonial governments and conquests, to foster overall development in their mother countries as well as to fund Cold War conflicts. These centuries-old practices laid the foundations for the international economies in cocaine and heroin, some of the main sources of income of international organized crime. This chapter also provides the necessary introduction to the case studies dealing with organized crime in China during the 1920s–1940s as well as Bolivia, Colombia, and Peru during the 1980s–1990s.

Introduction

Humans have used psychoactive substances for millennia. These traditional applications were relied on during religious ceremonies as sacred means to reach different stages of consciousness to enable communication with the divine, as facilitators for socialization for people belonging to the same group, and as medicines (Soberón 1995: 3).

The coca plant — from which cocaine is derived — has played an important role in the diet, religion, and culture of the indigenous populations of the Andean region, most significantly the Quechua and Aymara people, for thousands of years. The plant and its derivatives are still employed as medicines against altitude sickness, colds, stomach pains, colic, diarrhea, cramps, nausea, toothache, stomach ulcers, rheumatism, and asthma. Those who use it in the traditional manner, by chewing the leaves, claim that it is a stimulant which gives them stamina and strength and also relieves "feelings of hunger, thirst, cold, and fatigue" (Grinspoon and Bakalar 1981: 150–151). Coca leaves were a very valuable commodity in the Inca Empire, *Tawantinsuyu*, the 'land of the four quarters.' Apart from gold and cotton, coca was used to pay tribute to tribal chiefs and the Inca Emperor (Aguado 1956: 407). In Inca society, the plant was viewed as the gift of the gods (Henman 1981: 19–30). Most scholars maintain that the cultivation, distribution, and consumption of coca was a monopoly in the hands of the Inca elite who excluded the lower classes from using it, except for medicinal purposes. According to Henman, coca cultivation and usage began among the agrarian societies of Peru and Ecuador and spread north to Colombia by about 3000 BC (*ibid.*, 65). At the time of the Europeans' arrival in the 1530s AD, coca was used as far north as Panama, while Inca conquests of territories to the south had spread the custom to present-day northern Argentina. Coca use continued to spread after the Spanish conquest, and by the nineteenth century, tribes in Brazilian Amazonia, situated in the Portuguese colonial empire, also used it (*ibid.*, 72).

Opium, from which morphine and heroin derive, has been used since 8000–7000 BC and is probably the oldest drug known to humankind. Opium poppies were grown by the ancient Sumerians, Assyrians, Egyptians, and Chinese. It was also known to the Greeks and Romans (Thamm 1994: 10–11). The drug was used for medicinal, religious as well as recreational purposes, but it was also a tool of political assassination and murder. The Roman Empress Agrippina poisoned her stepson Britannicus with an overdose of opium in 55 AD to assure the ascension of her own son Nero (Booth 1999: 16–21). By 1500 BC, opium and hashish had become important items of trade and could be found on Egyptian and Phoenician marketplaces. These drugs were also commonplace in the late Roman Empire; however, sale and consumption were restricted. For example, Emperor Diocletian (243–316 AD) regulated the trade in opium and hashish by setting very high prices, which limited their availability to the upper classes. Accordingly, about 1.25 kilograms of hashish sold for eighty Roman dinars, while the same quantity of opium cost one hundred and fifty. At the time, a kilogram of wheat flour cost two dinars (Thamm 1994: 15).

Following the breakup of the Roman Empire after the fourth century AD, knowledge of drugs and their uses fell into oblivion in Western Europe. In the Byzantine Empire in Southeastern Europe and Asia Minor, the usages of opium and other drugs were not forgotten in the Greek schools of medicine established in antiquity, which continued to function and later merged with those of Arab medicine (Seefelder 1996: 49). Indeed, there are only a few references to opium in the historical records between the eighth and eleventh centuries in western Europe (*ibid.*, 77—78). Drugs were often associated with witchcraft, and practitioners were persecuted. Knowledge of the old usages returned to Europe following the crusades and contact with the more advanced societies of Islam. Moreover, the practices and regulations established during antiquity were reintroduced in the late Middle Ages. Drugs were viewed as luxury items and heavily taxed. The northern Italian city-states of Venice and Genoa grew rich from the trade in opium and hashish. Apparently, Venetian opium products were known all over Europe for their high quality (Thamm 1994: 12—16; Seefelder 1996: 90).

By the early sixteenth century, the Europeans had begun to establish overseas colonies where they provided large supplies of drugs to the colonized to finance the administration of these territories and to pacify the less cooperative among the new subjects. These practices, in turn, created large populations of addicts. In addition, sales contributed to widespread drug dependency in the mother countries, a process that was reinforced by the emergence of the pharmaceutical industry and large-scale narcotics manufacturing in Europe and North America by the mid-nineteenth century. This period ended only in the early twentieth century with the creation of an international regime on drugs administered initially by the League of Nations (LN), and following World War II, the United Nations (UN).

However, while narcotics became internationally controlled substances whose illegal production and distribution carried severe punishments, many states continued their involvement with drugs on a clandestine basis. Often governments failed to implement or enforce legislation to end the illegal drug sales of their nation's pharmaceutical companies. In other cases, states in today's developed world relied on narcotic sales to finance military operations, often in collaboration with criminal organizations. Examples include the large-scale drug production and distribution by the Japanese in Manchuria prior to and during World War II as well as the drug trafficking involving the French and US intelligence agencies in the Cold War conflicts in Indochina, Afghanistan, and Central America (Scholl-Latour 1979; Avirgan and Honey 1989; McCoy 1991; Porch 1995; Lyman and Potter 2000). Since the fall of Communism, the demons called in to fight the Cold War have come to haunt their former employers and collaborators. Fostered by Cold War practices, the new millennium has witnessed the rise of transnational criminal organizations, sometimes linked to militant terrorist groups with a multitude of agendas, as well as a revival of left-wing, counter-hegemonic movements with varying claims of legitimacy, who rely on some form of involvement in illegal drug economies to help finance their operations.

Coca, Incas, and Conquistadors

The coca plant has been an important component of the pre-Columbian Andean societies for millennia. After the conquest of the Inca Empire by the Spanish conquistadors Francisco Pizarro and Diego Almagro in the first half of the sixteenth

century, coca leaves came to play an important role in the colonial economy. The
Indian laborers in the gold and silver mines received coca as part of their wages
because it made them work better (Naranjo 1981: 168; Del Olmo 1992: 71; also see
Unanue 1794: 228). As a result, in Potosí, Spain's silver-mining capital in South
America, located in today's Bolivia, the coca trade alone was worth half a million
pesos annually during the second half of the sixteenth century (Keen 1974: 187).
Henman (1981) explained that a merchant bringing sixty thousand pounds of coca
leaves to Potosí could expect to make 7,500 pesos, the equivalent of over 34 kilos
in gold, sufficient currency to retire in comfort in sixteenth century Spanish
America (1981: 79). Prescott (1963) argued that coca "constituted a most important
item of the colonial revenue of Spain" (1963: 85). Another author referred to coca
as "one of the driving forces of the Andean economy" (Cook 1981: 223). The Latin
American historian, Eduardo Galeano (1982), wrote:

> Coca . . . . already existed in Inca times. But [it] was then distributed in
> moderation; the Inca government had a monopoly on it and only permitted its use
> for ritual purposes or for those who worked in the mines. The Spaniards
> energetically stimulated its consumption. It was great business. In Potosí in the
> sixteenth century as much was spent on European clothes for the oppressors as on
> coca for the oppressed. In Cuzco four-hundred Spanish merchants lived off the
> coca traffic; every year one hundred thousand baskets with a million kilos of coca-
> leaf entered the Potosí silver mines. The church imposed . . . . [a 10 percent tax]
> (1982: 72–73).

The Spanish American historian Garcilaso de la Vega, the son of a conquistador
and an Inca princess, pointed out in his *Comentarios reales que tratan del origen
de los Incas* [The Royal Commentaries of the Incas] written in the first decade of
the seventeenth century that "it would not be right to pass over the herb the Indians
call cuca and the Spaniards coca, which was and still is the chief source of wealth
of Peru for those engaged in the trade" (De la Vega 1966: 509). He also included
the observations of the Spanish priest Padre Blas Valera, who wrote that coca "has
another great value, which is that the income of the bishop, the canons, and other
priests of the cathedral church of Cuzco is derived from the . . . . [10 percent tax]
on the coca leaf; and many Spaniards have grown rich, and still do on the traffic in
this herb" (*ibid.*).

The Spanish conquistador Pedro Cieza de Leon, who spent some seventeen
years in Peru, recorded that "this coca was so valuable in Peru in the years 1548,
1549, and 1551 that there has never been in the whole world a plant or root or any
growing thing that bears and yields every year as this one does, aside from spices,
which are a different thing, that is so highly valued" (Cieza de Leon 1973: 221).

The so-called coca debate in the sixteenth century provides further insights.
Apparently, various factions of the Spanish colonial administration were at odds
over the question of coca. Abolitionists from the Catholic clergy, imbued by the
spirit of the Inquisition, viewed the Indians' consumption as a pagan practice and

considered the plant an "invention of the devil" (Gagliano 1963: 43–47; also see Unanue 1794: 215–216). A humanist faction of the Church did not object to the consumption of coca, which was considered part of the diet of Indian laborers. Rather, the group opposed the inhuman conditions in the Spanish-run coca plantations that caused the deaths of 30–50 percent of laborers annually. Yet, the lobby of Spanish coca growers strongly objected to any restrictions pointing to the enormous importance of the leaf to the colonial economy and its significance to the Spanish treasury. While the economic arguments proved strongest, by the second half of the sixteenth century, the Spanish crown issued legislation which apparently eased the conditions of laborers in coca plantations (*ibid.*). Still, coca production not only increased in the period following the conquest, after the Spanish had made the leaves available to everybody, it expanded further during the eighteenth century. According to Unanue (1794), between 1785 and 1789, the coca economy in Spanish-controlled Peru was worth almost 2.7 million pesos annually and by far surpassed the one that had existed in the sixteenth century (1794: 227). While it may be difficult to ascertain the leaves' precise economic importance, these observations nevertheless confirm their significance for the Spanish colonial economy.

There appears to be considerable disagreement as to how the conquered Indians used coca. Most authors concur that coca consumption had been strictly regulated by the Inca, permitting its use for religious and medicinal purposes only but not for mass consumption, which was introduced by the Spanish (Grinspoon and Bakalar 1976: 19; Cook 1981: 223; Naranjo 1981: 166; Galeano 1982: 58–59). Henman (1981), however, charged scholars with copying a "dubious claim" made by sixteenth-century Spanish American historian Garcilaso de la Vega, namely that the trade and use of coca was an Inca monopoly and that its consumption was limited to the ruling class (1981: 39).

This point is important in the debate on coca eradication today. If coca is a mind-altering drug, the Spanish turned the conquered populations of *Tawantinsuyu* and other parts of South America into addicts for their purposes. Hyams and Ordish (1963), for example, described coca as the "soma" of the Peruvian "Brave New World" (1963: 163). While the narcotics sold through the opium monopolies established by the European colonial powers in Southeast Asia — which will be discussed later — indeed had an intoxicating effect on the governed, the same cannot be argued in the case of coca. Given the properties of coca compared to those of opium, the explanation that the indigenous people in Peru, Bolivia, Colombia, and northern Argentina as well as their antecedents have been drug addicts for more than five centuries is inadequate. Yet, as Enrique Mayer (1986) points out, this is precisely the manner in which the inhabitants of the Andes have been depicted in much of the literature. The coca-chewing Indian is invariably described as "alienated" and "asocial," "solitary and taciturn," and also "stupefied and apathetic" because of this practice (1986: 9; also see Von Hagen 1957: 112; Henman 1981: 42; Cotler 1999: 81–85).

As Mayer observes, such views are contradicted by the realities of coca consumption. First, the leaves are hardly ever consumed alone but in shared rituals in the company of others prior to and during physical labor. The chewing of coca takes place within a specific cultural setting of established "courtesies, etiquette and good manners" (*ibid.*, 9). In addition, coca is chewed when there is the need for clear and precise appraisal and judgment. Finally, apathy can hardly be a characteristic of the Andean natives who have persisted in the harsh conditions of their environment "in the face of . . . . five centuries of exploitation and cultural domination" (*ibid.*).[1]

A number of authors challenged the notion of the Inca monopoly on coca. Henman (1981) claimed that the Incas' dominion over many different conquered nations required making concessions. Thus recently acquired subjects were permitted to continue their practices after they had accepted the new rulers, especially in those cases when coca played a significant role in a conquered nation's economy. The Inca rulers would not have risked antagonizing new subjects by disrupting their economic practices (1981: 72–77). The Peruvian researcher, Hugo Cabieses (1994) also disputed that coca was reserved for the elites and asserted instead that "the leaf was used extensively . . . . by the [Inca] elite and the common people alike" (1994: 3–4). He maintained further:

> While coca constitutes a fundamental part of Andean culture, cocaine was isolated, used and abused first by Europeans and later by North Americans . . . . [On the other hand,] millions of people in the Andean region continue to use coca for the same reasons it was used by their ancestors and they consider it a form of cultural affirmation and resistance against Western pressures. In addition, coca contains a series of nutritional and medicinal properties that cannot be taken advantage of because of the dark history that has been built around the leaf (*ibid.*).[2]

Myrna Cintron (1986) provided an additional explanation, a process which may be termed the *socialization of coca use* as a consequence of conquest. Thus, while coca consumption was likely subject to some restrictions during Inca times, she viewed it as an aspect of social control and an expression of social stratification. Given the religious importance of the plant, the availability of coca, the gift of the gods, depended on an individual's social status and occupation. While available to the common people for medicinal purposes, because coca extracts were seen as a chief remedy for many maladies, the consumption of the leaves by chewing was permitted only to members of the Inca class, priests, the long-distance messengers of the Empire, and the mine workers (Cintron 1986: 26–27; Galeano 1982: 72–73). When the Spanish made the leaves available to everybody, the gift of the gods that had been the symbol of the Inca upper class of *Tawantinsuyu* came to represent the Indian underclass of the Spanish Viceroyalty of Peru. This, however, does not imply that coca consumers are drug addicts.

This issue is significant considering the very different effects that coca and drugs such as cocaine, opium or its derivatives, exert on the human nervous system, which calls for different solutions. Although the traditional consumption of the leaves does not produce mind-altering effects among users in the Andes, both coca as well as cocaine are on the index of the UN's list of illicit drugs. In fact, the organization's Single Convention of 1961 called for the complete eradication of the coca plant. The 1988 UN Vienna Convention's article 14 acknowledges the "traditional legal uses" of coca, although the plant is still considered illegal (Mortimer 1974: 20; Plowman 1986: 6–7; Amboss 1994: 15; Painter 1994: 2). However, the scientific basis on which the assessment of coca rests is a 1950 study which by now should be considered dated. Moreover, a 1995 UN study on coca and cocaine, which was never published, pointed to the favorable health effects of the traditional methods of coca consumption (TNI 2003). Regardless, the cultivation of coca declined but did not end with the collapse of Spanish colonial rule in the 1820s. Coca has remained an important part of the culture and the diet of tens of millions of indigenous people in South America (Plowman 1986: 6–7; Spedding 2000: 47–70).

From Coca to Cocaine

The present consumption practices of cocaine can be traced back to the mid-nineteenth century, when the Austrian scientist Albert Niemann isolated the alkaloid cocaine chlorohydrate (Holmstedt 1981: 114–115). In 1863, Angelo Mariani produced his *Vin Mariani*, a Bordeaux wine with fresh coca leaves. The analysis of preserved bottles determined that *Vin Mariani* contained between thirty-five and seventy milligrams of cocaine (Gómez Ordoñez 1991: 74). This enterprising individual from the French Mediterranean island of Corsica also produced an elixir with a concentration of cocaine three times higher than the wine as well as a tea with a potency that was eight times higher than *Mariani* wine (*ibid.*).

Mariani published a book with the names and dedications of his most famous customers. Accordingly, Pope Pius IX always carried a little bottle of *Vin Mariani* with him (*ibid.*).[3] His successor, Pope Leo XIII, also had a fancy for Mariani's wine because it inspired his religious contemplations. Queen Victoria I and other crowned heads of Europe consumed the Corsican's products as well. The US inventor Thomas Edison, the French sculptor Auguste Rodin, the actress Sarah Bernhardt, and the writers Emile Zola, Henrik Ibsen, Jules Verne, and Arthur Conan Doyle were also famous Mariani customers (*ibid.*, 75). In 1886, the US chemist John Pembert Smith, created Coca-Cola, a drink containing cocaine, which became a major commercial success. Other commercially sold beverages laced with cocaine include Coca-Nola, Cerely-Cola and Dope-Cola (Arango and Child 1987: 99–100).

During the second half of the nineteenth century the availability of many products containing narcotics was enhanced by the emergence of the pharmaceutical industry that became a driving force in the development and marketing of new drugs. The commercial production of medical cocaine began in the mid-1880s following Austrian ophthalmologist Karl Koller's discovery that the drug was a good local anaesthetic for eye operations (Freud 1999: 16). The then German pharmaceutical company Merck was the first to manufacture cocaine industrially. The US company Parke-Davies "became one of the world's leading cocaine manufacturers, producing coca cordials, cocaine cigarettes, hypodermic capsules, ointments, and sprays" (McCoy 1991: 6–7; also see Musto 1973: 7). Hundreds of medications that contained coca leaves or cocaine to deal with ailments such as colds, digestive troubles, asthma, or impotence were available in the pharmacies of Europe and North America (Arango and Child 1987: 99–100).

The German military also took an interest. Physician Theodor Aschenbrandt dispensed cocaine to soldiers to test whether the drug enhanced their physical endurance on maneuver (Grinspoon and Bakalar 1976: 32). Aschenbrandt's study was read by a young Sigmund Freud, who subsequently came to play a role in the expansion of the German and US cocaine industries. In fact, Freud received payments from both Merck and its US competitor, Parke-Davies, to vouch for their respective brands (Freud 1999: 67–83).

After 1884, the demand for cocaine in Europe and North America was so great that coca came to be viewed as the "new and everlasting source of wealth" in the Latin American countries growing it (Arango and Child 1987: 102). In 1886, the influential Colombian writer and politician José María Samper wrote that

> there is no doubt that coca represents one of the many treasures with which the good hand of the Lord has provided us . . . . Already there are attempts to grow coca in the Caribbean, Algeria and Corsica but because the climatic conditions in these places are not the same as in the country of origin, the results achieved are not very satisfactory (*La Nación*. Jan. 1, 1886: 1; as cited in Arango and Child 1987: 102–103).[4]

Indeed, Europeans and Americans attempted to grow coca themselves. The Americans tried it in California, the French in Algeria and Corsica, the British in the Caribbean, Australia, their African colonies, and India and Sri Lanka. While most attempts to grow the coca plant outside of South America failed, Dutch planters on Java and Sumatra were able to challenge the monopoly of Colombia, Peru, and Bolivia. Between 1884 and 1910, coca production in these countries had steadily increased, then declined thereafter as the plant developed into a significant cash crop for the Dutch on Java by the beginning of the twentieth century (Plowman 1986: 21; Cotler 1999: 21). Maier (1987) claimed that coca produced in the Dutch Indies slowly replaced the South American variants to supply the pharmaceutical industries of Europe, North America, and Japan. "In 1922, Java alone exported 1250 tons of coca leaves" (1987: 255). Java was still referred to as a producer of coca leaves during the 1980s (*Oiga*. April 22, 1991: 43–45). Moreover, according to Gómez Ordoñez (1991), the Malay archipelago, today Malaysia, became one of the primary suppliers of coca leaves by the early twentieth century (1991: 76).

Cotler (1999) noted that Peru's coca exports dropped by 80 percent between 1905 and 1913, from 1600 to 200 tons (1999: 76).

Today Colombia, Peru, and Bolivia are again the largest producers of coca leaves. The Coca-Cola Company still uses the leaves from South America for its beverage, although the cocaine chlorohydrate has been removed. Thus, in the Yungas, Bolivia's traditional coca-growing region close to the capital La Paz, cultivation is designated for the legal domestic consumption of coca leaves as well as for export. Coca-Cola also imports coca leaves from Peru where the government maintains a monopoly, the Empresa Nacional de la Coca (ENACO), to which farmers with legal production quotas sell their harvests at set prices (Henman 1981: 77, 132–133; Filippone 1994: 329; Wisotsky 1990: 35).

In the medical communities of Europe and North America cocaine was also viewed as a cure for morphine addiction, which had become a serious social problem following various bloody military conflicts during the second half of the nineteenth century. Wounded soldiers had received morphine preparations and became addicted (Musto 1973: 1, 7; Thamm 1994: 25). In 1884, Freud wrote several glowing essays on cocaine in which he recommended cocaine therapy for the following:

- as a mental stimulant;
- as a possible treatment for digestive disorders;
- as an appetite stimulant in case of wasting diseases;
- as a treatment for morphine and alcohol addiction;
- as a treatment for asthma;
- as an aphrodisiac;
- as a local anaesthetic (Freud 1999: 67–83).

In later decades, Freud avoided discussing his earlier works on cocaine. In a 1936 letter to a colleague, he maintained that some of his studies should never have been published, including his endorsement of Parke-Davies' cocaine. In fact, he referred to these as "sins of his youth" (*ibid.*, 36). By the end of the nineteenth century, European and North American pharmaceutical companies had an international reach as physicians from different parts of the globe gave similar accounts of addiction to cocaine. In 1902, medical doctors from British India reported growing numbers of individuals habituated to cocaine, which had been produced in the Dutch Indies (Maier 1987: 31). Russian physicians also noted rising addiction levels to the drug after the turn of the century (*ibid.*, 39). Other reports pointed to the rampant cocaine use in the Russian armed forces during the first World War (*ibid.*, 46). Apparently, German fighter pilots were provided with cocaine to stave off fatigue (Thamm 1994: 27).[5] Cocaine abuse was acknowledged as a serious problem by the medical professions of France, Spain, England, Italy, and the United States at the turn of the century, and by their colleagues in Germany and other Central European countries during and after World War I (Maier 45–47,

257). At this time, Germany's pharmaceutical companies Merck, Bayer, and Boehringer were the largest global suppliers of the drug (*ibid.*, 45).

Opium and 'Foreign Devils'

As noted, opium use in Western Europe had declined with the collapse of the Roman Empire in the fourth century and vanished almost completely by the end of the millennium (Seefelder 1996: 48). Arab doctors and traders, and crusaders during the eleventh and twelfth centuries, brought back knowledge of the uses and abuses of opium to Europe (*ibid.*, 58). After the decline of Arab power, the merchants of the trading cities of Northern Italy, in particular Venice, imported opium from the Middle East and became the main suppliers of the drug in Europe during the late Middle Ages. By the sixteenth century, seafarers from Portugal had largely replaced the Venetians, importing large shipments of opium acquired through their trade on the Indian subcontinent. The Portuguese in turn yielded to the Dutch in the seventeenth century. At this time, opium was again widely used in Europe for medicinal and recreational purposes, and its addictive properties had been recorded by the medical profession of the time (Booth 1999: 22–25). Opium was consumed from the middle of the seventeenth to the nineteenth century in the form of laudanum, a "strong red wine or port in which a dosage of opium had been dissolved" (*ibid.*, 26–27). Booth concluded that opium use did result in widespread addiction, yet it also helped save many lives of those sick with dysentery and cholera generated by the unsanitary conditions in Europe's cities. Indeed, he pointed to opium as a substance that "provided an escape from the miseries and vicissitudes of working class life"(*ibid.*, 60; also see Parssinen 1983: 35–36; 42–58).

Between 1830 and 1860, British opium imports from India increased from twenty-two thousand pounds to ninety thousand (Seefelder 1996: 101–102). While the drug was freely available during this time, Booth (1999) noted that the attitudes toward opium in Britain began to change by the 1830s, because addiction was increasingly perceived as a medical problem. By the 1850s, opium use was viewed as a serious social issue, as mortality statistics showed the high number of deaths resulting from intentional or accidental overdoses, particularly small children who were given preparations containing opium as a sedative. These findings had several consequences which not only resulted in the formation of an anti-opium lobby but also brought about the first attempts in Britain to regulate domestic drug consumption. Legislation was introduced to ensure that only trained professionals would dispense drugs. Thus, the 1852 Pharmacy Act introduced "examinations and certificates to qualified pharmacists" who were regulated by the British Pharmaceutical Society (Kremer and Urdang 1963: 99). The 1868 Poisons and Pharmacy Act, although hardly repressive, reinforced the earlier legislation by governing that — aside from medical doctors — only pharmacists would be able to sell opium. Moreover, the drug was to be labeled as a poisonous substance. While the legislation did bring about only a small decline in the overall mortality statistics, it resulted in a significant reduction in the death rate of infants (Booth 1999: 61–65). These laws also represented important first steps toward controlling opium and other drugs, leading to the 1909 Shanghai Conference in China, the earliest international attempt at drug control.

Opium had been known in China for thousands of years and was largely used for medicinal purposes. Opium preparations were utilized prior to surgery or as cures for dysentery and diarrhea. Regarding its recreational use before the arrival of the Europeans in the sixteenth century, Booth (1999) noted that "opium use was not widespread and was restricted to an upper class elite who could afford it: most of the population, being semi-literate or illiterate, had not heard of it" (*ibid.,* 103–104). In the seventeenth century, Dutch and Portuguese sailors introduced the Chinese to the smoking of opium — which leads to addiction much faster than ingesting a product containing the drug in diluted form such as laudanum (*ibid.,* 105–106). Recognizing the harmful effects, consecutive Chinese emperors issued various decrees regarding its use. In 1729, the smoking of opium was prohibited and its use restricted to medicinal purposes only, while severe penalties were introduced for opium dealers. Yet, imports increased rapidly, a contradiction explained by the fact that the Chinese imperial government, while handing out harsh penalties to those selling the drug, also profited from taxing its import. In fact, the importation, sale, and domestic cultivation of opium were made illegal only in 1799 following an edict by Emperor Chia-ch'ing who ruled between 1796 and 1820 (*ibid.,* 109–110).[6]

While it had been the Portuguese and Dutch who initially supplied the Chinese with smoking opium, merchants from the British East India Company (BEIC) came to control the trade by the early eighteenth century, bringing increasingly large amounts of the drug into the Middle Kingdom.[7] In fact, the British colonial economy and administration in India depended heavily on earnings from opium exports to China, which expanded from thirteen tons in 1729 to one hundred and seventy tons in 1781 (*ibid.,* 107–115; Seefelder 1996: 138–139). In 1813, BEIC officials acknowledged that the commerce with China was the company's only trading operation that was profitable (Elton 1968: 90). Drug trading turned into drug smuggling after the imperial edict of 1799, while the amount of opium consumed in Chinese society kept growing. Between 1821 and 1837, imports of British and US opium increased almost eightfold. In addition, opium entered the country from Turkey, while domestic cultivation increased as well. Many Chinese, namely the dealers, middle men, and corrupt Manchu officials, grew rich from the trade. Only in 1838, as the detrimental effects of opium on Chinese society became an urgent issue with an addict population numbering millions, did the imperial government finally decide to enforce the laws mandated decades earlier. The move against opium trafficking was reinforced by the fact that the government no longer profited from taxing the trade since the 1799 edict. When the legal trade, which could be taxed, had turned into smuggling, it resulted in an outflow of funds and represented a serious loss to the imperial treasury (Booth 1999: 120–128; also see Tuchman 1972: 34; Seagrave 1985: 4; McCoy 2000: 197).

In 1838, the imperial high commissioner Lin Tse-hsü ordered the arrest of the dealers and the confiscation and dumping of 1.4 tons of British-imported opium (Thamm 1994: 20–21; Fay 1997: 142–161). The First Opium War (1839–1841) broke out shortly thereafter. The conflict resulted from Great Britain's intent to address its negative trade balance by selling opium to China, although the drug had been made illegal there. In the Second Opium War (1857–1860), in which the French also participated, the capital of Beijing was captured, and looting soldiers plundered and destroyed the Imperial Palace. As a result of the conflict, the Middle Kingdom, forced to legalize opium consumption, became a "nation of opium smokers" (Block and Chambliss 1981: 21–24; also see Stein 1974: 902; Thamm 1994: 20–21; Seefelder 1996: 136).

British exports of Indian opium to China increased from 170 tons in 1781 to 5,800 tons in 1880, and declined thereafter due to the growing Chinese domestic production. In 1902, Britain still exported some four thousand tons. In 1906, the year with the highest yield recorded, China itself harvested some thirty-five thousand tons of opium, while it imported several thousand more. At this time, "27 percent of its adult males" were considered addicted, which was "a level of mass addiction never been equaled by any other nation" (McCoy 2000: 198; also see Seefelder 1996: 138–139; Booth 1999: 168). According to another observer, by 1906, the country consumed 22,588 tons of opium a year, most of which had been cultivated in China (Smith et al 1992: 7). By contrast, according to UN statistics, the global annual opium production in 1999, which provided for the needs of the world's heroin addict population, was 6,100 tons (McCoy 2000: 191).

As noted, in Britain opium usage had been viewed as problematic since the 1830s, resulting in the implementation of domestic drug control legislation in the 1850s and 1860s. In other words, Britain engaged in two military conflicts to be able to sell opium without hindrance in China, while domestic forces were bringing about steps to restrict the very same drug, because its abuse was increasingly perceived as serious medical and social issues. Moreover, in 1895, the members of a British Royal Commission traveled to the Far East to study opium use at close hand. Despite the activities of the anti-opium lobby and the public health legislation implemented at home by this time, the commission's report concluded that Chinese opium consumption did not result in any worse problems than those created by alcohol use in Britain (Parssinen 1983: 77–88; Kraushaar and Lieberherr 1996: 55).

The Narcotization of Chinese Society (and some of its Consequences)

The late US historian Barbara Tuchman (1972) observed that access to the huge Chinese market, not opium, was the main cause of the opium wars, noting that "the

Chinese wanted to restrict, and the West to expand their intercourse" (1972: 33–34). Tuchman's assertion seems odd given the grave direct and indirect effects opium was to have on China for over a century to come. The opium wars marked the beginning of foreign domination of China signified by the imposition of 'unequal treaties.' Between 1840 and 1860 Britain, France, and Russia took advantage of China's political and military weakness. Britain gained Hong Kong in 1842. Tsarist Russia carved out large slices of territory in northern China, including the Amur and coastal regions with the port city of Vladivostok. Moreover, between 1854 and 1884, the Russians took over the territories that made up the former Soviet and, presently independent, republics of Kyrgystan, Tajikistan, Turkmenistan, and Uzbekistan. France took control of Indochina by 1885. Britain, France, and Russia were later joined by Germany, Japan, and the United States. In 1895, China suffered a humiliating military defeat at the hands of the rising power of Japan and lost Taiwan (Jackson 1962: 36–39, 113–114; Putzger 1970: 124–125; Kinder and Hilgermann 1977a: 91; 107; 113; Thiess 1987: 13). As a result of the weakness of the Chinese imperial government under the Manchu, these nations gained major economic and political concessions from the Middle Kingdom. Most important were the so-called treaty ports, which forced the Chinese to open their country to trade with the West. The Manchu regime had to accept the ports' extraterritoriality, meaning that they were under the administration of the Western powers, although situated on Chinese soil (Tuchman 1972: 34–35).

In addition, China experienced massive internal upheavals which cannot be divorced from the issues of opium and foreign domination. From 1850 to 1864, the country was rocked by the so-called *Taibai* (Tai-ping) rebellion in which tens of millions of people lost their lives. The rebellion was a popular insurrection against the corrupt Manchu rulers who had been weakened and exposed as such across China by the defeat in the First Opium War. The *Taibai* movement's teachings were based on a blend of nationalism, Chinese religion, and Christianity. Moreover, the movement aimed to introduce principles of social organization, which would have transformed the country in a way only the Chinese Revolution did after 1949. The proposed reforms included the abolition of private property and the common duty to participate in the cultivation of land, the banning of foot binding, equality for women including their access to all positions, the abolition of alcohol and opium consumption, and the repudiation of all treaties that the Manchu had concluded under foreign pressure. While the West was initially sympathetic to the *Taibai* because of their movement's affinity to Christianity, Western, especially British, military assistance to the Manchu — after the Second Opium War — played a pivotal role in its defeat during the 1860s. Muslim uprisings in Central China followed the *Taibai* rebellion and were quashed by 1878 (*ibid.*, 35; Lennhoff 1966: 516–536; Kinder and Hilgemann 1977a: 91; Seagrave 1992: 104–115; Thamm 1996: 38–39).

At the turn of the century, the *Fists of Justice and Unity Society* organized the Boxer Rebellion of 1899–1900 against the growing influence of the foreign powers in China. A multinational military force from Europe, the United States, and Japan brutally suppressed the rebellion. In turn, China suffered further humiliations, including the stationing of foreign troops in the treaty ports, and in the capital, Beijing (*ibid.*, 39–40; Seagrave 1992: 287–371; Thamm 1996: 24–25). The foreign interventions were a direct result of Chinese internal weakness, the corruption of Manchu rulers, civil conflicts, and opium. The Chinese revolution of 1911 led by the founder of the *Guomindang* (Kuomintang), Dr. Sun Yat-sen (Sun Yixian), resulted in the end of Manchu rule and the creation of the Republic of China, but left the country fragmented and ruled by warlords.

Following the death of Sun Yat-sen in 1925, the *Guomindang*, under the leadership of Chiang Kai-shek (Jiang Jieshi) had established some measure of central control. However, before long the country not only suffered the first round of the civil war between Communists and Nationalists but found itself subjected to further aggressions by Imperial Japan, which was devouring large tracts of Chinese territory. By 1931, the Japanese had created the puppet state of *Manchukuo* in occupied Manchuria, which they used as a launching pad for attacks on the rest of China during World War II.

After 1945, the country entered the final phase of the civil war between Nationalists and Communists, which ended in 1949. Only after Mao Zedong's victory did China finally put an end to opium growing and trafficking on its territory. The new regime imposed drastic measures, ranging from burning poppy fields to executing of opium dealers. In the early 1970s, the People's Republic of China (PRC) grew only what it required for its domestic medicinal uses and harvested "exactly 100 tons of raw opium" (Booth 1999: 168–169).

Taxes, Opium, and the Colonized (Part I)

A number of Western nations were deeply involved in the opium trade in other parts of Asia as well. The territories controlled by the British, Dutch, French, and Spanish were, to a large extent, financed through opium monopolies managed by their respective colonial administrations. British opium practices also led to increased addiction in India, for example, among units of the British-Indian army. In fact, habituation to opium spread to other locations of the empire, such as the island of Mauritius, where Indian army units were stationed. In addition, as noted, opium produced in the colonies was sold in the mother countries (Block and Chambliss 1981: 24–25; McCoy 1991: 77–93; Akbar 1996: 275–276; Booth 1999: 180). Thamm (1994) estimated that in 1855 some 400 million opium consumers existed worldwide (1994: 21–22).

While the cultivation and export of opium brought in revenues to the British administration in India, other colonial governments received their tax earnings by importing unprocessed Indian opium, which was then refined into smoking opium and sold to addicts through their respective monopolies. The opium was marketed at high prices generating large earnings. The colonial authorities continually hiked prices to increase profits, while they jealously guarded their opium monopolies against smugglers (McCoy 1991: 96). These opium monopolies were set up as early as the mid-seventeenth century, and remained in place until the mid-twentieth century. Britain and the other colonial powers agreed to abolish them only under US pressure in 1945 (Renborg 1972: 175).

The Dutch were one of the first colonial powers to establish an opium monopoly, on Java in today's Indonesia. Between 1640 and 1799, it is estimated that the Dutch East India Company imported fifty six tons of the drug per annum, thereby creating a large Javanese addict population. Apparently, the Dutch also used the drug, which was imported from India, as a weapon to soften up hostile tribal chiefs in Indonesia. In fact, opium imports increased to over two hundred tons by 1904. Although sales were cut back thereafter, by 1929, the Javanese still consumed close to sixty tons of opium in over a thousand opium dens generating considerable revenues for the colonial authorities. The Dutch opium monopoly remained in place until 1945 (McCoy 1991: 92–93; Booth 1999: 105).

In the 1860s, the French, ruled by Emperor Napoleon III, established an opium monopoly in Vietnam after forcibly annexing the country, which had been a Chinese vassal state. In the following decades, France expanded its control to other territories in Indochina and set up opium monopolies there as well. While sales initially produced few profits due to administrative inefficiency and waste, the restructuring process of the 1890s resulted in a 50 percent hike in revenues by the turn of the century. The reforms ushered in at the time included the creation of a centralized monopoly as well as the introduction of cheaper Chinese opium which was made available to the poor who lacked the means to purchase the more expensive Indian variant. The French colonial authorities also opened up new establishments where the drug could be bought and consumed (*ibid.*, 110–111). While the colonized were the targeted consumers of opium, the habit also spread to the French Foreign Legion units stationed in Indochina (Wellard 1974: 73).

The Spanish had been in the Philippines since the sixteenth century, yet established an opium monopoly only in the mid-nineteenth century, which provided solely for the Chinese minority in the country, a large percentage of which was addicted. The United States annexed the Spanish colony in 1898, and upon discovering the addiction problem phased in a drug regime that banned the importation of opium by 1908 (Musto 1973: 26; Booth 1999: 180).

Still, the opium export from British India "provided 18 percent of the [colony's] annual revenue . . . . in the late nineteenth century" which dropped during the 1880s due to the sharp increase in cheaper Chinese domestic production (Parssinen 1983: 147). Moreover, in 1905–1906, the sales of opium "provided 16 percent of taxes for French Indochina, 16 percent for Netherlands Indies, ... and 53 percent for British Malaya" and supplied the funding for the "construction of the cities, canals, roads, and rails that remain as the hallmarks of the colonial era" (McCoy 1991: 93).

International Drug Control, Narcotics, and Pharmaceutical Companies

As noted, the spread of narcotics and addiction was greatly augmented by the emergence of pharmaceutical industries as well as several military conflicts in Europe and North America during the mid-nineteenth century. Morphine was discovered and isolated in 1806, and marketed in North America and Western Europe in the 1820s. In its early history morphine was rarely abused by addicts; rather it became a drug of choice for committing suicide. The addictive qualities of morphine were discovered once it was applied not orally in liquid form like laudanum, but via a syringe. Many of the wounded soldiers of the armies who fought the Crimean War of 1853–1856, the American Civil War of 1861–1865, and the Franco-German War of 1870–1871, had become habituated to morphine. Warnings about its addictive qualities appeared as early as 1870, and morphinism, as this type of addiction was referred to, was recognized as a serious medical problem by the 1880s, resulting in the quest for a cure (Musto 1973: 69–90; Seefelder 1996: 153; Booth 1999: 68–76).

In 1897, two chemists working for the German pharmaceutical company *Bayer*, Dr. Felix Hoffmann — who in 1898 also discovered the pain killer Aspirin — and Dr. Heinrich Dreser created diacetyl morphine, more commonly known as heroin. The researchers were convinced that they found a medication that reduced any feeling of fear and prevented coughing even among patients suffering from tuberculosis. Most important, they believed that they had found a substance that could be used to treat morphine addicts — as Freud and others had mistakenly believed in the case of cocaine a decade earlier. Dreser referred to heroin as a "substance whose characteristics do not result in addiction, which is easy to use, and most importantly, it is the only [medicine] which has the capacity to cure morphine addicts most rapidly" (Kraushaar and Lieberherr 1996: 35). He did not believe that heroin was habit forming because its chemical formula differed from that of morphine (*ibid.*, 36).

The success of heroin and aspirin contributed greatly to Bayer's profit rates after 1889. The company opened up subsidiaries in "Vienna, Brussels, Barcelona, Milan, Lodz [Poland]," as well as Vilna [Russia], Shanghai, Melbourne, and Paris" (*ibid.*, 35). "The ads for heroin appeared worldwide," and Bayer also provided "generous samples" of its product to customers, which helped increase distribution and sales (*ibid.*). The drug took off very rapidly and was widely sold as a miracle cure. Heroin "was shipped in large quantities to India, Indochina, China, Japan, and the Philippines" while the "largest market was the United States" where it was used to treat opium addiction (*ibid.*, 36).

In 1904, a study by a French doctor challenged Bayer's claim that heroin was not addictive. Bayer prevented its publication in Germany and hired a renowned French pharmacology expert to produce a counterstudy which denied the addictive effects. However, only a year later, after further testing had been done, the company was forced to admit that heroin was indeed addictive (*ibid.*). The US medical profession acknowledged in 1910 that heroin "was even more habit forming than the drugs it was supposed to replace" (Shannon 1989: 32). The United States did not make the drug illegal until 1924, although access was restricted by 1914 (Kraushaar and Lieberherr 1996: 36).

Following the Spanish-American War and the takeover of the Philippines in 1898 where Americans had encountered a large population of addicts, and because of a perceived drug crisis at home, the anti-opium movement had become a powerful factor in domestic US politics. In turn, the United States also took a lead in international drug control. Washington policy makers believed that the creation of international mechanisms would decrease the importation of drugs into the United States (Bewley-Taylor 1999: 17–19). Moreover, the US laws against narcotics use, as necessary as they were to deal with important medical and social issues, had racist overtones. Drug use became identified with certain minority groups. As noted by Shannon (1989):

> Mexican itinerant workers — who competed for jobs with Americans — were condemned for dealing in marijuana, Chinese immigrants reviled for smoking and trading in opium. The use of cocaine by blacks aroused intense fears among whites, particularly in the South: cocaine, it was said, made blacks lustful, uninhibited, and impervious to pain (1989: 33; also see Lusane 1991).

The United States also based its position on economic grounds as American companies hoped to improve their access to the large Chinese market which was dominated by the European powers, particularly the British. The United States did receive support from the British anti-opium movement, which by now strongly opposed the opium trade from British India into China on moral grounds (Bruun, Pan, and Rexed 1975: 9; Bewley-Taylor 1999: 23). As a result of US diplomatic moves the so-called Great Powers met in Shanghai in 1909. However, the negotiations did not have the outcome the United States desired because "it was impossible to get general agreement that the use for other than medical purposes was evil and immoral" (Musto 1973: 36). Most of the governments present preferred a form of trade regulation rather than complete abolition, largely because they received considerable revenues from narcotic sales either by pharmaceutical companies or by colonial opium monopolies. The results of Shanghai were largely a compromise between Britain and the United States. Signatory countries agreed to make the application of opium for uses other than medical ones subject to "prohibition or . . . . careful regulation" (Bruun, Pan, and Rexed 1975: 10–11; 38; Bewley-Taylor 1999: 22).

While the Shanghai Conference focused largely on opium, follow-up meetings included other drugs as well. The various conferences at The Hague (1911–1912, 1913, 1914) included cocaine, opium, morphine, and heroin (*ibid.*, 38). The results at The Hague were more conclusive than those of Shanghai. Not only did the participating nations agree to limit the trade of drugs to "medical and legitimate uses" but to "bring about the gradual suppression of the abuse of opium, morphine and cocaine" and their derivatives (*ibid.*). Unfortunately, with the outbreak of World War I "the issue was suspended" (Parssinnen 1983: 129–130).

The conference results at The Hague became official only by 1919, in accordance with article 295 of the Versailles Treaty, which stipulated that all states joining the League of Nations (LN) automatically committed themselves to passing and turning into law the agreements made (Haffner 1988: 286). Yet, actual implementation was often delayed as long as possible, while loopholes in the treaties allowed pharmaceutical companies in the drug producer countries Britain, France, Germany, and others to go on manufacturing narcotics officially designated for medical use only. Substances like morphine, heroin, and cocaine were then exported to a second country where they would be procured by criminal organizations. Allegedly, German-made cocaine was even smuggled through Switzerland into France during World War I, where it was acquired by the French addict population, concentrated in Paris, a fact apparently reflected in the growing number of arrests of cocaine traffickers between 1916 and 1918 (Maier 1987: 45; 55). In addition, the pharmaceutical industries in the neutral countries, such as the Netherlands and Switzerland, not only greatly profited from the increased narcotics sales to medicate the wounded of the belligerent countries but from exports to illegal markets (*ibid.*, 45).

The British government had signed and ratified in parliament the agreements made at The Hague and was in the process of developing legislation to turn them into domestic law, when interrupted by the events of August 1914. One might assume, therefore, that the increased morphine production by British pharmaceutical companies in 1914 and thereafter served the purpose of easing the sufferings of wounded Allied soldiers. Yet, companies like Whiffen almost doubled their production of morphine destined for illegal markets, not for the battlefields of World War I. In the three years leading up to World War I, British pharmaceutical firms exported between 11.5 and 12.5 tons of so-called medical morphine annually that ended up on the black market. Between 1914 and 1918, this amount increased to an average twenty-two tons a year. Companies like Whiffen legally exported morphine designated for medical use to Japan, a British ally during World War I. There, the drugs were acquired by black marketeers who transferred them to China to be sold openly in the so-called concessions, the territories the Japanese — like the European powers — had taken over (Parssinnen 1983: 149). Also, Britain had withdrawn from the opium trade in China, not only on moral grounds but because cheaper domestic cultivation had made foreign imports unprofitable (Block and Chambliss 1981: 26–28). In other words, as opium sales declined, British pharmaceutical companies increased illegal exports of the far stronger drug morphine. The British government finally ended this illegal trade in 1923, several years after having put into place a domestic drug control regime, the Dangerous Drug Act of 1920 (Bruun, Pan, and Rexed 1975: 223; Parssinnen 1983: 159).

Following World War I, the Third Opium Conference took place in Geneva in 1925. The British, allegedly interested in diverting attention away from their own practices, managed to divide the agenda, which resulted in the holding of two separate congresses. The first focused on opium production and consumption. One of the important agreements made allowed for the retailing of opium through state and colonial monopolies with the requirement to phase out the trade within fifteen years. The other congress was devoted to the drug-producing nations. During the 1920s and early 1930s, Britain, British India, France, Germany, Holland, Japan, and Switzerland were the leading producers and exporters of illegal narcotics (Renborg 1972: 71; Kraushaar and Lieberherr 1996: 57; Sinha 2001: 12).

Countries like Germany and Switzerland had extremely relaxed regulations, which not only allowed pharmaceutical companies to produce but also to legally import and export drugs such as morphine or cocaine. For example, a British company sold morphine to a French business partner who shipped the drugs to Switzerland where they were bought by a local firm. The Swiss government, however, did not require any export licenses and hence the narcotics were sent directly to China, or indirectly via Japan (Bruun, Pan, and Rexed 1975: 224; Parssinnen 1983: 154–159).

In 1922, Switzerland was one of few countries which not only produced narcotics but which also completely neglected to regulate their export and import. The country did not sign and ratify The Hague Convention of 1912 until the mid-1920s (Kraushaar and Lieberherr 1996: 56). In fact, Swiss pharmaceutical companies such as Hoffman-La Roche were strongly opposed to the ratification which they viewed as a death knell for the industry (*ibid.*, 40). The pharmaceutical industry had been booming in Switzerland, as had those of other European countries. It profited from World War I, which had provided a market niche for Swiss companies producing morphine and cocaine. While Swiss drug production grew during the war, it increased again after 1918. In 1921, the country produced 2.5 tons of morphine, 0.7 tons of heroin, and 0.7 tons of cocaine (*ibid.*, 39). An official 1922 Swiss report on cocaine noted that the amount of cocaine manufactured domestically was "100 times as large as the amount required for medical and scientific purposes" (as quoted in Maier 1987: 57). Obtaining cocaine, and presumably other narcotics, was quite easy in Switzerland. According to the report,

> individuals . . . . passing themselves as physicians, or assuming other impressive and misleading titles, have been able to obtain up to ten kilos directly from the manufacturer simply by writing an order on a piece of paper with a fictitious letterhead. It goes without saying that the drug obtained soon finds its way onto the illicit market (*ibid.*).

Although the Swiss Psychiatric Association urged the government to adopt measures to deal with cocaine addiction in 1921, Switzerland failed to sign the Hague Convention until 1924 (*ibid.*, 59). Moreover, the country turned the accords into domestic legislation only in 1925, after the League of Nations and the United States had stepped up the pressure on Switzerland, and after economic boycotts were threatened against Swiss products (Kraushaar and Lieberherr 1996: 56–57). During the same year, Switzerland hosted the Third Opium Conference, which produced the 1925 Geneva Convention. The accord aimed to close the loophole that allowed for the overproduction of narcotics designated for medical use which subsequently ended up on the black market (Bruun, Pan and Rexed 1975: 38; Sinha 2001: 13). Even so, Swiss pharmaceutical concerns remained the world's leading producers as well as exporters of heroin as legislation remained unenforced until the early 1930s. Indeed, Swiss companies again increased their production of drugs, producing and exporting two tons of heroin annually between 1925 and 1929 (Kraushaar and Lieberherr 1996: 56–57).

The 1931 Limitation Convention, which followed the 1925 accord, further aimed to limit the "manufacturing of narcotic drugs to the world's legitimate requirements for medical and scientific purposes" (*ibid.*). The 1936 Convention of Illicit Traffic requested member states to punish violations of the law and "to combat . . . . the illicit traffic in . . . . drugs" (*ibid.*). Switzerland and Turkey did not sign the 1931 treaty because they deemed it too strict. The United States refused because it considered the treaty too lenient. Subsequent international agreements, such as the 1936 Convention, had few results as the encroachment of the Second World War turned international drug control into a minor issue (Ryan 1998: 147–148). Still, by 1937, Switzerland had reduced its heroin production to thirty-four kilos annually (Kraushaar and Lieberherr 1996: 56–57).

Germany was the largest drug producer in the post–World War I era, irrespective of the fact that the country had signed the Hague treaties in 1921. A kilo of 99 percent pure cocaine produced by Bayer, Merck or Hoechst could be obtained cheaply in Germany, but the same kilogram would fetch ten to fifteen thousand francs in neighboring France during the mid 1920s. The German-French traffickers of the period were able to sell the cocaine for up to twenty-five times the price of purchase. All the same, French companies in return sold narcotics to Germany, which subsequently disappeared on the black market (Gómez Ordoñez 1991: 77; Block 1994: 100; also see Maier 1987: 55).

Drug consumption was high in the Weimar Republic after 1918, as many Germans had problems coping with experiences of defeat, revolution, and economic turmoil in the post–World War I period (Wehrling 1994: 721–723; Schleich 1994: 723–724; Engelbrecht and Heller 1994: 724–726; Engelbrecht and Heller 1994a: 726–728; Landsberger 1994: 732–734). In 1926, Maier (1987) wrote of the necessity to control drugs in Germany and to end the availability of narcotics such as cocaine, yet he expressed pessimism that the proper mechanisms would come into place in the foreseeable future. He emphasized that following the implementation of a national narcotics control, cocaine "would . . . . vanish from the drugstores, thus eliminating the main source of the drug for the population at large. It should be added, however, that we are far from reaching this ideal situation, and that for a long time to come we shall have to rely on individual methods of prevention" (Maier 1987: 262).

However, by 1929, Weimar Germany had signed the 1925 Geneva Convention, which also resulted in the creation of domestic laws threatening to punish users with "imprisonment of up to three years" (Mach 2002: 380). Still, while the courts of Weimar Germany were relatively lenient when dealing with drug users, measures implemented by the National Socialist regime a few years later were much harsher. Narcotics users turned into "addicted perpetrators" of crime (*ibid.*, 382–383). In November 1933, new stipulations were added to the German criminal code which allowed for the option of "forced intramural treatment for . . . . addicted offenders" (*ibid.*). Further additions to the National Socialist anti-drug laws allowed that users "be committed for up to two years for forced withdrawal in special institutions" (*ibid.*). The Nazis viewed narcotics addicts as threats to the nation's health who had to be removed by various means including sterilization as well as their physical elimination in a concentration camp (*ibid.*, 383–384).

Regardless, the role of international pharmaceutical companies in the evolution of the international narcotics trade is very significant. Not only did the industry actually create new and more powerful drugs such as heroin, it spread addiction through their global export. In addition, pharmaceutical companies not only continued their practices after drugs were recognized as harmful but made every effort to evade regulation and detection in order to profit from their sales as long as possible, even when their own national governments had signed and implemented legislation criminalizing the production and export of narcotics unless strictly controlled. Finally, while pharmaceutical companies no longer participate in the actual production of illicit narcotics, they continue to profit from involvement in criminal economies by providing the precursor chemicals necessary to produce drugs. The Federal Republic of Germany (FRG), which today is no longer a producer but a market for illegal narcotics, is also an important manufacturer of precursor products. For example, during the 1980s, German-made chemicals required to produce cocaine were sold to Ecuador and then diverted to Colombian trafficking groups. In the 1990s, German pharmaceutical firms sold chemicals needed to produce amphetamines to countries in Western and Eastern Europe. US pharmaceutical corporations are also major suppliers of these chemicals. In addition, companies from the newly industrialized countries Brazil and Chile have begun to manufacture precursor chemicals (Castillo 1991: 147; OGD 1993: 109–122, 246–248; Boyer 2001: 304–307).

Taxes, Opium, and the Colonized (Part II)

As noted, drug trafficking from Germany was a major concern for French police (Gómez Ordoñez 1991: 77). While the French government enforced strict antidrug laws at home, the situation differed in Indochina where, in violation of international agreements such as the Third Opium Conference of 1925 in Geneva, drug sales were not reduced during the 1920s and 1930s. In contrast to the policies implemented by other colonial powers such as the Dutch, who gradually reduced drug consumption, the French continued to rely on opium (McCoy 1991: 111–112). By 1939, some "2,500 opium dens and retail shops" provided for tens of thousands of addicts who generated some 15 percent of annual tax revenues (*ibid.*, 113). In fact, the French authorities went a step further in 1940, after the defeat and occupation of France by Nazi Germany during the early period of World War II. During the same year, Indochina had also been taken over by Japanese forces, who allowed the French administration to continue to function. Regardless, as a consequence of the Japanese occupation, the British Royal Navy enforced a blockade on shipping to Indochina. Cut off from its traditional sources of opium, namely China and India, the French encouraged the domestic cultivation without interference from the Japanese occupiers (*ibid.*). In turn, opium production in French Indochina grew "from 7.4 tons in 1940 to 60.6 tons in 1944," which was sufficient to supply the existing addict population and substantially increase revenues (*ibid.*, 115).

Japanese policies were likely the most notorious. Like the French, the Japanese were concerned about the impact of narcotics on their society, and consequently they implemented strong antidrug policies in their own country and Korea and Taiwan, which they had acquired as colonies by 1905. Bergamini (1972) noted that the Japanese imperial government — in recognition of the negative impact of opium on China — had signed "an agreement with Great Britain to keep opium out" in 1858 (1972: 553). When the Japanese initially took over Taiwan in 1895, they found that some 14 percent of the population had an addiction problem. After the introduction of a control regime which aimed at gradual reduction, the addict population had been cut back "to less than one half of 1 percent" by the mid-1930s (*ibid.*). Bergamini wrote:

> The Japanese drug police licensed addicts, issued them three-day supplies of pipe poppy at prices far below the going rate on the illicit market, and saw to it by stringent detective work that no smugglers could compete with the government monopoly and no youngsters could find courage to try the habit. Eventually old addicts died and few new ones emerged to take their places (*Ibid.*).

In fact, Bishop Brent, the previously mentioned leader of the US delegation to the 1909 Shanghai Conference, had traveled through Asia in 1903–1904 to observe the practices regarding opium. In his report, he praised the Japanese for their restrictive domestic drug policies and for their success in reducing addiction in Taiwan (Musto 1973: 27).

However, in the territories occupied by the Japanese after 1905, they furthered the domestic cultivation and production of drugs as well as their importation. As noted, Japanese narcotics sales had already been a common practice in China during World War I (Parssinen 1983: 131). The Japanese used habit forming substances as a weapon of war to undermine China's capacity for resistance. Prior to and during World War II, Japan's military in occupied Manchuria (*Manchukuo*), faced with the task and cost of subjugating northern China, relied on drug sales to finance its operations (Bergamini 1972: 553; Chang 1997: 163; Jennings 1997: 79–81; 95). Japanese navy gun boats transported drugs, which had been manufactured in laboratories controlled by the army. In fact, the military had set up a system of some seven thousand pharmacies which sold opium and heroin to the population (McCoy 1991: 267).[8]

In their puppet state of *Manchukuo*, created in 1931, the Japanese not only promoted opium cultivation but its refinement into smoking opium and sale to the population. In 1931, it was estimated that one in 120 Manchurians was habituated to drugs. By 1938, "one of every forty Manchurians was addicted" (Bergamini 1972: 553). In fact, the League of Nations repeatedly admonished the Japanese "drug policies" in occupied Manchuria. In its 1937 report the League's Opium Advisory Committee specifically referred to the "clandestine manufacture and the illicit traffic in narcotic drugs" undertaken "by Japanese subjects in China" in the territories "under Japanese influences," claiming that the situation had "deteriorated to an alarming extent" (as quoted in Renborg 1972: 190–191). According to Booth (1999), Japan earned US$300 million annually during the 1930s from the "distribution and sale of Manchurian opium and heroin" (1999: 163).

However, not only did the Japanese occupiers rely on narcotic sales to fund their military operations, their Chinese enemies, notably the cash-strapped Nationalist regime of Chiang Kai-shek, established an alliance with an OC group, the *Green Gang* of Shanghai, and used the revenues from opium sales to finance its own armed forces. In accord with international agreements, Chiang established the National Opium Suppression Bureau (NOSB) with the official claim to control and ultimately eradicate opium consumption. However, the NOSB was a facade adopted to lessen domestic disapproval and protests from other signatory states of international narcotics treaties. It was a government-run monopoly that purchased and refined opium, which was then sold to the Chinese addict population in the areas under Nationalist control. By 1935, the NOSB was run by *Green Gang* leader Du Yue-sheng (Wakeman 1995: 131; Martin 1996: 136).

Nonetheless, despite the practices of drug-producing countries like Britain, Germany, or Japan, and others in the interwar period and thereafter, the creation of an international regime under the auspices of the League of Nations, and its further evolution under the United Nations after 1945, contributed to a slow, overall reduction of global drug production and consumption. For example, global opium production declined from 41,600 tons in 1907 to 16,000 tons in 1934, while the output of medical heroin fell from 20,000 pounds in 1926 to only 2,200 pounds in 1931. Indeed, following World War II and the reorganization of international drug control under UN auspices, which was strongly influenced by US prohibitionist policies, global opium production reached a low of one thousand tons in 1970, although it has increased substantially since that time (McCoy 2000: 202–211).[9]

The Single Convention of 1961 of the UN merged the previous conventions, such as those of Shanghai in 1909, The Hague in 1911–1914, and Geneva in 1925, into one. The Single Convention, which was instigated by the United States, instructed signatory states to take the required legal and organizational steps to limit the trade, manufacture, and possession of narcotics to scientific and medical endeavors, while all other activities were deemed as criminal offenses. Moreover, it asked signatory states to cooperate with each other and the international agencies in countering the illegal trade of restricted narcotics (Bruun, Pan, and Rexed 1975: 37–46). The 1988 UN Convention on Illicit Traffic in Narcotic Drugs and Psychotropic Substances not only added synthetic drugs to the illicit list, it was by far the furthest in scope addressing issues such as extradition and punishment of traffickers, interdiction of narcotics, confiscation of illicit profits, and mutual legal assistance between signatory states. Moreover, it allowed individual governments to implement the measures they deemed necessary for their countries (Thamm 1994a: 21–22). Still, as noted, the 1961 Single Convention had treated the coca plant as a drug to be eradicated, while the 1988 Vienna Convention broadened the licit use of drugs to include traditional practices, which acknowledged the customs of Andean peoples (Sinha 2001: 22, 36).

Drugs and Criminals

While the trafficking of opium and its various derivatives may have been reduced as a result of multilateral drug policies since the 1909 Shanghai Conference, criminal organizations, such as the *Green Gang* in 1920s–1930s China, moved in to provide for the addict populations that had been spawned by the European practices.[10] It supplied addicts not only in China but also in Europe, as half of the heroin produced by the *Green Gang* was exported to France through established links with Corsican criminals from the *Union Corse* (Booth 2000: 156). Freiberg and Thamm (1992) point to another international drug link involving Chinese organized crime. During the late 1920s, as domestically produced cocaine became a controlled substance even in Germany, the country's criminal groups, the *Ringvereine*, obtained the drug through links with the Shanghai *Green Gang* (1992: 80). The leaves used to produce the cocaine, which the *Green Gang* sold to German crime groups, likely originated from the Dutch Indies or the Malay archipelago (Gómez Ordoñez 1991: 76).

   Criminal organizations also took over the South American cocaine trade during the 1930s. Initially, it was controlled by the Cuban branch of the *Italo-American Mafia*, with Colombian go-betweens providing the cocaine. The US mob's financial wizard Meyer-Lansky had established this Cuban-American criminal association in the 1930s, which was based on good relations with Havana strong-man Fulgencio Batista (Gosch and Hammer 1976: 284; 304–325; Arango and Childs 1987: 115; Del Olmo 1992: 63; Cirules 1993). After the 1959 Castro revolution, Cuban criminals, who had emigrated to the United States, continued to import cocaine from their traditional Colombian suppliers. However, by the late 1970s, the

Colombians, with Bolivians and Peruvians as junior partners, pushed out the Cubans and took over the whole chain for themselves, including the profitable distribution in the United States, where cocaine use expanded four times between 1980 and 1988 (Couvrat and Pless 1989: 79; Wisotsky 1990: 43; Elias 1991: 43; Filippone 1994: 324–325). The Colombian crime groups managed to set up an international network for the "commercialization, processing and transport" of cocaine (Arango and Child 1987: 139). Between 1980 and 1992, the estimated global cocaine production increased from about three hundred to one thousand metric tons. It declined somewhat in 1993, but remained stable since at approximately eight to nine hundred metric tons (Farrel 1995: 138–139; UNODCCP 2002: 55). In addition, Colombian criminals had moved into the heroin trade by the early 1990s (Soberón 1992: 40–44).

The 1980s and 1990s witnessed the rise and decline of the so-called cartels of Medellín and Cali. Yet despite the measures taken by the Colombian authorities against these and other crime groups, there have been few consequences for the cocaine trade. For example, after the successes against the cartels in 1992–1993, traffickers reorganized quickly. By the time Medellín drug lord, Pablo Escobar Gaviria, had been killed in December 1993, the *Cali Cartel* had already taken over the rival's markets. Likewise, the 1995 capture of *Cali Cartel* leader Gilberto Rodríguez Orejuela had no "repercussions for the market" (*Frankfurter Rundschau.* Dec. 4, 1993: 3; *Der Spiegel.* June 19, 1995: 128–129). Again, other crime organizations emerged almost instantly. Not only has the removal of a trafficker little to no impact because those who are arrested or killed are quickly replaced, the capture or death of crime bosses indirectly causes elite circulation, often bringing a new, improved, and more ruthless leadership to the top. Moreover, since the early 1990s cocaine production has also become decentralized and moved to other Latin American countries (Arango and Childs 1987: 131; OGD 1993: 217; *Frankfurter Rundschau.* April 13, 1994: 30; Rumrill 1996). Finally, Mexican criminal organizations took advantage of the reduction of the large Colombian trafficking groups in the mid-1990s to become the suppliers of much of the cocaine entering the United States, after having established direct supply routes with Bolivian and Peruvian trafficking groups. In the late 1990s, estimates of the US Drug Enforcement Authority (DEA) put the annual profits of Mexican trafficking groups at US$7 billion (Smith 1999: 196–197).

Cold War Drug Trafficking and Drug Control

While pharmaceutical companies undermined the drug control system established by the League of Nations by spreading narcotics and addiction through informal collaboration with criminal partners after World War I, the intelligence services of various nations played a similar role during the Cold War. Following World War II, the French attempted to re-establish their colonial authority in Indochina. In

1945, the Paris government finally agreed to the abolition of the opium monopoly, being the last of the colonial powers to do so. However, upon their return, the French faced a militant anticolonial resistance movement, the Communist *Vietminh* under Ho Chi Minh. This fact greatly contributed to the financial dilemma the French experienced as they tried to recover from the defeat, devastation, and humiliation of World War II. In turn, the military in Indochina took over the administration of the opium trade, which was then illegal even under French law. As noted by McCoy (1991): "The opium monopoly had gone underground . . . ." (1991: 133).

Through drug trafficking managed by the French Secret Service, the Service de Documentation Extérieure et du Contre-Espionage (SDECE), France helped fund the conflict against the *Vietminh* in the late 1940s and 1950s (*ibid.*, 127–161; Porch 1995: 319–357). It did so by becoming allies with a regional mafia group, the *Binh Xuyen*. The French would buy the raw opium from Hmong tribes people. It was then processed into smoking opium by their partner in crime to whom the French had ceded the administration of the red-light districts of Saigon, today Ho Chi Minh City. In turn, the gangsters shared the profits with French intelligence who used the funds to finance their clandestine military operations. Opium that could not be sold locally was either shipped to the British crown colony of Hong Kong or acquired by gangsters from the *Union Corse*, who exported it to Marseilles, France, where it was converted into heroin and subsequently re-exported into the United States. Meanwhile, the United States provided almost 80 percent of the costs to keep the French army in the field in Indochina (McCoy 1991: 48–49,135,155–157; Morton 1999: 623).

Peter Scholl-Latour, a German national who spent time in Vietnam in 1946 with the French Foreign Legion and who returned many times afterwards as a journalist, described the alliance between the French and the *Binh Xuyen*. Scholl-Latour (1979) wrote:

> These cutthroats were not only given policing powers over Saigon, but also the colossal profits of the red light districts of Cholon. The Binh Xuyen were feared and hated by the population. They were of gruesome efficiency, and there were ghastly rumors about their interrogation methods (1979: 87–88).

The *Binh Xuyen* profited from the opium trade, prostitution, and extortion. Moreover, the French relied on the gangsters to crack down on the Vietnamese Communists. The *Binh Xuyen's* leader, General Le Van Vien, had been given 'carte blanche' and his "heavily armed gangsters" were feared more than the "Communist partisans and . . . . succeeded in eliminating the active Communist resistance in the Saigon region" (*ibid.*, 47; also see Karnow 1984: 181). Even so, colonialism in Indochina ended following the disastrous French military defeat at the hands of the *Vietminh* at Dien Bien Phu in 1954. McCoy (1991) maintained that the collaboration between the French SDECE and organized crime represented an informal counterinsurgency model. He noted:

For more than eighty years French colonialism had interwoven the vice trades with the basic fabric of the Vietnamese economy by using them as legitimate sources of government tax revenue. During the late 1940s the French simply transferred them from the legitimate economy to the underworld, where they . . . . [became] a tempting source of revenue . . . . By exploiting the rackets for the French, the Binh Xuyen had developed the only effective method ever devised to countering urban guerrilla warfare in Saigon. Their formula was a combination of crime and counterinsurgency; control over the municipal police allowed systematic exploitation of the vice trade; the rackets generated large sums of ready cash; and money bought an extensive network of spies, informants and assassins (1991: 161).

Regardless, after the French withdrew from Indochina, the United States become embroiled in the Vietnam War, while its Central Intelligence Agency (CIA) became involved in trafficking of heroin, turning a blind eye even when the mother country was the final destination (*ibid.*, 193–261).

During the 1980s, the CIA found itself in a similar relationship with the Nicaraguan right-wing rebels known as *Contras* and Colombian drug traffickers. This particular collaboration is so well known that it has made its way into an actual textbook on organized crime (Lyman and Potter 2000: 385–389). As determined after a three-year investigation by the US Senate Subcommittee on Terrorism, Narcotics, and International Operations, also known as the Kerry Committee, the *Contras* had been deeply involved in cocaine smuggling. The committee report further determined that the CIA and the National Security Council (NSC), in an operation directed by Lieutenant Colonel Oliver North, had relied on the same pilots, planes, and military infrastructure to maintain the covert *Contra* operations against the *Sandinistas* in Nicaragua, which drug traffickers with direct links to the highest echelons of the Colombian cartels used to smuggle narcotics into the United States (US Senate Committee 1989: 2; also see Scott and Marshall 1991). Inquiries by several Costa Rican commissions confirmed the findings of the Kerry Committee and concluded that the part of the *Contra* supply network which was run from Costa Rica and administered by North was connected to drug traffickers (Avirgan and Honey 1989; Lee and Solomon 1992: 290; Weir 1996: 455–465; Chossudowsky 1997: 15–16).

Following the 1979 Soviet invasion of Afghanistan, the CIA became involved with the Afghan resistance, which partly financed its operations through the trafficking of heroin that ended up in North America and Western Europe. Moreover, most of the military assistance delivered by the United States ended up in the hands of the most radical Islamic fundamentalist groups within the Afghan resistance. In fact, the Islamic radical terrorists responsible for attacks on US targets during the 1990s, as well as the horrific events of New York and Washington on September 11, 2001, quite possibly derived from groups who benefitted from the CIA assistance (McCoy 1991: 436–460; Chossudowsky 1997: 15–16; Pott 2001: 260–278).

Meanwhile, the flow of heroin and cocaine into the United States and other

Western nations has for some time caused many drug-related social problems. These contributions of intelligence agencies to international drug trafficking should not be underestimated. For example, according to a DEA estimate "perhaps one-third of all the cocaine consumed in the [United States]" during the mid-1980s was provided by the Honduran gangster Juan Ramón Matta Ballesteros, only one of a number of drug traffickers associated with the *Contras'* supply network (Scott 1991: 100).

Von Bülow (1998) noted that 60 percent of the Afghan heroin produced during the 1980s ended up in the United States and Western Europe where it resulted in hundreds of heroin deaths. Moreover, as a result of the Afghan trade the number of heroin addicts in neighboring Pakistan rose from 5,000 in 1980 to a staggering 1.3 million by 1986 (1998: 210–214; also see OGD 1993: 31–37). In addition, these links between traffickers and Cold Warriors greatly contributed to economic losses resulting from factors such as missed work or medical costs. Former US drug czar William Bennett estimated that in 1988, "approximately $100 billion of productive output was lost [nationally] due to narcotics consumption" (Grosse 1990: 145).

While it is generally difficult to provide precise figures on drugs and drug profits, it is safe to assume that these intelligence agencies' involvement with drug trafficking into their own countries or those of their allies have inflicted great damages on these societies. Still, not only had those French or US officials who condoned or even encouraged these trafficking activities an odd understanding of the meaning of national security but they also never faced justice, or if they did, then only after their contributions were no longer required. Indeed, the media was often a willing partner in downplaying and covering up these events (Scott and Marshall 1991; Lee and Solomon 1992: 290).

While the practices described have been perpetrated by Western intelligence agencies during the Cold War, it was the ideological enemy who was accused of drug trafficking, even when these allegations were completely unfounded. The People's Republic of China was denounced for being a major drug producer in the 1950s, even as the Communist regime imposed harsh measures to eradicate the cultivation, production, and trafficking of opium and its derivatives (Booth 1999: 168–169; Bewley-Taylor 1999: 108–114). This is not say that the agencies of former East Bloc nations did not engage in the sale of narcotics in one form or another. However, no credible evidence has emerged to date which indicates that former Soviet or East European intelligence operatives participated in drug trafficking activities as large scale as those involving the French in Indochina during the late 1940s to the mid-1950s or the United States in Vietnam during the late 1950s–1970s and in Afghanistan and Central America during the 1980s.

Cuba has also been accused of collaboration with drug traffickers. Yet, the Cuban attitude to drugs is rather harsh. This was demonstrated by the case of general Arnaldo Ochoa Sánchez, who was executed in 1989 for involvement in the cocaine trade. Ochoa had commanded the victorious Cuban expeditionary forces in Angola during the 1980s and was a 'hero of the revolution' (*LAWR*. Sept. 21,

1989: 3; also see *Case 1/1989*). The alleged cooperation between drug traffickers and Marxist rebels, also largely a product of Cold War propaganda, will be discussed in chapter 5.

Moreover, while *narcodollars* may contribute to economic growth and development, assuming that today's producer countries of drugs profits most would be erroneous. Rather, as pointed out by Castillo (1991), the drug trade brings death to his native Colombia, while others fill their 'noses and pockets' (1991: 147). Cabieses (1994; 1996) maintained that most of the money laundering and subsequent investments takes place in the developed countries. Accordingly, only some 8−10 percent of cocaine profits actually return to the producer countries, and a mere 0.4 percent go to the coca-growing peasants. Incidently, the 8−10 percent return rate is similar to the earnings received by Bolivia, Colombia, and Peru for their legal exports (1994: 51; 1996: 2).

According to the International Monetary Fund (IMF), global money laundering amounts to "somewhere between two and five percent of the world's gross domestic product" (FATF 2002). Based on 1996 statistics, these percentages would indicate that money laundering ranged between US$590 billion and 1.5 trillion (*ibid.*). The United States is considered to be the final destination of most of the illegal funds from many parts of the world. Another address is the Federal Republic of Germany. Cash-strapped due to the costs of reunification after 1990, the FRG maintained very lax banking laws which allowed mafia investments to enter especially eastern Germany. According to the DEA, Germany is ideal for money-laundering because "the Deutsche Mark is stable, inflation practically does not exist, and the banking system is one of the best . . . . in the world" (*Der Spiegel.* Feb. 24, 1992: 141−142). It is unlikely that much has changed since the country introduced the euro in the new millennium.

Finally, while the US leadership and participation in multilateral drug eradication efforts between 1900 and 1970 may be described as necessary and, although problematic, generally positive, the same cannot be maintained for the period after President Nixon embarked on the first modern Drug War, which was subsequently renewed by his successors. Since the 1970s, the United States largely engaged in bilateral drug eradication efforts, which had the adverse effect that successes in one country boost production elsewhere. This dilemma, also referred to as the 'balloon effect,' is similar to the 'hydra effect' recognized by scholars associated with the Enterprise paradigm of organized crime discussed in chapter one (McCoy 1991: 484−490; Bertram, Blachmann, Sharpe and Andreas 1996: 18−19; Bewley-Taylor 1999: 165−209). In fact, Elias (1991) claimed that drug consumption in the United States grew by 1750 percent between 1970 and 1990 (1991: 43). US drug policies also failed because of the contradictions of the Drug War and the Cold War, which pitted agents of the DEA against those of the CIA (Castillo III and Harmon 1994).

Regardless, while opium production had fallen considerably as a result of an, albeit imperfect international cooperation, from over forty thousand tons in the early twentieth century to some sixteen thousand tons in the 1930s and one thousand tons in 1970, it has increased since (McCoy 2000: 202, 206). According to UN statistics, global opium production has doubled in every decade since the early 1970s "from 1,200 tons in 1971 to 2,200 tons in 1987, 5,300 tons in 1996," and "6,100 tons in 1999" (*ibid.*, 191). Based on these projections, McCoy deemed it entirely possible that global production would reach some "ten thousand tons in 2007 and a daunting forty thousand tons in 2027" (*ibid.*). McCoy's dire predictions were at the very least delayed by political developments. First, after the 1999 record harvest of 4,600 tons in Afghanistan, the Taliban regime moved against opium cultivation, which resulted in a reduction to an estimated 3,300 tons in 2000. Second, opium production declined even further to 185 tons in 2001, likely a consequence of the military intervention of the United States. Nonetheless, by 2002, it had recovered to 3,400 tons (UNODCCP 2002a: 33). By 2004, according to UN sources, almost 90 percent of the global opium production derived from Afghanistan (*La República.* May 19, 2005: 26).

While the statistics for cocaine seem to indicate a reduction in annual global production since the mid-1990s, there has been an increase in heroin coming from South America, which not only makes up for some of the difference but also demonstrates the flexibility of the marketing strategies of Colombian trafficking groups (Soberón 1992: 40–44, also see Henman 1981: 138; Farrel 1995; UNODCCP 2002: 47). It is almost certain, however, that 'Plan Colombia' as well as the 'Plan Patriota,' the most recent US Drug War strategies implemented in Colombia since 1998–1999, had relatively little impact on coca farming and cocaine production in that country but resulted in cultivation increases in neighboring Peru and Bolivia by hiking up prices (BBC Feb. 17, 2001; Reyna Izaguirre 2001: 1–2; *La República.* June 13, 2004: 10; *El Comercio.* June 26, 2004: A22). The enormous increment in global drug production, which McCoy (2000) fears, would also imply growing populations of addicts. Indeed, the numbers of drug addicts have increased globally from an estimated 20–50 million in 1987 to approximately 190 million by the new millennium (Roth 2001: 11). Finally, such developments would have the result that crime groups come to play increasingly powerful roles in the future, a topic discussed in a later chapter of this book.

Conclusion

The present international drug economy evolved in a centuries-long process to which today's developed countries greatly contributed. Those very nations that are presently fighting drug wars have in their past, colonial or not, been producing, and profiting from the same drugs or their derivatives which they now condemn. The sales by opium monopolies, and later on, pharmaceutical companies, created addiction in many parts of the world. Moreover, by financing Cold War conflicts through the sales of internationally banned narcotics, agencies of the same countries continued to contribute to the present international drug economy, even if it included the import of narcotics into their own countries or those of their allies. Indeed, this form of collaboration between intelligence agencies and criminal organizations may be described as an informal counterinsurgency model, which was initially tried out by the French in the first Indochina War and then replicated by the United States in its various Cold War conflicts from Vietnam, to Central America, to Afghanistan.

Endnotes

1. For a good description of the cultural and social importance of coca see Allen 1986: 35–48.

2. Two hundred grams of Peruvian coca leaves contain one gram of cocaine. One bag of coca tea with one gram of coca leaf contains 0.005 milligrams of cocaine, which is many times less than what is allowed by the 1988 Vienna Convention on Drugs for products made from coca (Cabieses 1994: 42–43). Similarly, the amount of cocaine consumed by those who chew coca leaves is lower than the ceiling set by the 1988 Convention because of the low quantities used. It should also be kept in mind that the cocaine in the leaves is released over an extended period of time when chewed. In addition, according to a study comparing the nutritional value of Bolivian coca to the fifty average Latin American foods, coca was "found to be higher in calories, protein, carbohydrates, fibers, calcium, phosphorus, iron and vitamin A" (Plowman 1986: 6–7). W. Golden Mortimer examined the effects of coca chewing by the Indians in his classic work entitled *History of Coca*, published originally in 1901. He also mentioned the findings of a physician and maintained: "After being intimately associated among the natives for nearly a year, where he had witnessed the constant use of coca, failed to find a single case of chronic cocaism, although this one subject chiefly occupied his attention, and he searched assiduously for information. Speaking of the amount used, he says: What it does for the Indian at fifteen it does for him at sixty, and a greatly increasing dose is not resorted to. There is no reaction, nor have I seen any of the evil effects depicted by some writers and generally recorded in books" (Mortimer 1974: 20). Finally, I too have consumed copious amounts of coca tea to treat an upset stomach or altitude sickness in the Peruvian Andes without experiencing what a medical dictionary would term addiction and mind-altering effects.

3. *Vin Mariani* may have had considerable effect on the activities of Pope Pius IX. Larger amounts of cocaine apparently stimulate the central nervous system resulting in a feeling of well-being, pleasant hallucinations, a wealth of ideas, and overestimation of one's abilities (*Brockhaus* 1968: 94; also see Thamm 1994: 45–47). It is noteworthy in this context that the same pope is also the author of the dogma of papal infallibility of 1870, which essentially conveyed that the Holy Father viewed himself as God's representative on earth, a stance that could indeed be perceived as having an exaggerated notion of one's own importance. While I did not come across any direct links between this pope's consumption habits and patterns of behavior, the descriptions of contemporaries do provide some insights. For example, various cardinals and bishops described him as "insane," "mentally ill," and "megalomaniac"

(Deschner 1980: 101–102). José Fernando Ximenes, the Spanish ambassador to the Vatican, thought he was "really crazy" (*ibid.*). His German counterpart, von Arnim, related the following anecdote to Chancellor von Bismarck in a diplomatic letter: "It is common knowledge that last year the Pope while walking past a church . . . . ordered a disabled person in front to get up and walk. But the experiment failed" (*ibid.*). Modern-day psychiatrists and psychologists concluded that Pius IX had an "abnormal personality" and exhibited "symptoms of schizophrenic behavior" (*ibid.*). The late Pope John Paul II beatified Pius IX in September 2000 (BBC Sept. 3, 2000).

4. In the same article, Samper also gave tips on how to properly grow and pack coca leaves for export.

5. Incidently, the US Air Force issues amphetamines, also called 'go pills', to its pilots to help against fatigue. This fact came to light during the investigation of the 'friendly fire' incident in Afghanistan, which killed four Canadian soldiers on April 17, 2002 (CBC March 19, 2003).

6. This approach differed little from the one taken by some governments in Latin America and elsewhere. Officially participants in the War on Drugs, they simultaneously encourage the inflow of drug money into their coffers.

7. Edmund Burke, whom political scientists acknowledge as one of the founding fathers of their discipline, was very critical of the British East India Company (BEIC). The British politician and political thinker compared the company's practices to looting, and participated in various parliamentary investigations into its activities during the 1770s and 1780s. In 1786, for example, Burke was a key figure in the failed attempt to impeach BEIC chairman Warren Hastings (Elton 1968: 57).

8. A Japanese army manual explained the strategy as follows: "The use of narcotics is unworthy of a superior race like the Japanese. Only inferior races, races that are decadent like the Chinese, Europeans, and the East Indians, are addicted to the use of narcotics. This is why they are destined to become our servants and eventually disappear" (as cited in Wakeman 1995: 272).

9. Still, a study done by the Secretariat of the League of Nations (LN) noted that "not less than one hundred tons of drugs . . . . had passed to unknown destinations (i.e., into illicit traffic) in the five years 1925–1929" referring to narcotics that "had disappeared without trace" from "authorized factories" in the producer countries (Renborg 1972: 96–97). Henman (1981) observed that as late as 1971, cocaine produced by the pharmaceutical company Merck was available on Colombia's black market (1981: 98).

10. In their discussion on the early career of Sicilian-American gangster 'Lucky' Luciano, which included a narcotics arrest in 1916, Gosch and Hammer (1976) noted that following the 1914 Harrison Act in the United States — which did not ban outright access to narcotics but made them more difficult to obtain — many Americans habituated to substances like heroin "were forced . . . . to seek drugs illegally and to pay higher prices for them than ever before. A new breed of criminal rose to fill the demand, not just from pimps and prostitutes,

the most notorious and well-publicized users, but from the addicted housewives deprived of their patent medicines" (1976: 22).

Chapter 4

A Tale of Two Coups: Shanghai 1927 and La Paz 1980

Overnight it became the weirdest place imaginable,
with creeps with carbines running around
and everybody normal off the streets. It was as though
the Mafia had taken over in downtown Washington.

(A diplomat describing La Paz, Bolivia, after the military coup of July 17, 1980; as quoted in Levine and Kavanau-Levine 1994: 59).

The Shanghai Coup of April 1927 resulted from the alliance between China's Nationalist Party and the country's most powerful organized crime group, the *Green Gang*. It took place as China's elites were under pressure from the organized and revolutionary left during the 1920s. In Bolivia, left-wing insurgencies had not been a threat to the elites since the 1960s. However, the 1980 Cocaine Coup was directly linked to the planned return to democracy after over a decade of military rule. It prevented the inauguration of the newly elected center-left civilian government that would have probed into the criminal activities and human rights abuses committed by the previous military regime.

Introduction

The 1927 and 1980 coups in China and Bolivia, although separated by time and place, are archetypes of mafia-elite cooperation. The Shanghai Coup stemmed from the alliance between Nationalist Chinese dictator Chiang Kai-shek and Du Yue-sheng, the leader of the Shanghai *Green Gang*, during the 1920s. In turn, China became a country where criminals were given a leading role in government (Thamm 1996: 80–81). After a decade of military control, Bolivia was on the verge of returning to democracy when General Luis García Meza led a "National Revolution" to prevent the country's return to civilian rule (Hargreaves 1993: 177). While military coups were indeed a common feature in this impoverished Latin

American country, the 1980 coup differed from previous ones. Not only had leading Bolivian drug dealers financed the coup, turning the country into a *narcocracy*, one of its chief organizers was the Nazi war criminal Klaus Barbie (*ibid.*, 177–178).

The events surrounding the 1927 Shanghai Coup cannot be understood without prior reference to secret societies, their role in Chinese history and the historical circumstances that resulted in the coup and brought about organized crime involvement in that episode. Likewise, the origins of the 1980 Cocaine Coup requires some mention of the 1952 Bolivian revolution and of the *Banzerato*, the 1971–1978 dictatorship of General Hugo Banzer Suárez.

The Origins of Chinese Organized Crime:
A Brief Introduction to Chinese Secret Societies

The existence of secret societies in China, the *Hung Mun*, can be traced back to the second century AD. They often grew out of religious or mutual aid organizations who protected peasants against plundering soldiers, brigands, exorbitant taxes, and the oppression and corruption of Confucian state bureaucrats as well as resisted foreign rule. Chinese secret societies were formed either through the merger of several families into clans or when unrelated persons established organizations which were arrayed hierarchically like clans. Members had to swear an oath to the clan and to its head. These orders operated in secrecy as 'societies within society,' with their own internal systems of authority, moral code, and justice. High membership numbers made it essential to develop verbal and nonverbal forms of secret communication that nonmembers would not comprehend (Freiberg and Thamm 1992: 9; Chin 1995: 55; Thamm 1996: 19–20).

Secret societies have played an important role in Chinese history as the nuclei of resistance against foreign domination and/or domestic oppression. For example, the *White Lotus Society* was a driving force behind the uprisings during the thirteenth and fourteenth centuries, which ultimately overthrew the Mongol rulers and ushered in the Ming dynasty in 1368. The *White Lotus* re-emerged during the second half of the seventeenth century after the foreign Manchu dynasty (1644–1911) had taken over China, although these rebellions failed (Daraul 1969: 281–282; Kuhn 1980: 38–39; Tefft 1992: 324).[1]

By far the largest insurrection against the Manchu was the previously noted *Taibai* (Tai-ping) rebellion which took place in China between 1850 and 1864 and cost an estimated twenty million in lives and was carried out by an organization that initially began as a secret society. The previously mentioned *Fists of Justice and Unity Society*, also known as the Boxers who organized a rebellion in 1900, had descended from the *White Lotus* and was another secret order set up to resist 'foreign devils' (Daraul 1969: 281–282; Kuhn 1980: 38–39; Seagrave 1992; Tefft 1992: 324). In northern China, the *Red Spear Society* arose after the collapse of the imperial government in 1911. In response to the lack of government troops to the presence of thousands of bandits who terrorized the countryside, peasants organized the *Red Spear Society*, a self-defense movement. The peasant militias operated with considerable success against the outlaws. During the 1920s, the *Red Spear Society* "played a significant role" in the country's civil war (Kuhn 1980: 34). Later on, it participated in the resistance against the Japanese invaders. The Chinese Communists viewed the militias as potential allies and "did succeed to some extent in infiltrating them" (*ibid.*, 34–35; also see Tai Hsün-chih 1985: 103–114).

It is important to recognize that these and other secret societies were initially set up as associations with specific political or economic goals. Charles W. Heckethorn's (1966) early study, published originally in 1900, viewed them primarily as political societies (1966: 131–132). Some of these groups, or factions of them, developed into criminal organizations between the 1850s and World War I, either after they had achieved their objectives or after their causes had been defeated. Only a few started as outlaw organizations (Freiberg and Thamm 1992: 9).[2] Such conversion was enhanced by the sort of economic turmoil and civil conflict, experienced by large parts of the Chinese population between the First Opium War of 1839–1842 and the Communist victory in 1949, which generated the conditions of social disorganization that would provide a breeding ground for organized crime anywhere on the globe.

It was in this environment that the *Green Guild* mutated into the *Green Gang*. The guild had been set up during the mid-nineteenth century to represent the interests of the many thousands of sailors and laborers who made their living on the barges and boats of the Grand Canal shipping grain to Beijing. Initially, this organization had been created to end the unrest among the laborers. However, due to the trade interruptions that resulted from the country's civil conflicts as well the introduction of steam ships allowing transport by sea, they lost their livelihoods (Martin 1996: 12–13; Ter Haar 1998: 393). In consequence, the society changed from an organization with an economic agenda to one with political goals. This transition occurred between the late nineteenth and the early twentieth century, as China experienced massive economic and social upheavals. What started out as a guild to protect the interests of laborers and sailors, became an anti-Manchu political society, which participated in the 1911 revolution (Chesneaux 1971: 47–51; Deacon 1976: 275). The final metamorphosis into the *Green Gang*, a criminal fraternity, was complete by the early 1920s. Under the leadership of Du Yue-sheng and Huang Jing-yang, the *Green Gang* was estimated to have between twenty and one hundred thousand members. At that time, Shanghai had become well-known "as the major center of large-scale criminal activity in China," while the *Green Gang* was involved in labor racketeering, gambling, prostitution, and arms and drug trading (Martin 1996: 35).[3]

The Roots of the Bolivian Cocaine Economy (I)
The Bolivian Revolution

The Revolution of 1952 brought about the overthrow of Bolivia's traditional elites, namely, the oligarchy comprising tin-mining barons and large-estate owners who had dominated the country since the turn of the century. Three companies, Patiño, Aramayo, and Hochschild, had controlled tin mining, the source of more than 70 percent of the country's annual export earnings since the end of World War I. Moreover, 95 percent of agricultural land was owned by an agrarian elite, while approximately 60 percent of the peasants shared less than 1 percent. Prior to 1952, the Bolivian power structure displayed some resemblance to South Africa's system of apartheid. By making literacy a prerequisite to vote, the regime excluded the 95 percent of the native population, which "lived in a state of near-serfdom," from participating in elections. The oligarchy relied on the military to preserve "increasingly fossilized" social and political structures (Bernard 1966: 109; Nohlen and Mayorga 1992: 184–185).

After Bolivia's defeat by Paraguay in the so-called Chaco War (1932–1935), and following the negative repercussions of the global economic crisis in the interwar years, a nationalist opposition emerged against oligarchic rule, which received its support from the growing urban middle class and the small, but militant labor unions from the country's mining sector. These groups organized themselves politically in the *Movimiento Nacionalista Revolucionario* (MNR) (Hennessy 1968: 28–29). The April 1952 revolution, carried out by the MNR's union of nationalist middle classes and organized labor, resulted in following transformations:

- the extension of civil rights to the indigenous population;
- the nationalization of the mining industry;
- the introduction of agrarian reforms that resulted in a massive redistribution of land from the large-estate owners to the indigenous peasantry;
- the government-sponsored creation of strong miners and peasant unions, which were united under the roof of the *Central Obrera Boliviana* (COB);
- the complete collapse of the military as an institution and the distribution of weapons to workers and peasant militias created by the regime (Nohlen and Mayorga 1992: 185–186).

Scholars consider the Bolivian Revolution as one of the true revolutions in Latin America. Not only did it end the political dominance of mining barons and hacienda owners, it destroyed their bases of social and economic power in most of the country. After the revolution, the alliance between middle class and organized labor split apart, as the MNR increasingly moved to the right. Also, unlike in Costa Rica where the military remained abolished after that country's 1948 revolution, the Bolivian armed forces were rebuilt in 1953 as a counterweight to the militias. The MNR tried to assure the loyalty of the new military by setting up party cells as well as through a selection process in promoting new officers (Hennessy 1968: 29; Aspiazu 1989: 50–56).

Also, while the agrarian reforms resulted in the abolition of the hacienda system in the areas inhabited by the indigenous peasants, the less populated regions in the northeastern part of the country called the *Oriente*, namely, the departments of Beni, Cochabamba, and Santa Cruz, were excluded.[4] From the beginning of Spanish colonialism in the sixteenth century to the mid-1950s when the Bolivian government built a transportation infrastructure, the *Oriente* had been cut off from the central authorities. The city of Santa Cruz, the regional capital, founded in 1561, could be reached only by horse or mule. The *Oriente* was finally united with the rest of the country after 1952, through the construction of roads and railway lines which also created links to Argentina and Brazil. And it was in the *Oriente* where the Bolivian cocaine industry eventually emerged (Abecia Baldivieso 1985: 232–237; Klein 1992: 235; Hargreaves 1993: 98).

The Roots of the Bolivian Cocaine Economy (II)
The *Banzerato*

The leader of the 1971 military coup, General Hugo Banzer Suárez, originated from Santa Cruz province and was on familiar terms with the regional agrarian elites. Banzer himself possessed a large hacienda and shared the elites' fears of a possible extension of the agricultural reforms of the 1952 Bolivian Revolution to the *Oriente*. Banzer's brother also owned large tracts of land in the *Oriente* and was involved in cotton cultivation. The general launched his 1971 coup from the department of Santa Cruz with the support of elites in the *Oriente*, and he could rely on their continued backing thereafter. In return, they received economic favors and benefits which brought economic growth and prosperity to the once neglected region. Bolivia recorded a 238 percent expansion in the value of its foreign agricultural sales between 1971 and 1974, most of which derived from the *Oriente* (Ladman 1982: 329–330; Aspiazu 1989: 80; Klein 1992: 254). The government also maintained its support base in the *Oriente* by supplying cheap agricultural credits. These policies amounted to "a substantial transfer of income to the large commercial farmers of the *Oriente*. It was a policy that favored the large-scale farmers of the *Oriente*, who in turn provided political support for the government" (Ladman 1982: 330).

It is also noteworthy that Bolivia's Fascist Party, the *Falange Socialista Boliviana* (FSB), had solid support in the department of Beni from where some drug-trafficking families originated (Reid 1989: 163). The FSB was founded in 1937, and based on the principles of Spanish Fascism, it emerged in Bolivian politics after the anti-oligarchic revolution of 1952. Despite its relatively small size, the FSB played a strong role in the country's politics, because it received the support of those "who had been victims of the revolution — dispossessed landowners, professional people who had worked for the now nationalized mining companies, [and] army officers transferred" to duty in the provinces (Bernard 1966: 127−129; also see Domich Ruiz 1978). Initially, the Popular Nationalist Front, the government set up by Banzer after the coup, which lasted until November 1974, included the *Falange Socialista Boliviana*. After an unsuccessful coup attempt by militant members of this extreme right-wing party, the military took over completely and abolished all political parties (Arnade 1984: 228). The *Banzerato* ended in 1978, and a period of political instability followed which was to end with the handover of power to a civilian government produced by the elections of June 29, 1980. However, the July 1980 coup prevented the would-be president, Hernán Siles Zuazo, the leader of the victorious center-left *Unión Democrática Popular* (UDP), from forming a government. Thus, the era of the military dictatorship of General Banzer was directly linked to the coup.

Elites and the Left in Republican China

The *Green Gang* cannot be separated from the turmoil that gripped China between the 1911 overthrow of the Manchu dynasty, the foundation of the Republic of China under Dr. Sun Yat-sen, the founder of the Nationalist Party (NP) or *Guomindang* (Kuomintang), and the 1949 victory of the Communists under Mao Zedong. During the early 1920s, the Chinese Communist Party (CCP) was a growing force, albeit a junior partner of the Nationalists, as Communist Party members could also join with the *Guomindang*, which was under Sun's leadership. The NP was then a radical party based on the so-called Three Principles developed by Sun, namely "Nationalism, Democracy and the People's Livelihood" (Tuchmann 1972: 87). None of these was ever fully developed. However, the third principle, which advocated "the restriction of capital" and the "equalization of rights in the land," attracted the Chinese Communists and suited the interests of the Communist Internationale, or Comintern, directed from Moscow (Isaacs 1962: 61−64). Following its mandates, the Communists, therefore, entered the NP and ultimately emerged as the left wing of the party. CCP and NP were official allies (Deutscher 1970: 394−396; Chesneaux, Le Barbier, and Bergère 1977: 146−149).

The Soviet Union played an important role in reorganizing China's military during the early 1920s. Not only did the Soviets supply the regime with weaponry, they were also instrumental in setting up the Whampoa military academy in 1924 (Tuchman 1972: 116). The academy was "supplied and operated with Russian funds, staffed by Russian military advisors," while Chinese troops were armed with weapons from the Union of Soviet Socialist Republics (USSR). Sun Yat-sen's principal military advisor, Soviet General Vasily Blücher, had helped found the Whampoa academy (Isaacs 1962: 64, 257). Chiang Kai-shek's second wife also refers to the "Soviet . . . . aid in the form of finances, arms, and ammunition" which allowed the Nationalists to successfully campaign against the northern warlords in

1926 and 1927 (Chieh-ju 1993: 203).

The cordial ties between Nationalists and Communists did not continue long after Sun's death in 1925. The *Guomindang's* new leader, Chiang Kai-shek, had initially maintained the good relations with his Communist ally as well as Moscow, relying on the CCP activists and on Soviet weaponry in 1926 to defeat the warlords who had established their rule in the northern parts of the country. Yet he also feared the CCP's growing infiltration of the NP and of the military. After re-establishing some form of central control in China, Chiang turned against his Communist allies in the spring of 1927 (Isaacs 1962: 142–143, 153–155; Jordan 1976: 67–106).

To suppress the organized and revolutionary left in China, Chiang Kai-shek relied on assistance from the *Green Gang*. The alliance between the *Green Gang* and the *Guomindang* was furthered by the personal relationship between Chiang Kai-shek and Du Yue-sheng. Chiang was introduced to the gang as early as 1906 and was sponsored for membership in 1908. He participated in gang activities as an officer of the Chinese army prior to the 1911 revolution. Accordingly, the future Chinese leader had a police record in the British-administered international settlement in Shanghai, which included murder, extortion, and armed robbery (Booth 1990: 77). While it is difficult to determine the exact date of their first encounter, Chiang Kai-shek and Du Yue-sheng had apparently formed a personal friendship by 1911 that resulted from their carousing together in the brothels of Shanghai (Lennhoff 1966: 484; Seagrave 1985: 156–158). The relationship between the future ruler of China and the gang leader was to have serious repercussions for the evolution of Chinese politics.

Sun Yat-sen's nomination of Chiang Kai-shek as commander of the Whampoa military academy in 1924 was a key development. Not only was the position a prestigious one, it also put him in charge of admissions. Seagrave even alleged that some seven hundred cadets were "drawn directly from the *Green Gang*, or indirectly through family membership or dependency" (1985: 186–187). Even if Seagrave's claim is exaggerated, it would seem that Chiang Kai-shek's position permitted him to admit candidates of his choosing to the school. These future officers of the Nationalist army came to play an important role after Chiang Kai-shek succeeded Sun Yat-sen in 1925.

By the 1920s, Shanghai had become China's most important city. It contained about half of the country's modern industrial capacity and was home to its burgeoning bourgeoisie. The city was the nation's banking center as well as the focus of Western economic interests and investments (Coble 1980: 17). Shanghai contained the majority of the country's industrial workers, including the largest base of Communist support in China. The CCP maintained a strong position because of its role in the organization of strikes that had led to the downfall of Shanghai's local warlord in March 1927. An armed worker's militia comprising some three to five thousand members, which had been set up by the Shanghai General Labor Union (SGLU), carried out most of the policing and guarded important locations, such as the SGLU's headquarters. In addition, the CCP dominated Shanghai's municipal government (Snow 1974: 78−79; Martin 1996: 98; Thamm 1996: 81). Chiang Kai-shek "realized that whoever held Shanghai would hold the purse of China and ultimate power" (Berkov 1970: 63). *Green Gang* backing was therefore decisive for success because the NP's military presence in Shanghai was weak. In fact, Chiang felt he could not rely on Nationalist troops stationed nearby because their commanders had apparently displayed "leftist tendencies" (Martin 1996: 99).

The Shanghai Coup and the *Guomindang* Dictatorship

The operations that aimed at eradicating Shanghai's Communists and left-wing union activists unfolded in the early morning hours of April 12, 1927. Although NP and CCP were officially still allies, the workers' militias guarding union offices and safe places were attacked by *Green Gang* members furnished with "Nationalist uniforms," armed with guns and even tanks, and supported by regular Chinese troops loyal to Chiang Kai-shek (Snow 1974: 79). The militias were taken by surprise by 'soldiers' whom they considered allies (*ibid.*). Isaacs (1962) writes correspondingly:

> Together or separately, in accordance with . . . . prearranged plans, ... [the gangsters and Nationalist soldiers] attacked the head-quarters of working class organizations scattered throughout the city. In most cases . . . . the objectives were won after sharp but brief battles . . . . Every man who resisted was shot down where he stood. The remainder were lashed together and marched out to be executed . . . . (1962: 105−106).

The 'White Terror' that ensued thereafter culminated in the massacre of thousands of Communists and labor activists and resulted in the end of open organized left-wing activities in Shanghai, driving the CCP underground. The renowned American journalist Edgar Snow relied on figures provided by Chou En-Lai — who himself barely escaped death in Shanghai and went on to become the Foreign Minister of the People's Republic of China's after 1949 — claimed that some five thousand CCP members and union activists were killed in the city (Snow 1974: 79−80; also see Martin 1996: 111; Thamm 1996: 80−81). Moreover, the events that transpired in this Chinese port city were part of a larger design that was put into operation across the country and resulted in the establishment of Chiang Kai-shek's military dictatorship, the Nanking regime, in 1927. Within six months the entire Chinese Communist movement was ruined as "hundreds and thousands of Communists perished in Shanghai, Nanking, Wusih, Soochow, Changchow, Hangchow, Canton" (Berkov 1970: 66; Eastman 1974: 7; Wu 1976: 157−158; Kinder and Hilgemann 1977: 173). The respected German-Hungarian journalist Georg Paloczi-Horvath claimed that "about twenty-five thousand Communists were executed" in all of China during this time (1967: 65).[5]

Chiang relied on his underworld associates in those areas where he could not officially use the army. For example, the *Green Gang* was instrumental in setting up what can be described as the Chinese precursor to a Latin American death squad. It consisted of Communist deserters, and according to Shanghai Municipal Police reports, the group was responsible for the assassination of some 4,500 members of the Communist underground between July 1933 and July 1934 (Martin 1996: 165). Another report refers to the so-called C. C. Corps, which "quickly became known as Chiang's OGPU," a reference to the Soviet secret police because of its alleged involvement in "countless acts of terror" (Berkov 1970: 132).[6] In 1932, the *Green Gang* leadership, in collaboration with the Nationalist Party, also created the Action Club, a "highly secret organization" strongly inspired by the "Italian Fascist Party" and "German National Socialism" (Martin 1996: 165). Its goal was to inculcate Fascist doctrines into the Nationalist Party and to enhance the status of Chiang Kai-shek. The *Green Gang* leadership was also instrumental in establishing the *Blue Shirt Society* in the early 1930s, which was strongly influenced by Fascist teaching and set up to emulate the German and Italian models (*ibid.*; also see Caldwell 1972; Deacon 1976: 281). The *Blue Shirts* were about ten thousand strong and were allegedly led by *Green Gang* members who had been cadets at the Whampoa military academy (Seagrave 1985: 294). In her memoirs, Chiang Kai-shek's second wife claimed that the members of the *Blue Shirt Society* "were to recognize only the orders of the leader . . . . were told to forget about all other duties except fealty to the boss and to be ever ready to arrest, kill, torture, or mutilate any suspect or culprit that fell into their hands" (Chieh-ju 1993: 201). Seagrave (1985) wrote that it was the *Blue Shirts'* task "to reform China the hard way, by knocking heads together, carrying out political assassinations, liquidating corrupt bureaucrats and enemies of the state" (1985: 294). While officially dissolved in 1935, the *Blue Shirts* continued to exist under different designations. For example, Du Yue-sheng and the organization's leader Dai Li planned operations which sent *Blue Shirts* as assassins and guerrillas behind enemy lines after Shanghai had fallen to the Japanese in 1937 (Wakeman 1996: 19–24).[7]

The *Green Gang* was also made responsible for labor peace (Chesneaux 1971: 166–169). The SGLU was put under gang control, who enforced the new labor legislation of the NP regime. The 1928 Law of Expediency licensed the apprehension of any strike organizer for being a "troublemaker" (Bergére 1981: 18–19). In 1929, the *Guomindang* introduced new repressive labor legislation which included

- government approval as a precondition to unionization;
- compulsory notice of union meetings and handover of minutes;
- a ban on union organization beyond the local level;
- the designation of government "watchdogs" in public sector unions;
- the obligatory arbitration to settle disputes (*ibid.*).

Shanghai labor was managed largely through violence or the threat of violence inflicted by organizations established by the *Green Gang*, such as the "Workers' Action Battalion," which was described as an assortment "of black-shirted bully-boys" (Martin 1996: 165). Organized crime was "integrated into the system of state power" and became "part of the formal structures of labor organization" set up by the Nationalists (*ibid.*, 224; also see Thamm 1996: 80). Chesneaux (1972) observed: "However archaic the organization of the Green Gang may have remained, and however disreputable its activities in the eyes of the 'honorable' bourgeois of the Guomindang, those activities clearly belong to the capitalist development of Shanghai in the twentieth century" (1972: 14).

As a result, the labor system of the Nationalists displays great similarity to the one observed within the corporatist structures of Fascist states. The stipulations of the *Deutsche Arbeitsfront* (DAF), the Nazi organization created to manage German workers after 1933, had the same consequences as those imposed by the *Green Gang*. Not only were labor representatives and industrial manufacturers merged into one and the same organization, all union structures beyond the factory level were eliminated. By 1938, the German worker had been turned into a "soldier in the economy," regimented by a powerful bureaucracy intent on rapid rearmament (Broszat 1981: 138–156; also see Salvemini 1971: 50–58).

Chiang's shift to the right was also apparent in his choice of military advisors and sources of armaments. Until 1927, Nationalist forces had received most of their weaponry from the USSR, whose military advisors had set up the Whampoa academy. The cooperation between the Soviets and the *Guomindang* had been the continuation of Leninist policies in the attempt to help foster revolution abroad during the early Stalin era. However, the failure of these revolutions resulted in fundamental changes in the Soviet Union's foreign and domestic policy agenda, which were introduced by Stalin in his bid to build 'Socialism in the Soviet Union first.' These policies — notably, the push for rapid industrialization and the collectivization of agriculture — were set into motion after Stalin had achieved a position of control in 1928. The Soviets' 'loss of China' greatly contributed to this shift. As noted by Rostow and Levin (1960), "the failure of the German Revolution in 1923 and of the Chinese Revolution in 1927 strengthened the nationalist bias in the Russian Communist Party, as it took shape under Stalin's rising authority" (1960: 52).[8]

In 1934, when Chiang Kai-shek launched his fifth offensive against the Chinese Communist Red Army since the 1927 break, the NP leader's military advisors came from the West, notably Nazi Germany, while his armaments were supplied from Europe and the United States. The 1934 offensive succeeded in destroying the Soviet Republic of Kiangsi, established three years earlier which forced the Communist troops onto the famed Long March.[9]

Cocaine and Elites in Bolivia

While the suppliers of raw coca were, and still are, from the peasantry, the Bolivian trafficking organizations, in contrast to most mafia groups, originated from the traditional landowning elite in the departments of Beni and Santa Cruz and the military. Kevin Healy (1986) wrote:

> Two principal groups of this economic elite included owners of large cattle ranches and merchants (e.g., exporters of cattle, rubber and Brazil nuts) in the eastern department of the Beni, and the agro-business elite (whose wealth and income derived primarily from sugar cane, cotton, soy beans, cattle production, commerce and agro-industries, such as sugar and rice mills) in the Santa Cruz region. Their multiple economic interests . . . . extend into import houses, banks, automobile dealerships, retail stores and money exchange houses (1986: 104−105).

Roberto Suárez Gómez, who emerged as the country's leading drug dealer in the late 1970s, was a cattle rancher, a "traditional latifundista . . . . of Spanish descent" (Painter 1994: 26−28). Suárez owned large tracts of land in the department of Santa Cruz and had originally used his fleet of small airplanes to deliver beef to the capital, La Paz. Another rancher from Beni known to have turned drug trafficker was Hugo Rivero Villavicencio (*ibid.*).

A second group of drug dealers emerged from the military. During the 1970s, the government had issued land concessions in the Beni region of northern Bolivia to officers who later entered the cocaine economy. For example, Erwin Guzmán and Jorge Flores Moisés, leading drug dealers who gave themselves up in the early 1990s, were former officers and pilots in the Bolivian air force. It is generally assumed though that this group was responsible for transportation rather than production (*ibid.*). The military officers involved in the Cocaine Coup, such as Luis Arce Gómez, also belong into this category.

The evolution of Bolivia's cocaine industry cannot be divorced from the price fluctuations of the products with which the country enters the global economy, confirming the claim made by US criminologist William J. Chambliss (1988) that "criminal behavior is a response of groups and social classes to the resources and constraints that exist in the social structure" (1988: 208). It also fits Chambliss' assertion that organized crime may be created by "law and government" and may be "a hidden but nonetheless integral part of the governmental and economic structures of the society" (*ibid.*, 6).

After the collapse of the price of cotton in 1975−1976, which was accompanied by the decline of the prices of other commodities on the global market, the landowning and agribusiness elites moved into cocaine trafficking (Leóns 1993: 125; Hargreaves 1993: 98−99; Leóns and Sanabria 1997: 9−10). Scott B. Macdonald (1989) pointed out that many wealthy landowners "in the Santa Cruz area had invested in cotton when prices were up . . . . [in the early] 1970s;

when prices fell on the international markets, increased coca production as well as selling cocaine on the contraband market, became attractive" (1989: 73).

Bolivian economist Valentin Abecia Baldivieso (1985) noted that the twenty thousand metric tons of cotton exported in 1974 amounted to earnings of just over US$21 million. By 1977, cotton exports had dipped to some nine thousand metric tons, while export earnings totaled US$13.5 million. By comparison, in 1963, Bolivia produced approximately five thousand metric tons of coca destined for traditional domestic consumption and legal exports. By 1977, coca production totaled almost twenty thousand metric tons (1985: 263).

Moreover, circumstantial evidence suggests that the Banzer regime came to the aid of the *Oriente* elites, facilitating the shift to cocaine. The Bolivian author, René Bascopé Aspiazu (1989), claimed that the Banzer government took an active role in the conversion from cotton production to participation in the cocaine economy. Following the collapse of cotton prices in 1975–1976, both the government and the Asociacón de Productores de Algodón (ADEPA), Bolivia's Association of Cotton Growers, allegedly conducted a feasibility study to research the conversion to cocaine (1989: 64–74).

Although Dunkerley (1985) discounted this version, he maintained that "some degree of high-level planning" occurred (1985: 315). For example, the acquisition of chemical precursors for coca paste production "required a major commercial operation and some state assistance" (*ibid.*). In her study of Bolivian cocaine trafficking, Hargreaves (1993) claimed that the Banzer government, via the state-owned Banco Agrícola [Agriculture Bank], gave credits worth millions of dollars to the members of ADEPA following the collapse of cotton prices, "a repayment of political debts" (1993: 99). Some of the ranchers and plantation owners used these funds to acquire the necessary infrastructure to enter the cocaine economy, such as materiels constructing secret jungle runways, buying planes, and hiring security services. All the same, it was the collapse of cotton prices during the mid-1970s which set into motion processes that contributed to the emergence of Bolivian crime groups and the creation of a trafficking infrastructure (*ibid.*).

The Bolivian cocaine industry was shaped by another even more severe economic crisis: the dramatic decline of the country's main source of income due to the collapse of the tin industry during the early 1980s. Bolivia lost 20 percent of its GNP between 1980 and 1985, while the official unemployment figures rose from 6 to 20 percent. In 1985, inflation had reached the astronomical height of 24,000 (!) percent annually. Thousands of unemployed miners migrated to the Chapare region in the department of Cochabamba to cultivate coca as an alternative source of income (*ibid.*, 65). From Bolivia's predominant areas of coca cultivation, the Yungas and Chapare, the leaves were moved to secret laboratories in the *Oriente* for conversion to coca paste. The half-finished product was then transported to Colombia for final processing. However, Bolivian traffickers also produced cocaine themselves, which they exported to Colombia or directly to the United States (Léons and Sanabria 1997: 4–10).

The Military, Organized Crime, and the Cocaine Coup in Bolivia

In 1980, Bolivian elites did not face threats from the revolutionary left. Ernesto 'Che' Guevara, the most notable of Latin America's Marxist-style guerillas, had attempted to generate Cuban-style revolutionary warfare in Bolivia. However, Guevara and most of his rebels were killed in 1967, while a second attempt to set up a rebel group failed in 1969 (Waldmann and Zelinsky 1982: 57; Anderson 1997: 682–739). Still, the election victory of the center-left Unión Democrática Popular (UDP) threatened the links between Bolivian drug traffickers and some of the elites established during the Banzer dictatorship, a regime which had "assured official passivity toward . . . . [the formers'] activities" (Reid 1989:163). The new democratic government would undoubtedly have looked into these and other activities that transpired during the Banzer regime. Indeed, leading left-wing politicians had called for investigations into the human rights violations of the dictatorship (*LAWR.* July 25, 1980: 1–2; Dunkerley 1986: 149; Hargreaves 1993: 167). Finally, it must be considered that the return to democracy after a decade of military rule coincided with the imposition of a structural adjustment program by the International Monetary Fund (IMF) which caused "widespread popular protest," especially in the rural regions where the country's peasants had established the Confederación Sindical Unica de Trabajadores Campesinos de Bolivia (CSUTCB), a powerful union organization (Dunkerley 1985: 273).

Just as *Green Gang* members had been involved in the execution of Chiang Kai-shek's coup, an identical role was played by a paramilitary force financed and organized by drug traffickers in Bolivia. The so-called 'Fiances of Death' had been set up by the previously mentioned Klaus Barbie and financed by the Bolivian drug baron Roberto Suárez (Wilson 1984: 262–268). The internationally sought Nazi war criminal had already been employed as security advisor to the military regime where he allegedly refined the torture and interrogation techniques of the Bolivian Secret Service. He, however, switched to work for Suárez after Banzer's overthrow. Hargreaves (1993) wrote:

> Barbie recruited a gang of young Neofascists and Neonazis . . . . The outfit, which called itself the 'Fiances of Death,' included the Italian terrorist Stefano delle Chiaie (who had been trained by the Chilean Secret Police), his friend Pier Luigi Pagliai, the young [German] Neonazi Fiebelkorn and Manfred Kuhlmann, a Rhodesian mercenary. Most had been trained by the Argentinean Secret Service and had worked for it. In Bolivia they belonged to the dubious, newly formed organizations within the Interior Ministry . . . . (1993: 175–176).

Former DEA agent Michael Levine, who worked in Bolivia at the time, described the 'Fiances of Death' as "a group of more than six hundred paramilitary, swastika-wearing, Nazi-worshiping mercenaries recruited by . . . . Barbie" (Levine and Kavanau-Levine 1994: 57). A Swiss journalist referred to a blend of Bolivian generals, "German-descended Nazis, Italian Neofascists, Argentinean torture specialists, and domestic cocaine traffickers" (Rey 1983: 143). The paramilitary also included militants from Bolivia's Fascist Party, the FSB (Reid 1989: 163).

As in Shanghai, the first targets of the coup leaders in La Paz included the offices of the leftist political parties, the Movimiento de la Izquierda Revolucionaria (MIR), and the Partido Socialista (PS), and of Bolivia's powerful labor union, the COB. The other locations of importance were the government palace, the Catholic radio station, *Fides*, and the offices of the weekly *Aquí* (Gumucio Dagron 1982: 11). Socialist Party boss, Marcel Quiroga Santa Cruz, the country's most prominent left-wing politician, was assassinated, as were some twenty trade union leaders. Quiroga was on the paramilitary's blacklist because of his attempt to impeach the previous president and military dictator, General Banzer, for human rights violations (*LAWR*. July 25, 1980: 1–2; Dunkerley 1986: 149; Hargreaves 1996: 167). After gaining control in the capital, the military and the death squads rushed to overcome the resistance in the rest of the country, particularly among the mine worker and peasant unions. Apparently, miners and peasants blocked roads, and were even initially successful in repelling army attacks. Gumucio Dagron (1982) mentioned poorly armed peasants who, with a few old guns from the 1930s Chaco War, resisted repeated attacks by tanks and air force planes (1982: 42). After the troops had gained the upper hand, they massacred dozens of striking workers in the Andean mining town of Caracoles. Military and paramilitary units scouted the countryside, "disappearing peasants" to suppress any resistance among the rural population. Several thousand people were arrested immediately after the coup. Many were tortured. In September 1980, around 1,500–2,000 people were still imprisoned without arrest orders (Hargreaves 1993: 171). The terror against the left continued for some time as exemplified by the massacre of eight MIR leaders in January 1981 (Reid 1989: 164).

The García Meza regime also attempted to reorganize Bolivia's powerful union movement along corporatist lines. Shortly after the coup, the regime "outlawed all trade union activity" (Dunkerley 1985: 290). It then set up a new organization comprising "the only legal representatives of the working class . . . ." (*ibid.*, 296) These representatives, called *relacionadores*, were not elected but appointed by the government. They vowed to uphold a "social pact," based on "harmony . . . . between capital and labor on terms determined by the regime" (*ibid.*, 296–297). The delegates were "long standing 'nationalists' or tame, unknown . . . . White-collar workers," old union activists, who thought they could do some good by staying, and members of the paramilitary (*ibid.*). Given the regime's short time in power, the attempt to reorganize the labor movement did not succeed while many of its activities continued clandestinely. In fact, Bolivian organized labor played an indispensable role in bringing down the dictatorship (*ibid.*, 343).

Organized Crime Groups in Power in Nationalist China and Bolivia:
a Comparison

Shanghai elites had apparently reached an understanding to deal with the threat from the left, not so much with the *Green Gang* leadership itself but with the NP. Chiang Kai-shek had received funding "from Shanghai bankers" to bankroll the coup, while "professional gangsters" in cooperation with Nationalist troops crushed Shanghai's revolutionary left (Snow 1974: 79).[10] Shortly after April 12, 1927, Chiang received word from the sixty-three most important business groups in the country who applauded the actions taken and praised the *Green Gang* leaders as "saviors of the country" (Wu 1976: 156–157). China's business leaders also hoped that "the whole country would imitate the example of Shanghai and slaughter all the Communists" (*ibid.*).

The persecution did not stop once the Chinese Communists had been defeated and Nationalist rule was secure. In fact, the terror turned against Shanghai's economic elites, the third partner in the alliance. Although Chiang Kai-shek had already received some 30 million Chinese dollars from the Shanghai business groups, he unleashed the *Green Gang's* terror against the same bankers and industrialists who had previously supported him to extract more finances for his military. *Green Gang* members turned into NP proxies, who moved against wealthy merchants unwilling to comply (Coble 1980: 28–35; Bergére 1981: 16–17). *The New York Times* wrote:

> The plight of the Chinese merchant in and about Shanghai is pitiable. At the mercy of General Chiang Kai-shek's dictatorship, the merchants do not know what the next day will bring, confiscations, compulsory loans, exile, or possible execution (*The New York Times.* May 4, 1927; as quoted in Seagrave 1985: 234–235).

Berkov (1970) likewise noted in his work, originally published in 1938:

> Men were kidnaped and forced to make heavy contributions to the military funds. Others were seized because they had corresponded with friends in Hankow [where the constitutional government resided]. They were granted no hearings. Men with millions of dollars to their names were held as Communists (1970: 66).

Isaacs (1962), whose work was also published for the first time in 1938, wrote:

> The Chinese bankers and merchants had found it necessary to call in Chiang Kai-shek and the gangsters against the workers. Now they were forced to submit themselves to the predatory raids of their rescuers. Like the French bourgeoisie which in 1852 "brought the slum proletariat into power, the loafers and tatterdemalions headed by the chief of the Society of December 4th," the Chinese bourgeoisie in 1927 elevated over itself the scum and riffraff of the cities headed by the chiefs of the Green Gang and the man who was sometimes called the Ningpo Napoleon, Chiang Kai-shek. Like the French prototype, the Chinese

bourgeoisie had now to pay heavily for professional services . . . . Like Louis Napoleon, Chiang Kai-shek ordered the moneyed men of Shanghai to flee, to be silent or submit. More explicitly, he added: Pay! (1962: 181).[11]

As in the Chinese case, the Bolivian upper and middle classes, who had initially supported the regime, as they had hoped for a return to the stability of the Banzer dictatorship, were also subsequently subjected to the same terror as the political left. Interior Minister Arce Gómez created a new organization, the Servicio Especial de Seguridad (SES), set up with members of Barbie's paramilitary, which he used for arbitrary arrests, torture, and the "disappearing" of suspects. James Malloy and Eduardo Gamarra (1988) pointed out:

The malevolence of the García Meza government repelled Bolivia's civil society, ... It had a sustained, systematic nature . . . . [while in] the past repression tended to be episodic, and violence was mainly a characteristic of the heat of the moment . . . . However, Arce Gómez and his Argentine-trained paramilitary groups drawn from the youth of Bolivia's lumpen proletariat were not inhibited by the traditional constraints of . . . . conflict among Bolivia's political class (1988: 145).

Drugs and Regime Finances in Nationalist China and Bolivia

Both the Chinese Nationalist government and the Bolivian regime depended strongly on funds from the drug trade. The NP–*Green Gang* alliance provided the cash-strapped regime with important revenues from the opium trade, which it needed to keep its troops supplied. In accordance with international agreements signed at the 1925 Opium Conference in Geneva, Switzerland, the drug had been declared illegal. Chiang established the National Opium Suppression Bureau (NOSB), which had the official mandate to control and ultimately eradicate opium cultivation and consumption. The NOSB was merely a facade adopted to lessen domestic disapproval and protests from other signatory states of international drug prohibition treaties. It was a government-controlled agency that bought opium from local producers which was then refined and sold to the large Chinese addict population. Indeed, in 1935, the agency was even run for a short while by Du Yue-sheng, the leader of the *Green Gang* (Wakeman 1995: 131; Martin 1996: 136).

While any computations on the drug trade are sketchy and difficult to verify, there can be little doubt that these revenues were of extreme importance to running the Nationalist regime. According to estimates, government income through participation in the opium trade amounted to as much as thirty million Chinese dollars monthly in 1933 (*ibid.*, 260–263). Another source claims that between 1934 and 1937, overall profits must have been beyond US$500 million (*ibid.*, 272–275).

The US military attaché, General Joseph Stilwell, maintained that the Nationalists' control over the drug trade deprived unruly provincial governments of important incomes preventing them from revolting against the regime in Nanking. The profitability of the opium trade can also be deduced from the fact that the NP government was not the only one in the region financing its operations through the officially illegal drug trade. In fact, the Chinese opium monopoly had been set up specifically to compete with the one established by the Japanese. As noted, the Japanese military in occupied Manchuria, faced with the task and cost of subjugating northern China, relied on drug sales to finance its operations. At the same time, the Japanese used opium and heroin as weapons of war to undermine China's capacity for resistance. After their conquest of Shanghai in 1937, the Japanese were unable to control the opium trade and unsuccessfully tried to tempt Du Yue-sheng, who had fled to Hong Kong, to manage it for them (*ibid.*, 260–263, 272–275; also see Chang 1997: 163; Jennings 1997: 79–81, 95; Booth 1999: 163).

In the Bolivian case, the regime also attempted to monopolize the cocaine trade. Colonel Luis Arce Gómez, a relative of drug lord Roberto Suárez, became Minister of the Interior. He had been connected to the drug trade since the early 1970s and owned an air transport company operating eight planes which largely moved cocaine. In fact, Arce Gómez, like Du Yue-sheng, was put in charge of the country's antidrug operations, including those involving the DEA (MacDonald 1989: 74; Hargreaves 1993: 174–175). Levine and Kavanau-Levine (1994) pointed out that "all Bolivian cocaine trafficking was put under the control of a small group of drug barons — those who had financed the coup . . . . A percentage of the drug proceeds was paid to Arce Gómez, and each of the drug barons was given a squad of Neonazis for protection and to suppress competition" (1994: 59–60).

The García Meza regime was a drug dealer protection racket that had seized the power of the state. It not only repressed the political left and other opposition groups as well as the media but monopolized the cocaine trade by violently eliminating the competition. Traffickers who did not pay protection money were killed by henchmen from Arce Gómez' security service, the SES. Their drugs were then confiscated and transferred to traffickers who paid into the racket. Arce Gómez and the paramilitary also sold previously seized cocaine themselves. Allegedly, they stored the drugs in the vaults of Bolivia's national bank. Drug dealers also directly contributed to the running of the Bolivian narco-military racket and its agencies of repression. Allegedly, Bolivian drug traffickers were willing to finance the military government for several months and paid the regime some US$200 million annually. However, after the trade's monopolization by Arce Gómez, drug revenues, according to the regime's own estimations, were expected to rise to US$600 million (Linklater 1984: 289–293; Shannon 1989: 404; Hargreaves 1993: 176–179).

Conclusion

The Shanghai Coup and subsequent events initially resulted in the decimation of the Communist Party in most of the large cities of China. These developments also caused a complete change of strategy on the part of the CCP, which ultimately proved successful. Most important was the rise of Mao Zedong and the shift from the urban struggle based on an industrial working class to rural revolutionary warfare by the peasantry, which made up most of the Chinese population. In 1926, Mao had opposed the Comintern strategy of only organizing China's small industrial proletariat which, in his opinion, could not be victorious without its "most powerful and strongest . . . . ally, the peasantry" (Palozci-Horvarth 1967: 60–61). The Shanghai Coup likely also produced some of the first ripples in the relationship between Chinese and Soviet Communists, which culminated in the split of the 1960s.

Both regimes may stand as examples of criminalized states, where the integration of organized crime has resulted in criminal power structures. In return for their help in eliminating the Communist Party and union organizations in Shanghai, Chiang not only gave the *Green Gang* and its most prominent leader, Du Yue-sheng, free reign in Shanghai's underworld and the narcotics trade, gang members also became officers and members of the Nationalist army and police. The three most prominent *Green Gang* leaders, including Du Yue-sheng, were appointed as advisors to Chiang Kai-shek and given the rank of Major General. Other gang members were also employed by the regime as military officers, soldiers, or secret service agents (Martin 1996: 111; Thamm 1996: 81). Shanghai elites had financed the coup and became the silent partner in the anti-Communist coalition, at the mercy of the other two. The gang's involvement with the *Guomindang* should be viewed as an evolving process that began with the friendship of Chiang Kai-shek and Du Yue-sheng, formed initially in the brothels of Shanghai and continued after the 1927 coup. The links to the *Green Gang* persisted until after their 1949 defeat at the hands of the Communists. However, the *Green Gang*, which had moved to Hong Kong after Mao Zedong's victory, did itself not survive long after Du Yue-sheng's death in 1951. The Nationalists continued their close ties to criminal groups in Taiwan where Chiang Kai-shek had relocated to with the remnants of his defeated army (*ibid.*, 109–110, 128–130; Booth 1999: 258–259). The *Green Gang's* leader's body was denied interment in Hong Kong and was buried in Taiwan where he is considered "a hero of the people," and "a patriot who fought the evil of Communism" (Booth 1999: 178).

In the Bolivian case, there was also little distinction between state and organized crime, considering, for example, the direct involvement of Arce Gómez who ran his own trafficking operation as Minister of the Interior. The military regime was finally brought down by a general strike organized by the COB in September 1982. This allowed the constitutionally elected president, who had been prevented from taking office by the coup, to return from Peruvian exile (Rey 1983: 143). General Luis García Meza was put on trial in Bolivia in 1986 for the crimes committed by the regime. The trial turned out to be a drawn-out affair, and he disappeared in 1988, when a verdict of guilty became increasingly likely. After a seven-year trial in absentia for murder, human rights abuses, and other crimes, in

April 1993, the court sentenced former dictator García Meza to thirty years in prison. He only began serving his term in 1995, after being extradited from Brazil. Luis Arce Gómez, the Minister of the Interior, was handed over to the United States, where he received a thirty-year prison sentence in 1991. Nazi war criminal Klaus Barbie, who had been under the protection of the Bolivian military, was extradited to France in 1983. He was put on trial in Lyon and received a life sentence for his crimes as Gestapo chief of that city during World War II. Barbie died in prison in 1991 (Bedürftig 1997: 33–34). Bolivian drug lord Roberto Suárez Gómez was captured in 1988 and sentenced to fifteen years in a Bolivian jail. He was released from prison in 1996 and died in 2000 (Hargreaves 1993: 133–134; Leichtmann 2000: 63). Most of the other drug dealers involved in the coup were imprisoned after giving themselves up in return for light sentences following a government amnesty in the early 1990s (Painter 1994: 83–84). Bolivia's cocaine trade did not subside, though. The government in La Paz was initially elated about the 1991 surrender of drug dealers, until it became apparent that their business continued from jail, while Colombian traffickers tried to take over from the jailed Bolivian crime bosses (*ibid.*, 33–34).

Also, in China in 1927, as well as in Bolivia in 1980, mafia-paid paramilitaries performed the same role which was initially played by the *Sturmabteilung* (SA), or Brownshirts, then by the *Schutzstaffel* (SS) and the *Geheime Staatspolizei* (GESTAPO), in the establishment and maintenance of Nazi rule in Germany, or by similar agencies in Fascist Italy. The practices of mafia groups and of the organizations they finance resemble those of the security services of Fascist and other repressive regimes because they suppress identical opponents; namely, the organized left, the institutions of democracy, and the media. However, the similarities with Fascist practices went beyond the social function performed in the maintenance of a repressive regime. Both the Nationalist–*Green Gang* alliance in China and the narco-military coalition in Bolivia demonstrated the potential extremist ideological leanings of members of organized crime to people, groups, and political parties proclaiming great regard for the Fascist models in Germany (1933–1945), Italy (1922–1943), or Spain (1939–1975).

Finally, *Green Gang* leaders showed their ideological preferences not only by supporting the initial coup against the Communists but by integrating into the Shanghai elites. However, the integration of gang members into the highest echelons of society inevitably had the detrimental effect of criminalizing and corrupting the Nationalist Party, which ultimately contributed to its defeat in 1949. The García Meza regime in Bolivia lasted only for some eighteen months. Still, the case of the *Oriente* elites is unique because they did not give up political power to criminals, like their counterparts in 1927 China; rather, they turned criminals themselves in order to maintain their social power.

Endnotes

1. Dr. Sun Yat-sen, who led the first Chinese Revolution in 1911 and is considered the founder of modern China, was himself a member of a secret society called *T'ung Meng Hui*, which eventually evolved into the country's official ruling party, the *Guomindang* (Snow 1974: 142).

2. Given the history of antigovernment resistance by secret societies, the reaction of the present regime in Beijing to the emergence of a new secret society, the *Falun Gong*, in the late 1990s, is hardly surprising. The *Falun Gong* mixes Buddhism, Taoism, and New Age beliefs of a coming apocalyptic end of the world. The Beijing government has branded the *Falun Gong* as counterrevolutionary and evil and has been cracking down on this movement for some time. In late 1999, the authorities introduced and passed a new anticult law which allowed handing out long prison terms and even capital punishment. Members of *Falun Gong* were put on trial for treason. According to its founder, Li Hong-zhi, a former minor government official who presently resides in New York, the sect has one hundred million followers all over China. However, expert opinion puts the number of supporters at fifteen to thirty million, while official Chinese sources claim that the sect has only two million members. The *Falun Gong* spooked the authorities in Beijing with its ability to stage protests and its apparent popularity among military and police, students, and in society at large. While initially the sect did not seem to be political, the repressive policies initiated by the Chinese government against *Falun Gong* may turn sect members into political dissidents. After all, in April 1999, some ten thousand *Falun Gong* members staged a protest in front of the compound housing the Communist Party elite, the "largest challenge to the government since the Tiananmen Square protests" of 1989 (*The Globe and Mail.* Oct. 28, 1999: A11; *The Globe and Mail.* Nov. 1, 1999: A13; *The Globe and Mail.* Nov. 3, 1999: A19).

3. According to Martin (1996), the higher number was cited most frequently in the literature. He maintained that Shanghai gangsters, most of whom belonged to the *Green Gang*, numbered about one hundred thousand and that they "represented just over 3 percent of the population" of this port city (1996: 35). Chesneaux (1971), on the other hand, believed that their number was closer to the lower estimate of twenty thousand (1971: 164; also see Thamm 1996: 38–40; 80). Deacon (1976) provided the largest estimates, claiming that the *Green Gang* had "as many as a hundred thousand members in Shanghai," in addition to "a million members in the Yangtze Valley" (1976: 275).

4. 'Department' is the term used for the administrative units of Bolivia, Colombia, and Peru. There are nine departments in Bolivia, thirty-two in Colombia, and twenty-four in Peru.

5. While Moore (1966) made no mention of the *Green Gang's* role during the coup, he referred to Chiang's pact with the elites as an "agrarian-bourgeois alliance" that "turned upon the workers" (1966: 189).

6. C. C. stands for Ch'en Kuo-fu and Ch'en Li-fu, two brothers who were some of Chiang's closest political allies (Seagrave 1985: 293–294).

7. The renowned China specialist Lloyd E. Eastman (1974) provided an extensive account of the *Blue Shirts* and their Fascist leanings, without mentioning the links to the *Green Gang* (1974: 31–84). This is a serious shortcoming considering the existing overwhelming evidence to the contrary. Author Maria Hsia Chang (1985), however, denied not only the *Blue Shirts'* Fascist leanings, but also the links to the *Green Gang*. Her perspective on the *Blue Shirts*, while informative, on the whole is not very convincing, if somewhat frightening. For example, she contended that the *Blue Shirts* lacked the "culture of death" of Nazi Germany and Fascist Italy (1985: 20–22). In fact, she argued that the "terror or assassinations" committed by the *Blue Shirts* did not demonstrate any affinity to Fascist practices because such activities are routine in intelligence agencies and even part of "CIA" operations (*ibid.*).

8. It was Joseph Stalin who had backed Chiang Kai-shek, while Leon Trotsky had opposed the alliance with the *Guomindang*. Stalin was taken by surprise by the events of April 12, 1927, and his position was endangered for several months thereafter. However, he managed to regain support and it was Trotsky, as well as Zinoviev and Kamenev, who were expelled from the Soviet Communist Party in late 1927 (Deutscher 1970: 396–399).

9. Thus, Chiang Kai-shek relied on a "corps of German advisors headed by General Hans von Seeckt" (Isaacs 1962: 303). Meanwhile, Chiang's half-a-million-strong Nationalist army was "schooled by . . . . General von Seeckt and armed with weapons of the latest design from the munitions factories of Europe and the United States" (*ibid.*, 349).

10. Apparently, the CCP leadership was surprised by the coup. Indeed, the NP officially called off their alliance with the CCP on April 21, 1927, nine days after the event (Martin 1996: 99).

11. Ningpo refers to Chiang's place of birth, a port city near Shanghai.

Chapter 5

Elites, Cocaine, and Power in
Colombia and Peru

But that they try to present me
as an associate of the guerrilla,
. . . hurts my personal dignity. . . .
I am a man of investments, and therefore
I cannot sympathize with the [leftist] guerrillas
who fight against [private] property.

(The late Colombian drug trafficker Pablo Escobar Gaviria;
as quoted in Camacho 1988: 144)

The collaboration between elites, most importantly the military, and organized crime in Colombia and Peru served the purpose of setting up local anti-insurgency fronts to address the threat from the revolutionary left. In Colombia, this cooperation is entrenched and has existed since the late 1970s. In Peru, organized crime collaborated largely with the military in the civil conflict against *Sendero Luminoso*, the Shining Path, during the 1990s. This partnership, although of shorter duration than that in Colombia, also served the purpose of channeling drug profits to the country's military, which desperately needed funds to finance the conflict against the rebels.[1]

Introduction

Although Colombia has received most of the international attention, the cocaine economy, as it existed between the 1970s and the early 1990s, cannot be illustrated without mentioning Bolivia and Peru. The cultivation of coca and its refinement into coca paste and cocaine had largely been restricted to the activities and associations of organized crime in these countries. It has, however, diversified considerably since. As noted by the Observatoire Géopolitique des Drogues (OGD) institute in Paris, France, in its 1993 annual report, the cocaine trade had developed beyond these three nations. By the early 1990s, every country in Latin America was involved in one aspect or another of the cocaine economy, regardless whether in "cultivation, processing, commercialization, money-laundering, financing of political parties or of conflicts" (OGD 1993: 217).[2]

The various groups and actors involved in the Andean cocaine economy, including coca peasants, trafficking organizations, agrarian elites, business groups, Marxist rebels, militaries, and right-wing paramilitaries, cannot be separated from the means employed in each of these countries to manage the one issue central to most of Latin America: the distribution and the redistribution of arable land (Bonilla 1993: 162; Barraclough 1994: 17–22; Tanaka 2002: 27–29). There are conflicting views about guerrillas and the violence they employ; it should be understood, though, that such movements are often attempts to address legitimate grievances. It is largely because Colombia has experienced very few land reforms that the country is home to the oldest, strongest, and most numerous guerrilla organizations in Latin America (Bascone 1991: 199). Likewise, the inadequacy of the land reforms in Peru contributed to the re-emergence of the guerrillas in that country during the 1980s (Barraclough 1994: 20). Moreover, the participation of the peasantry in Peru and Colombia in the cultivation of coca, the first link in the chain of the cocaine economy, equally resulted from the lack, or failure, of agrarian reform. This problem is reinforced by the vulnerability of peasants to global market forces, which further induces them to enter the drug economy.[3]

The most powerful left-wing guerrilla organizations in Colombia today are the *Fuerzas Armadas Revolucionarios de Colombia* (FARC) and the *Ejército de Liberación Nacional* (ELN). Other rebel groups of import include the *Ejército Popular de Liberación* (EPL), and the *Movimiento de Abril 19* (M-19), both of which are largely defunct now. In Peru, where the government was able to suppress the left-wing insurgencies for the moment, the most significant rebel groups of the 1980s and 1990s were *Sendero Luminoso*, a.k.a. the Shining Path, and the *Movimiento Revolucionario Tupac Amaru* (MRTA).[4] The lack of guerrilla organizations in Bolivia during the 1960s and thereafter is likely a result of the agrarian reforms carried out in the years following the 1952 revolution. Bolivian peasants came to express their interests through different channels, notably, the unions set up after 1952. This contributed to the demise of 'Che' Guevara in 1967, as the guerrilla leader was unable to rouse Bolivia's peasantry into rebellion.

It is necessary to provide a brief analysis of Colombia's elites, especially its political parties, who not only differ considerably from those in other Latin American countries but have a history of involvement with drug-trafficking organizations that is decades long. A similar approach is not a necessity in the Peruvian case because the country's party system is much weaker than Colombia's, while the cooperation largely involved organized crime and the military during the conflict against *Sendero* in the early 1990s. The end of the conflict not only resulted in the Peruvian state's withdrawal from this temporary alliance with criminals, which had helped to finance the war, it also created the necessity to conceal this involvement. This is not to say that Peruvian OC groups have not managed to integrate into local power structures. Yet these organizations, given their specific location in the drug economy as suppliers of raw coca paste rather than of the far more profitable final product, did not gain the economic and political clout of their counterparts in Colombia and Bolivia (Rospiglioso 1993: 161; Cotler 1999: 171).

The Colombian study will focus on the years between 1980 and 2000, to account for the larger depth of criminal integration into elite structures. The Peruvian study will concentrate on the years between 1990 and 2000, the Fujimori era. This chapter will also examine the most important rebel movements in these countries and their involvement in the drug economy.

Notes on *Narcodollars*

Although the amounts may differ, and while it is certain that profits have declined due to overproduction and market satiation, the economic impact of *narcodollars* in Bolivia, Colombia, and Peru has been substantial. Colombia may be seen as representing an alternate model of development, namely *narcodevelopment*, not unlike the 'legal' drug trafficking by the Europeans which transpired from the sixteenth to early twentieth century.

The figures that follow should be viewed with some caution. They indicate trends but are not precise observations. After a thorough investigation of economic studies on the size of the cocaine economy in Colombia, Thoumi (1995) noted that the studies often fail to mention various participants who are "part of the illegal industry and who have profited from it" (1995: 199). Thus, "the estimates only indicate that the amount of income and capital that has been tainted by illicit drug activity is quite high; but neither the distribution of that capital today nor the proportion that has been legitimized in the Colombian economy is known" (*ibid.*).

For the scholar who explores the impact these funds have on the economic and political landscape in Colombia and elsewhere, it is not essential to have precise computations at hand. While it is difficult to provide exact figures for the illicit funds which enter the various Andean economies, it seems clear that this wealth provides trafficking groups with the resources to infiltrate their nations' power structures. In addition, the *narcodollars* contribute to financing the Colombian and Peruvian civil conflicts.

Hardinghaus (1989) offered some of the highest figures and claimed that the profits made by Colombian drug traffickers amounted to US$9 billion in 1989. By comparison, Colombia's official Gross National Product (GNP) in 1990 was US$ 41 billion (1989: 98; *Fischer Weltalmanach* 1992: 426). Lessmann (1996) provided appraisals for the early 1990s which ranged from US$1.5 billion to 7 billion annually (1996: 203). Filippone (1994) estimated that the 1987 profits made by Colombian criminal groups were between US$2 and 4 billion (1994: 324). The figures used by De Rementería (1995) were lower still. He estimated that in 1990 about US$2.34 billion remained as profits in Colombia, while the consumers of cocaine paid an approximated US$74 billion worldwide (1995: 17). The authors of the 1993 OGD report supplied some of the lowest numbers. In their estimate the illicit funds repatriated to Colombia during the 1980s amounted to US$800–1.200 million annually, which rose by another US$500–600 million by 1991. This figure, however, does not include drug monies invested elsewhere (OGD 1993: 241). The earnings of Colombian crime groups declined during the 1990s following the dismemberment of the *Medellín* and *Cali Cartels*, which may explain some of the economic problems the country has been experiencing of late. Even so, the impact on the availability of cocaine was marginal as Mexican criminal organizations moved in to take over the Colombians' positions in the United States, earning some US$7 billion annually by the mid-1990s. The Colombian traffickers, once the main distributors of cocaine in the US market, in effect, were reduced to suppliers of the very Mexican crime groups who once had been their junior partners (Smith 1999: 196–197; Morton 1999: 543; Boyer 2001: 165).

Peru is dependent on funds from the cocaine economy. The Peruvian economist, Humberto Campodónico (1994), believed that the country made approximately US$500 million from its involvement in the cocaine economy in 1993 (1994: 153–162). The 1993 OGD report estimated that the trade was worth between US$1–2 billion (OGD 1993: 226). According to Fuhr and Hörmann (1992), Peru earned between US$1.3–3 billion. Of this amount only between US$170–240 million ended up with the Peruvian peasants cultivating the plant (1992: 456). De Rementería (1995) allotted US$362 million to peasant earnings in 1992, but he emphasized that this was the highest amount they had received in seventeen years. In 1989, for example, after a major crackdown against the *Medellín Cartel*, the peasants' earnings came to only US$86 million (1995: 102).

Peru's cocaine industry has evolved since. Having once furnished the criminal networks in Cali and Medellín with coca paste for final refining in Colombia, today's Peruvian minicartels often bypass Colombia altogether and directly supply the final product to large Mexican organizations who are responsible for distribution on the North American and even European markets (*The Toronto Star.* March 22, 1997: A1; *El Comercio.* July 13, 1997: A1; *El Sol.* Aug. 2, 1997: 8A; BBC June 11, 2002).

Hardinghaus (1989) further maintained that the drug economy created jobs on all levels of the chain of production and distribution. According to his estimates, approximately six to seven hundred thousand Bolivians, nine hundred thousand Peruvians and two hundred and fifty thousand Colombians were 'employed' by the drug economy by the late 1980s. He also calculated that between 2.5 and 2.7 million people throughout Latin America earned their livelihood in the cultivation, production, and trade of drugs. These, in turn, provided a living for another 12–15 million people (1989: 100).[5]

In addition, Hardinghaus pointed out that the Gross Domestic Product (GDP) as well as the monetary basis grew due to the stimulating effects of the cocaine economy. Still, while the drug economy was invariably inflationary because of its size and illegality, large amounts of *narcodollars* were absorbed by imports, which lowered inflationary pressures (*ibid.*, 104–105). Thus, the drug trade had become an important factor in maintaining economic stability in Bolivia, Colombia, and Peru. It should not be surprising that the three Andean nations at the core of the cocaine economy, in need of foreign exchange to finance their debts or their conflicts, have openly encouraged the flow of *narcodollars* into their financial institutions, while taking part in the US-sponsored Drug War. As pointed out by a leading Bolivian economist, the inflow of *narcodollars* is "the only way we've been able to balance the balance of payments" (as quoted in Andreas 1993: 28).

The Colombian economy gained the most from the trade due to the position the cartels had won as distributors in the US market. Moreover, the growth of the drug economy in Colombia cannot be separated from economic crisis, confirming Chambliss' (1988) observation that "criminal behavior is a response of groups and social classes to the resources and constraints that exist in the social structure" (1988: 208). Arango (1988) claimed that the modern Colombian cocaine trade originated in the economic recession which impacted in the country during the 1970s. Antioquia, Colombia's most industrialized region since the 1940s, was hit the hardest. The textile industry, centered in the regional capital of Medellín, suffered severe losses in production and jobs. The city's economic output declined by 15 percent, while its unemployment rate was three times higher than that of other major Colombian cities. These developments prompted local entrepreneurs to seek involvement in the cocaine economy (1988: 87–97; also see Strong 1996: 32–33).

The growth of this criminal economy was also enhanced by Colombian fiscal policies. In 1968, the government imposed severe restrictions on external trade and foreign exchange after its foreign currency reserves had fallen to US$35 million. This move gave new impetus to the already well-established Colombian tradition of smuggling contraband. Other factors that contributed to the emergence of Medellín's drug trade included the growing cocaine markets in the United States, the promise of high profits from exporting to that country, and Colombia's ideal geographic location for such ventures (*ibid.*, 91–94). Finally, Colombian traffickers had already set up well-established networks in the United States as suppliers of marijuana (Pearce 1990: 110–111).

Between 1979 and 1993, Colombia's economy expanded by an "average of 3.6 percent" annually because the drug trade stimulated other industries, such as construction, soft drinks, and agriculture (Strong 1996: 184–185). The country therefore avoided the economic adversities suffered in the rest of Latin America. Salomón Kalmanovitz, a respected economist who worked on the board of the Colombian central bank, wrote that "cocaine stopped the balance of payments from collapsing, which would have pushed us into the spiral of hyperdevaluation and hyperinflation that shook most of the rest of the continent . . . . [during] the 1980s . . . ." (as quoted in Strong 1996: 184–185).

The Colombian Senator Ivan Marulanda asserted in like manner that the "drug traffickers bring narcodollars and invest them in the country. In Colombia, they reactivated the economy . . . . They are in industry, business, finance, agriculture, construction and the government" (as quoted in Collett 1989: 128). Arango (1988: 136) also described the drug trade as an "economic reactivator" for Antioquia and its main city, Medellín. He claimed that, in 1987, some US$311.7 million, or 60,000 million Colombian pesos, "irrigated" the city's economy and generated approximately twenty-eight thousand new jobs in Medellín's commercial, service, and informal sectors (*ibid.,* 136–140).

By the early 1990s, Colombian crime groups, the *Cali Cartel* in particular, had also moved into the production of heroin for the US market. Indeed, most of the heroin available in the United States today derives from Colombia, not Southeast Asia (Henman 1981: 138; Soberón 1992: 40–44, Farrel 1995; *The Economist.* March 4, 2000: 23; UNODCCP 2002: 47; *La República.* May 21, 2005: 21). Colombian drug dealers were initially far more export-oriented than their Bolivian or Peruvian counterparts. The commercial success of the cartels prompted the country's Minister of Development during the Barco Administration (1986–1990), Carlos Arturo Marulanda, to write that "Colombia's industrials should imitate the model set by the drug dealers . . . . The[ir] strategy . . . . of aggressively opening new markets should serve as an example for our national industrials who are afraid to appear on foreign markets" (*El Siglo.* Aug. 18, 1989: 1; as cited in Duque Gómez 1991: 208.).

Regardless, as noted, the developed countries of North America and Western Europe benefit most from money laundering and subsequent investments, not the drug-producing countries in the developing world (Castillo 1991: 147; Cabieses 1994: 51; 1996: 2).

A Short History of Political Violence in Colombia

The dominant political forces in Colombia and homes to the country's economic elites are the *Partido Liberal* and the *Partido Conservador*, the Liberal and Conservative parties. The country differs from many others in Latin America in that it has not experienced revolutionary changes from below or above which would have transformed its oligarchic power structures. Bolivia, Costa Rica, Cuba, Mexico, and Nicaragua had revolutions. Peru was ruled by a left-wing military that introduced important reforms, as did the Peron and Vargas regimes in Argentina and Brazil respectively. Colombia's political structures, however, have changed little since the middle of the nineteenth century. The elites from the *Partido Liberal* and the *Partido Conservador* have maintained their strong positions, which may explain why Colombia has experienced only two military coups as opposed to almost two hundred in Bolivia. Nevertheless, Colombia's past has been very violent. Liberals and Conservatives have fought a series of civil wars since the establishment of the two-party system in the middle of the nineteenth century, a generation after gaining independence from Spain (Andreski 1966: 216–256; Krumwiede and Stockmann 1992: 382–384; Zelik and Azzellini 2000: 46–50).

Both parties claim to follow the legacy of key figures in the independence struggle against Spain. While the Conservatives consider the *Libertador* Simón Bolívar, the South American equivalent of George Washington, to be their founding father, the Liberals attribute this position to General Francisco Paula de Santander. The labels of Liberals and Conservatives cannot be ascribed to recognizable social groups, and the common identification of the Liberals with traders and merchants and of the Conservatives with large-estate holders may not be important. After all, there were Liberal landowners as well as Conservative merchants. Historically, the two parties differed on three points: The Conservatives defended the Catholic Church and its property, they were protectionist, and they believed in strong central government. The Liberals advocated the separation of state and church and the partitioning of church property, and opposed clerical privileges, while they favored a federal state and a free trade economy (Lyonette 1968: 76–77; Meschkat, Rohde and Töpper 1983: 71–72; Bergquist 1986: 8; Pearce 1990: 183; Bushnell 1993: 92–93; Zelik and Azzellini 2000: 47).

The civil wars between the two parties were bloody conflicts because Liberals and Conservatives had created mass followings. These should not be mistaken with the modern mass parties in Latin America, such as the *Alianza Popular Revolucionaria Americana* (APRA) in Peru, or even the European political parties like Germany's Social Democrats. Rather, the campesinos' physical presence in a given Liberal or Conservative party boss's locale implied acceptance of his or her political credo as well as recruitment into the respective party militias who fought the civil wars (Gott 1970: 175; Pearce 1990: 20, 183; Krumwiede and Stockmann 1992: 385).[6] Zelik and Azzellini (2000) refer to a "vertical division of society" whereby the "lines of separation do not run across social polarities but between party camps whose social composition is largely identical" (2000: 49).[7]

In 1852, the Conservatives revolted after the Liberal government abolished slavery (Meschkat et al 1983: 74). During the 1880s, the Liberals rose against the Conservative government of Rafael Nuñez after it had intervened in the country's economy by setting up a national bank and by increasing import tariffs, which challenged the Liberals' free trade credo (*ibid.*, 86–87). A Liberal revolt in 1899 resulted in the so-called Thousand Day War of 1899–1902. It ended in a Conservative victory and cost the lives of tens of thousands of people (*ibid.*, 90–95; also see Pearce 1990: 25; Zelik and Azzellini 2000: 48–49). This conflict was a precursor to the *violencia* period of the 1940s and 1950s, which took an even higher toll in lives.

The Period of Violence

The guerrilla movements as well as the cocaine trade are linked to the *violencia* period, as Colombians call the last civil war (1948–1957) between the two oligarchic parties. In 1948, the unpopular Conservative government was confronted with the increasing electoral power of the Liberals and their charismatic leader, Jorge Eliécer Gaitán, who promised to be the easy winner of the next election and whose support came largely from the majority of peasants and urban poor. The populist leader was gunned down in the streets of the capital, Bogotá, on April 9, 1948 (Meschkat et al 1983: 121–124; Mayer 1990: 32–33; Zelik and Azzellini 2000: 53).[8] The responsibility for the murder has never been determined. Still, the Conservatives pointed to internal divisions within the Liberal Party. Gaitán, on the left of the party, had certainly caused considerable friction, and right-wing Liberals feared his populist agenda. The Liberals, though, as could be expected, charged the Conservatives with his murder. After the assassination, the city erupted into an urban revolt known as the *Bogotázo*, which police crushed after three days of rioting. The Colombian Communist Party, the *Partido Comunista de Colombia* (PCC), was blamed for the revolt, although its members had been caught by surprise because the violence in the capital was a spontaneous explosion which lacked any organization. While the *Bogotázo* may have been an instinctual response to Gaitán's shooting, the fighting that gripped the country thereafter was not. Local Liberal party bosses armed the peasants in their villages and organized them to fight as guerrillas against matching forces set up by the Conservatives in power, who were supported by the police and army. Traditional loyalty to a local strong man, whether Liberal or Conservative, sustained a horrifying violence that engulfed many parts of the country. Estimates of the number of *violencia* victims range between 80,000–300,000 (*ibid.*, 125; Guzman, Borda and Luna 1963: 287–293; Gott 1970: 173; Gerassi 1973: 152; Szulc 1987: 183; Pearce 1990: 52; Krumriede and Stockmann 1992: 387; Zelik and Azzellini 2000: 53–54).

When the conflict threatened the economic bases of Liberal and Conservative elites, both parties initially supported the June 1953 military coup led by General Gustavo Rojas Pinilla and even joined his government to put an end to the fighting. However, Rojas Pinilla's policies shifted toward populism, nationalism, neutralism, and the establishment of personal rule, similar to the Peron regime in Argentina. This led to further rapprochements between Liberals and Conservatives, and in 1958, both parties agreed to an accord, the *Frente Nacional*, which divided power between them for sixteen years, while Rojas Pinilla was forced into exile. Government positions were equally divided and occupied by members of both parties, while the presidency alternated between the two. Until 1985, the arrangements of the *Frente Nacional* were continued in spirit by the practice of offering government positions to the second strongest party. The *Frente Nacional* officially ended the *violencia* period. It further cemented oligarchic rule by excluding other groups from the political process, particularly those representative of the urban poor and the peasants (*ibid.*, 130–136; Krumriede and Stockmann 1992: 383; Zelik and Azzellini 2000: 54–55; Tanaka 2002: 29).

Dimensions and Problems of Protection-Racket Maintenance in Colombia

Constitutionally legal attempts to break the *Frente Nacional's* stranglehold on power largely failed. After his return from exile former Colombian President Rojas Pinilla founded the populist *Alianza Nacional Popular* (ANAPO), which mounted a serious challenge against the oligarchic parties. The new party had been set up as a third force capable of breaking the Liberals' and Conservatives' hold on power. ANAPO aimed at domestic reforms, such as the nationalization of large banks, as well as improvement of the living conditions of the country's poor. It professed a nationalist and neutralist agenda and can be characterized as a Colombian brand of Peronism. However, during the presidential elections of April 19, 1970, Rojas Pinilla was narrowly beaten. Many assume that the election results were rigged. Convinced of electoral fraud, the former general's most radical supporters formed the previously mentioned M-19 (Sukup 1988: 80–81; Pearce 1990: 170; Zelik and Azzellini 2000: 61).[9]

The 1984 peace accord with the guerrillas, during the administration of Colombian President Belisario Betancur (1982–1986), represented another attempt to open up the political system. During the election campaign, Conservative presidential candidate Betancur, himself of humble origins, vowed to initiate peace talks with the rebels. It was his goal to democratize society by encouraging the large number of Colombians not involved in the electoral process to participate in politics. To do so, Betancur permitted the rebels to form their own political parties and made changes to the electoral laws, such as introducing municipal elections. He also hoped to initiate sweeping agrarian and administrative reforms. In short, Betancur wanted to eliminate the conditions that created the milieu in which the rebels flourished (Vazquez Carrizosa 1986: 358; Thoumi 1995: 53, Vargas Meza 1998: 24; Tanaka 2002: 31).

In the spring of 1984, the government signed agreements with the FARC, and with the EPL and M-19 several months later. Only the ELN and two smaller groups refused to join the process. By August 1984, 90 percent of Colombia's rebels had agreed to a truce with the government (*LAWR*. Sept.7, 1984: 5). However, the military and its paramilitary allies successfully managed to derail the peace process through selective assassinations and massacres, and everyone went back to war. Betancur's reforms had alienated the members of the oligarchy because they threatened the dominance of the traditional parties. Successful peace negotiations would also have deprived the military of its raison d'etre. Colombia's generals had pledged many times over to eradicate the insurgents but had been unable to follow through on their promise. Although the strong positions of the oligarchic parties had prevented the military from playing an important role in early Colombian politics, it became increasingly instrumental since the *violencia* because of the growing size of the rebel movements. This position was institutionalized in the country's various constitutions (Vazquez Carrizosa 1986: 319–348, 360–363; Watson 1991: 26–27; Richani 1997: 51).

The latest attempt at peace with the rebels was initiated in 1998 by Conservative President Andrés Pastrana, who ordered the military to evacuate a safe zone of more than forty thousand square kilometers as a precondition for talks with the FARC. Similarly, he created such a domain for the ELN. However, the government again proved unable or unwilling to control the paramilitaries, which had been a key rebel demand. Right-wing death squads — in direct collaboration with army units — once again engaged in peasant massacres and assassinations of suspected leftists in order to end the talks. As noted by Amnesty International (AI), the activities of right-wing paramilitaries increased during the Pastrana Administration (1998–2002). The negotiations, which started officially in early 1999, never got off the ground and ultimately failed like previous endeavors at peace (BBC June 5, 1998; BBC Nov. 7, 1998; BBC Jan. 8, 1999. BBC Jan. 8, 1999a; BBC Jan. 19, 1999; BBC Feb. 23, 2000; BBC March 2, 2000; BBC April 25, 2000).

The peace negotiations also fell victim to the Colombian government's ill-timed October 1999 pronouncement and the subsequent launching of the controversial 'Plan Colombia,' with US$1.3 billion in mostly military funding from Washington. While the project was ostensibly aimed at reducing coca cultivation and cocaine production, it targeted the left-wing FARC, who control the large territories under coca cultivation in the Putumayo region in southern Colombia. The arrival of a rapid deployment force, especially trained in antiguerrilla warfare in the United States, and brand-new military hardware from Washington, gave fresh courage to the Colombian military, which had suffered some serious setbacks in the late 1990s. In April 2001, the commander-in-chief of Colombia's military, General Jorge Enrique Mora, further undermined President Andrés Pastrana's peace process when he charged that the FARC dominated the country's drug trade (BBC Sept. 13, 1999; BBC Dec. 8, 1999; BBC Aug. 31, 2000; BBC April 5, 2001; Richani 2002: 17–20; Tanaka 2002: 30). Talks with the FARC collapsed in January 2002, while negotiations with the ELN ended in June of 2002 (BBC Jan. 13, 2002; BBC June 1, 2002). The depiction of the rebel movements as drug cartels whose members aimed to become wealthy by producing and exporting narcotics brought the peace process to an end because it turned the FARC and ELN, internationally recognized political actors, into criminal ones.[10]

In hindsight, Pastrana's endeavor to bring peace to Colombia was a replay of Betancur's attempt during the 1980s: a period of reduced fighting which both the military and the rebels used to replenish their forces for the next round of hostilities. Renewed fighting began with the introduction of 'Plan Patriota' implemented by Pastrana's successor, the hawkish Alvaro Uribe, with the goal of finishing off the rebels or forcing them to the negotiating table (*La Republica.* June 13, 2004: 10; *El*

Comercio. June 26, 2004: A22).[11] By 2005, Washington had spent over US$3 billion without achieving the desired results. After some initial setbacks the rebels recovered and even went on a counteroffensive against the Colombian army, killing dozens of troops. Moreover, the FARC rebels — under pressure in the southern regions of the country which they controlled for decades — responded with mobile warfare attacking areas where they had never established a permanent presence (*El Comercio.* April 28, 2005: A14; *La República.* April 28, 2005: 24; *Correo.* April 30, 2005: 17; *La República.* May 5, 2005: 37; *El Comercio.* May 29, 2005: A32).

In addition, 'Plan Colombia' also included the presence of some eight hundred US troops and six hundred civilians in the country. These have been the cause of scandal and embarrassment as several US soldiers have been accused of involvement in drugs and arms trafficking, the sale of pornographic videos, and the illegal trade in ancient artifacts. Based on a 1974 US-Colombian treaty these individuals enjoy immunity and impunity because they will not be brought to court in that South American country but returned to the United States. This fact has caused indignation among Colombians because Washington insists on the extradition of all drug traffickers, while refusing to hand over American soldiers who violate Colombian law (*La República.* May 5, 2005: 27; *El Comercio.* May 7, 2005: A25).

Colombia had been in a state of siege between 1948, the beginning of the *violencia* period, and 1991, the year the Gaviria Administration (1990–1994) introduced a new constitution. The 1991 constitution differed between two states of emergency which justify a form of martial law. It can be introduced during an external war. Moreover, according to article 213, the so-called *estado de conmoción interior*, the state of internal commotion, allows for the introduction of martial law in the whole country, or parts thereof, in cases where public order is threatened. Once invoked and approved by Colombia's Congress, the president rules by decree for a three-month period, which can be extended twice (Meschkat et al. 1983: 136; *Nueva Const.* 1991: 55–57). It is generally applied in zones where the military clashes with the guerrillas. For example, the government of Cesar Gaviria first implemented the state of internal commotion during a guerrilla offensive in November of 1992; it was also declared in August 2002 following the violence surrounding the inauguration of Alvaro Uribe as president (*El Tiempo.* Nov.7, 1992: 5A; BBC Aug.12, 2002). Knoester (1998) points out that the introduction of the state of internal commotion allows the Colombian president to "limit internationally recognized human rights, within the constitution" (1998: 99; also see Tanaka 2002: 30).[12]

While officially a democracy, the Colombian state is part of a protection racket that employs violence against the excluded to maintain the supremacy of the oligarchic structures. The situation differs little from that in El Salvador where the military's violence was "the currency of relations between state and nonstate elites" (Stanley 1996: 6–7). In response to the increasing numbers of guerrillas, Colombia's oligarchic elites handed over political power to the military in order to maintain their social power. Ironically, the increase in state violence resulted in more guerrillas producing more state violence in return, and so on. The authors of the 1990 report on human rights in Colombia published by the Comisión Andina de Juristas (CAJ), the Andean Commission of Jurists, observed in this context that "the indiscriminate use of force and repression augmented the popular base of the guerrilla groups [and] increased their offensive capacities" (CAJ 1990: 95).

In fact, Colombian military spending — due to increased aid from Washington — went up considerably between 1991 and 1996, while Colombian military performance actually decreased. Defense spending in Colombia grew 14 percent in real terms, from 1.79 percent to 3.17 percent of the country's GDP. Still, while the military budget rose, the number of guerrillas killed did, in fact, decline (taking into consideration the growing numbers of rebels). For example, between 1992 and 1995 military spending increased from US$422 million to almost US$1.4 billion. Despite the increases, rebel casualties actually fell from 934 in 1992 to 669 in 1995 (Vargas Meza 1999). Similarly, despite the military aid of 'Plan Colombia,' the FARC have not been weakened but have gone on the counteroffensive in the spring of 2005 (*La República.* April 28, 2005: 24; *Correo.* April 30, 2005: 17; *La República.* May 5, 2005: 37).

At any rate, already by the 1980s, a situation had been created in which the military no longer sufficed to contain the rebels. This, in turn, led to the collaboration between the military, local elites, and criminal organizations in the regions most affected. As noted, organized crime is "compatible with the continued existence of the formal state structure and can even be employed to defend it" (Naylor 1993: 22). In Colombia, this collaboration was in part made possible by Law 48, the legislation implemented during the 1960s that empowered the military to create so-called *autodefensas*, or armed self-defense groups. Law 48 permitted the military to "authorize the use of arms considered only for the exclusive use of the armed forces by private individuals" when deemed necessary (*LAWR.* Aug.13, 1987: 6; CAJ 1990: 91). Although the military has never officially admitted to its reliance on paramilitaries, the existing proof is overwhelming (Carrigan 1995: 6–10; *Semana.* Jan.14, 1997: 24–25; Zelik and Azzellini 2000: 88–89).

In Colombia, this collaboration is illustrated by the conversion of mafia-paid paramilitary organizations, such as MAS, into death squads aligned with the military. MAS stands for *Muerte a Secuestradores*, which translates as 'Death to Kidnappers.' It was originally established in 1977, after the abduction of Martha Nieves Ochoa Vásquez by M-19 rebels. She was the sister of Jorge Luis Ochoa, one of the leading Medellín mafia bosses alongside Pablo Escobar Gaviria. Initially organized to protect cartel leaders and their families against Colombia's leftist guerillas, MAS transformed into a right-wing death squad linked to the military (*LAWR.* Feb.11, 1983: 5; Castillo 1987: 111–114). As one observer noted:

> MAS evolved into an instrument for the indiscriminate persecution of leftists, including labor organizers, peasants who collaborate with guerillas. . . . Some Colombian army officers have been members of MAS; in fact, the organization

seemingly served as a communication channel of sorts between the mafia and the military (Lee III 1988: 117–118).[13]

The *Asociación campesina de agricultores y ganaderos del Magdalena Medio* (ACDEGAM), the Association of Peasants and Ranchers of the Magdalena Medio, in the Department of Antioquia, was another organization directly linked to the *Medellín Cartel*. Cartel leaders Pablo Escobar Gaviria, Jorge Luis Ochoa, and Gonzalo Rodríguez Gacha were members of ACDEGAM and helped finance its activities (*LAWR*. Aug. 24, 1989: 9; Medina Gallego 1990: 219–229; *The Miami Herald*. July 18, 1990: 4A; Strong 1996: 162–163). ACDEGAM was initially not set up by traffickers but by middle- and large-estate owners and cattle ranchers. However, the acquisition of land by the *Medellín Cartel* leaders brought the traffickers and agrarian elites into direct contact. By 1988, traffickers had allegedly acquired one million hectares of Colombian real estate worth an estimated US$5 billion. Other sources claimed that the drug traffickers had bought up to 2.5 million hectares by the late 1980s (*LAWR*. Dec.8, 1988: 12; *LAWR*. Dec.15, 1988: 10–11; Filippone 1994: 335; Thoumi 1995: 239–240). According to Carrigan (1995), drug traffickers owned 21 percent of Colombia's arable land in 1994–1995 (1995: 9; also see Zelik and Azzellini 2000: 107).

MAS and similar groups who helped derail the Betancur peace process have their antecedents in the so-called *Pajaros*, who were responsible for human rights abuses during the *violencia* period. The *Pajaros* were gangs of paid killers who murdered peasants and amnestied rebels, often in direct collaboration with government security forces (Guzman, Borda and Luna 1963: 165–169; Zelik and Azzellini 2000: 74–75). Modern groups like ACDEGAM and MAS came to represent a "plethora of mostly local death squads who used anti-communism" to defend the murder of a wide range of victims (Pearce 1990a: 22). These included "petty criminals, prostitutes and homosexuals," members or supporters of the rebel groups, "artists, intellectuals, journalists, and lawyers" (*ibid.*).

A report by the Departamento Administrativo de Seguridad (DAS), the one Colombian intelligence agency directly responsible to civilian rather than military authority, claimed that some hundred and forty death squads operated in the country by 1987 (*LAWR*. Oct. 15, 1987: 8). According to Amnesty International, more than one thousand people were murdered for political motives by death squads in 1987. In the following year, this number doubled to 2084 (AI 1988: 7; also see *LAWR*. Jan. 19, 1989: 8). Massacres of peasants as well as selective assassinations of activists and candidates of the leftist *Unión Patriotica* (UP) party became weekly events between 1985 and 1988 (AI 1988a: 17). According to a report by the Colombian section of the respected Comisión Andina de Juristas, nearly three quarters of the more than twenty-five thousand political killings between 1986 and 1994 can be attributed to the army, police, and paramilitaries, while the rebels committed the remainder (Carrigan 1995: 9). The same observer notes also that in

Colombia, the toll of political victims of state terrorism demonstrates that every year since 1986, more citizens have been killed, disappeared, or suffered death from torture at the hands of the State or its paramilitary allies than the total of all victims of political repression in Chile during the entire seventeen years of the Pinochet military dictatorship (*ibid.*).

The collaboration between criminals and elites in Colombia likely qualifies as a form of *trasformismo* as understood by Gramsci (1973), namely, the integration of adversarial groups into the existing structures of domination for the purpose of maintaining them (1973: 243). Colombian scholar Alejandro Reyes (1996) described the relationship from the traffickers' perspective:

Many narcotraffickers [had begun] to invest in large haciendas in those regions where property was concentrated and where there was frequent guerrilla harassment of the landowners. As a consequence, what was expected to be a way to defend the traditional social order against subversion opened a political and legal space for some narcotraffickers to join the task of counterinsurgency for their own benefit, as allies of the armed forces (1996: 126).

A German human rights lawyer wrote on ACDEGAM, the *Medellín Cartel*, and right-wing politics in the Magdalena Medio in the Department of Antioquia, that

the . . . . mafia, in an expedient alliance with ranchers, local politicians and the military, succeeded to set up one of the most powerful paramilitary units of Colombia, [and] to turn the region of the Magdalena Medio into . . . . an independent paramilitary mafia republic [as well as] to legalize its right-wing terror with the founding of their own political party (Mayer 1990: 199).

In 1989, Colombia's supreme court declared illegal the 1960s law which permitted the creation of self-defense groups and legitimated paramilitary activities; however, the move had little effect (Chernick 1998: 32; Ruiz 2001: 174). By the mid-1990s, the paramilitaries in Colombia had consolidated into the *Autodefensas unidas de Colombia*, the United Self-Defense Forces of Colombia, or AUC. Chernick also notes that the "paramilitaries have . . . . come to replace the armed forces, which are mired in crisis as a result of their failure to defeat the insurgents" (*ibid.*, 29). While the paramilitaries are increasingly responsible for massacres and human rights abuses, military involvement is evidenced by the fact that these outrages tend to occur in areas "heavily patrolled or occupied by the army" (*ibid.*). Moreover, the AUC attempts to present itself as a "third party" in the conflict which allows the Colombian government and its military to appear as untainted victims of the violence generated by the extreme left and right (Zelik and Azzellini 2000: 104; BBC Nov. 25, 2002).

The Revolutionary Left in Colombia

The *Fuerzas Armadas Revolucionarios de Colombia*, the Revolutionary Armed Forces of Colombia (FARC), Latin America's oldest left-wing insurgency movement, was born in the *violencia* years. The *Ejército Liberación Nacional*, the National Liberation Army (ELN), emerged as part of the revolutionary fervor which swept Latin America after the 1959 Cuban Revolution. The *Ejercito Popular de Liberación*, the Popular Liberation Army (EPL), as well as the *Movimiento de Abril 19*, the Movement of April 19 (M-19), were established in opposition to FARC's political line, and even with the help of FARC combatants who had switched allegiance.

The FARC guerrillas are very strong militarily and control large tracts of Colombian territory. The movement's origins lie in the so-called independent republics set up mainly by former Liberal peasant guerrillas who had turned to the left during the *violencia*. In fact, most of FARC's original leadership derived from this background. Accordingly, some sixteen republics were founded during the *violencia* over which the central government in Bogotá had no control. These were zones of self-defense, self-governed by the peasants, who had also set up their own security forces. Shielded from the violence in the rest of the country, these areas turned into safe havens for refugees. A typical republic was Marquetalia, on the borders of the departments of Tolima and Huila. It was approximately two thousand square miles in size and was home to some four thousand peasants who had fled the violence (Gott 1970: 174–179; Arenas 1985: 68–73).

While Liberals and Conservatives were at each others' throats, Colombia's Communist Party, the PCC, made strong inroads in the republics. The PCC's role differed from that of other Latin American Communist parties, who had distanced themselves from the guerrilla movements in their respective countries following directives from Moscow. For example, the Cuban Communists did little to support Fidel Castro's *26th of July Movement* and labeled him "adventurist" (Szulc 1987: 458). For some time, even after Castro's launch of guerrilla warfare against the Batista dictatorship, Cuba's Communists maintained that there was no cause for rebellion and demanded democratic elections instead (*ibid.*). The Colombian Communists allied themselves with the guerrillas in order not to lose influence among the peasantry. Also, many peasant rebel leaders themselves, including the renowned Manuel Marulanda Velez, who apparently died of cancer in May 2004 and was the FARC's commander-in-chief for some four decades, held prominent positions in the party which had many peasant members (Gott 1970: 192–194; BBC March 3, 2000; *La República.* June 13, 2004: 33). The PCC's stance was a compromise solution that took into account Colombian reality and the belief of Soviet leaders that the region was not yet ready for a socialist revolution. Kremlin leaders strongly opposed the goal of Cuban leader Fidel Castro to overthrow the governments of Latin America and disliked 'Che' Guevara's revolutionary fervor because they did not want to provoke the United States. Furthermore, the Soviets feared that successful revolutions might be taken over by the Chinese. Finally, there was strong disgruntlement in the Union of Soviet Socialist Republics (USSR) with the amount of "fraternal assistance" given to Cuba and other developing socialist countries. Simply put, the Kremlin could not afford further revolutionary successes (Salisbury 1965: 47; Shevchenko 1985: 187; Szulc 1987: 669).

The independent republics that were dominated by the PCC existed well into the 1960s, when the Bogotá government decided to eradicate them with US backing. In fact, Colombia became the first Latin American country where the United States tested its new antiguerrilla tactics, developed after the 1959 Cuban Revolution. After several unsuccessful attempts, the Colombian army destroyed these enclaves by 1965 (Gott 1970: 188–189; Pizarro 1992: 180–181).[14] Yet, the fall of the territories did not spell the end of the Communist guerrillas. While the republics had relatively little cohesion, a merger of all rebel groups in southern Colombia in 1966 established the FARC. Moreover, the rebels changed tactics from the apparently unsuccessful self-defense zone to mobile guerrilla warfare. In Colombia, guerrilla warfare became the strategy officially adopted by the Communists, although it was not the only form of struggle. According to the PCC, Colombia was not in a revolutionary situation. Conversely, the party's leadership argued that the guerrillas could not simply stand by in the face of the military's aggression but strike back with their own form of warfare (Gott 1970: 192–193; *Movimientos revolucionarios de America Latina.* 1972: 115, 158; Casas 1987: 190; *El País.* May 30, 1999: 8).

The strength of the FARC has grown considerably during the 1980s and 1990s, largely due to the polarization of the struggle over land between local elites in league with criminal groups on one side and peasants on the other. In fact, FARC officially acknowledged the existence of a "revolutionary situation" in Colombia in 1982 (Pearce 1990: 173). The movement has increased its presence from fifteen fronts in 1982 to sixty-six in 1996, with each front comprising some one to two hundred guerrilla fighters (Richani 1997: 41–42). By the late 1990s, it was estimated to have between fifteen to twenty thousand active combatants operating in most parts of Colombia. However, figures regarding the military strength of the different Colombian rebel organizations are difficult to verify. The late rebel commander Manuel Marulanda even claimed in 1985 that the FARC could launch forty thousand armed combatants, which then was clearly beyond the FARC's capabilities (*LAWR.* May 24, 1985: 8; *Cambio 16.* Dec.18, 1993: 6–10; *The Globe and Mail.* May 30, 1998: A12; *The Globe and Mail.* Aug. 1, 1998: A8).

Still, as a result of its increased military capacity, FARC has repeatedly humiliated the Colombian military. One such embarrassment was the 1997 handover of soldiers captured by FARC. Receiving international media attention, the rebels released their eighty prisoners to the International Red Cross (IRC) after lengthy negotiations, and after the military temporarily evacuated some fifteen thousand square kilometers in the Department of Caquetá in the south of the country. In 1998, during peace talks between the Pastrana government and the

FARC, the military had to vacate a territory the size of Switzerland, which it did only grudgingly (*El Sol.* June 16, 1997: C1; *El Sol.* June 16, 1997a: C1; *Semana.* June 16–23, 1997; Miller 2001: 1; *The Globe and Mail.* Jan. 17, 2002: A14).

Other rebel groups emerged in Colombia following global events and changes in the Communist world. While the Cuban Revolution of 1959 produced the ELN, the rift between Soviets and Chinese brought about the creation of a Beijing-oriented Communist party in Colombia, which also launched its own rebel movement, the EPL. The foundation of the ELN, in 1964, was strongly influenced by the writings of 'Che' Guevara, and the movement derived much of its initial support from left-wing students. One of its most famous members was the priest Camillo Torres, who was killed in 1966. His decision to become a guerilla is still controversial in Colombia. The ELN based its guerrilla struggle on the strategy of the insurrectional focus, which would spread and eventually engulf the whole country. The ELN thus differed from the FARC in its analysis of the revolutionary situation and how to go about creating one. While the FARC doctrine proclaimed that revolutionary conditions developed over time, ELN fighters were confident about creating them, even if the existing situation did not favor that outcome (Gott 1970: 195; Meschkat et al 1983: 144–145; Blomström and Hettne 1988: 37). This optimism was based on the thinking of 'Che' Guevara, who, inspired by Mao Zedong's works on revolutionary warfare, believed that it was not required to wait until all conditions for revolution had developed because guerrilla warfare would induce them. While this approach may have worked in Cuba, 'Che's' revolutionary strategy did not succeed in Bolivia, where the famed guerrilla leader was captured and executed in 1967. The ELN leaders initially attempted to cooperate with the FARC; however, a working relationship was not established because of the former's unwillingness to submit to PCC control. Unlike the FARC, the ELN considered revolutionary warfare the only important form of struggle, and as a result, the movement did also not participate in the previously mentioned peace process initiated by President Betancur. Presently, the ELN has an estimated three to five thousand fighters operating mostly in northern Colombia (Debray 1967; Sully 1968: 80–81, 205–206; Gott 1970: 195–227; Richani 1997: 42; BBC Jan. 4, 2002).

The Maoist EPL stemmed from the 1963 Sino-Soviet split. In 1965, after the PCC adopted positions opposed to the Chinese Communist Party, a faction of pro-Chinese members broke away and established the *Partido Comunista Marxista-Leninista* (PCML), with a program influenced by Maoist teachings. Accordingly, the struggle for liberation was seen as inevitable and necessary, and revolutionary violence was viewed as the 'midwife of history.' In 1968, the party launched its own rebel movement, the EPL. Some of Marulanda's FARC fighters switched over to help the new group organize. The EPL aimed to emulate the Maoist strategy of popular war and had some initial successes in the 1960s. However, due to military defeats and internal divisions, the EPL never gained the significance of either FARC or ELN (Gott 1970: 225–226; Meschkat et al 1983: 145; Pizarro 1992: 179).

The EPL signed a peace accord with the government in the spring of 1991, and most of its two thousand combatants surrendered. The EPL transformed into a political party called *Esperanza, Paz y Libertad* [Hope, Peace and Liberty] and continued to use the acronym EPL. The military force of the EPL, however, was integrated into Colombia's rural police force, the CONVIVIR, and the AUC. The former Maoist rebels turned right-wing paramilitaries who were accused of massive human rights abuses among the banana workers in the Urabá region. However, one dissident group of the EPL did not submit and came to form one of the smallest of the rebel organizations presently active in Colombia. It was estimated to have seven hundred combatants in 1996 (*LAWR*. Feb. 21, 1991: 3; *LAWR*. March 7, 1991: 2; *LAWR*. April 1, 1993: 146; *LAWR*. Feb. 3, 1994: 38; Richani 1997: 42; Zelik and Azzellini 2000: 15–23, 216–221).

One last guerrilla movement of import, although now largely defunct, was M-19, an offspring of the previously mentioned populist ANAPO founded by former Colombian President Rojas Pinilla after returning from exile. The movement's name derived from the presidential elections of April 19, 1970, when Rojas Pinilla had been narrowly defeated in a vote many Colombians believed to have been fixed (Meschkat et al. 1983: 135; Sukup 1988: 80). In turn, the most radical supporters of Rojas Pinilla, who were joined by dissatisfied FARC rebels formed M-19, which called itself nationalist and anti-imperialist. From the outset, M-19 acquired a reputation for actions which looked more like publicity stunts than revolutionary warfare. Pizarro (1992) refers to "the group's tendency to substitute audacious political-military feats for the patient building of a political movement" (1992: 183). In 1974, M-19 stole the sword of *Libertador* Simón Bolivar from a Bogotá museum. In January 1979, M-19 combatants took over Bogotá's military arsenal, making off with thousands of firearms, most of which were later recovered. On February 27, 1980, M-19 raided the embassy of the Dominican Republic, taking dozens of diplomats hostage, including US Ambassador Diego Ascencio. The rebels involved escaped to Cuba with over US$2 million, after the government had freed more than three hundred political prisoners. M-19 also became known because of its Robin-Hood like activities, such as distributing stolen food to the inhabitants of slums (Sukup 1988: 81).

M-19 declined after its ill-fated attack on the Palace of Justice in Bogotá, in November 1985. The rebels occupied the building, taking twenty-three Supreme Court judges and hundreds of clerical workers and clients hostage. However, instead of negotiating, the army staged a bloody counterattack in which more than ninety people perished, including eleven judges and most, if not all, the guerrillas involved (Shannon 1989: 195; also see Pearce 1990: 181). The group was seriously weakened after the assault. This may have been one of the reasons M-19 returned to the negotiating table in 1989, and signed a peace agreement with the Barco government turning itself into a political party. As *Alianza Democrática M-19* (ADM-19), it made significant gains in the December 1990 elections. Nonetheless, while ADM-19's candidate Antonio Navarro Wolff, a former guerrilla leader, received 27 percent of the vote in 1990, the party's poor showing in 1994 again demonstrated the difficulty of ending oligarchic politics in Colombia. A dissident group split from M-19 and did not surrender but continued the armed struggle as *Movimiento Jaime Bateman Cayón* (MJBC) (*LAWR*. Aug. 3, 1989: 4; *LAWR*. Dec. 20, 1990: 1; Pizarro 1992: 184–185; *LAWR*. March 24, 1994: 13; Zelik and Azzellini 2000: 207; Tanaka 2002: 75).

The strength of Colombia's guerrilla forces, especially the FARC, has been growing considerably since the failure of the Betancur peace negotiations described earlier. As one observer noted in the early 1990s, before the 1984 peace talks "the frequency of guerrilla attacks . . . . was, on average, two a month . . . . Today it is daily" (Apuleyo Mendoza 1992: 8). Alfredo Rangel Suárez (1996), security advisor to former Colombian President Ernesto Samper, warned that the combined Colombian rebel movements could field a force of "some thirty thousand combatants" in the new millennium, carrying out military operations from "300 fronts" (1996: 74).[15]

The present situation in Colombia may for the moment be characterized as a protracted stalemate between military and guerrilla, in which neither side can destroy the other. This situation is partly explained by the inability of the rebel movements to form a united front. While the various rebel groups did set up the *Coordinadora Guerrillera Simon Bolivar* (CGSB) in the 1980s to harmonize their activities, collaboration amounted to little. The CGSB was initially compared to El Salvador's *Frente Farabundo Martí para la Liberación Nacional* (FMLN), an umbrella organization created by that country's five rebel groups in 1986. However, the *Coordinadora* never achieved the FMLN's cohesion and at best provided a united forum in negotiations with the government (Bejarano 1993: 7).[16]

Colombia suffered staggering losses as a result of the civil war. According to a government report, between 1990 and 1994 alone, the conflict cost the country US$13.5 billion. This amount was based on military spending, kidnapping and extortion by the guerrillas, attacks on oil pipelines, and the human costs of the conflict (*El Tiempo*. Oct. 24, 1992: 10A; *The Economist*. Jan. 13, 1996: 40). Strong (1996) provided a portrait of a society in the grip of continuous violence. He traced the country's ills back to the *violencia* period, the last civil war between Liberals and Conservatives between 1948 and 1957, when tens, if not hundreds of thousands, of Colombians lost their lives. This conflict, he claimed, spawned a "culture of violence" that thrives to this day (1996: 9).[17]

The Colombian case also illustrates the validity of US sociologist Robert K. Merton's (1970) observation that both crime and rebellion are two of several possible reactions to exclusion from the riches of society (1970: 238–246). While criminal activity becomes a vehicle for social mobility and integration into elite structures, rebellion aims to destroy and replace such structures. Moreover, political science scholars have argued that frustrated expectations in a given populace could result in political violence and rebellion (See, for example, Davies 1962). The Colombian political establishment has made it impossible for opposition groups to assert themselves without the use of violence. As described by one observer, "it seems that . . . . in Colombia real opposition is only possible as subversion" (Schultze-Kraft 1982: 16; also see Tanaka 2002: 29).

The Military, Elites, and Political Power in Peru

While Colombia's traditional elites, and the party institutions through which they rule, have managed to maintain their dominance, albeit by sharing power with the military and by integrating criminal elites, the same cannot be maintained for their Peruvian counterparts. Peru's traditional oligarchy included bankers, large coastal-plantation owners, and the landholders of the middle and high Sierra in the Andes. Traditional Colombian elites have gathered in two political parties, however, their Peruvian counterparts have not represented their interests on a party platform since the demise of the *Civilista* party in the early twentieth century. The country's political parties have not been strong, self-perpetuating institutions, except for the center-left *Alianza Popular Revolucionaria Americana* (APRA), which was founded in 1924. In contrast to Colombia, where the military slowly gained ground and acquired its prominence only since the *violencia* period, Peru's armed forces historically have been involved in their country's politics. In fact, of the seventy-six presidents who governed Peru between independence in 1821 and the 1968 revolution, fifty came from the military. Peru's oligarchy traditionally maintained good relations with the military (Philip 1978: 15−16; Cleaves and Pease García 1983: 214; Skidmore and Smith 1984: 206; Durand 1997: 173). Thus, the coziness between the Fujimori government and the dominant clique within the armed forces during the 1990s was not a novel experience. Still, the military should not be perceived as a tool of the Peruvian elites, or of other social groups, but as a historically independent institution.

The era of military rule between 1968 and 1980 exemplified this autonomy. Peru's armed forces, under General Juan Velasco Alvarado, took over the government and introduced a 'revolution from above' which aimed at modernizing society and economy. The reforms were largely instituted to forestall the left-wing insurgencies which the oligarchic system was expected to produce after the shock waves which swept Latin America following the Cuban Revolution had reached Peru. Rebel groups emerged from the Rio Grande to Patagonia, including the previously mentioned ELN in Colombia. In Peru, a movement also called the ELN, as well as the *Movimiento de Izquierda Revolucionaria* (MIR) emerged during the early 1960s but were squashed by the military in 1965.[18] Both MIR and ELN never collaborated (Béjar 1970: 75−87). Although these rebellions and others were defeated, it was understood within the officers' corps that only a transformation of Peru's fossilized socioeconomic system would prevent revolution. North (1983) quoted one of the generals involved in the 1968 coup as saying that "the guerrillas . . . . rang the bell that awakened the military to the reality of the country . . . . The moment the . . . . [rebels] appeared it was the army that said that this problem was not going to be solved with bullets" (1983: 250).

The reformist military regime initiated sweeping changes which ended the power of the old oligarchy. Agrarian reforms introduced in 1969 broke up medium-sized and large estates and redistributed the land to peasant cooperatives set up by the regime. The military nationalized foreign companies, notably in the petroleum and mining sector. It also re-established diplomatic ties with Cuba, increased trade and commerce with the Soviet Bloc and Socialist Yugoslavia, and even bought weapons from the USSR and Czechoslovakia (Rangel 1982: 375–386; Fuhr and Hörmann 1992: 444–446).

While the old power structures were indeed removed, the reforms largely benefitted the peasants on the coastal lands, not the Indian communities in the Andes, which became the breeding ground of the *Sendero* rebellion. McClintock (1983) maintained that the highland communities "were the last to be affected by the agrarian reforms," which were implemented there only between 1973 and 1975, although these regions had experienced most of the peasant unrest (1983: 289). Eckstein (1983) also pointed out that the "earning power of highland Indian communities did not improve as much as that of coastal cooperatives" (1983: 373). Sukup (1988) blamed the military's reforms for causing the "social and economic disintegration" that contributed to *Sendero's* support base (1988: 114). He also noted that the Sierra departments received less than 1 percent of government spending during the period between 1968 and 1980, when the military was in power (*ibid.*).[19]

The generalization that the emergence of the guerrillas and the drug trade are linked to issues of land distribution and agricultural reform, or the lack thereof, holds true in Peru as well. The *Sendero* rebellion and drug trafficking resulted from the manner in which the peasants were organized by the military government and also from the official neglect after the implementation of these changes. Moreover, the government's failure to act in the highland departments reflected the racism of Peruvian society which treated — and still treats — the Indians, such as the Quechua, Aymara, or Amazonian tribes people, as second-class citizens (Strong 1992: 74). *Sendero Luminoso* first emerged in the departments Apurímac, Ayacucho and Huancavelica. These were among the poorest regions of the country where between 50–90 percent of the population had no running water, sanitation, or electricity. A health infrastructure did not exist, and up to 50 percent of the population were illiterate (Fuhr and Hörmann 1992: 465). The military government removed the oligarchic structures, yet failed to replace them.

The growth of the drug economy in the Huallaga Valley, which became the world's largest area of coca cultivation, was also due to government neglect. To colonize the interior during the 1950s and 1960s, successive Peruvian governments had attracted settlers to the region by promising continued development funding. However, finances ran out. The project came to a halt and finally was discontinued under the military regime in 1975. By that time, however, coca had already become the major cash crop, as peasants turned to cultivating the plant, whose byproduct was in growing demand in the United States (Rumrill 1992: 81–83). Thus, coca cultivation increased "from a few hundred hectares in 1973 to some eighteen thousand in 1978 and to over one hundred and twenty-five thousand by 1990" (Kay 1999: 101).

Finally, the emergence of *Sendero* and the drug trade cannot be separated from the misrule of political parties in power following the era of military rule. The center-right *Acción Popular* (AP) and the center-left *Alianza Popular Revolucionaria Americana* (APRA) governed Peru between 1980 and 1990, and were discredited because of their corruption, their failure to contain the *Sendero* threat, and their disastrous economic policies. Between 1980–1990, the country's debts rose from US$9.6 to 17.6 billion. The amount represented 63 percent of Peru's GDP and was five times larger than its 1990 exports. The country suffered hyperinflation, which climbed over 7,000 percent in 1990 and resulted in large income reductions. Between 1985 and 1990, the minimum monthly pay declined by almost 70 percent to the equivalent of US$36. Between 1985 and 1987, official employment increased from 34 to 60 percent, but rapidly declined to 5.3 percent (!) in 1990, the last year of the APRA government under Alan García as president. In the capital, Lima, underemployment figures rose correspondingly from 34.9 percent in 1987 to 86.4 percent in 1990. These developments greatly augmented the growth of the informal economy. Further, the country's democratic left offered little hope. The *Izquierda Unida* (IU), an alliance of six parties which had combined forces, made gains during the 1980s. Yet it split resulting in the creation of another party on the left, the *Izquierda Socialista* (IS). Indeed, support for Peru's traditional party system declined from almost 100 percent in 1980 to less than 20 percent in 1992 (*The New Internationalist.* July 1989: 24–25; Fuhr and Hörmann 1992: 444–461, 477; Tanaka 2002: 42–54).[20]

The 1990 election victory of political outsider and son of Japanese immigrants, Alberto Fujimori, and the regime established in turn, resulted from the failures of the traditional parties. Indeed, attempts to revive the old political forces failed largely because they had been discredited, and for almost a decade the increasingly dictatorial Fujimori regime, and the military clique sustaining it, remained unchallenged. A credible alternative emerged in the late 1990s, with the *Perú Posible* party led by Alejandro Toledo. However, without the unfolding political scandals and the obvious election fraud in the year 2000, Fujimori may have remained president far longer.[21]

In 1990, however, Fujimori never expected to win the presidency. Apparently, he declared himself a presidential candidate only to receive free television coverage to improve his chances for a seat in the Peruvian Congress. Hence, Fujimori had no plan for government action when elected into his country's highest office (*Oiga.* May 28, 1990: 30–34; Jochamowitz 1994; Caretas Dossier 2000: 22; Taylor 2000: 392). Meanwhile, unrest was brewing in the military because of the disastrous situation in the country. In fact, important members of the officer corps, particularly within the army, had been contemplating a military coup and the establishment of an authoritarian regime, or a so-called directed democracy (*ibid.*). The project was also known as 'Plan Verde,' the Green Plan. What transpired next was the marriage between a president without a plan and the dominant faction within the military led by General Nicolás de Bari Hermoza, brought together through the courtesy of a shady former army officer and lawyer, Vladimiro Illich Montesinos Torres. During the 1970s, he was dishonorably discharged from the Peruvian military for spying for the CIA and then, after earning a law degree while in prison, turned lawyer, gaining notoriety for defending drug traffickers (*ibid.*, 392–393; also see Rospiglioso 2000; Caretas Dossier 2000: 20–22; Picasso and Martin 2001).

Fujimori essentially adopted the 'Plan Verde,' and the military became a partner in the regime. After Peru's Congress rejected various measures aimed at increasing the military's powers to deal with the *Sendero* insurgency, Fujimori, Montesinos — who became the president's security advisor — and the military responded with a coup. The *autogolpe*, or self-coup, of April 5, 1992, dissolved the Congress and the country's constitution and allowed for the implementation of the most important components of the 'Plan Verde.' According to opinion polls, the coup had the support of over 80 percent of the population because of the chaotic economic and political situation in the country (*ibid.*; Tanaka 2002: 48).

Revolutionary Movements in Peru in the 1990s

The Peruvian rebel movements are younger than their Colombian counterparts, although both *Senderistas* and the *Emmertistas*, as members of *Sendero Luminoso* and MRTA, respectively, are referred to in Peru, can trace their roots to organizations active during the 1960s. Established in the 1970s and dubbed Peru's equivalent of Cambodia's *Khmer Rouge*, *Sendero* had grown into a serious threat to the Peruvian state and elites by the late 1980s (Palmer 1992). *Sendero Luminoso* was founded by Abimael Guzmán Reynoso, a university professor from the Andean city of Ayacucho. As with Colombia, after the Sino-Soviet split the Peruvian Communist Party separated into pro-Soviet and pro-Chinese factions. By 1970, Guzmán controlled the pro-Beijing party, or Red Flag faction, turning it into the *Partido Comunista del Perú — por el Sendero Luminoso de José Mariátegui* (PCP–SL) (Neira 1973: 457).[22]

Various observers of the Peruvian situation have described the *Sendero Luminoso* uprising as an ethnic rebellion against a racist society which treats highland Indians as second-class citizens. Strong (1992), for example, wrote:

Shining Path rebels are mainly young Quechuan-speaking Indians in a country where their language is considered a sign of inferiority. On the one hand, they are those whose communities have been little exposed to the market economy and who have never had the benefit of education. For the young, Shining Path offers an escape, a chance of change, modernity, a challenge to their own elders and a stab at ethnic revenge. But the movement also attracts those who have been able to acquire an education and have fought to learn Spanish in an attempt to escape their linguistic and economic domination (1992: 74).

Starn (1998) downplayed the notion of an ethnic peasant rebellion. He noted that this perspective disregarded that *Sendero* was founded "by privileged intellectuals in the city of Ayacucho" (1998: 229). Moreover, the rebels operated and received support in the coastal regions, where the populations largely consists of mestizos, as well as in the Sierra since 1983 (1998: 229). He observed further that "the party operated through a rigid hierarchy by race and class that replicated the social order it sought to overthrow. Dark-skinned kids born in poverty filled the bottom ranks under a leadership composed mostly of light-skinned elites" (*ibid.*).

Sendero spent the 1970s preparing its insurrection by organizing, indoctrinating, recruiting, and creating a support structure. This phase was referred to as stage one of "agitation and propaganda" (Tarazona-Sevillano 1990: 29–30). The movement entered the second phase of its struggle of "sabotage and guerrilla action" in 1980 (*ibid.*). Stage three, namely, "generalized violence and guerrilla warfare," involved the extension of the conflict to most of Peru (*ibid.*). According to *Sendero* propaganda leaflets, this phase had been realized in 1982. Moreover, the rebels claimed to be in the process of attaining the next step, "conquest and expansion of support bases," as they had set up strong networks in some parts of the country, such as the Huallaga Valley (*ibid.*). The Maoist guerrilla indeed reached the fourth stage as it had set up a strong presence "in at least fifteen of Peru's twenty-four departments" (*ibid.*). Even so, *Sendero* never achieved the last phase, "the fall of the cities and total collapse of the state" (*ibid.*; also see *Sí.* June 12, 1989: 30–34; Inca 1994).

A 1991 official Peruvian study claimed that the rebels' military forces numbered three thousand fighters with a support network of forty to sixty thousand activists (Fuhr and Hörmann 1992: 469). Fuhr and Hörmann themselves estimated the strength of the rebels to be five thousand combatants (*ibid.*; also see Tapia 1993: 158). On the face of it, *Sendero's* strategy followed the maxims of Maoist guerrilla warfare; however, its leadership ignored the most important lesson: namely, to assure itself of the loyalty of the peasantry. *Sendero's* ruthless approach toward those it claimed to fight for, combined with its policy of liquidating representatives of Marxist persuasions other than its own, greatly contributed to its decline (Degregori 1997: 182–188).

The Maoist rebels not only assassinated the leaders and activists of the democratic organizations on the left but they also fought Peru's other rebel group, the pro-Havana *Movimiento Revolucionario Tupac Amaru* or MRTA, over ideology and the proceeds of the coca economy in the Huallaga Valley (Tapia 1996; also see *Sí.* July 12, 1989: 18–21; Poole and Rénique 1992: 12, 185). *Sendero* declined after the 1992 capture of its leader Abimail Guzmán. It was reduced to a few hundred guerrillas in the country's remote jungle regions. In the summer of 1999, Peruvian security forces also captured Guzmán's successor, Oscar Ramirez, a.k.a.

Feliciano. However, the rebels have made a comeback as attacks on government troops have been increasing since 2003 (Manrique 1996: 43; *The Globe and Mail*. July 15, 1999: A11; Tanaka: 2002: 48–49; *La República*. June 25, 2004: 20; *El Comercio*. May 10, 2005: A11).

The MRTA was formed in 1984, and viewed itself as the successor to the earlier-mentioned MIR and the Peruvian ELN. Ideologically the MRTA was linked to the Cuban Revolution, 'Che' Guevara, and the Nicaraguan *Sandinistas*. Unlike the *Senderistas*, many *Emmertistas* derived from a white middle-class background. However, the movement could also rely on support from organized labor and had established networks among the peasantry. In contrast to *Sendero*, the MRTA viewed the other organizations of the left, such as labor and peasant unions, as well as political parties such as the *Izquierda Unida*, as potential allies. The MRTA began as an urban group but moved into the jungle regions of the central Huallaga Valley by the late 1980s. It was initially successful, yet did not gain the significance of its Maoist rival and was, for a time, immersed in internal squabbles. At the height of its strength in 1990–1991, the MRTA's fighting force numbered around one thousand combatants (*LAWR*. March 2, 1989: 4; *LAWR*. March 2, 1989a: 4; Poole and Rénique 1992: 182–185; Strong 1992: 216–219; Anderson 1997: 753; Manrique 1998: 211).

Like *Sendero*, the MRTA has suffered decisive defeats. After serious losses to government troops and *Sendero* rebels and the arrest of its most important leaders, MRTA activity had already been significantly reduced by 1992 (*LAWR*. June 25, 1992: 2). Following the takeover of the Japanese ambassador's residence in Lima in December 1996 and siege which lasted until April 1997, Peruvian special forces counterattacked. In the operation, which was masterminded by Montesinos, all participating MRTA rebels were killed. Since then, the Peruvian organization of the MRTA appeared destroyed and without leadership. Purportedly, Rodolfo Eduardo Klein Sañamez is the last surviving *Emmertista* leader of significance in liberty. Formerly a member of an internationalist guerrilla unit that participated in the 1979 *Sandinista* Revolution, he allegedly lives in Nicaraguan exile (Inca 1994; Gutierrez 1997: 6–7; Burt 1998: 35).

After the collapse of the Fujimori regime, interim President Valentín Paniagua established the Peruvian Truth and Reconciliation Commission, which was to investigate the human rights abuses committed by rebels and government forces during the years of civil conflict. It was revealed by the commission's final report, released in August 2003, that the number of killings, particularly by members of *Sendero Luminoso*, exceeded those of the Peruvian security forces. Peru's experience thus stands in contrast to those of other Latin American societies in civil conflict, for example, in neighboring Colombia, where the abuses and extralegal killings by the military and their paramilitary allies by far outstrip those of the rebels. Indeed, in Peru, most of the victims derived from the country's indigenous peoples (*La República*. Aug. 26, 2003: 8; Diáz. Interview. Aug. 27, 2003; *La República*. Aug. 29, 2003: 9).

The Peruvian Military, Organized Crime, and the War Against
Sendero Luminoso

The following analysis derives largely from fieldwork and research in Peru. It is based in part on a reconstruction of events which may not be accurate in every detail. After all, it is impossible to scrutinize all particulars of information under the best of circumstances, and Peruvian reality during the 1990s was certainly not the best of circumstances. The analysis is, however, in accordance with the previously noted dictum of a famous fictional detective who claimed that "once one has eliminated the impossible, then whatever remains, however improbable, must be the truth" (Doyle 1987: 185).[23]

The trafficking organizations in Bolivia, Colombia, and Peru occupied specific positions in the cocaine economy. The Bolivian groups discussed earlier were in an intermediary position. They provided the Colombian cartels with coca paste for further refinement and also with the final product, cocaine. Moreover, Bolivian trafficking groups set up their own distribution networks in the United States. Traditionally, Peruvian traffickers were suppliers for the Colombian cartels. The Peruvian drug economy emerged during the late 1960s and early 1970s in line with Colombia's. So-called Peruvian minicartels also engaged in the sale of the final product cocaine in the United States and Canada, but their involvement was rather small compared to their Bolivian and Colombian counterparts (Poole and Rénique 1992: 169–174; Morales 1996: 162). Still, at the height of the *Sendero* conflict in the early 1990s, some forty trafficking groups operated in Peru, playing a powerful role in the regions in which they were active. These gangs allegedly controlled 90 percent of the trafficking industry, supplying mostly coca paste and some Peruvian-produced cocaine to Colombian cartels (*Oiga.* May 30, 1994: 17; *Sí.* Nov. 21, 1994: 26).

During the Fujimori era, a large number of Peruvian military officials were put on trial and received stiff prison sentences for their involvement with traffickers. However, this prosecution of individual cases of corruption served only to conceal the true links that existed between Peruvian military officials and criminals. In any case, the dramatic increase in the number of military officials who were prosecuted even by the inefficient and crooked Peruvian judicial system for involvement in the drug trade attested that corruption was systemic rather than individual. Between 1980 and 1985, eight members of Peru's armed forces were put on trial because of links to the drug trade. This number grew to thirty-one for the period between 1985 and 1990, but increased tenfold between 1990 and 1996 to three hundred and nine (*Gestión.* Aug. 25, 1996: 15).

After the *autogolpe* of April 5, 1992, Peru underwent a process of *narcotization* of its security apparatus in general and of the army in particular. Although not a *narcogolpe*, or drug coup, as in Bolivia, the existing evidence suggests that the central government gave its military commanders a free hand to participate in the drug trade as part of an unofficial strategy to defeat the rebels.

Peruvian organized crime and the military collaborated to deprive *Sendero* of the very same resource: the coca grown in the Huallaga Valley, which provided income through 'revolutionary taxes' to the rebels but which the military also needed to help pay its war against *Sendero*. While some of the available evidence is circumstantial, it is certain that these activities could not have transpired without the knowledge and approval of the highest circles of the Peruvian government.

The goal of financing the conflict against *Sendero* with funds from the drug trade conflicted with the alternative-crop project that was to be implemented by the Fujimori government to wean peasants off coca cultivation. The person in charge of the project was Hernando de Soto, the neoliberal economist and author of *El otro sendero* [The Other Path], a well-known if not controversial work on Peru's informal economy. However, the regime's unofficial policy undermined the crop project, as peasants were seemingly encouraged to grow coca to earn funds for the war. At the same time, Peru, like other Andean nations, was — and still is — involved in the US Drug War. Yet, while Washington had put considerable pressure on Colombia because of government corruption, little was said about Peru, although numerous credible allegations were brought forward. Moreover, military officials who denounced these activities were demoted, intimidated, and imprisoned. Others received death threats, were beaten, kidnapped, or assassinated, unless they escaped into exile.

The origins of the organized crime–military collaboration can be traced to 1989–1990, when General Alberto Arciniega Huby was commander-in-chief in the Huallaga Valley, one of the most important theaters of conflict in the war against *Sendero Luminoso*, and at the time, the largest coca-growing area in the world. Arciniega Huby changed the approach taken by previous commanders in the Huallaga Valley. Instead of persecuting the coca peasants, or *cocaleros*, he allowed them to grow coca and relied on armed peasants to fight *Sendero*. This, however, caused an uproar in Washington, where the general was accused of protecting drug dealers. Arciniega saw the situation as follows:

> What Sendero wants is to win the support of a population who depend on monocrop coca agriculture and who are repressed [by the police] . . . . which eradicated their crops, ... because they consider coca farming to be a crime. We are talking about 80 percent of the population! What we must do, therefore, is to change this situation in order to prevent the cocalero peasant — the base on which Sendero thrives — from being harassed (as quoted in Poole and Rénique 1992: 187–189; also see *Caretas*. Oct. 29, 1990: 13; Arciniega Huby 1994).

Palmer (1996) also described organized crime–military cooperation in the war against *Sendero Luminoso* guerrillas. The Peruvian military suffered greatly due to the country's economic woes. It was ill-equipped, underpaid, and lacked basic supplies.[24] In 1989, the military budget had been slashed by more than half and "the resources to support field operations were severely curtailed. . . ." (1996: 183–184). Consequently, Arciniega relied "to a significant extent, on local resources (i.e., drug money) to finance his military operations" (*ibid.*). Although the general succeeded in pushing *Sendero* out of the Upper Huallaga Valley in 1989, he was replaced due to US pressure. The three commanders who successively took over on the Huallaga front did not follow Arciniega Huby's example. The regional military headquarters was relocated to the north, where the troops fought MRTA rebels instead. This left the antidrug police in charge of operations, a move which allowed *Sendero* to return to the region and consolidate once again (*Caretas.* Oct. 29, 1990: 13; Gonzáles 1991: 48; Arciniega Huby 1994).

Determining all of the factors that contributed to the shift in Peruvian policies is difficult. Nevertheless, one significant issue was the difference in threat assessment regarding *Sendero* and drug trade by the Fujimori regime and the administrations of US presidents George Bush senior (1988–1992) and Bill Clinton (1992–2000), respectively. The role and activities of General Arciniega illustrated the fundamental contradiction in perceptions of the conflict as it was seen from Washington and Lima. While the United States focused wholly on fighting the Drug War, Peruvians were preoccupied with winning the conflict against *Sendero*. From the Peruvian perspective, the American demand for coca eradication played directly into rebel hands. *Sendero* not only received funding through taxing the coca trade in the Upper Huallaga Valley, the eradication policies also drove peasants to support the rebels, who protected them against the police, the military, and abusive traffickers (Arciniega Huby 1994).[25]

Moreover, the lack of funding for alternative development from the United States and elsewhere, which the bankrupt Peruvian state could not provide itself, was likely an additional factor in the decision that fostered the military's alliance with drug traffickers. Economist Hernando de Soto, in charge of an extensive plan designed to bring rural development to the Huallaga Valley, had called for the investment of US$2.5 billion over a ten-year period. The project, which also emphasized environmental protection, included the creation of an infrastructure by constructing roads, hospitals, and electrical power plants. However, without funding it was doomed. The United States, for example, offered only US$95 million, of which a mere 2 percent were designated for crop substitution (*LAWR.* March 28, 1991: 4; *Oiga.* Sept. 16, 1991: 39–42).

The timing of the cooperation between military and drug traffickers is also significant. Between the Fujimori *autogolpe* in April 1992 and 1995, the US government cut military aid, which had been slashed by Congress because of Peru's sordid human rights record. The US Congress, however, released some funding for nonmilitary purposes (Roberts and Peceny 1997: 217–220; Cotler 1999: 204–205). Regardless, given the existing budgetary problems, this development likely reinforced the Fujimori government's need for funds, irrespective of the source, to acquire armaments and equipments. From a position that favored alternative crop projects, the government moved to one of collaboration with traffickers for the purpose of defeating *Sendero*, following the model set by General Arciniega. Circumstantial evidence suggests that this shift in policy came about in the period between the replacement of General Osvaldo Hanke in the summer 1991 by General Jaime Ríos Araico, as commander-in-chief in the Upper Huallaga Valley, and the *autogolpe* of April 5, 1992.

The following events were indicative of these developments:

The July 1991 assassination of peasant leader Walter Tocas López evidenced the existence of strong resistance to de Soto's alternative-crop project within the Peruvian government itself. Tocas represented some fifty thousand coca peasants in the Upper Huallaga Valley who were willing to sign a deal with the government to obtain aid for alternative development and crop-substitution programs. In fact, after receiving death threats, the peasant leader had asked General Ríos Araico for protection only days before his assassination. However, the general refused (*La República.* July 7, 1991: 3; *Caretas.* July 8, 1991: 28–29). Following the murder, the independent Peruvian researcher Roger Rumrill (1991) claimed that "many people are not in agreement with a solution of the cocalero problem. One ought to recall that similar activities take place in Colombia where the members of the forces of public order also intervene by eliminating the leaders of coca peasant unions" (1991: 16).

The alternative-crop program was finally cancelled after the departure of Hernando de Soto on January 28, 1992. In his letter of resignation, he claimed that Tocas had been killed by "the state," and that "there are places from where planes loaded with drugs leave regularly" (*La República.* Jan. 29, 1992: 8). Furthermore, de Soto asserted that people in the government were not interested in alternative-crop projects and attempted to impede them (*ibid.*).[26] He reaffirmed this point in an interview given to the Peruvian daily newspaper *La República*, in March of the same year. Accordingly, "the problem is the . . . . [chronic] corruption which affects the whole country which frustrates any progress in the strategy of crop substitution" (*La República.* March 21, 1992: 2).

The collaboration between traffickers and military continued to develop after President Fujimori's *autogolpe*. On April 10, 1992, shortly after the coup, the airports in the coca cultivation areas were declared emergency zones and placed under direct military control (*La República.* April 10, 1992: 4).[27] The relations between the military and traffickers are best illustrated by the example of one of the country's foremost drug traffickers, Demetrio Chávez Peñaherrera, a.k.a. *Vaticano,* a major supplier for the *Cali Cartel*. In 1991, *Vaticano* had been arrested by agents of the US Drug Enforcement Authority (DEA) operating in Peru. However, he was claimed by and handed over to the Peruvian military, who let him go although the drug trafficker had various outstanding arrest warrants dating back to 1979 (OGD 1993: 224–225). In fact, *Vaticano* received a certificate of good conduct from the police (*Gestión.* Aug. 25, 1996: 17). He was finally caught in Cali, Colombia, and extradited to Peru in 1994, where he was sentenced to a thirty-year prison term (*El Tiempo.* Jan. 14, 1994: 3A; *La República.* Aug. 6, 1996: 10).[28]

Vaticano described his relationship with the military in his official court testimony as follows:

> The military did not interrupt our . . . . [operations], [but] . . . . protected us well
> because we paid them US$5,000 for every airplane of drugs . . . . It was known
> that what took place was drug trafficking . . . . no trafficker could act unless he
> was on good terms with the army. . . . I was on good terms with the army (*La
> República.* Aug. 31, 1996: 16–17).

Similarly, the Colombian trafficker Waldo Simeón Vargas, a.k.a. *El Ministro,* like
Vaticano, a supplier of the *Cali Cartel* operating in Peru, acknowledged that he
experienced no difficulties because he "knew how to manage the Peruvian police
and military" (*La República.* Aug. 12, 1997: 8; also see Picasso and Martin 2001).

While the testimony of convicted drug traffickers may not be convincing, other
sources have confirmed these claims. The respectable Paris-based Observatoire
Géopolitique des Drogues received information that several hundred kilos of coca
paste were flown daily to Colombia from the military base at Campanilla in the
Huallaga Valley from where *Vaticano* operated during the early 1990s. In October,
1992, *Vaticano* changed locations and moved north to another military post, where
his trafficking organization was again allowed to operate freely (OGD 1993: 225).

Peruvian journalist Adolfo Isuiza Urquía was the first who reported on
trafficking at the Campanilla military base, and who made *Vaticano's* name public
when he wrote several articles for the Peruvian daily *La República* between January
and March 1992. Isuiza was subsequently murdered in August of that same year (*La
República.* Jan. 27, 1992: 14–15; OGD 1993: 225; *La República.* Aug. 30, 1996:
16–17).

A multiparty commission of the Peruvian Congress investigating military
corruption confirmed that *Vaticano* operated freely with the assistance of high
officials (*La República.* Aug. 20, 1996: 6). Describing the arrangements between
the military and *Vaticano,* Peruvian Congressman Julio Castro Gómez maintained
that "the armed forces are the highest authority in the emergency zones, and the
other institutions and powers are practically subordinated under the military
command. Consequently, there is no control . . . . It is evident that D.C. Peñaherrera
operated without problems [at the] Campanilla [army base] . . . . because of
protection offered by the special military commandos of the zone" (*ibid.*).

A member of the army's intelligence service, the *Servicio de Inteligencia del
Ejército* (SIE), identified only as *Chanamé,* leaked a report to the media which
confirmed the links between traffickers and the military. The *Chanamé* document
claimed that four drug-trafficking organizations were operating in the vicinity of
Campanilla in the Upper Huallaga Valley, the most important of which was
Demetrio Chávez Peñaherrera's. The report's author asserted that the antisubversive
Battalion No. 30 (BCS-30) stationed at Campanilla, *Vaticano's* base of operations,
collaborated with the trafficker and protected his organization. *Chanamé* claimed
that the base commander received US$3,000–4,000 for every drug flight. He also
noted that the whole population of Campanilla was openly working in the drug
economy, without fear from the army. The document even referred to a clash
between the Peruvian police and the military. In this incident, the Peruvian antidrug

police ambushed a group of traffickers. These traffickers, however, traveled under the protection of soldiers in civilian clothing, several of whom died during the ensuing shootout. The event was subsequently covered up as a clash between the army and rebels (*La República*. Feb. 29, 1992: 14–15; *Oiga*. Jan. 24, 1994: 18–22).[29]

Other instances of cooperation between the military and drug traffickers include the following:

In the fall of 1991, Colonel Gustavo Ríos-Pita Yanulaque had been given command of an antidrug base in the Upper Huallaga Valley near *Vaticano's* Campanilla headquarters. Working together with DEA officials, he ordered the destruction of a secret airfield used by the drug trafficker. Ríos-Pita was replaced two days later, and his career in the army was ruined thereafter (*El Comercio*. Aug. 29, 1996: A21).

Shortly after the 1992 *autogolpe*, General Eduardo Bellido Mora replaced the previously mentioned Ríos Araico on the Upper Huallaga Valley (*La República*. June 24, 1995: 4). Allegedly, in April 1992, Bellido Mora rebuilt a clandestine airfield that had been used by *Vaticano* during the previous year and which Ríos Araico claimed to have destroyed (*El Sol*. Sept. 28, 1996: A6). However, in May 1994, Araico and eleven other officers were charged and subsequently imprisoned because of their dealings with traffickers. The general described himself as the "fall guy" who was being sacrificed to hide the complicity of other officials in the narcotics trade (*Oiga*. May 30, 1994: 14–16). Meanwhile, his successor, General Bellido Mora, who had also been linked to the drug trade, was never charged but was sent to Israel as a military attaché. Bellido Mora was being protected by then commander-in-chief of Peru's armed forces, General de Bari Hermoza, who described him as a "gentleman" (*ibid*.).[30]

In 1992, Colonel Alejandro Sime Castillo was appointed the army's official investigator to inquire into military corruption in the Upper Huallaga Valley. His report, linking Bellido Mora to traffickers, was sent to General de Bari Hermoza, without any consequences (*La República*. Aug. 23, 1996: 17).

Similarly, in October 1992, Major Evaristo Castillo Aste denounced military corruption and involvement with drug traffickers to both Bellido Mora and de Bari Hermoza. However, instead of an investigation into these allegations, his claims resulted in a visit by SIE army intelligence officers, who confiscated his documents (*La República*. June 27, 1994:17–19; *La República*. Sept. 22, 1996: 2; *La República*. Aug. 12, 1997: 8).[31] In February 1993, Castillo was kicked out of the army and fled to Spain. In an article written from exile, the Major pointed out that President Fujimori had named Bellido Mora Peruvian military attaché to Israel to remove him from the country and prevent him from being investigated (*Oiga*. Feb. 14, 1994: 35; *La República*. Sept. 22, 1996a: 20–22).

During his 1994 trial, *Vaticano* was also accused of dealing with *Sendero*, a charge which he vehemently denied. He claimed instead that he supported the Peruvian military. Allegedly, *Vaticano's* men even fought a three-day battle against

Sendero in 1991 at Campanilla using weapons they received from the army, which itself had withdrawn from the area. The trafficker's mercenary 'troops' succeeded in holding off the rebels, who took heavy losses and retreated. Afterwards, during the victory celebrations, *Vaticano* ordered the hoisting of the Peruvian flag.[32]

General Ríos Araico affirmed in his 1996 trial that *Vaticano* "virtually fed the troops stationed in his region" (*La República*. June 26, 1996: 3; *El Comercio*. Aug. 21, 1996: A14; also see *Oiga*. May 30, 1994: 14−16). The previously mentioned report by *Chanamé* also stated that the "food for troops and officers" was supplied by traffickers (*La República*. Feb. 29, 1992: 14−15). Relying on drug traffickers, such as *Vaticano*, the Peruvian military netted a considerable portion of annual drug profits. These funds were used to finance the war effort against *Sendero*. However, as a result, the military became a player in the drug trade and grew highly corrupt (OGD 1993: 219−226; Dammert Ego Aguirre 2001: 283−294; Zapata 2005: 257).[33]

The US government was certainly aware of the Peruvian military's activities. In October 1991, General Ríos Araico faced an angry US Ambassador, Anthony Quainton, as well as US Congress representatives visiting the Upper Huallaga Valley, who demanded to know: "Why does the Peruvian army fire with machine guns at DEA helicopters? Why does the army not allow that the antidrug police enter . . . . [areas] where drugs are loaded onto planes which leave for Colombia?" (*Oiga*. Jan. 24, 1994: 22; also see Cotler 1999: 172).

The allegation that drug trafficking and drug funds were part of an informal strategy adopted by the Peruvian military in its conflict with left-wing insurgents is corroborated by the fact that some of the *rondas campesinas* utilized the same approach. These were peasant militias set up independently, or with government assistance, to combat the rebels.[34] The *rondas*, initially created by the Alan García government in 1989, played an important part in the Fujimori regime's defeat of *Sendero Luminoso*. More precisely, the *ronderos* provided some two hundred thousand additional combatants to the counterinsurgency effort, whose presence freed the army for more urgent tasks (*LAWR*. March 5, 1992: 1; Bauer 1995: 28).

One of the regions where *Sendero* initially arose was in the river valleys of the Apurímac and Ene in the eastern jungle regions of the country. However, because of brutal *Sendero* policies, the movement lost its support base. Indeed, the *rondas campesinas* in the Río Apurímac and Ene region, cultivated coca, and produced coca paste, which they sold to drug traffickers. With the profits, the campesinos acquired arms to fend off attacks by *Sendero*. This approach by the *rondas* became a necessity, given the complete absence of the state in the region, and the brutal treatment by *Sendero* rebels. Del Pino (1996) observed that

> between 1985 and 1987 the indifference of the state and of the armed forces concerning the massacres of peasants at the hands of [Sendero], ... [induced the ronderos] to establish alliances with the drug trade, in return for arms and resources with which they [not only] defeated the . . . . [rebels] but also kept the zone clear of police and military. In the mid of the adversities of war and poverty

arose this dangerous alliance between ronderos, coca peasants and drug traffickers
. . . . financing the struggle against . . . . [Sendero]. [This is] a very different
scenario from the Upper Huallaga where the drug trade finances the . . . .
[insurgency]" (1996: 119).[35]

These observations mirror those of the Peruvian antidrug police. A 1993 internal
police document claimed that 90 percent of the inhabitants of the districts on the
Apurímac River engaged in various aspects of the drug economy, and that *ronderos*
"controlled and protected" the airports from where traffickers shipped drugs.[36]
Investigative journalist Francisco Mattos confirmed that the *ronderos* played a
crucial role in defeating the *Sendero Luminoso* rebels. However, he also pointed to
future troubles for the Peruvian state. In 1994–1995, after the great decline in the
price of coca leaves, the *ronderos* demanded immediate assistance programs for
alternative products from the government. In an interview, Hugo Huilca Ovalle, the
president of the Federation of Coca Growers in the valleys of the Apurímac and Ene
rivers, threatened the Peruvian state. He claimed that

> the government seems to have forgotten that we have fought the . . . . [rebels] with
> weapons we bought with the proceeds earned from cultivating coca. Now that we
> defeated the rebels, we do not want to abandon coca cultivation unless we are
> being offered a possibility of subsistence . . . . Given our resources, these weapons
> not only point at the rebels but also at another direction (*La República*. Aug. 13,
> 1995: 2).

Indeed, Peru's coca farmers have continued to protest government policies (BBC
April 22, 2003; *La República*. May 14, 2005: 8). Regardless, the *rondas*, even those
financed through their participation in the cocaine economy, differ greatly from the
Colombian paramilitaries financed by drug traffickers, although both engaged leftist
rebels. Organizations like ACDEGAM, and the AUC were set up by the agrarian
elites and traffickers to combat rebel movements generated by the struggle over land
distribution. The Peruvian *rondas* were created by, or with the help of, peasants
against an insurgency movement of which they themselves wanted no part.

Finally, Peru's return to democracy did not change the country's unstable
economic situation or its dependence on the drug trade. The country's coca
production saw a considerable reduction from some three hundred thousand tons in
the early 1990s to less than one hundred thousand tons in 1999–2000, as a result
of the combined effects of overproduction and low coca prices, as opposed to
government repression. However, as noted by Peruvian analyst Carlos Reyna
Izaguirre (2001), 'Plan Colombia,' the US operation which aimed at suppressing
coca production in neighboring Colombia, actually resulted in increased coca
farming in Peru. According to UN estimates, the coca-growing areas of Peru
increased by 6.5 percent between 2000 and 2001. The implementation of the plan
boosted the price of the leaves, which induced farmers who had abandoned the trade
largely due to the low prices to return to it. Moreover, coca cultivation has again

increased due to the drop in prices for coffee of which Peru is one of the major producers in South America (2001: 1–2; BBC Feb. 17, 2001; BBC Sept. 18, 2002; UNODCCP 2002b: 2).[37]

In the year 2004 alone, Peruvian coca cultivation increased from 30,000 to 50,000 hectares. More important, productivity levels have risen, and according to Peruvian researchers the existing coca fields produce higher yields than the 130,000 hectares which were cultivated during the early 1990s. In addition, it was estimated that the area dedicated to coca and opium poppy cultivation in Colombia, Ecuador, and Peru had grown to 250,000 hectares. Indeed, 'Plan Colombia' included the fumigation of poppy plants and increased interception in the Peruvian-Colombian border, the Putumayo. As a consequence, Colombian traffickers moved into Peru where they contributed to the emergence of a growing heroin industry. By 2004, the country's antinarcotics police intercepted four hundred and fifty kilograms of heroin compared to less than three hundred and fifty in 2003. Traffickers also diversified their transportation routes, operating through Ecuador and Brazil as well as Colombia (*La República.* May 14, 2005: 8; *La República.* May 20, 2005: 8; *La República.* May 21, 2005: 21; *La República.* May 23, 2005: 8; Toche. 2005).

In Peru, the infiltration of organized crime into the state and the economy may not have been as deep as in Colombia. Still, the impact of the cocaine economy has been considerable to this day. The corruption of the military had an infectious effect on other sectors of Peruvian society and economy during the 1990s, such as the banking and transportation industries. Economist Lamas Puccio claimed in an interview that some US$500 million were being laundered annually in Peru's banking system during the mid-1990s (*La República.* Aug. 25, 1996: 24A). Likewise, various airlines and maritime companies were involved in the transportation of drugs from the coca-growing regions to the coastal cities and for further shipping abroad (*La República.* May 14, 1997: 7A; *El Comercio.* May 18, 1997: A17; *El Sol.* Aug. 2, 1997: 8A). According to an observer from one of the country's leading dailies, *La República*, despite the celebrated successes of the Drug War, the country "is infected with drug trafficking at all levels" (Gutiérrez, Pers. Comm. Sept. 19, 2002; also see Ugarteche 2005).

Observations on *Narcoguerrilla, Narcoterrorism, Narcofascism,* and *Narcobourgeoisie*

The terms *narcoguerrilla* and *narcoterrorism* were coined by the US State Department and the Pentagon during the Cold War in the 1980s. They referred to an alleged alliance between drug traffickers, arms dealers, terrorists, guerrillas, and the Marxist governments in Cuba and Nicaragua, which reflected the growing Soviet influence in Latin America (Collett 1989: 125–126). However, the term *narcoterrorism* is a misnomer and may more appropriately be ascribed to the terrorist practices of traffickers, for example, during the *Medellín Cartel's* war against the Colombian government and public in the early 1990s. *Narcofascism* describes the activities of the paramilitary units set up and, to a large extent, financed by drug traffickers in Colombia and Bolivia. These groups are often used to eliminate the political opposition, mostly organizations of the democratic and revolutionary left (Medina Gallego 1990: 331). Finally, *narcobourgeoisie* describes the traffickers as a newly emergent social group who challenge the traditional elites for 'a place in the sun' (Meschkat et al 1983: 166; Zelik and Azzellini 2000: 111–132).

The term *narcoguerrilla* has its origin in the Colombian police's 1984 discovery of *Tranquilandia*, a giant jungle cocaine laboratory run by the *Medellín Cartel*. There is considerable disagreement on the subjects of the *Tranquilandia* raid and the *narcoguerrilla* conjecture. Several days after the raid, the US ambassador to Colombia Lewis Tambs announced that *Tranquilandia* had been under military protection of the FARC, which allegedly earned some US$3 million weekly from cocaine trafficking. General Miguel Antonio Gómez Padilla, the commander in charge of the Colombian police unit responsible for the raid, denied that any trace of rebels had been detected at the site. Nevertheless, the *narcoguerrilla* became part of the reality of the Reagan Administration (1980–1988) as far as Latin America and the Caribbean were concerned (Collett 1989: 125–126; Zelik and Azzellini 2000: 135).[38]

It was likewise embraced by the Colombian military. A former Colombian Minister of Defense, General Manuel Jaime Guerrero Paz, described the guerrillas as a threat equal to, if not greater than, the cocaine cartels, already during the late 1980s:

> [F]or some years a third cartel has been in existence which economically is as strong, if not stronger than the cartels of Medellín and Cali, and which politically is more vicious, damaging and dangerous for our internal stability: This is the cartel of La Uribe through which the FARC finances itself. Most of the coca which is grown in Colombia derives from there. Meanwhile [the FARC] controls cocaine production in other parts of the country through a 'medical tax,' or by providing transportation and the technologies necessary for production and commercialization (Guerrero Paz 1989: XV; as quoted in Duque Gómez 1991: 212).

According to Castillo (1987; 1991), some links existed between the FARC and Medellín drug trafficker Rodríguez Gacha. He also believed that the guerrillas were present at *Tranquilandia,* providing security in the coca cultivation areas in return for 'taxes' (1987: 235; 1991: 68). Notwithstanding these claims, Peruvian author Manuel Taxa Cuadros (1987) discussed the raid without mention of the FARC or the allegations that rebels were present at the site (1987: 35–36).[39] The generally reliable *Latin America Weekly Report* also did not report any FARC presence (*LAWR.* April 6, 1984: 4–5). Other sources even indicated that the FARC was in conflict with the paramilitary MAS, set up by drug traffickers from Medellín, when the guerrillas were allegedly guarding the *Tranquilandia* complex (Medina Gallego 1990: 186–195; Mayer 1990: 71–73).

Shannon (1989) claimed that a FARC deserter had informed the US Embassy in Bogotá about the guerrillas' presence, while the DEA declared that the intelligence had been provided by a pilot who was captured by FARC but managed to escape. The DEA, however, rejected allegations that the guerrillas obtained US$3 million monthly from their involvement. Furthermore, DEA analysts "were not convinced that the guerrillas were engaging in cocaine refining on a significant scale or that they were using trafficking as their primary source of money for weapons . . . . " (as quoted in Shannon 1989: 161–166). Shannon also dismissed the Cuban and *Sandinista* connections due to the lack of evidence (*ibid.*). Conversely, Krauthausen (1997) believed that the Cubans and the *Sandinistas* in Nicaragua were involved "at least temporarily" in providing safe routes to traffickers (1997: 215; also see *Case 1/1989*). However, even if these allegations were true, the participation of the governments of Cuba and Nicaragua paled in comparison to the activities of the US agencies in Central America during the *Contra* War in the 1980s (US Senate Committee 1989; Scott 1991).

The existence of an alliance between drug traffickers and rebels was also alleged in the attack on the Palace of Justice in Bogotá, Colombia, in November 1985, by M-19 rebels (Shannon 1989: 195). According to Strong (1996), the rebels had taken over the Palace of Justice on behalf of the *Medellín Cartel* to destroy the files on cocaine traffickers to be extradited to the United States. Burning the archives destroyed the proof against the traffickers (1996: 9). Tarazona-Sevillano (1990) also claimed that the Medellín traffickers were in league with M-19 rebels (1990: 99).

Mayer (1990), though, did not mention any involvement of criminals. Rather, he pointed out that the events surrounding the Palace of Justice effectively amounted to a military takeover. As noted, the military was strongly opposed to the peace negotiations initiated by the Betancur government in 1982–1983, and attempted to derail the process. After a bomb attack against the M-19 leadership, the rebels returned to war, and the attack on the Palace of Justice was the outcome (Mayer 1990: 45; also see *LAWR*. July 19, 1985: 4). Zelik and Azzellini (2000) likewise noted that M-19 was responding to the cease-fire violations by the military. In addition, the devastation of the archives profited not only the drug traffickers but also the Betancur government and the military because it eliminated the evidence of their involvement in corruption and human rights violations (2000: 68).

Furthermore, a special commission headed by two justices inquiring into the affair failed to find any proof of drug traffickers' involvement in the attack on the Palace of Justice, contradicting earlier claims by the government. While the report absolved the president, it pointed to some irregularities. For example, it was baffling to the authors why the customarily heavy security at the Palace of Justice had been withdrawn and replaced by lightly armed private security guards on the very day the assault took place. Colombia's Attorney-General, Carlos Jiménez-

Gómez, also released a very critical report which pointed to more inconsistencies, including the unexplained disappearance of two M-19 rebels and eleven Palace of Justice employees who had survived the army's assault (*LAWR*. July 3, 1986: 3).

According to Thoumi (1995), the alleged alliance between M-19 rebels and drug traffickers was a Cold War myth created by the Reagan Administration in its attempt to link the War against Communism in Latin America with the Drug War. Accordingly, "exhaustive journalistic and judicial enquiries have shown that the mindless repetition by US officials that the takeover was financed and engineered by the drug traffickers has no basis in fact" (1995: 159–160; also see Chernick 1990: 31).[40]

Colombian author Gómez Ordoñez (1991), another advocate of the *narcoguerrilla* hypothesis, even alleged that the Colombian FARC and the Peruvian *Sendero Luminoso* maintained an alliance. While the Colombian guerrillas owned the production techniques as well as the net of distribution in Europe and the United States, the *Senderistas* controlled the Upper Huallaga Valley in Peru, then the world's largest coca cultivation region (1991: 315). However, in interviews with several Peruvian experts, any link between FARC and *Sendero* was strongly denied. The two groups were separated by geography as well as ideology. Moreover, as indicated, *Sendero* did not cooperate with the MRTA, Peru's other rebel group of significance, but fought it instead (Robles 1996; Tapia 1996; also see *La República*. Jan. 31, 1992: 13–14; OGD 1993: 222–223).

Colombian author Diana Duque Gómez (1991) provided an insightful perspective. This strongly anti-Communist author not only defended the drug traffickers as good 'cocaine capitalists' who stayed on guard against Marxist rebels, she also applauded the efforts by the cartel-financed paramilitaries to eliminate the guerrillas. She did not mention, however, that these organizations committed severe human rights abuses. Duque Gómez was highly critical of Colombian government attempts to rein in the paramilitaries financed by drug lords, claiming that these groups had eradicated the guerrilla in the country's coca-growing regions. However, once the *Medellín Cartel* was fighting a war against the government as well, its military capacities were directed elsewhere and the rebels could return to these areas. Duque Gómez quoted directly from the book *Un narco se confiesa y acusa*, allegedly written by a Colombian narcotics dealer, when she claimed that "the majority of drug traffickers in the mentioned regions are . . . . good . . . . people, simple business men . . . . [but] when the government [initiated] its extraordinary measures [against the cartel], the [drug] business was restored to the FARC and other subversive groups" (1991: 211; also see Anónimo 1990: 69; Carrigan 1995: 6–10; *Colombia Alert*. 1997: 1–6; Vargas Meza 1998a: 25–30).

The information provided in *Un narco se confiesa y acusa* should be treated with scepticism, yet the book has value because of the author's view of himself and of his associates. Drug dealers are not criminals but Colombian patriots, who invest capital and create jobs. In other words, what is good for the cartels is good for Colombia. As well, the author viewed the government's war against the *Medellín*

Cartel as an intra-class war of the oligarchy against fellow capitalists (Anónimo 1990: 43−44).

Other authors refer to the drug traffickers as the *narcoburguesía*, the drug bourgeoisie, or the *clase emergente*, the emerging class (Meschkat et al 1983: 166; Zelik and Azzellini 2000: 111−132). Amboss (1996) observed that the cartels used different methods of integrating into Colombian elite structures. While the Rodríguez Orejuela brothers, who led the *Cali Cartel*, aimed "to integrate into the largely urban traditional bourgeoisie, their counterparts in Medellín attempted a territorial integration through acquisition of land" (1996: 30). Moreover, Medellín drug traffickers, such as the late Pablo Escobar Gaviria, attempted to use violence to force their way into the upper ranks of Colombian society. Meanwhile, the Rodríguez Orejuela brothers from Cali, acquired a bank, became the owners of Colombia's biggest drugstore chain *La Rebaja*, and relied on their links to important political personalities in both the Liberal and Conservative parties (Castillo 1991: 59; Strong 1996: 169).

In fact, the Cali bosses cooperated with the Colombian authorities in the war against the trafficking groups in Medellín. The 1989 assassination of the Liberal Party's presidential candidate, Luis Carlos Galán, an outspoken critic of the drug trade, had brought about a complete reversal of government policies vis-à-vis the *Medellín Cartel*. While the regime had tolerated, if not encouraged, the activities of right-wing paramilitaries financed by drug traffickers until then, the traditional elites viewed Galán's murder as an attack on themselves, and the government went on the offensive (*ibid.*, 251−252). Andreas (1993) wrote: "Colombia . . . . did not carry out a full-scale attack on the Medellín trafficking cartel until the organization's terror tactics had become a direct threat to credibility and political authority of the state. Meanwhile, the Cali Cartel remained unharmed" (1993: 23).[41] One observer commented in the prominent Colombian weekly *Semana*: "It is an undeniable fact that the government moves constantly against everything that smells of the Medellín Cartel, while it seems less preoccupied with the [one] in Cali" (*Semana.* No. 404. Jan. 30−Feb. 6, 1990: 30; as quoted in Duque Gómez 1991: 214). This preoccupation, though, seemed justified considering that assassins from the *Medellín Cartel* exploded some two hundred bombs between August and December 1989 alone, killing and injuring hundreds of police, military, and innocent bystanders (*La República.* Dec. 11, 1989: 21).

While the links between government agents and the cartels have been readily apparent, the rebels, most importantly the FARC, have denied any involvement in the cocaine economy (*Resistencia.* 1998). However, existing evidence indicates otherwise. Nonetheless, the majority of researchers who analyzed the links between rebels and drug traffickers believed that the rebels' involvement was small and paled in comparison to that of the traditional elites. Thoumi (1995), for example, does not repudiate "that there have been connections" between rebels and drug traffickers, yet he finds that "these relationships have been fundamentally unstable because the long-term goals of the two groups are diametrically opposed" (1995:

160). Morales (1990) maintains in the case of Peruvian rebel groups that it is "a myth that revolutionary guerrilla movements are financed by drug traffickers" (1990: 107–108). While guerrillas are present in the coca-producing regions, they "are not operating in the same league with international drug traffickers" (*ibid.*).

Determining the precise figures for Colombian guerrilla economics is difficult; however, it is certain that the revolutionary left of the country obtains a considerable portion but not necessarily most of its overall income from participating in the drug economy. According to Alfredo Rangel Suárez, a Colombian military analyst, profits from the drug trade amounted to 48 percent of the rebels' income, or close to US$180 million annually (*Houston Chronicle*. Aug. 3, 2001). Other figures run far higher. Alfonso Lopez Caballero, a former Colombian Ambassador to Canada and Minister of the Interior during the administration of Ernesto Samper (1994–1998), estimated that the FARC made between US$600–800 million annually in revenues from the drug trade and kidnapping ransoms. The BBC's Colombia correspondent Jeremy McDermott provided estimates between US$300–600 million (*The Globe and Mail*. May 30, 1998: A12; BBC May 28, 2001).

It is rarely discussed, however, that particularly the ELN and FARC guerrillas of Colombia receive considerable income from noncriminal sources as well. The guerrillas enjoy annual returns from investments made in the Colombian economy, especially in the transportation, banking, and agriculture sectors. According to Colombian sources, in the early 1990s, the rebels had over US$500 million at their disposal and maintained an additional annual income of over US$200 million through criminal activities, such as kidnapping and extortion (*El Tiempo*. Nov. 15, 1992: 3A; *El Espectador*. Dec. 13, 1992: 6A; also see Richani 1997: 45–46). In addition, both FARC and ELN receive funds through international donations, although the precise amounts are difficult to determine.

While the FARC does take in considerable income from taxing the drug trade, the same cannot necessarily be maintained for the ELN. Since 1989, directives from the ELN leadership to all units under its command made it illegal to participate in any aspect of the cocaine economy, and the rebels reduced the coca plantations in the areas under their control. Indeed, the rebels' successes prompted the director of Colombia's official state agency in charge of coca eradication to suggest in 1998 that the ELN be included in government programs. The FARC relies on income from the drug economy and protects the coca farmers against abuses from government security forces and traffickers. However, the FARC also compels farmers to grow foodstuffs in addition to coca. Moreover, even scholars critical of the rebels admit that the FARC is not involved in the actual production of cocaine, while it successfully managed to escape the adverse effects of drug use among its members. In fact, the consumption of drugs is illegal in the areas controlled by FARC (Zelik and Azzellini 2000: 195–197; Antezana 2005). Amboss (1996), referring to a confidential UN report, claimed that the FARC even implemented the Colombian government's policy of coca substitution. Hence, the rebels moved against drug consumption in the regions under their control while they encouraged, or possibly forced, peasants to reduce coca cultivation and grow foodstuffs instead (1996: 29–30).

Sendero's income during the height of the conflict in the late 1980s and early 1990s was far lower than the FARC's. According to a 1990 report by Peru's antiterrorist police, *Sendero* was not involved in drug trafficking. However, the movement did exact taxes from the drug traffickers, "charging for permission to pass through certain key zones and for providing security" (Manrique 1991: 29). Gonzáles (1987) estimated that *Sendero's* annual income from taxing the coca trade amounted to US$30 million in 1987 (1987: 72; also see Rospiglioso 1993: 164). Tarazona-Sevillano (1990) merely referred to "tens of millions of dollars" (1990: 121). Naylor (1993) wrote "if Sendero Luminoso is really earning that much money from the cocaine trade, it has produced neither any significant symptom of corruption nor any sign of modern, heavy weapons from the international black market" (1993: 37–38).

It is possible to reconcile the two sides of the *narcoguerrilla* debate. Naylor points out that rebel groups' "most important sources of income will be from taxation of commerce and/or from the exploitation of the natural resources of the area . . . . under control" (*ibid.*, 21–22). He argues that "the objective of the guerrillas is to build a parallel economic system to support their assault on the status quo, though . . . . they may have no moral or ideological objection to financing those activities by taxing the drug trade" (*ibid.*). Thus, the rebels impose a levy on *any* economic activity in their area of control. The FARC also "taxes" the illicit gold smuggling between Colombia and Brazil, while the smaller ELN extracts 'revolutionary taxes' from the multinational oil companies operating on its 'territory' (*ibid.*, 30–31; also see *El Espectador.* Nov. 10, 1992: 11A).

Naylor, therefore, believes that the "notion . . . . [of] a strategic alliance" between Marxist rebels and drug cartels goes against "logic and evidence" (*ibid.*, 37). He affirms that drug lords "are insurgent capitalists, seeking to beat or buy their way into participation into a hitherto largely closed social system, while the guerrillas are insurgent Communists, seeking to . . . . overthrow that system" (*ibid.*).[42] Although Naylor occupies a position on the opposite side of the political spectrum, his analysis of drug traffickers and rebels differs little from that of Duque Gómez, who distinguishes between 'good capitalist' and 'bad Communist' drug dealers.

As noted in a previous chapter, only an estimated 8–10 percent of cocaine profits actually remained in or returned to the producer countries, while a mere 0.4 percent went to the coca-growing peasants during the mid-1980s (Cabieses 1994: 51; also see Cabieses 1996: 2). Likewise, De Rementería (1995a) estimated that in 1990, the coca-growing peasants in Colombia, Peru, and Bolivia together earned 0.41 percent or US$305 million (1995a: 95). In Colombia and Peru, the guerrilla gain 'taxes' from the coca peasants and the traffickers, namely the lowest levels of the cocaine economy. These levies can be collected only in the regions under control. At this point, it would appear that the allegations of left-wing rebels' involvement in the drug trade are greatly exaggerated, certainly when compared to the participation of Colombia's or Peru's elites and militaries. FARC's income is higher than *Sendero Luminoso's* because the Colombian rebels tax not only the peasants who cultivate coca leaves and produce coca paste but also the traffickers who refine and export the final product. However, no Latin American rebel group is directly involved in the sale of narcotics in the developed countries.[43]

The FARC rebels have gained support among coca-growing peasants by protecting them against the military, the paramilitaries, the drug police, and the drug traffickers. Moreover, the guerrillas provide a number of services as they take over some of the functions of the state they replace such as policing, as the FARC imposes its own brand of law and order in areas often reigned by lawlessness and violence (Pearce 1990: 173; Zelik and Azzellini 2000: 195–196; *The Globe and Mail.* July 19, 1999: A11; Tanaka: 2002: 30). The Colombian rebel groups supply services, such as giving peasants cheap credits, providing health and education, issuing land registrations, and dispensing justice. Allegedly, the rebels are even involved in protecting local culture and the rain forest's ecosystem (Richani 1997: 43).

Morales (1996) made an interesting comparison when he wrote:

> In the event there exists an alliance between the radical political movements and narco-traffickers, the cocaine underground economy's support for the armed insurgents would not be that much different from the Reagan Administration's secret arms deals with Iran to support the anti-Sandinistas in Nicaragua. In principle, they both support anti-government forces to fight ideological adversaries (1996: 168).

The emptiness of the *narcoguerrilla* conjecture is very well demonstrated by the previously mentioned collaboration between the US Central Intelligence Agency (CIA), the Nicaraguan right-wing rebels known as *Contras*, and Colombian drug traffickers whose activities were exposed during the Kerry Committee hearings and subsequently confirmed by several Costa Rican enquiries (Avirgan and Honey 1989; Scott 1991; Lee and Solomon 1992: 290; Weir 1996: 455–465).

As far as present-day Colombia is concerned, allegations of FARC involvement with drug trafficking also clash with DEA reports, which maintain that most of the cocaine that leaves Colombia does so through the seaports in the Urabá region in the northern part of the country, which are controlled by paramilitary and army units (DEA 1998; 2001; also see Zelik and Azzellini 2000: 219). Colombian paramilitary leader Carlos Castaño admitted publically that drug trafficking and drug traffickers likely funded 70 percent of AUC operations (CNN Sept. 6, 2000). Moreover, Stokes (2001) noted that coca cultivation in the areas controlled by FARC largely involved peasant producers working on small plots. Conversely, in northern Colombia, powerful landowners and paramilitary groups grew coca on large plantations—without interference from the authorities (2001: 65–67).

Indeed, it should be noted that despite previous claims made by US officials that the FARC was a *narcoguerilla*, the DEA did not accuse the rebels of strong involvement in the drug economy until after the September 11, 2001, terror attacks against the United States, which evidently resulted in fundamental policy shifts in Washington. Already in the late 1980s the DEA had denied accounts that FARC rebels were deeply involved in the production of cocaine. In early 1998, the DEA still reported to the US Congress that there was little proof that the "insurgent groups . . . . [were] trafficking in cocaine themselves, either by producing cocaine . . . . and selling it to Mexican syndicates, or by establishing their own distribution networks in the United States" (Shannon 1989: 161–166; DEA 1998). In its report to Congress in February 2001, the DEA again noted that "no reliable information existed which demonstrated that the FARC . . . . was involved directly in the shipment of drugs from Colombia to international markets" (DEA 2001).

Also, a study authorized by Myles Frechette, the US Ambassador in Bogotá during the Clinton Administration, concluded that the guerrillas' involvement was largely confined to protecting coca crops and cocaine laboratories. In the meantime, the right-wing paramilitaries linked to the military guarded many more such laboratories and trafficking routes. Indeed, a Colombian law enforcement source referred to in the Frechette report claimed that drug trafficking was the paramilitaries' main source of funding (Smyth 1997), a fact corroborated by the CNN interview with AUC leader Carlos Castaño. A 1999 report produced by the Council on Hemispheric Affairs (COHA) found no evidence of the FARC's export of drugs to the United States but did point to the extensive drug smuggling to the US mainland by "right-wing paramilitary groups in collaboration with wealthy drug barons, the armed forces, key financial figures and senior government bureaucrats" (COHA 1999).

Regardless, in April 2002, some six months after the attacks of September 11, the DEA had determined that Colombian rebels were involved in various aspects of drug-trafficking activities including the "purchasing, transporting, and reselling [of] cocaine within Colombia; and the distribution of cocaine to international drug trafficking organizations" (DEA 2002). In the same year, the DEA accused the FARC of involvement in international drugs-for-arms deals, although the information on which the charge was based remained "uncorroborated" by the organization's own admission (DEA 2002a).[44]

In other words, 'Plan Colombia' was implemented officially in August 2000 with aid from Washington but had effectively begun a year earlier with the arrival of elite antiguerrilla forces trained in the United States. Also, the plan was largely directed against the FARC, although the US administration's own drug-fighting agency did not identify the rebels as seriously involved in international drug trafficking until after September 11, 2001. Finally, 'Plan Colombia', and the more recent 'Plan Patriota,' have targeted the Marxist rebels in the south of Colombia, even though the bulk of the cocaine available in the United States and Canada derives from the northern parts of the country, which are under direct military and paramilitary control.

Conclusion

The term *clase emergente*, the emerging class, refers to drug traffickers who integrate into the traditional elites. In Colombia, the *clase emergente* managed to do so by taking part in the war against the left waged by the military (Meschkat et al 1983: 166). In both Colombia and Peru, drug traffickers demonstrated their ideological preferences by collaborating with elites against left-wing rebels.

Gramsci's (1973) concept of *trasformismo*, namely, the understanding that elites stay in power by admitting adversarial groups into the existing structures of domination for the purpose of maintaining them, has considerable explanatory capacity in the case of Colombia (1973: 243; also see Femia 1981: 47). The country's regime qualifies as a classical protection racket run by elites in a permanent crisis of hegemony. In response to the growing guerrilla threat, Colombia's intransigent elites, like their counterparts in El Salvador during the 1980s, handed over political power to the military in order to maintain their social power. Except that the military, as the vehicle of repression relied on by elites, generated more of the very thing it was devised to subdue, namely, the guerrillas, and ultimately no longer sufficed to contain it. Consequently, OC groups were also allowed to share political power in order to preserve elites structures. In return, these groups and the paramilitaries they financed applied nonstate violence to the enemies of the regime.

Conversely, Colombia's guerrilla evidently differs considerably from the general perceptions idealistic left wingers may harbor about revolutionary movements. Most important, the Colombian guerrilla movements, particularly the FARC, while not flourishing criminal business empires as suggested by some, are nonetheless economically self-sustaining units. The availability of large financial resources has had consequences for the relationship between the rebels and those who back them. The wealth has turned the guerrilla groups into organizations less dependent on the people they once relied on for support and for whom they claim to fight. While Mao Zedong's and Fidel Castro's guerrillas relied on the ability to live like fish in the water, the Colombian rebels control and supply the water and the fish. Today, participation in the guerrilla represents an alternative to military service, their parents' subsistence agriculture, the drug economy, or the paramilitary for many young men, and women in rural Colombia (Zambrano Perez 1993: 8; Richani 1996).[45] Colombia's rebels are buying the revolution as well as fighting for it, as both the FARC and the ELN possess the financial means to obtain weapons on the international black market while they can pay the willing recruits to operate them. Even so, the demonization and labeling of the Colombian rebel movements as *narcoterrorists* obscures the fact that both rebellion and drug trafficking have grown independently as direct consequences of Colombia's social conditions. Eliminating one is unlikely to have a lasting impact on the other.

Moreover, the activities of rebel movements, terrorist groups, and criminal organizations may indeed overlap as all three participate in drug economies; however, one should not confuse them. Colombia's FARC rebels are involved in the cocaine economy as they 'tax' the coca peasants as well as the cocaine traffickers on their territory, but the guerrillas are not involved in the actual production of cocaine. And even if they were, the FARC would still differ from drug traffickers as long as they use the funds not for personal enrichment but to finance their conflict and to supply a minimum of services in the territory under their control.

Furthermore, the FARC relies on terrorist practices to achieve its goals, but its overall organization and approach to the conflict is that of a regular military force. Meanwhile, the terrorism by Colombia's paramilitary groups, although far worse than that of the rebels, is played down (CAJ 2002: 70–74). While a victory by FARC or ELN would not be the answer for Colombia, there is no solution unless it involves the rebels. Official Colombian and US sources may call the FARC a criminal organization because it occupies a strong position in the chain of the cocaine economy. Still, whether the rebel movement is indeed mutating into one can ultimately be measured only by the degree of internal corruption as a result of its participation in the drug economy, not simply because of that involvement or by the fact that it relies on terrorist practices. It is oversimplified, therefore, and in the final analysis counterproductive, if not dangerous, to view rebel movements with thousands, if not tens of thousands of combatants merely as drug-trafficking and terrorist organizations. It is worthwhile recalling that the *African National Congress* (ANC) and its leader Nelson Mandela were also once labeled terrorist and criminal by the apartheid regime in South Africa.

Nonetheless, the potential for the gradual criminalization of the FARC does exist unless peace negotiations and successful reforms lead to the guerrillas' integration into society in the foreseeable future. If not, the rebels, who have been in conflict since the 1950s, may turn from an organization with a political and social agenda to a criminal one, not unlike the previously discussed conversion from *Green Guild* to *Green Gang*. This is evidenced, for example, by the growing number of human rights abuses committed by the rebels against poor peasants (Diáz Interview. Aug. 27, 2003; also see Castro Caycedo 2001).[46]

In Peru, the infiltration of criminals into the state and the economy has not been as deep as in Colombia. As a result of the country's position in the cocaine trade, far fewer *narcodollars* have entered its financial system than that of Colombia. Peruvian traffickers are and have been, for the most part, suppliers of larger Colombian and, more recently, Mexican organizations, who make far larger profits (*El Comercio.* July 13, 1997: A1). It follows that Peruvian crime bosses have not been not able to accumulate the political muscle of their Colombian and Bolivian counterparts. Peru's main handicap has therefore not been the entrenchment of criminal elites within its power structures, as in Colombia. Rather, it is the criminalization of state agents ensuing from the collaboration with traffickers and from other activities, such as corruption, which reached new levels even for Latin American standards, or the human rights abuses during the government's dirty war against *Sendero*. Since the fall of the regime in 2000 and the subsequent inauguration of President Alejandro Toledo, Peruvian society has to deal with the crimes committed during the Fujimori era (Reyna Izaguirre 2001: 1–2; Tanaka 2002: 106–108; *The Globe and Mail*. Feb. 19, 2003: A23; Quiroz 2005).[47]

The country's return to democracy following the demise of the Fujimori regime has not changed the volatile economic situation. Peru's economy remains dependent on the production and sale of narcotics. In fact, hundreds of thousands continue to depend on the cocaine economy for their livelihood. Given the importance of coca for economic survival, a solution based on repression is unlikely to work and may create another insurgency problem for Peru (Coffin 1998: 2; *La República*. June 18, 2004: 10; *La República*. May 14, 2005: 8).

Finally, the respective collaborations between the Colombian and Peruvian militaries and criminal organizations for the purpose of defeating the Marxist rebels appear to be Latin American versions of the informal counterinsurgency model used by the French in Indochina. McCoy's (1991) reference to the "combination of crime and counterinsurgency," and the access to "large sums of ready cash" which "bought an extensive network of spies, informants and assassins" is certainly descriptive of Colombia and Peru (1991: 161).

Endnotes

1. This chapter is based largely on research done during my field work in Colombia between August 1992 and April 1993, and in Peru for the month of August 1996, between May and August 1997, August 2003, June 2004, and May–June 2005. During these stays, I acquired information from individuals who have since received threats to their lives and their families, or who may be exposed to such. While I will rely on the information provided, these individuals will not be named, even if they specifically allowed me to do so.

2. Cecilia Rodriguez, then *The Globe and Mail's* special correspondent for Latin America, gives a graphic depiction of OC penetration in the region: "Try to find a taxi driver in Rio de Janeiro, Cali, La Paz or Buenos Aires who cannot show a visitor the luxury apartment buildings, upscale shopping malls and five-star hotels erected to launder billions of dollars of dirty profits. Progress comes with *narcomoney*, as people call it; they also talk about *narcoshopping centers*, *narcomansions*, *narcoranches*, *narcoriches*, *narcojustice*, *narcocampaigns* and — the latest phenomenon in the drug-tainted era of Latin electoral freedom — *narcodemocracy*" (*The Globe and Mail*. Feb.10, 1996: D4).

3. This situation of peasants in the developing countries does not differ greatly from that of small agricultural producers in developed nations, who are equally at the mercy of global market forces. Having grown up on a farm myself, I might add the following observations: Farmers do not get paid regularly, except for those who are in the possession of a milk or egg quota, but once a year. However, expenses, such as machinery, seeding materials, fertilizers, fuel, repairs, etc., occur all year-round. In my estimate, a person who farms one thousand hectares will have fertilizer costs of tens of thousands of dollars alone. In many cases, farmers obtain credits to finance their operations during the planting season in hopes that the price of the crops they grow will be high enough at harvest time. Farmers, unlike car manufacturers, for example, cannot determine the price of what they produce. They cannot charge the costs they incur when selling their crops or other products. Farmers are at the mercy not only of market forces, but those of nature as well. Drought, rain, or frost can easily damage or destroy next year's crop. Farmers often consider themselves fortunate if they make ends meet for the year, but many survive only on the meager government compensations they receive for their losses.

4. Instead of SL, I will use *Sendero* or *Senderistas* when referring to the Maoist Peruvian rebels. Members of the MRTA are called *Emmertistas*, which I will utilize as well.

5. Other sources point to far higher numbers. According to the author of *Un narco se confiesa y acusa*, an alleged drug trafficker, over 1.7 million Colombians alone lived off the drug trade by the late 1980s, while the number of those indirectly involved, such as bankers, merchants, industrials, and professionals of any type, was far higher (Anónimo 1990: 11).

6. This affiliation between *campesino* and *haciendero* is reflective of the doctrine of *Cuis regio, eius religio* introduced by German Emperor Charles V at the 1555 Augsburg Peace treaty, that was to end the civil strife between Catholics and Protestants in the country. Accordingly, subjects were to have the same religious convictions as their feudal overlords (Tenbrock and Kluxen 1976: 322–323; Kinder and Hilgemann 1977: 235).

7. According to a Colombian acquaintance of mine, the only difference between the two today is that Conservatives go to Sunday church at 8 a.m., while Liberals attend at 10 a.m.

8. Gaitán was murdered only minutes before attending a second meeting with a young unknown Cuban radical who was in Bogotá with a student delegation: Fidel Castro (Szulc 1987: 183).

9. The counting of the vote was televised nationally showing Rojas Pinilla with a strong lead over the National Front candidate, Misael Pastrana Borrero, from the Conservative Party. Suddenly, the broadcast was cut off and on the next day, the Conservative candidate was declared the winner (Meschkat et al 1983: 135).

10. One incident which greatly contributed to the collapse of the talks was the necklace bomb affair of May 2000. Allegedly, members of FARC had put an explosive device around the neck of fifty-five year old farm woman, Elvira Pachon Cortez, to extort money from her family. The bomb exploded killing her as well as a bomb disposal expert. The FARC was immediately accused of the atrocity by the Colombian and US governments, while the rebels

denied their involvement. Further investigations which received far less media coverage revealed that it was more likely the work of paramilitaries. Also, members of the victim's own family "told reporters on condition of anonymity that they did not believe" that the attackers had been members of the FARC (*The Irish Times.* May 22, 2000). Another affair which brought bad press to the rebels was the capture of three alleged members of the Irish Republican Army (IRA) who were accused of training FARC rebels in terrorist techniques. Subsequent press reports, though, appeared to indicate that the case was not as clear-cut as initially proclaimed. For example, an Irish diplomat testified on behalf of one of the accused, Niall Connolly, that she had met him on a leave in Cuba when he was allegedly training FARC rebels in Colombia. Also, a British forensic scientist, with many years of experience, testified that there was no indisputable proof that the three handled ammunition because explosives' traces on the suspects' clothing could also have come from the military base where they were kept after their arrest. In April 2003, a video was submitted as evidence for the defense which showed another of the three accused, James Monaghan, in Belfast, northern Ireland, on February 22, 2001, when he was allegedly observed training rebels in Colombia (BBC Aug. 19, 2001; RTÉ News Feb. 17, 2003; BBC April 10, 2003; BBC April 12, 2003).

11. In December 2004, the government of Colombian president Alvaro Uribe expressed that it would accept the creation of so-called zones of trust where prisoners could be exchanged (*El Caribe.* Dec. 20, 2004: 52).

12. While is true that many developed countries have created legislation of this kind, it is rarely employed. One such occasion has been the implementation of the War Measures Act in Canada during the so-called FLQ crisis in 1970.

13. The role of the military was confirmed by Colombia's Attorney General, Carlos Jiménez Gómez, in a report to his nation's congress. He referred to "the vicious habit of the military of relying on private citizens to carry out its counterinsurgency" in order "to make up for its own limitations . . . . " (Pearce 1990a: 24).

14. Marquetalia fell after the air force dropped some twenty thousand bombs and the army attacked with sixteen thousand soldiers against the small rebel force, which allegedly numbered only forty-eight combatants, led by Marulanda (Galeano 1982: 166; FARC-EP 1999: 17, 143).

15. A member of the FARC's International Commission told me during an interview in Halifax, Canada, in the summer of 2001, that the movement's military strength amounted to some twenty-five thousand active combatants.

16. Some sources have claimed that the Colombian revolutionary movements in the *Coordinadora* are gradually inching closer to military cooperation and possibly a united military command (see for example, Pizarro 1992: 175–176). However, in discussions with the previously mentioned member of the FARC's International Commission in 2001, I was told that little cooperation transpired between the different organizations except for political contacts. The situation appears fluid as guerrillas belonging to FARC and ELN reportedly joined forces since on several occasions in operations against Colombian military and paramilitary units (BBC April 30, 2001; BBC Dec. 28, 2002).

17. Violence kills tens of thousands of Colombians annually. Between 1980 and 1990, the murder rate increased from 2 murders per 100,000 citizens to 8.5 per 100,000 (*El País*. Cali, Colombia, Nov. 22, 1992: C10). According to a Colombian police report, the annual number of killings increased by 19 percent to 31,808 from 1996 to 1997 (*The Globe and Mail*. May 5, 1998: A12). There were over thirty-two thousand murders in 2002, most of which resulted from criminal violence. Over ten thousand homicides were either politically motivated or resulted from social cleansing operations that victimize drug addicts, prostitutes, and homosexuals, or the homeless. Most of these killings have been attributed to right-wing paramilitary organizations (BBC April 24, 2003).

18. On Peruvian rebel movements during the 1960s, see Gott 1970: 231–290.

19. Little changed under the populist President Alan García, who was elected in 1985. Sukup (1988) pointed out that in 1985–1986, the Peruvian government spent more on one large irrigation project on the country's northern coast than on the whole Andean region, although the civil war against *Sendero* had been heating up for several years (1988: 121).

20. The emergence and outlook of *Sendero Luminoso* contributed to the crisis on the Peruvian left. The rebels moved against all left-wing organizations, including labor and peasant unions, and the *Izquierda Unida*, by assassinating its leadership. According to Carlos Tapia, a Peruvian expert on the subject, *Sendero* did more to destroy the left than the neoliberal policies and the repression of the Fujimori regime (Poole and Rénique 1992: 12, 185; Tapia 1996).

21. The election of April, 2000, turned out to be a fraudulent affair of massive proportions, the likes of which Peruvians had not experienced since the 1930s. Apparently, 1.4 million more votes were cast than there were eligible voters. The obvious vote rigging resulted in massive protests and, ultimately, the end of the Fujimori regime (Taylor 2000).

22. José Carlos Mariátegui (1895–1930) may be best described as one of Peru's foremost left-wing intellectual whose main contribution was the reinterpretation of Marxism to fit Peruvian realities, providing a perspective which likely differed from that of the Communist Internationale (Comintern) run from Moscow. His 1928 work *Siete ensayos de interpretaciones de la realidad Peruana* [Seven Essays of Interpretations of Peruvian Reality] is a classic of Marxist literature (Mariátegui 2002).

23. After receiving threats researching this topic in Colombia, I decided to rely largely on reviewing what had been written in the Peruvian press since 1990, while I interviewed contacts whom I met through the journalists I cooperated with. These informants specifically asked not to be identified. Moreover, in May and June 2005, I had the opportunity to review my work with a number of retired Peruvian military officers who witnessed some of these events and who completely concurred with my analysis. These former officers will remain unidentified to protect their personal security.

24. Obando (1998) referred to "the incredibly low and compressed" earnings of Peruvian military officials during the early 1990s. For example, the monthly pay of a division general amounted to about US$283 while a second lieutenant received some US$212 (Obando 1998:

397).

25. The observation that *Sendero* rebels received support in the Huallaga Valley does not contradict statements made earlier. Coca peasants in the valley preferred the presence of *Sendero* rebels over that of the antidrug police who eradicated their crops and destroyed their livelihood. Conversely, the rebels protected the peasants from the police and from the exploitation of traffickers but taxed them in return, while imposing their brand of revolutionary justice. However, given a choice, peasants, whether they grew coca or a legal crop, preferred to cooperate with the military as long as it behaved, and even organized militias against the rebels (Isbell 1992; Del Pino1996).

26. Shortly before his resignation, de Soto pointed out that there was "no political will to solve the problem" (*LAWR*. March 28, 1991: 4). He maintained further that the Peruvian air force was not shooting down the drug dealers' airplanes "because they don't want to" (*ibid.*).

27. According to one of my media contacts, Vladimiro Montesinos, who was in charge of Peru's several intelligence services including the *Servicio de Inteligencia Nacional* (SIN) or the *Servicio de Inteligencia del Ejercito* (SIE), used traffickers to fight *Sendero*. The army relied on the logistics and intelligence of traffickers and on their money to supply food and weapons to troops. To facilitate the trafficking activities at a given airport in Peru's coca-growing regions such as Upper Huallaga Valley, the military simply would shut off their radars for ten to fifteen minutes to allow drug flights to land or take off.

28. One of my sources alleged that there existed a list of drug dealers who were not touched by the police, although sometimes traffickers were sacrificed to maintain good relations with the United States. Thus, military officials connected to Vladimiro Montesinos were safe from persecution. The same informant also referred to an alleged 1994 reunion between Fujimori, Montesinos, and several generals from Peru's intelligence services in the *Pentagonito*, or 'Little Pentagon,' as Lima citizens like to call their country's headquarters of the army. At the meeting, it was decided to sacrifice *Vaticano* after his 1994 arrest in Colombia because of his notoriety and knowledge of the existing links between the military and drug traffickers.

29. The *Chanamé* report has been translated into English and reprinted in a US publication. (See Chanamé 1998). The drug trade may have created even stranger bedfellows. According to a report by the Peruvian daily *La República*, MRTA rebels maintained a temporary local alliance in the Upper Huallaga Valley with army and police units. Their collaboration served the purpose of ensuring that the proceeds from the sale of coca leaves and paste would not fall into the hands of advancing *Sendero* rebels. Allegedly, MRTA and police jointly administered secret air strips and patrolled jungle towns (*La República*. Jan. 31, 1992: 13–14).

30. According to his lawyer, General Ríos Araico became the victim of a political vendetta because he refused to sign a document which denounced another Peruvian military, General Robles, as a traitor. The latter had made public the human rights abuses by the *Grupo Colina*, a military death squad (*El Comercio*. Oct. 14, 1996: A16). Conversely, an arrest order for General Bellido Mora was only issued in January 2003 (*El Peruano*. Jan. 4, 2003).

31. Similarly, Captain Gilmar Valdivieso Rejas denounced military corruption and links to drug traffickers on the Huallaga front in November 1994. However, his witnesses all died "strange" deaths that were never investigated (*El Comercio.* Nov. 24, 1994: A16).

32. The identity of the source cannot be revealed to assure his/her personal security.

33. During his interview in August 1996, retired General Rodolfo Robles denied that Peru's military had been involved in any drug dealing. Yet, in an article written from exile in Argentina, to where Robles had fled after having exposed human rights abuses of a military death squad, the so-called *Grupo Colina,* he expressed a different view. Among other, the *Grupo Colina* was responsible for a massacre of students and their professor, at La Cantuta University in Lima. In his article, Robles pointed to a group of politicians and military officials who were seriously compromised by corruption and drug trafficking (*LAWR.* May 30, 1993: 22; *Oiga.* May 30, 1994: 22; Robles 1996). However, Robles' initial 'disinformation' was likely based on his apprehension of recriminations against his family and himself on the part of the country's secret service, the SIN. In fact, this fear was justified, as the ex-general was kidnapped by agents of the SIN and illegally detained for several months in late 1996 (*Caretas.* Nov. 28, 1996: 10–14).

34. For valuable insights into the role played by urban and rural self-defense groups, see Degregori, Coronel, del Pino, and Starn 1996.

35. This rather complex situation was completely misinterpreted in a number of journalistic publications. For example, *The Economist's* Peru correspondent failed to notice the activities of the *rondas campesinas* in the Apurímac y Ene region and informed its readers that *Sendero Luminoso* was behind the drug trade in both the Huallaga Valley, and the Apurímac y Ene region (*The Economist.* March 4, 2000).

36. The author of the document cannot be named here to protect his/her identity. However, a Swiss journalist who researched the drug trade in the Río Apurímac region confirms these findings. Accordingly, the *ronderos* had defeated *Sendero* by 1993, with weapons they acquired from the proceeds of drug trafficking. Even when the military finally moved in, it did not seriously interrupt the trade (Bauer 1995: 28).

37. 'Plan Colombia' had a similar effect on coca cultivation in Bolivia. After reaching a low of less than fifteen thousand hectares in 2000, the area under cultivation once again increased to 24,400 hectares by 2002 (UNODC 2003: 5).

38. In a letter to the Colombian government after the *Tranquilandia* raid in 1984, the country's hundred leading drug traffickers also denied any links to the rebels and wrote: "Our activities have never intended to replace the democratic and republican form of government" (Filippone 1994: 326–327). Incidentally, Lewis Tambs later became the US ambassador to Costa Rica, where he was accused of involvement in cocaine trafficking with the Nicaraguan *Contra* rebels operating in that country (Lee and Solomon 1992: 290).

39. In his version of the event, published only three years later, Taxa Cuadros (1987) gave a very detailed account of all that was found at the site. *Tranquilandia* was a giant complex designed for the mass production of cocaine, where up to one thousand people worked, including electricians, plumbers, and cooks. Local farmers provided a daily supply of fresh food for those working at the site. Taxa Cuadros mentioned a large eatery as well as a dormitory which could hold more than eighty people, bathrooms with white and orange tiles imported from Italy, luxurious furniture, microwave ovens, a library with popular and pornographic magazines, and so forth. Given this preoccupation with detail, it seems odd that he neither alluded to the alleged FARC presence nor mentioned the debate on the subject (1987: 35–36).

40. As noted, during the 1950s, the United States also accused the People's Republic of China of being a major drug producer, even as the regime imposed harsh measures to eradicate the cultivation, production, and trafficking of opium and its derivatives (Bewley-Taylor 1999: 108–114; Booth 1999: 168–169).

41. The investigation into Galán's murder was recently reopened as the Colombian politician Alberto Santofimio Botero was arrested and charged with participating in the assassination. Santofimio's links to the *Medellín Cartel* have been known since the mid-1990s when he lost his seat in the Colombian Congress after it it was revealed that he had received money from Pablo Escobar. Santofimio had presidential ambitions himself and allegedly urged Escobar to kill Galán because of the presidential candidate's stand against drug traffickers. Galán's family has long maintained that he was the victim of a conspiracy between drug traffickers and Liberal Party politicians (*La República*. May 13, 2005: 27; *El Comercio*. May 14, 2005: A 20; *La República*. May 15, 2005: 36).

42. Fabio Castillo, a journalist for the Colombian daily *El Espectador*, provided a wealth of information on the cartels and their infiltration of Colombia's governing structures. In *Los jinetes de la cocaína* (1987), the author paid special attention to the infiltration of the Colombian political system by organized crime. In a chapter titled "Mafia and Politics," he discussed the kickbacks paid to representatives of the Colombian Congress and the political activities of Medellín drug traffickers Pablo Escobar Gaviria and Carlos Lehder Rivas. Escobar, for example, ran and was elected as an alternative candidate for the Colombian Congress (Castillo 1987: 224–244). Castillo is one of the best-known Colombian authors on government corruption and the cartels. Strong (1996) referred to Castillo's 1987 book *Los jinetes de la cocaína* as "the first and bravest exposé of the Colombian cocaine trade" (1996: 61). In fact, the author was forced to leave the country after receiving death threats following the book's publication. Castillo's 1991 book, *La coca nostra*, was written in exile (*ibid.*, 165).

43. It does not take complex mathematics to discredit some of the claims that the rebels make huge profits from the cocaine economy. The average amount paid for a kilo of cocaine while still in Colombia, I came across in the literature, was US$2000. In 2002, the estimated global cocaine production stood at approximately 800 metric tons, or 800,000 kilos. Regardless, at a 10 percent 'revolutionary tax' or US$200 per kilo, FARC would earn US$160 million, if it were able to tax the whole global production of Bolivia, Colombia, and Peru. At 15 percent FARC revenues would amount to US$240 million. Even if the rebels tax the precursor chemicals and other materials needed to produce cocaine, they can impose such

levies only in the areas under control inside Colombia, but they do not operate laboratories nor do they own distribution networks outside of the country. Still, the figures on FARC's income from the drug economy often quoted in the media tend to be far higher. In my estimate, the FARC is not able to impose 'revolutionary taxes' on more than a third of cocaine made in Colombia, namely, from those traffickers it can tax in its area of control. The amount of taxation received from the coca-growing peasantry must be far lower because the product is worth far less at that stage of its production and distribution cycle. In other words, the FARC may indeed have an annual income of US$800–1000 million, which, however, is derived from a variety of sources, not all of which are criminal like drug trade or kidnapping. Moreover, a far larger amount of the drug leaves from the laboratories in areas controlled by military and paramilitary forces, while a substantial amount of cocaine, originating from Bolivia and Peru, bypasses Colombia altogether.

44. The DEA also described the weaponry which were exchanged for drugs. These included items such as Kalashnikov rifles, M-60 machine guns, or Stinger missiles. However, the report also referred to so-called STRELA (DEA 2002a). The only explanation of a STRELA I came across referred to a converted intercontinental ballistic missile, called SS-19 in NATO jargon. Of the one hundred and sixty SS-19s in Russian possession, fifty-five must be taken out of service by 2007 under the START 2 treaty. The Russian company *NPO Mashinostroyeniya* has the contract to convert the missile into the STRELA rocket which is to carry satellites into space. The STRELA is capable of carrying a payload of up to 1,700 kg into low orbit. *NPO Mashinostroyeniya* is offering the STRELA with a launching fee of US$10.5 million, not including the payload, which usually runs into the hundreds of millions of dollars (Space and Tech 2003). While the FARC are probably interested in Kalashnikov rifles or Stinger missiles, the rebels, in all likelihood, would find a converted intercontinental ballistic missile less useful for their purposes. Another story regarding the acquisition of some ten thousand Kalashnikov assault rifles by FARC supplied by Russian black marketeers in 2000 is therefore a more likely occurrence. Allegedly, Ilushin-16 cargo jets flew from Russia and Ukraine loaded with antiaircraft missiles, small weapons, and ammunition. The planes landed and refueled in Jordan, crossed the Atlantic to Colombia, where they landed on remote landing strips or airdropped the weapons, which then ended up in the hands of FARC (Bagley 2001). The Colombian journalist, Germán Castro Caycedo (2001: 135–168), confirmed that the delivery of Kalashnikov rifles did indeed take place but claimed that it involved the CIA and served the purpose of justifying 'Plan Colombia.' Oddly enough, the DEA failed to mention this account in its February 2001 report (DEA 2001). What makes this story even more peculiar is the proven involvement of the previously mentioned Peruvian spy master Vladimiro Montesinos, who masterminded the operation (Bagley 2001; DEA 2001; *La República.* May 1, 2005: 10).

45. In a number of conversations about the country's military which transpired during my stays in Colombia in 1988 and 1992, as well as with Colombian exiles in Canada, certain facts were brought to my attention. Officially, Colombia has the universal draft, however, it is common practice for the eligible sons of the country's middle and upper classes to avoid conscription through bribery, which is not affordable for the male offspring from lower-class families. In Canada, I even came across a young Colombian male who complained that he had to serve in the military because his father refused to pay the bribe, although he could have easily afforded to do so. Regardless, Colombia's military is a drafted lower-class army fighting for elite interests, a fact which may prove potentially dangerous in the long term for

those holding the reigns of power in that country.

46. The criminalization of the FARC may indeed be under way. In late May 2005, the Colombian and Peruvian press reported the largest drug bust in Colombia's history, over fifteen tons of cocaine. According to police reports, the owners of the drug were several Colombian, Ecuadorian, and Peruvian criminal organizations as well as the FARC and the paramilitaries (*El Comercio.* May 24, 2005: A13). Conversely, alliances of convenience, formal or informal, between the extreme left and right are not uncommon. The best known example is the Hitler-Stalin pact of 1939.

47. The regime attempted to cover up its crimes by bullying the Peruvian media, particularly during the second half of the Fujimori era. In fact, the president denounced his country's press for collaborating with corrupt elements because journalists exposed wrongdoings by his government (*El Sol.* June 15, 1997: 11). In other cases, the regime's response to its critics was much harsher. For example, the so-called 'Plan Narval,' an attempt by the Fujimori regime to silence media opposition through intimidation and, if necessary, assassination. The details of 'Plan Narval' became known after two female agents of the army's intelligence service, the SIE, secreted a document to an opposition daily. When discovered, they were tortured. One of them was killed and her body mutilated. The other, Leonor La Rosa Bustamante, was saved only because human rights groups found out about her in time prompting the US ambassador to intervene on her behalf (*La República.* June 25, 1997: 15; *La República.* Aug. 12, 1997a: 13).

Chapter 6

Beyond Modern Capitalism: Soviet and Post-Soviet Organized Crime

"There is no Mafia in the Soviet Union."

(The editor-in-chief of the Soviet daily
Literaturnaya Gazeta in 1980;
as quoted in Waksberg 1992: 18)

Not only capitalist practices generate forms of organized crime. This examination is the first of two studies of very different forms of social organization and the unique forms of organized crime generated in them. The Russian *Mafiya* and the various other ethnic mobs in the former Soviet Union did not suddenly emerge after the 1991 collapse of Communism. Rather, they had existed before and were the direct consequences of the contradictions produced by the Soviet system.

Introduction

Officially, organized crime did not exist in the former Union of Soviet Socialist Republics (USSR) (Chalidze 1977: 34; Handelman 1994: 1).[1] Yet shortly after the 1991 collapse Timofeyev (1992) claimed that entire segments of the economies of the USSR's successor states, in the Commonwealth of Independent States (CIS), were under the control of "purely criminal structures," while complete areas of entrepreneurship, such as the sale of computers, had surfaced with the support of funds from organized crime (1992: 169). Likewise, Mikhail Yegorov, from the Russian Ministry of Internal Affairs (MVD), claimed that organized crime had merged with legal entrepreneurism and owned some forty thousand companies. In 1993, Russian economists estimated that criminal organizations controlled 30–40 percent of their country's Gross National Product (GNP) (*Focus.* Jan. 25, 1993: 44). Handelman (1994) quotes Russian law enforcement estimates, which claimed that "organized crime allegedly accounted for between 30–40 percent of the national turnover in goods and services" (1994: 305).

The existence of organized crime was not officially acknowledged prior to Mikhail Gorbachev's 1985 rise to power and his introduction of the policy of *Glasnost*, or openness. By 1990, a year before the Soviet collapse, 1,641 gangs had been identified (Gleason 1990: 87–88; Serio 1992: 85).[2] In 1994, MVD officials estimated that some 5,700 criminal gangs operated in the territory of the Russian Federation alone, 30 percent more than in the previous year. The Canadian Security Intelligence Service (CSIS), adopted this figure but added "another one thousand" gangs who were operating in the other former Soviet republics (Hensler 1994: 24).[3] Roth (1996) maintained that these numbers were exaggerated and stemmed from the tendency of Russian security agencies to classify even "a small gang of thieves" as organized crime (1996: 40). Handelman noted likewise that his sources were unable to verify the figures he was given because his contacts failed to concur on a definition of what constituted criminal activity (1994: 305). Still, former Russian President Boris Yeltsin himself believed that "crime . . . . [had] become the number one problem" in Russia (Handelman 1994a: 88). The rise of post-Soviet organized crime in the early 1990s also alarmed the Central Intelligence Agency (CIA), whose former director, James Woolsey, claimed that criminal groups not only controlled large segments of the Russian economy but also threatened the security of the world (*Die Woche.* May 11, 1994: 22).[4]

Organized Crime in the Russian Federation and the 'Near Abroad' after 1991

As is generally the case with organized crime, it is also difficult to provide precise measurements of the extent of the criminal infestation of the former USSR's political and economic structures. Still, a brief examination of the reach and scope of OC activities since 1991 provides some insights on the extent of this criminal encroachment which must have been considerable prior to that time. Notable in this context are the illicit trade in arms from the former Soviet army, the illegal sale of raw materials and art treasures, and drug trafficking.

The former USSR's best military fighting force, which until 1994 had been stationed in eastern Germany, was the so-called Western Group of Forces (WGF). Most of the heavy military equipment of these troops was evidently sold by those in command who were in league with criminal organizations. The WGF's military command was implicated in the illegal sale of Antonov-72 transport planes, MI-8 helicopters, tanks, and artillery pieces (Schmidt-Häuser 1994: 6; Turbiville 1995: 63). The president of the Parliamentary Committee for Defense, Sergei Yuchenkov, raised the issue in the Russian Parliament, the *Duma*:

> The trains with the military equipments which came from Germany to Russia could have been sent directly to the garbage dump. But where remained all the

equipments which recently had been procured especially for our troops in Germany and which were sent there? (*ibid.*)

Many weapons stolen from the former Soviet army found their way to the ethnic conflicts on Russia's borders. Given its scope, the sale of Soviet military hardware on the international arms markets after 1991 was described as "the biggest and most dangerous arms bazaar in history" (Handelman 1994: 216; 1994a: 84). The Russian military in eastern Germany also became involved in drug trafficking. According to law enforcement sources from the Federal Republic of Germany (FRG), WGF military planes flew narcotics into the former German Democratic Republic (GDR) (Turbiville 1995: 77). The *Moskovsky Komsolets* journalist, Dimitri Kholodov, who was assassinated prior to a hearing in the *Duma* on his investigations into shady deals conducted by WGF commanders, wrote in one of his last articles: "When they say that a whole army of Mafia is operating in Russia, they can't imagine how close that is to the truth. Our Russian army is really descending into the world of organized crime" (*Moscow News*. Oct. 21–27, 1994: 2).

According to the German weekly *Die Zeit*, former President Boris Yeltsin was aware of these activities. However, Yeltsin did not dismiss General Matvei Burlakov, the commander of the WGF, but fired Yuri Boldyrev, the chief inspector of the Russian Federation, whom he had appointed to investigate military corruption. Yeltsin also elevated Burlakov to the post of Deputy Minister of Defense (Schmidt-Häuser 1994: 6; *Moscow News*. Oct. 28–Nov. 3, 1994: 1; Kolesnikow and Sidorow 1994: 364–365; *The Globe and Mail*. Nov. 28, 1998: A12). Burlakov was finally dismissed, likely because he became an embarrassment after being directly linked to the Kholodov assassination (Turbiville 1995: 79).[5]

Similarly, post-Soviet organized crime has been involved in the illegal trade of raw material. For example, in 1992, criminal groups illegally shipped approximately five million tons of nonferrous metals to the West via the Baltic states, with an estimated profit of US$3 billion. Miraculously, Estonia became the world's sixth-largest exporter of copper, although the country has no such metal deposits on its territory. The most important buyers turned out to be FRG companies (*Die Woche*. May 11, 1994: 22). Handelman (1994) noted for the period between July and December 1992, "Russian border police intercepted trucks and cars carrying a total of 1.5 million tons of oil and petroleum products, 77,000 tons of metal, 43.8 thousand cubic meters of forest and timber materials, and 2.4 billion rubles' worth of industrial chemical products" (1994: 172–173).[6]

The illegal traffic of precious art and religious objects such as icons, which are sold off to willing customers in the West, has done great damage to Russia's cultural heritage. Russian sources claimed that this illegal trade was worth anywhere from US$30 million to hundreds of millions of dollars annually during the early 1990s (*ibid.*, 172–173; also see *Moscow News*. Sept. 1992: 12).

Organizations capable of transporting tens of thousands of tons of metals or military hardware are easily capable of smuggling a few hundred or even a thousand tons of drugs. In fact, drug trafficking and abuse had already been growing social problems during the late Soviet era. The former USSR's Ministry of Health had reported that the number of addicts rose by more than 70 percent between 1985 and 1990. During the Afghan War, Soviet soldiers had acquired drug habits, and soon thereafter opium and hashish became available in the USSR. This stimulated the domestic cultivation and production of these drugs in Soviet Central Asia. Turbiville (1995) claimed that the Soviet republics in Central Asia had already turned into centers for the "cultivation, transit, and processing" of drugs after 1985 (1995: 61). Also, Gorbachev's antialcohol campaign, which was aimed at reducing violence in society and improving economic efficiency, contributed to growing narcotics abuse, especially among young people who switched from alcohol to drugs (*ibid.*; Lee III and Macdonald 1993: 98).

In 1993, fifty-four tons of narcotics were confiscated in Russia, compared with twenty tons in 1992, the year following the USSR's disintegration (*Die Woche.* May 11, 1994: 22).[7] In the Central Asian republics, the cultivation and production of drugs have also increased. Azerbaijan, Kazakhstan, and Uzbekistan have turned heroin producers, while some 70 percent of the West European heroin supply in 1992 allegedly came from or via the CIS (*Focus.* Jan. 25, 1993: 45; *Die Woche.* July 15, 1993: 16). The expansion of the narcotics trade in the former USSR corresponded to the growing interceptions in the West. Between 1989 and 1991, German seizures of heroin on the German-Czech border increased from 8.5 to 616 kilos annually (Lee III and Macdonald 1993: 94). These figures may not necessarily provide an accurate index of its magnitude; however, they do suggest that the drug trade, which had come into existence during the last years of the regime, particularly after the 1979 Soviet invasion of Afghanistan, rapidly increased after the 1991 collapse (Paoli 2001: 1007).

Moreover, the growing involvement of post-Soviet OC groups in the drug trade has provided them with links to other criminal fraternities who operate internationally. For example, the February 1993 confiscation of one ton of cocaine in a Russian Baltic port indicated that Colombian crime groups had discovered the former USSR as a transit route for drugs into Western Europe. Allegedly, there have even been 'summits' between post-Soviet and Western crime groups to establish a division of labor and profits, illustrating the "importance of post-Soviet gangs in the international hierarchies of crime" (Handelman 1994: 180, 239; *Die Woche.* May 11, 1994: 22; Roth 1996: 48–52).

The growing power of organized crime in post-Soviet Russia was also evidenced by the establishment of a money-laundering industry, as the country's lax banking laws allowed domestic and international crime groups to set up their own financial institutions. Until 1994, anyone with US$100,000 was allowed to start operating a bank. After 1994, the funds required increased to roughly US$1.2 million. However, some three thousand private banks or banking affiliates had already been founded by 1993. According to estimates, "40 percent of the movement of capital in Russia is now linked with narcotics" (Handelman 1994: 122, 180–182). Moscow offers great opportunities for money laundering. Leonid

Fituni, from the Moscow Center for Global and Strategic Studies, claimed that US$10 billion annually were being laundered in Russia by international crime groups during the early 1990s (*Die Woche*. May 11, 1994: 22). In 1997, MVD officials alleged that approximately five hundred banks were in the hands of criminals (Volkov 1999: 748).[8]

To make matters worse, the police forces suffered greatly from the effects of the administrative changes that took place after the Soviet Union's breakup. Police lack fast cars, modern investigative equipments, and communication systems while their low pay also makes them easy targets for corruption. In fact, tens of thousands of corrupt policemen and militia soldiers had already been charged and dismissed during the last years of the Soviet era (Shelley 1991: 253; Galleotti 1993: 783; *Die Woche*. May 11, 1994: 22; *The Globe and Mail*. Oct. 3, 1994: A6).[9] Although the previous figures have to be treated with caution, one may conclude that organized crime had reached substantial proportions in Russia and the rest of the CIS with which authorities could not cope.

Author Stephen Handelman (1994b), in the discussion of his book, *Comrade Criminal*, during a radio interview with the Canadian Broadcasting Corporation (CBC), described that corruption was prevalent in all ministries in Russia and the CIS. After observing the cooperation between the mafia and government officials, he concluded that bureaucracy and organized crime were the same. It stands to reason that criminal organizations did not suddenly emerge after the 1991 collapse of the Soviet state. Rather, the manifest infiltration of power structures by semicriminal and criminal elements suggests that this process had already occurred during Soviet times. As Kelly (1986) notes, organized crime grows "in many kinds of societies" that "differ politically, economically, and culturally," yet it "is intimately linked to political structures and economic infrastructures" (1986: 14).

The Success and Failure of Soviet Economic Development

The introduction of Socialism to the former Tsarist Empire was not in accordance with Marxist thinking. Unlike Marx and Engels, who had foreseen a socialist takeover in the advanced capitalist nations, such as Great Britain or Germany, a party seeking to build Socialism came to rule the former Imperial Russia, a country which not only lacked a large industrial working class but, for the most part, was a backward agricultural society. Hence, the victory of the *Bolsheviks* did not turn into a project of reapportioning the wealth of an advanced capitalist country. Indeed, there were few things left to hand out in the former Russian Empire after the horrendous losses incurred during World War I (1914–1918) and the Civil War (1918–1921), and Marxism in practice became a specific strategy devised to catchup with the economically advanced West.

Senghaas (1982) addressed this issue in his history of economic development. He differentiated between several types of development, considering criteria such as a country's population, size, available resources, and the period in which economic takeoff was achieved. Economic development in Europe was not a simultaneous process; rather, different countries applied distinct strategies to catch up with more developed ones. Also, the later a country developed, the stronger state involvement became in that process (1982: 7–17). Senghaas styled the path used by latecomers, France and Germany during the second half of the nineteenth century as "disassociative–domestic–dynamic" (*ibid.*, 42). This is the strategy used by the economic policymakers in these two nations to catch up with Great Britain, which had undergone its industrial revolution during the early nineteenth century. These latecomers developed their economic potentials by using protectionism and other economic policies to nurture their young industries and shield them from the more advanced competition (*ibid.*).

Senghaas (1982) argued that unlike most countries of Western and Central Europe, Tsarist Russia could no longer develop on a capitalist path. The infringement of the more advanced capitalist countries threatened to push Russia into a position of economic dependence in the early twentieth century. Thus, development on the "disassociative–state socialist" path, implemented after the 1917 revolution, was the strategy selected to catch up (*ibid.*, 52–53). This course initially implied disassociation from the global market to develop. The Soviet Union did maintain economic relations with the outside world, including capitalist countries; however, these were selective and generally limited to trade deals viewed as advantageous and useful for development. Moreover, the state already played a significant role, together with other agents such as domestic banks and private companies, in the course taken by countries such as France and Germany. In the Soviet Union, however, the state became the sole vehicle for development (*ibid.*, 52–53, 277–278).

Yugoslav dissident scholar Milovan Djilas (1959) had expressed similar ideas already a generation earlier in his classic work *The New Class*. He pointed out that underdeveloped countries like Russia were confronted with a dilemma: They either industrialized or became part of the periphery controlled by foreign capital. Djilas wrote further

> revolutions did not occur because new, let us say socialist, relationships were already existing in the economy, or because capitalism was 'overdeveloped.' On the contrary. They did occur because capitalism was not fully developed and because it was not able to carry out the industrial transformation of the country (1959: 11–14).[10]

Prior to 1914, Tsarist Russia had generated the essential components for the country's development: an enterprising bureaucratic state, small formations of indigenous wealth associated with large amounts of foreign capital, sources of Western technology, and established trade relations. Russia also owned — and still owns — huge reserves of natural resources (Luke and Boggs 1982: 99).[11] Yet, this path of development also caused Russian dependency on the advanced capitalist countries. Before the outbreak of World War I, foreign interests controlled 21 percent of textile production, 26 percent of leather processing, 32 percent of lumber processing, 41 percent of all chemical industry and 63 percent of mining, metallurgy, and machinery production (Rostow 1979: 426–437). Prior to 1914, Germany was Russia's biggest trading partner. In fact, in 1913, some 47 percent (!) of Russian imports derived from that country (Dederichs 1989: 223).

Wilber and Jameson (1988) argued that the application of the Soviet model created the preconditions for development by ending the domination of foreign capital and by eliminating the existing socioeconomic power structures in the former Tsarist Empire. Peasants and workers did not receive these powers. Instead they were transferred to a one-party state and its institutions, which ruled only ceremonially on their behalf. The Soviets' victory did end Western dominance, and destroyed the old class system, both of which had frustrated economic development (1988: 20). While this extensive industrialization was largely successful, the collectivization of agriculture did not yield the desired increase in food production but became a considerable problem.[12] By contrast, Socialism created good education as well as health and social security systems (Senghaas 1982: 294–295).

However, the human costs of the Soviet experiment were horrendous. In addition to the victims of the *Bolshevik* terror during the Civil War, Stalin's drive for modernization cost the lives of many millions such as the victims of the Ukrainian famine — the *Kulaks*, or rich farmers — and the many others who were made to perish in the work camps of Siberia because they were deemed unfit for the new society. No lasting social order can likely be built whose very foundations rest on the bones of tens of millions of victims. Yet, without this forced industrialization would the Soviet Union have been able to withstand the onslaught of Hitler's armies in 1941 and 1942?

Furthermore, development on the socialist route also occurred in the countries of Central and Eastern Europe after World War II, although these nations had not adopted the Soviet path by choice. Prior to 1944–1945, Germany had been the economic, military, and political hegemonic power in the region. Nazi Germany had penetrated the economies of Eastern and Southeastern Europe to an overwhelming extent. Due to trade manipulations and economic pressures, Germany had obtained a share of roughly 50 percent of the total foreign trade of Bulgaria, Greece, Hungary, Rumania, Turkey, and Yugoslavia between 1933 and 1936. These trade policies primarily served the purpose of war preparations (Schacher 1937: 158–161). By 1938, the Bulgarians sent 58 percent of their exports to Germany, while they received 63 percent of imports from the same direction. Romania was of special interest because it had the oil reserves Hitler needed to run the Nazi war machine (Holsti 1977: 254–255).

After 1945, post-war Eastern Europe became part of the Soviet sphere of interest, and the countries of the Socialist Bloc achieved high rates of economic growth. These were based on the establishment of heavy industries and the mobilization of large workforces, in particular, through the collectivization of agriculture, which turned surplus rural labor into an industrial workforce (Senghaas 1982: 294−295). Development did take place, considerably changing these nations' economies. Centralized planning brought about the conditions for economic takeoff; however, East Bloc countries failed to grow beyond an early stage. Senghaas also noted though that the application of the Soviet model was the most successful in the least developed nations of Central and Eastern Europe. Countries like East Germany and Czechoslovakia which had already experienced considerable development prior to the Soviet takeover, were the first to experience problems once the post-war reconstruction phase had been completed (*ibid.*, 298).

Still, the first stage of industrialization succeeded well enough despite, rather than because, of Stalinist policies. Conversely, the same system became an impediment to the further development of the East Bloc societies. Particularly, the switch from an economy based on extensive industrial growth and heavy industry to intensive growth built on the application of modern technologies was not possible without a decentralization of economy and state structures (*ibid.*, 298). Marcuse (1961) identified the problem with the structural shortcomings of the Stalinist system: "The Stalinist construction of Soviet society rested on the sustained priority of heavy industry; a fundamental shift in the balance would mean a fundamental shift in the structure itself — in the economic as well as political system" (1961: 98).

The Soviet Protection Racket and the Period of Stagnation

The main resistance to these necessary reorganizations came from the Soviet elites, the new class of bureaucrats and technocrats (Koestler 1945: 171−174; Djilas 1959: 37−41). Created by the Stalinist regime to carry out the USSR's transformation from an agrarian to an industrial society at high speed, this entrenched group became the stumbling block on the road to a post-industrial one. A relationship exists between the refusal of Soviet elites to introduce meaningful reforms to counter the economic decline, the rise in corruption, and the growth of the shadow economy out of which organized crime arose.[13]

Of particular interest in this context are the political and administrative elites of the old Soviet Union in general as well as those representing the steel, petroleum and heavy construction industries, and the military, in particular. Khrushchev had called the members of these circles the "metal eaters" due to their ever-increasing demands for the allocation of resources for heavy industry and armaments (Salisbury 1965: 70). The "metal eaters" had become entrenched during the Stalin era and considered any attempt to change economic priorities a direct threat (*ibid.*).

Djilas (1959) identified a "new class" which had emerged in the USSR (1959: 37−41). Similarly, Nove (1976) referred to a "ruling class" in the Soviet Union. Wagenlehner (1978) discussed a "high bureaucracy" which ruled the USSR during the late 1970s through some "three hundred thousand functionaries in key positions of party, state, the economy and society" (1978: 790–792). This elite regenerated itself by recruiting new blood from a select list, the *nomenclatura* (*ibid.*). Harasymiw (1977) calculated that the *nomenclatura* list for the central committees of all union republics amounted to "between one hundred and ninety thousand and two hundred and sixty thousand positions" during the height of Brezhnev era (1977: 585).

According to Pakulski (1986), the administrative elites of the East Bloc nations differed greatly from those in the West. He argued that it would be misleading to apply a classical Weberian framework to the Soviet-type administrative model.[14] While he conceded that Western administrative experiences also conflict with the Weberian ideal type, he concluded that the digressions "constitute not the exception or 'anomaly' but the rule" in Soviet-type administrations (1986: 4–11). These include the discrepancy between the real and the formal command structure as well as the dominant position of party organizations compared with those of the state. Moreover, Pakulski referred to overlapping responsibilities and obscure jurisdictional divisions between — and within — party and government hierarchies, and the general preference of political favoritism over defined regulations. Additional factors included the weight given to ideology in the decision-making process as well as the central role of "(quasi)-charismatic elements in political leadership," as well as the importance of a mobilizational system based on a blend of exhortation and force (*ibid.*). Finally, he included the commonplace acceptance of extralegal and illegal activities, and of patronage, that resulted from the *nomenklatura* selection system. Thus, Pakulski described the Soviet-type administration as "quasi-bureaucratic" and "politocratic" (*ibid.*).

Although the necessity for reform was already generally acknowledged during the Khrushchev era, no major changes were introduced. According to Prybyla (1980), reform was viewed in the limited sense of increasing component productivity, stepping up the momentum of innovation, increased pay for workers, and higher standards in research, science, training, and technology. Still, the imperative modification of conceding to individual consumers, workers, and factory managers the right to have allocative alternatives was never implemented. Prybyla wrote further:

> Administrative decentralization took the place of proposed economic decentralization; the vertical structure of information flows, administrative coordination, and the center's detailed regulations of the incentive system were not significantly altered . . . . The partial reforms . . . . distorted the behavior of consumers, workers and managers in novel ways. In short, Soviet reforms [before Gorbachev] suggest that the Soviet political-economic establishment is organically incapable of surrendering meaningful decision-making powers to anyone. The retention of the monopoly of allocative power at the center remains a basic principle of Soviet conduct to this day. Plus ça change, plus c'est la même chose (1980: 35).

Not only did the failure to reform the apparatus prevent the Soviets from entering the stage of intensive industrialization, it also had serious consequences for the overall functioning of the economy. This became manifest in the years of stagnation during the Brezhnev era (1964–1982). Ministries and government agencies merely set quotas without considering the quality of the product, or the actual need for and consumer satisfaction with it. Plans were often badly coordinated, which caused bottlenecks, unused capacities, unnecessary inventories, and waste. The centralization of the decision-making process meant that corrections could be implemented only slowly and with difficulty. Given the pressure on management to maximize output and meet prescribed targets, the quantity of production became more important than product quality. This emphasis on maximal output prevented Soviet managers from modernizing outdated machinery because of their fear that innovations would disrupt production and endanger fulfillment of the plan. Furthermore, enterprises gained little from reorganizations that increased production and profits, as returns were siphoned off by the central government. In fact, Moscow would set higher quotas for the next planning period. Hence, Soviet industrial management avoided innovating their plants, because it resulted in the increased pressure of having to fulfill higher quotas. Conversely, management had to bear responsibility if changes did not have the desired effect (Grossman 1977: 114; Stiglitz 2002: 138).

These managerial practices had a large impact on the way Soviet industries worked. Administrators favored repairing obsolete machinery over replacing it. By the late 1970s, one-third of Soviet industry was geared toward producing machine tools designed for making repairs or spare parts, instead of manufacturing new machinery for production. Therefore, large segments of Soviet industry were unproductive. Some 30–50 percent of machinery was outdated by 1985, and the typical age of a factory machine in the USSR reached twenty-seven years (Hunter 1978: 16; Ferenczi 1987: 84–85). East Bloc industries were generally only half as productive but used three times the energy compared to those in the West (Oschliess 1990: 9–10).

The failure of the East Bloc economies was also caused by their inability to integrate the new technologies acquired from the West during the 1960s and thereafter. This was in contrast to the newly industrializing countries (NICs) of Southeast Asia, where the absorption of Western technology resulted in improved efficiency and greater export volumes (UN 1989: 91–97). This outcome also differed from the earlier successful application of Western technology, particularly from Germany and the United States, that the regime had relied on during Stalin's modernization drive of the 1920s and 1930s (Luke and Boggs 1982: 104). However, the introduction of foreign technology into the Soviet economy during the 1960s and 1970s had the opposite effect. The centrally planned economy, which did not encourage innovative processes, was also not adept at incorporating foreign technologies. These were of use only in domains where the Soviets had achieved parity with the West, such as aircraft or heavy equipment, and were thus able to absorb them. In most other areas, foreign technologies, if at all applicable, proved to be temporary solutions which blinded administrators from realizing the need for profound structural reforms (*ibid.*, 113).

Moreover, the brutal nature of Stalinist totalitarian rule shaped the initial modernization drive during the 1930s and the subsequent reconstruction period following World War II. After all, the goal of modernization was to be attained by 'primitive socialist accumulation,' squeezing the population for rapid capital buildup (Rostow and Levin 1960: 80–89). This included the leadership's willingness to expend the lives of millions to build a 'new' society. However, Stalinist central planning worked only as long as the tasks it had to administer were relatively simple during the early stages of economic modernization. Conversely, the same economic system could not provide the tools to continue on the path of development, which prevented Soviet society from entering the next stage of intensive industrialization.

The environment of terror and fear likely had implications for the functioning of the administrative apparatus, the management of information, and the economic decision-making process. In order for an economy of the size of the Soviet one to be productive, those running it must not only obtain but also process vast amounts of information. These data flow up from the various industrial and agricultural production units through layers of bureaucracy and form the basis for a decision-making process at the top. However, information losses increase with the size of the apparatus, because miscalculations at any layer are passed on to all subsequent ones, whether it is information on the way up or a decision based on this information on the way down (Murrell and Olson 1991: 257). Management had a monopoly on information, while the decision-making ability of the leadership depended on the quality and quantity of information received. It was, however, in the collective interest of Soviet industrial managers that the central leadership underestimated the productive potential of their enterprises to conceal shortcomings and mistakes. Thus, a significant incentive existed for management to withhold information as well as to overstate problems and understate production potential. Distorted information was used at every level of the apparatus (*ibid.*, 256–258).

In Stalin's totalitarian state, this problem remained manageable because the oppressive apparatus imposed negative incentives, which could take the form of a firing squad or a Siberian labor camp, yet made the system function. Show trials were held against hapless members of the Soviet managerial elite who were accused of being "wreckers" and "saboteurs" (Deutscher 1970: 136). However, the vertical decision-making process became less functional once the negative incentives were removed following Stalin's death and once the state of economic development reached required the conversion to decentralized forms of economic and political organization. The command economy could not cope with horizontal decision making and decentralization, which became requirements after the foundations for further development were laid. Oddly enough, Stalin (1947) himself realized this need and called for a decentralization of decision-making processes to adapt to the new conditions of production in the USSR (1947: 423).

Decentralization, however, was not in the interest of the new elites whose primary concern was the preservation of their status and privileges, albeit without the environment of fear and repression. Nikita Khrushchev's reforms failed because they went too far in the eyes of many members of the new class in the USSR, who saw their status and privileges endangered. His overthrow in 1964, and replacement by Leonid Brezhnev, basically implied a return to Stalinism without Stalin, and without the excesses of the secret police (Waksberg 1992: 35; Clark 1993: 276–277). All the same, corruption became an important element of the system.[15]

After the early 1980s, economic decline became manifest, as all Soviet Bloc nations experienced low growth rates. These had been 5 percent or higher during the 1960s but fell to between 1 and 2.5 percent in the late 1970s. This trend of declining growth rates ran parallel to the increasingly higher debt burdens these countries accumulated, as they implemented growth strategies of import substitution, applying Western technology to restructure and modernize their outmoded industries during the latter part of the 1960s to the mid-1970s. To finance this largely unsuccessful modernization drive, they relied on loans from Western banks (Pascal 1989: 99). By 1988, the cumulative debt of the USSR and its European allies reached roughly US$150 billion (Berrios 1990: 1686).

The Shadow Economy

It is important to mention the notion of property rights practiced in the USSR and other former East Bloc countries, a factor that greatly contributed to the growth of corruption. In a capitalist society, private individuals are the owners of property, although other forms of ownership exist as well, e.g., cooperatives. According to Marxist theory, the existence of private property is the primary cause for the division of society into antagonistic classes, which is manifested by the exploitation and oppression of the nonpropertied classes by those who own the means of production. In a socialist society, property is *social property*, belonging to the workers and peasants. According to Marxist thinking, this form of ownership is the power base of workers and peasants. Socialist societies allowed for a form of private property, or rather *personal property*, which refers to the individual consumption or use of goods, properties, etc., for personal use. Nonetheless, the sources to acquire *personal property* were limited to personal earnings, financial awards, inheritances, or gifts (Klaus and Buhr 1983: 293–294; Gregory and Stuart 1986: 379; Böhme et al 1988: 213).

Yet, as previously noted, peasants and workers were not running their own affairs in the former East Bloc. Rather, a one-party state and its institutions ruled on their behalf (Wilber and Jameson 1988: 20). Those in charge of *social property* were not its owners, but their positions allowed them to gain access to the benefits as if they were, although doing so represented a criminal offense according to the Soviet Constitution of 1977 (Harris 1986: 17). Still, the management of *social property* by Soviet elites permitted its use as well as abuse as if it were *private property*. As discussed by Djilas (1959), the control over property was the foundation of ownership, and as a result, those in charge effectively became a new class of proprietors (1959: 35–39). Indeed, for its increasingly corrupt elite, the Soviet economy became a place of pillage. Millar (1984) wrote that the regime "tolerated the expansion of a wide range of petty private economic activities, some legal, some in the penumbra of the legal, and some clearly illegal, the primary aim of which was the reallocation by private means of a significant fraction of Soviet national income according to private preferences" (1984: 697).

Soviet economic decline resulted from the failure to modernize the economy, as elites opposed the reform and decentralization of the decision-making process, fearing they would lose power and status. Throughout its history, the Soviet economic system served both the aims of production and the perpetuation of party power. The *nomenklatura* was the guarantee of the second function but also the cause of economic inefficiency and corruption. This at least partly explains the failure of the reforms initiated by Mikhail Gorbachev after 1985. His attempts to reform the economy and make it more efficient aimed at suspending the second function and met the resistance of the elites (Jancar 1991: 117). The new class who controlled the USSR, although spawned by a revolutionary regime, had turned into a protection racket primarily interested in maintaining itself.

When elites came to view innovation and decentralization with their loss of power and privilege, it became difficult to maintain productivity at reasonable levels. To keep producing within such a system, connections, extralegal practices and ultimately, corruption became important, even in running day-to-day affairs. Thus, the emergence of the *tolkachi*, or expediters, is hardly surprising. The term referred to private individuals hired by enterprises who used their special connections to supply businesses with equipment, tools, and raw materials, outside the official channels (Salisbury 1965: 72–73; Stiglitz 2002: 138). Beerman (1962) already pointed out in the early 1960s that the *tolkachi* operated in a gray zone between legal and illegal, and that "their activities . . . . may have the odium of criminality" (1962: 201–202). Journalist Barbara Kerneck wrote in this context:

> The principal person of the Socialist planned economy . . . . was the tolkach, the fixer . . . . [who could supply] any commodity: On behalf of his boss he was constantly driving around . . . . to obtain missing parts to continue production, not without payoffs, of course. The perverse element of the whole situation was the fact that the exchanged goods belonged to nobody (As quoted in Raith 1994: 158–159).[16]

The need for the *tolkachi* was fostered by the priority given to military production, which resulted in shortcomings in other sectors of the USSR's state-run economy, particularly in the agricultural sector. Katsenelinboigen (1977) maintained that agriculture suffered "the most from failure to receive spare parts" (1977: 79–80). Conversely, those in charge of agricultural production units were also under great pressure to deliver during harvest time. He noted that "kolkhoz managers . . . . [urged] . . . . workers to steal" badly needed spare parts, or tried to obtain them through 'special' arrangements with factory directors who produced the required supplies by diverting materials from their own production lines (*ibid.*; also see Rosner 1986: 6). The importance of the *tolkachi* was also demonstrated by the fact that they faced little to no interference from Soviet law enforcement officials and the justice system. According to Clark (1993) only two *tolkachi* were convicted for their activities in the twenty-five year period between 1965 and 1990 (1993: 265).

The emergence of the shadow economy since the 1950s, whose 'managers' tried to fill the gaps of the plan, should thus be considered a logical progression. Rather than private individuals, who would have been eager to fill the gaps left by the central plan but were prevented from doing so by the authorities, Soviet 'entrepreneurs' who evolved from the *tolkachi* as well as criminals took over the organization of underground factories, and with it the nonstate production of commodities, mostly in the area of consumer goods. The shadow economy became an integral part of the system. Officials from party and state were usually bribed, or even turned criminal themselves, and took part in the plunder of state and economy (Passas 2000: 28). Apparently, some "20 million Soviet citizens" found employment in the shadow economy (Clark 1993: 260). Girling's (1997) differentiation between "functional" and "dysfunctional" corruption is descriptive of the Soviet case (1997: VIII, 24). Corruption may be viewed as useful if it helps to surmount the "rigidities of an over-regulated economy" and remains beneficial while it is "wealth-producing," but becomes "wealth-consuming" when it wastes resources (*ibid.*).

The Emergence of Soviet Organized Crime

Passas (2000) referred to several criminal and semicriminal elements who formed part of the OC milieu in the former Soviet Union. These included "former company directors, the *nomenklatura*, professional criminals, and new entrepreneurs with a black market experience" (2000: 32). McCauley (2001) pointed to the "unholy troika" of "the mafia, the nomenklatura, and current and former members of the government, military, and security services" (2001: 75). In their analysis of organized crime in post-Communist Russia, Finckenauer and Waring (1998) also described different groups who belonged to the OC milieu in the USSR. First, they included the corrupt officials — an important requirement for the functioning of organized crime anywhere. Furthermore, they pointed to the *avtoritey*, or "thieves in authority" (1998: 92–93). The term referred to government and party officials who turned criminals themselves and pillaged the state economy. An example for the *avtoritey* was the so-called "Uzbek Mafia." These members of the highest party and bureaucracy in Soviet Uzbekistan misappropriated billions of rubles by systematically overstating the figures on the cultivation of cotton in their republic. The profits were used to fund the shadow economy (Gleason 1990: 93). According to Finckenauer and Warring (1998), some "thieves in authority" emerged as "major actors in the current organized crime scene in post-Soviet Russia" (1998: 92–93, 98–100; also see Waksberg 1992: 147–159; Roth 1996: 109–111).

The third group was organized crime proper, namely, the *vorovskoy mir*, or "thieves' world," in which the *vory v zakone*, the "thieves professing the code" played the most dominant roles (*ibid.*, 92–93). The origins of crime groups predate the USSR and include, for example, seventeenth-century outlaw peasant bands and nineteenth-century beggars' and thieves' societies, with their own laws, customs, and forms of communication, similar to the Chinese secret organizations discussed earlier (Chalidze 1977: 34–60).[17] Chalidze portrayed the *vorovskoy mir* in the Soviet Union as an evolved "social institution" with "its own internal cohesion and ethical code" (*ibid.*, 34). Handelman (1994) described it as an organized professional underworld, which had "existed on the margins of Russian life for centuries," with a "complex paramilitary culture" and "exclusive rituals and codes of honor" (1994: xix).

Organized crime in the Soviet Union evolved in accordance with the unique conditions of time and place. The thieves' world was traditionally an 'institution' which was strongly antistate. In fact, its code of honor promised severe punishment, including expulsion and death, for any type of collaboration with agents of the state (Varese 2001: 150–152). However, during the Stalin era this position changed, leading not only to the cooperation between criminals and the authorities, but also to great internal divisions within the *vorovskoy mir* (Chalidze 1977: 71; Handelman 1994: 30–31). As noted, organized crime was severely repressed during the regime's totalitarian phase under Stalin (Kelly, Schatzberg, and Ryan 1997: 176). This statement needs some qualification. While great numbers of criminals were imprisoned in the USSR during the 1920s and 1930s, their incarceration did not destroy the *vorovskoy mir*, which continued to function within the prisons and work camps. In fact, it was strengthened in some respects. The regime even relied on common criminals to oppress and eliminate the political prisoners. Chalidze (1977) wrote:

> In the twenties and thirties, common-law criminals were far from constituting the majority of camp inmates. The regime was conducting a campaign to change the class composition of society, and among the millions of class aliens in the camps were many whom the Bolsheviks wanted to get rid of but preferred to liquidate with the aid of criminals rather than openly (1977: 70; also see Frisby 1998).

After the June 1941 attack on the Soviet Union by Nazi Germany, many criminals joined the Red Army, against the thieves' world's stipulations, as Stalin had promised them their freedom if they fought the invaders. After the 1945 victory, Stalin did not keep his pledge and returned them to the labor camps, where the majority of Soviet and post-Soviet criminals have been and still are housed traditionally, as opposed to prisons. However, the returning criminals were viewed as traitors by the members of the traditional underworld who had stayed behind. The so-called Scabs' War erupted between the two groups within the labor camps costing many lives. Ultimately, the *vorovskoy mir* changed its law to permit the scabs back in and to accept involvement with the authorities. Still, the conflict, which took place during the early 1950s, contributed to the appearance of a new type of criminal, who like his Western counterparts, collaborated with and subverted state agents and who was immersed in society (*ibid.*, 71). Given their experiences in the labor camps, many former members of the thieves' world cut their ties with the traditional criminal underworld. They moved into the shadow economy, an area which required cooperation with and corruption of state agents. From there, according to Handelman (1994), they emerged as the

> most successful wheelers and dealers of the Perestroika era . . . . [who had] established working alliances across the black economy with businesspeople and government officials . . . . A new type of Russian godfather now challenged the tsars of the underworld. Having less regard for gang traditions . . . . the new-style crime boss . . . . transformed the cosy environment of the Soviet underworld. He moved into more risky spheres of criminal behavior, such as bank frauds and drug trafficking; and he commanded wealth beyond the dreams of the old . . . . [crime bosses] (1994: 31).

Zile (1976) claimed that the criminalization of Soviet society was likely enhanced by the regime's preference to pardon criminal rather than political prisoners, a tendency that was evident throughout the Stalinist era and thereafter (Zile 1976: 46). Shelley (1991) also believed that the increase in crime during the Brezhnev era resulted from the release of prisoners after Stalin's death (1991: 256–257).

The nature of the relationship between organized crime and state agents has undergone fundamental changes in Soviet history. From being antistate, it became an informal instrument of the state that played a role in the persecution of the regime's political enemies and even fought on its behalf. However, it is the regime which controlled this association, at least during the Stalin era. Subsequently, with growing corruption and the emergence of the 'thieves in authority' came about the collaboration between parts of the elite and members of the Soviet criminal underworld who had met in the management of the shadow economy. At this stage, however, the regime no longer merely used criminals for its purposes but had grown dependent on them, while the Soviet state and economy had been infested with corrupt and criminal elements.

In the former East Bloc, the informal economy referred to the "production and distribution of licit products outside the channels of centralized planning and direct state control" (Portes and Böröcz 1988: 17). These products were illegal not in themselves but in the manner in which they had been produced or acquired. Some might disagree, therefore, that the Soviet black market organizations indeed represent forms of organized crime. Still, as noted by a former Russian police official:

> In contrast to organized crime in a number of Western countries which developed by providing illegal [goods and] services — prostitution, lotteries, narcotics — our organized crime formed itself in the domain of the [legal] economy (as quoted in Raith 1994: 140).

The licit nature of the goods provided by Soviet crime groups likely enhanced their ability to integrate into the system. After all, criminals seemingly made the economy work. The services and goods provided by the Soviet *Mafiya* differ little from the activities that Naylor (1993) ascribes to organized crime in its "symbiotic" phase. While the goods provided were not necessarily criminal, they were furnished by individuals deemed criminals in the eyes of Soviet law. After all, participation in black market activities was considered unlawful as it implicitly resulted in the accumulation of private property. Hence, those attracted into this activity were primarily criminals, former labor camp inmates, and corrupt officials, not ordinary Soviet citizens.

Block and Chambliss (1981) argue that people react to the discrepancies that are inherent in their respective historical conditions. Individual acts result from the innate contradictions that people experience within the respective socioeconomic formations in which they exist (1981: 7). Ordinary citizens greatly contributed to the growth of organized crime in the former USSR. While Soviets were earning money, they were unable to spend it in the formal economy where few consumer goods of quality were available. To locate these products, Soviets shopped in the shadow economy, which became a "necessary escape valve for excess rubles" (Holtbrügge 1991: 47; also see Birman 1980: 88; Bremmer and Taras 1992: 72).

Due to growing corruption, signified by the emergence of the *avtoritey*, the shadow economy grew beyond a gray area where one would buy only consumer goods. Many daily necessities and food items which should have been sold within the framework of the state economy were diverted onto the black market, where greater profits could be reaped. By the 1980s, it had grown so large that according to estimates, 83 percent of the USSR's population acquired essential food items and services through the shadow economy (Clark 1993: 261). Official estimates claimed that this economy of the USSR was worth between 150–200 billion roubles annually by the 1980s. However, Soviet economists put the figure at some 400 billion roubles, which seemed exaggerated given that the official national income of the USSR in 1986, for example, amounted to 568 billion roubles (*Knaur's Weltspiegel* 1988: 383; Waksberg 1992: 169). Although official Soviet records are unreliable, it can be taken for granted that the shadow economy and corruption in the USSR had reached immense proportions. Moreover, Konstantin Simis (1982), a specialist on Soviet law and himself a former USSR citizen, noted during the early 1980s that the "massive and ubiquitous corruption . . . . of the party state apparat has forged such close ties between it and the criminal world that there is every justification for saying that a system of organized crime has come into existence in the Soviet Union . . . ." (1982: 94).

Indeed, this union of criminal groups managing the shadow economy with the *nomenklatura* was identified as the "greatest danger" to the USSR before the 1991 collapse (Wolkow 1991: 38). Thus, it is not implausible to argue that organized crime significantly hastened the USSR's economic collapse. After all, the commodities used in the shadow economy were misappropriated from the formal economy and were thus lost. One of the fundamental contradictions of the Soviet system was the growth of the shadow economy and ultimately the criminal one, which emerged to compensate for the shortcomings of central planning. Block (1987) observed in his analysis of capitalist elites in state and economy that "those who accumulate capital are not conscious of what is necessary to reproduce the social order" (1987: 54–55). Conversely, "[t]hose who manage the state apparatus" are preoccupied "with the reproduction of the social order because their continued power rests on the maintenance of political and economic order" (*ibid.*). In the USSR, the two groups were identical, while neither was conscious of the need to reproduce the system.

The Soviet power structures likely contributed to an important difference between organized crime in the former USSR and the capitalist West. For example, in Colombia and the United States criminal groups acquired political power only after attaining economic clout. In the former Soviet Union, the situation was more complex. On one hand, criminals released from the prison camps came to occupy positions of prominence through their economic role first, namely their participation in the shadow economy. On the other hand, the 'thieves in authority' used their political positions to gain economic power and to have access to the privileges that came with power. In addition, the integration of Soviet organized crime into elite structures was far simpler than similar efforts by their Western counterparts. OC groups in capitalist societies need to corrupt agents in both the state and the economy. However, in the USSR, state and economic actors were the same.

While the Soviet Union displayed many contradictory facets that contributed to its collapse, the role organized crime played in this process, at the very least, suggests an investigation of how immune a modern capitalist system would be to such encroachment. These developments may be possible in any socioeconomic system, where the criminal economy merges with the legal one, a notion that will be revisited.

From Soviet to Post-Soviet Organized Crime

The Soviet *Mafiya* emerged so rapidly after the beginning of reforms in 1985 because it had already been part of the system. The failure of the command economy created the shadow economy, which was controlled by criminals and semicriminal bureaucrats. The Soviet *Mafiya* prior to 1991 represented the product of a gradually evolving association of criminals emerging from below and semicriminal elites submerging from above. The USSR's 1991 collapse did not end the old power structures, corruption, or organized crime. Rather, what took place was a process of restructuring due to the new economic conditions, which strengthened the links between the former Communist elite and the new "entrepreneurial" *Mafiya* (Timofeyev 1992: 168).

Gorbachev's reform politics greatly contributed to this outcome. The Law on the State Enterprise of 1987 had the purpose of forcing market discipline on enterprises by impelling them to turn "self-financing or face closure," but also gave more leverage to administrators in utilizing company assets for private gain (Kneen 2000: 353). The 1988 Law on Cooperatives had similar results. It allowed the managers of state companies to set up "private subsidiaries to which they could assign equipment and sell subsidized resources, the products of which could then be sold at market prices" (*ibid.*). It was possible to establish cooperatives without providing a tax declaration and proof of the legal origins of funds, which provided an opening for the legalization of capital from the shadow economy (Kolesnikow and Sidorow 1994: 354). In a country without private property or a market economy, the funds gained by organized crime were of little use, unless they could be converted. Therefore, once it became possible to open businesses, such as joint ventures or banks, these turned into outlets for illegally acquired wealth, including funds gained through black marketeering (Timofeyev 1992: 169).

Even before the beginning of privatization in 1991, members of the *nomenklatura* used party funds and state property to set up different banks, associations, stock corporations, private limited liability companies, and joint ventures. These organizations were controlled by former party *apparatchiks* and state officials, who turned into company presidents and vice presidents (Waksberg 1992: 331; Silverman and Yanowitch 1997: 108–109). The process accelerated after the Soviet collapse. This appropriation of government holdings allegedly led Russia's minister in charge of privatization to comment that "property in this country belongs to whoever is nearest to it" (Kneen 2000: 357). Russian sociologist Olga Khryshtanovskaya used the term "nomenklatura privatization," and wrote: "Whereas formerly, property was at the disposal but not in the possession of the nomenklatura, it was now legally defined property" (as quoted in Silverman and Yanowitch 1997: 125). Within a few years after the 1991 collapse, Russia's wealthiest citizens were former members of the Communist elite. This group enjoyed an advantage because of its links to the old power structures. When state property was being privatized, control was often transferred to those who had managed it during Soviet times. Simultaneously, the Soviet *Mafiya* was able to channel its illicit profits into the same legal business ventures (*The Globe and Mail.* Sept. 17, 1994: A1; Handelman 1994a: 87; Khryshtanovskaya and White 1996; Silverman and Yanowitch 1997: 114).

Post-Soviet Organized Crime and Power after 1991

Russian economists had foretold in 1992 that the national income of the Russian Federation would be reduced by 43 percent between 1991 and 1995. In contrast, the decrease in national income during the Great Patriotic War (1941–1945) had amounted to 34 percent for the whole USSR (Kolesnikow and Sidorow 1994: 360). As noted by Stiglitz (2002: 143), Russian industrial output actually dropped by 60 percent between 1990 and 1999, while its Gross Domestic Product (GDP) declined by 54 percent. This unprecedented economic collapse greatly contributed to the conditions under which organized crime thrives the most. Given the strong presence achieved by criminal groups in the old USSR and their access to substantial finances and foreign cash supplies, they were able to strongly influence the economic and political structures that emerged in the Commonwealth of Independent States since 1991.

Most important, the increase in organized crime had negative consequences for the development of democracy and the rule of law. Like developed criminal organizations elsewhere, the post-Soviet *Mafiya* obtained political clout by influencing economic development. Illicit funds — as in Latin America — created significant local political support bases for mafia bosses, who secured political power by corrupting officials, financing political campaigns, and running their own candidates (Lee III 1985–86: 148). Wolkow (1991) even claimed that the independence declarations of the republics after the August 1991 coup mainly aimed at perpetuating the "mafioso-clientelist party apparat structures" (1991: 39). Former Russian President Boris Yeltsin used the term "nomenklatura separatism" to describe the attitude of regional crime bosses and bureaucrats to defy the central government (Handelman 1994: 99).

Moreover, the criminalization of the power structures in the Soviet successor states contributed to the slow pace of economic reform (Frisby 1998: 37). As part of its conversion to capitalist ways of 'doing business,' mafia-controlled enterprises may attempt to monopolize the market through threats and violence. Criminal violence might also be employed against political parties, institutions, and groups who form the opposition. The *Mafiya* is also likely to use violence against trade unions (Timofeyev 1992: 169–170; Shelley 1999: 41). Varese (2001) noted that criminals participated in running mining operations in Russia. During the mid-1990s, OC involvement allegedly ended a strike in the mining city of Vorkuta "at gunpoint" (2001: 71).

The insufficiency of legal mechanisms in Russia's business law, combined with the lack of resources to enforce them, led scholars to anticipate that many legal companies would "be forced to rely on the mafia . . . . suggesting the possibility of greater entrenchment of the mafia in the economic and social life in Russia in the future" (Hendley, Ickes, Murrell, and Ryterman 1997: 39). Varese (2001) notes that this has indeed happened. Accordingly, the weakness of the Russian state contributed to the emergence of other actors providing protection. These include individuals in private security firms, law enforcement officials who offer private protection, and members of criminal organizations who render identical services, while the methods employed do not appear to differ between the three. For example, private banks make use of legal security companies whose employees are commissioned to recover debts without relying on legal channels. They are engaged in what Varese (2001) refers to as "the violent recovery of assets outside the provision of the law" (2001: 64). Even so, banks also hire members of criminal organizations for the same purpose. In fact, criminal groups, law enforcement agencies, and private security companies compete with each other for the provision of such services (*ibid.*, 65; also see Volkov 1999).

The emergence of the private security industry is also a consequence of the escalation of common criminal delinquency in Russia and other CIS republics. The USSR was drowning in a crime wave during the late 1980s. In 1989, more than two and a half million crimes were committed, 32 percent more than in 1988, and 61 percent more than in 1980 (Serio 1992: 55). Juvenile crime in the Soviet Union rose by 62 percent between 1980 and 1989, and by 21 percent from 1988 to 1989 (*ibid.*, 58). Violent crimes also increased rapidly. Murder and attempted murder increased by almost 29 percent during 1988–1989, rape and attempted rape by 24 percent, and violence resulting in serious bodily injury rose by over 38 percent during the same period (*ibid.*, 74). Crime rates continued to rise after the Soviet collapse and stabilized only during the mid-1990s. Still, Russia's 1999 murder rate was topped internationally only by that of Colombia (Varese 2001: 19–22).

Conclusion

In chapter 2 I proposed a synthesis of Frankfurt School and Gramscian concepts to explain the emergence of protection racket regimes. While the Soviet Union represents a very different socioeconomic system, perspectives by Gramsci and Horkheimer are nevertheless useful. Gramsci aimed to resolve in his work why a socialist revolution took place in Tsarist Russia but did not come about in the more advanced capitalist countries like Germany or Great Britain, as had been predicted by Marx. He concluded that the relative strength of hegemonic structures in the latter was key. Gramsci did not design his concepts with the Soviet experience in mind. It is debatable, for example, whether Soviet elites ever enjoyed hegemonic rule in the Gramscian sense, and whether the notion of *integral* hegemony is applicable in the Soviet case given the brutal nature and the immense human costs of the Stalinist experiment.

The concept of dominance is more fitting in the description of the Soviet experience. In Gramsci's understanding of hegemony, the agents of coercion, such as the law enforcement agencies and the militaries in advanced capitalist countries, may be indirectly present, while the hegemony of Soviet elites has relied on a far stronger dose of dominance. The Soviet experience, to use Gramscian terms, may be described as 'hegemony through dominance.' Regardless, the notion of *trasformismo*, the practice of "incorporating the leaders . . . . of potentially hostile groups" into the elite network for the purpose of broadening their power base, is applicable to the Soviet Union as well given the role played by criminals in the shadow economy (Femia 1981: 46). However, not only did black marketeers and criminals incorporate into the country's power structures, Soviet elites underwent their own criminal transformation and created the preconditions for the collaboration with black marketeers. Soviet elites were therefore similar to the Bolivian agrarian elites discussed in chapter 4, who turned criminal themselves and entered the drug trade to preserve the economic order and their social status in it.

Finally, Horkheimer (1988e: 132) viewed the Soviet Union as a racket. Protection, as previously noted, was the "archetype of domination," a principle that was evident irrespective of time and place, although it would manifest itself in accordance with the stipulations of that time and place (Horkheimer 1982: 35). The "new class" of the USSR was not only "a conspiring group" who put "their collective interests" before those of the public, but was in fact a structure of rackets rooted in a particular mode of production which contained and guarded the "lower orders" (Djilas 1959: 37–41; Horkheimer 1985a: 288; 1988e: 334). In the Soviet case, Horkheimer's (1985) comparison of the means of production to the weapon of a criminal is as applicable as his observation that coercion and injustice are the key attributes of racket rule (1985: 86,102; Stirk 1992: 142).[18]

The decline of Soviet elites may not be strictly definable in Gramscian terms; however, it went hand in hand with the evolution of Soviet organized crime as it became part of the power structures of the old USSR. According to Naylor (1993), an OC group evolves from a "predatory" to a "parasitical" and ultimately to a "symbiotic" stage (1993: 20–22). His model is useful, because it recognizes evolutionary processes at work. However, the stages of the evolution of Soviet mafia groups differ from those of their capitalist counterparts. To begin with, organized crime existed in prerevolutionary times and flourished during the Civil War in the *traditional* or first phase of its development (Chalidze 1977: 34–67; Handelman 1994: XIX; Frisby 1998: 32).[19] In the second stage, organized crime was largely confined during Stalin's totalitarian rule, in a fashion differing little from Nazi Germany and Fascist Italy. Even so, it continued to exist and grow within the Soviet prison system. Stage two, the *hibernation phase*, took place within the prison system itself. The next phase began after Stalin's death in 1953, the end of terrorist rule, and ushered in Khrushchev's program of liberalization. The new elites created by Stalin no longer wanted to live in fear but wished to maintain the economic system that preserved their social positions. However, their unwillingness to reform caused the economic stagnation that culminated during the Brezhnev era and resulted in the emergence of the shadow economy out of which Soviet organized crime ultimately arose.

Stage three, the *re-emergence phase* of the 1950s and 1960s, was represented by the appearance of the *tolkachi*, the informal local fixers, who did not misappropriate commodities per se but filled the gaps of the formal economy by overcoming the rigidities of the apparatus and the return of criminals into society after being released from the prison camp system. However, while the *tolkachi* contributed to the functioning of that system, the 'Soviet entrepreneurs' and the *avtoritey* in charge of the black market operations, who evolved in stage four, or the *consolidation phase*, were dysfunctional and parasitic because they fed off the formal economy which furthered economic decline. The merger between criminal groups and semicriminal elements in state and party occurred during this stage. Soviet organized crime was symbiotic in its integration into power structures and by turning into an important ally of elites. Yet, it remained parasitic because its resources were not geared toward the maintenance of the Soviet economy. The less productive the formal economy grew, the more important the crime groups in the shadow economy became. But the more the shadow economy grew, the less productive the formal one became.

The fifth stage may be called *ecliptic* as Soviet organized crime not only integrated into structures of power, as, for example, its counterparts in the United States or Sicily managed to do; but it came to play an important role, while remaining parasitic. In the process, however, criminal groups undermined the formal economy to such an extent that the latter essentially self-destructed. Thus, while the informal dealings of the *tolkachi* initially filled the gaps of the Soviet economy, the growth and the increased criminalization of the shadow economy reduced the latter to a supplier of its own needs. The last stage is the *transformative* one. It is a mirror image of the processes the former USSR has been undergoing since 1991. Like the formal economy, the Soviet *Mafiya* has also adapted to the conditions of capitalist methods of accumulation as well as the methods of modern capitalist crime groups. This is manifested, for example, by the participation of criminal groups in the drug trade, an activity in which Soviet organized crime partook only marginally until the 1980s. In addition, post-Soviet *Mafiya* groups internationalized their operations relatively quickly after the collapse of 1991 and, among others, established a presence in Germany, the United States, the Caribbean, and Latin America (*Die Woche.* May 11, 1994: 22; *Focus.* May 6, 1996: 52–64; Finckenauer and Waring 1998; Paoli 2001).

As previously argued, criminal organizations are scarcely ever equal or principal partners because elites generally do not abdicate control to preserve social power, but share it. Yet, there have been cases of organized criminal infiltration into state, economy, and society where the partnership has produced a new and qualitatively different phenomenon, the criminalized state. In such a regime strong OC groups become part of elite structures as equal and even principal partners. It remains to be seen whether the activities of organized crime in the former Soviet Union are temporary phenomena that will wane as the economic transformation continues and a civil society emerges. Will these criminal elites become 'civilized' after having secured their positions and the economy continues to recover? If not, the Russian state's continued evolution may have unforeseen consequences for domestic and international affairs.

Such developments may be furthered by the high crime rates the country has been experiencing. Many ordinary people in Russia, and other parts of the CIS, have come to associate crime and corruption with democratic and capitalist practices and feel insecure in their cities. Hence, they call for governments of law and order which place restrictions on civil and democratic rights. The strength of post-Soviet organized crime suggests that only a repressive solution, not unlike the totalitarian regimes of the 1920s and 1930s, may be able to subdue it. Given the volatile nature of present Russian politics, such a solution cannot be ruled out. In fact, developments in Russia since the March 2000 election of former secret service agent Vladimir Putin for president indicate that such a process may be under way.

Endnotes

1. Czech dissident author and former president Václav Havel does not refer to organized crime in his essay. Rather, he characterizes the sort of society which pretends that it does not exist to avoid contradicting the official truth of the "post-totalitarian" regime in the former East Bloc. He writes: " . . . . Life in the post-totalitarian system is corrupted by a web of deceit and lies: The power of the bureaucracy is called power of the people. The working class is enslaved in the name of the working class; the all encompassing humiliation of people is regarded as . . . . [their] definitive emancipation. The isolation from information is called access to information; manipulation by power is labeled public control of power, and the arbitrariness is referred to as the preservation of the rule of law. The suppression of culture is praised as its development; the extension of imperialism is coined assistance to the oppressed; the lack of freedom of expression [is called] the highest form of freedom. The election farce [is referred to as] the highest form of democracy; the prohibition of independent thinking [is taken as] scientific ideology [and] occupation [is] fraternal assistance. Power has to distort because it is caught in its own lies. It falsifies the past, the present and the future. It forges statistical data. It pretends there is no powerful police apparatus that is capable of anything. It pretends human rights are respected [and] that nobody is ever persecuted. It pretends that it is not afraid. It pretends that it does not pretend. People . . . . do not have to believe all the mystifications. [But they] have to behave in such a way as if [they] did. At least [they] have to accept it quietly, or maintain a good rapport with those who operate the mystifications. Therefore . . . . [people] have to live the lie. [A person] does not need to accept the falsehood. It suffices, that he [she] accepts life with it and in it. By doing so, he [she] already confirms the system, serves and creates it . . . . he [she] is the system" (Havel 1980: 18–19).

2. Yet McCauley (2001), in a more recent work, claimed that "nine thousand" criminal gangs "with thirty-five thousand members" had already existed in Soviet times "controlling" up to "60 percent of the economy" (2001: 75). Frisby (1998) also points to the existence of some nine thousand groups with a membership of 100,000 in the late 1990s (1998: 40). Renowned mafia scholar Letizia Paoli (2001) believes that some "ten thousand organized crime groups"

are operating in the Russian Federation, "one thousand six hundred" of which are involved in drug trafficking (2001: 1010).

3. One hundred and fifty of them were considered large, with a membership between one thousand five hundred and two thousand (Raith 1994: 89).

4. It may seem exaggerated that Russian organized crime could threaten the security of the world. One officer from the former Soviet Union's military intelligence service, the *Glavnoye Razvedyvatelnoye Upravlenye*, (GRU), who defected to the West following the country's disintegration, even claimed that Russia was "a nation led by gangsters — gangsters who have nuclear weapons" (Lunev 1998: 12). The possible availability of weapons-grade plutonium to criminal groups and their sale to terrorist organizations and so-called rogue states has been considered such a threat (*Frankfurter Rundschau.* July 14, 1993: 1). However, Russian journalist Victor Orlov strongly doubted that criminal groups had access to nuclear materials (*Moscow News.* Oct. 21–27, 1994: 3). Moreover, during the so-called Plutonium Affair in Germany of the mid-1990s, the German Secret Service, the *Bundesnachrichtendienst* (BND) had allegedly prearranged the sale of weapons-grade plutonium from the Russian black market, which was subsequently 'captured' with great fanfare (Ulfkotte 1997: 241–242). Also, while there may be high profits for criminal organizations in the nuclear materials trafficking, it is a risky business. Other activities, such as drug trafficking or prostitution, while not quite as profitable, are less likely to arouse the attention of Russian security forces. The same logic does not necessarily apply to some of the Chechen criminal organizations.

5. Former President Yeltsin had been deeply implicated with corruption. Allegedly, there existed a "circle of cronies surrounding President Boris Yeltsin" that funneled large amounts of money into their private coffers (*The Globe and Mail.* June 15, 1999: A1, A16). Kneen (2000) pointed out that former Russian Prime Minister Primakov was removed, as was his government in May 1999, after he gave the go-ahead to investigations "into the financial affairs of the presidential family" (2000: 360).

6. The Observatoire Geopolitique des Drogues' 1993 annual report also noted that post-Soviet OC groups shipped two hundred and thirty-eight thousand tons of nonferrous metals from the Ural mines to Latvia where it was sold to Western buyers. However, the report also pointed out that these criminal groups had switched to drug trafficking (OGD 1993: 86).

7. This source does not differentiate between different drugs.

8. In 1993, there were thirty-one casinos in the Russian capital, while even Las Vegas in the United States had only twenty-five (OGD 1993: 87).

9. The breakup of organizations, such as the *Komitat Gosudarstvennoi Bezopastnosti* (KGB) allegedly had the result that first-rate intelligence professionals who can go "through 90 percent of existing alarm systems, and who know how to disappear without any trace, in any society, under any conditions" joined criminal organizations who offer a more attractive pay (Maximenkov and Namiesniowski 1994: 12).

10. In a speech held at the First All-Union Conference of Socialist Industry, February 4, 1931, Soviet leader Joseph Stalin talked of the necessity to catch up quickly: "One feature of the history of old Russia was the continual beatings she suffered because of her backwardness. She was beaten by the Turkish beys. She was beaten by the Polish and Lithuanian gentry. She was beaten by the British and French capitalists. She was beaten by the Japanese barons. All beat her — because of her backwardness, military backwardness, cultural backwardness, political backwardness, industrial backwardness, agricultural backwardness. . . . Do you want our socialist fatherland to be beaten and to lose its independence? If you do not want this, you must put an end to its backwardness in the shortest possible time and develop genuine Bolshevik tempo in building up a socialist system of economy. There is no other way. That is why Lenin said on the eve of the October Revolution: Either perish, or overtake and outstrip the advanced capitalist countries. We are fifty or a hundred years behind the advanced countries. We must do good this distance in ten years. Either we do it, or we shall be crushed. This is what our obligations to the workers and peasants of the USSR dictate to us" (Stalin 1947: 398–399).

11. The former Soviet Union had one of the largest resource bases on the globe. It pumped more oil and gas out of the ground than any other country. In 1977, it was assessed that the Soviets controlled 32 percent of global oil and 40 percent of global gas reserves. Similarly, the former USSR's share of the raw materials on earth was roughly calculated to be 35 percent of the total. At that time, the Soviets had the global production of 35 percent of manganese, 32 percent of chromium, 28 percent of uranium, 27 percent of iron ore, 20 percent of nickel, 20 percent of vanadium, 15 percent of copper, and 14 percent of bauxite (*Informationen zur Politischen Bildung.* 1979). On the territory of the CIS one can still find nearly all strategic metals and other important resources on the globe. For example, chromium, magnesium, nickel, platinum, silver and titanium, six of the twenty-five mineral raw materials needed to build the US space shuttle, were imported from the former USSR. In the case of silver and titanium, the former USSR sold more than half of its annual production to the United States (Kidron 1983: 28; see also The Economist Intelligence Unit. 1996–1997).

12. The great failure of the collectivization of agriculture was demonstrated by the fact that two generations after the 1917 Revolution the privately owned plots in the USSR, representing 3 percent of the total arable land, produced over 25 percent of the annual output of Soviet agriculture (Grossman 1977a: 26).

13. It is necessary to differentiate between the actors who managed the informal economy of the former Soviet Union and those of other informal economies. While an informal economy may contain criminal elements, these activities in the USSR were overwhelmingly conducted by real criminals and semicriminal representatives in state and party. For the purpose of distinguishing between the two informal economies, I will use the term *shadow economy* in the case of the Soviet Union.

14. According to Max Weber, the ideal type of bureaucracy is based on (a) a high degree of specialization and a clearly defined division of labor, with tasks distributed as official duties; (b) a hierarchical structure of authority which clearly circumscribed areas of command and responsibility; (c) the establishment of a formal body of rules to govern the operation of the organization; (d) administration based upon written records; (e) impersonal relationships

between staff and clients; (f) recruitment of personnel on the basis of ability and technical knowledge; (g) long-term employment, promotion on the basis of seniority or merit, and a fixed salary (Gerth and Mills 1958: 196–244).

15. Timofeyev (1992) describes the situation in the post-Soviet successor states as "meta-corruption . . . . a stage beyond corruption; it is the corruption of the corrupters, when corrupt power no longer conceals its corruptness . . . . This is the process now under way in the CIS. [It] is a new form of anomie, anomie squared" (1992: 163–164).

16. Raith (1994) observed that the intermediary function of the Soviet *tolkachi* was similar to the task performed by the Sicilian *gabellotti* from whom the *Sicilian Mafia* evolved (1994: 159). The *gabellotti* were the local strong men on which Sicilian absentee landowners relied to manage and suppress the peasants on their estates.

17. For a useful description of Russian criminal organizations from the Tsarist to the Brezhnev era, see Varese 2001: 145–166.

18. Horkheimer (1988e) certainly viewed the Stalinist Soviet Union as a racket regime. He wrote: "If the goal of society according to Marx and Lenin is the [creation of the realm] of freedom, then the so-called Communist countries are no closer to it than the capitalist ones . . . . [The difference is that in the Communist countries] not even the ruling dictatorial rackets enjoy any pleasures because their individual members feel insecure with each other because of the brutal competition. Nobody is certain in the evening, if he [/she] still belongs to the privileged the next day, or if he [or she] has to share the miserable fate of the dominated, assuming nothing worse happens. If in Russia, a bourgeois society had emerged instead of the false proletarian one, without having been interrupted by Fascism, those on top and on the bottom would do a lot better" (1988e: 132).

19. For example, in early 1919, Lenin's entourage was stopped by bandits on the outskirts of Moscow, where the furious revolutionary leader was relieved of his wallet and means of transportation (Payne 1964: 526–527).

Chapter 7

Beyond Modern Capitalism: Mercantile Piracy

War, trade and piracy,
are triune, not separable.

(Johann Wolfgang von Goethe 1972: 329).

Organized crime is not limited to modern times but has existed historically. This examination focuses on one of the oldest criminal practices known to humanity: piracy. The analysis of mercantile piracy practiced from the sixteenth to the eighteenth century as a form of organized crime which developed in a socioeconomic formation other than modern capitalism is relevant. Piracy shares important features with modern organized crime, including the linkage between criminal groups and elites. Of particular significance is the practice of privateering, which represented a legalization of piracy by the emerging European nation-states during this period.

Introduction

Piracy has existed for thousands of years and ended as a large-scale activity only during the nineteenth century, although it has been occurring sporadically since. Of late, the practice has had a revival, particularly in some of the coastal regions of Southeast Asia (Gottschalk and Flanagan 2000: 92). Unlike most forms of organized crime in existence, the dimensions of crime, state, economy, and society overlap to such an extent in the case of piracy in general, and mercantile piracy in particular, that it leads one to conclude that this phenomenon qualitatively developed beyond organized crime. Pirate economies practiced a mode of production based on appropriation without exchange, while a political leadership — directly or indirectly — commanded the raids, contributed to the gear, and/or shared in the spoils. Indeed, their societies fully accepted and even endorsed the practice.

Piracy: A Short History

The *Brockhaus Enzyklopädie*, the German equivalent of the *British Encyclopaedia*, describes piracy, or sea robbery, as "acts of violence, kidnapping, or plunder on the high seas committed by a private ship or airplane against another ship or airplane. It also includes the seizure of a ship by a mutineering crew or passengers" (*Brockhaus* 1972: 637).

Today, piracy is viewed as a romantic and adventurous trade. This image has been produced by Hollywood swashbuckling movies, such as *Captain Blood* (1925), *The Sea Hawk* (1940), *Hook* (1991), and *Cutthroat Island* (1995). In the imagination of Western peoples, this activity is often identified with the several generations of criminal enterprises of some 1,500–2,000 English, French, and other European pirates prowling the Caribbean and the North American coastline on a few dozen ships at one time or another between the mid-sixteenth and early eighteenth century. Most of the known pirate captains who inspired these images, such as Francis Drake, Henry Morgan, Edward 'Black Beard' Teach, William Kidd, Bartholomew Roberts, and 'Calico' Jack Rackham — whose crew included the women buccaneers Anne Bonny and Mary Read — can be traced to this time and place (Schreiber 1983: 48; Cordingly 1997: 202). Cordingly pointed out:

> Reason tells us that pirates were no more than common criminals, but we still see them as figures of romance. We associate them with daring deeds on the Spanish main, with rakish black schooners and tropical islands and sea chests overflowing with gold and silver coins . . . . The picture which most of us have turns out to be a blend of historical facts overlaid with three centuries of ballads, melodramas, epic poems, romantic novels, adventure stories, comic strips, and films (*ibid.*, xiii– xiv).[1]

Indeed, the lack of information and the dubious nature of much of what has been written shows another similarity between piracy and organized crime. Very little modern historical research on piracy exists. Pleticha (1997) wrote: "For historical scholarship piracy remains a . . . . marginal issue largely overlooked by . . . . historians. In the literature, one is more likely to encounter a few traces, a few meager [primary] sources and accounts from witnesses, and more minimizations and idealizations" (1997: 8).[2]

Although the focus of this investigation is piracy in the Caribbean from the sixteenth to the eighteenth century, the topic merits some general observations as the trade has not been confined to that time and place. As Gosse (1946) indicates, "it may be assumed that very shortly after men began the transport of goods from one point to another various enterprising individuals arose who saw profit in intercepting these goods on the way" (1946: 1). The oldest historical reference to robbery at sea is the travel log of one *Wên-Amon* found in an ancient Egyptian papyrus dating back to 1100 BC. It described piracy on what was then called the coast of Phoenicia in the eastern Mediterranean (Ormerod 1924: 75; Pleticha 1997:

9). The ancient Greek historian Thucydides (1985) also reported on piracy. The mythical King Minos of Crete "was the first person to organize a navy" to rule the eastern Mediterranean and as the Greek historian deduced, to "put down piracy" (1985: 37). Thucydides portrayed piracy as an age-old practice and as a "common profession both among the Hellenes [Greeks] and among the barbarians [foreigners] who lived on the coast and the islands" in his classic work on the Peloponnesian War (431–404 BC) (*ibid.*).

The chronicler Plutarch, who lived in the first century after Christ, recounted the naval campaign of the Roman General Pompey against the Cilician pirates in the Mediterranean in the year 67 BC. These pirates from Asia Minor had played a secondary role in the slave uprising of Spartacus a few years before. Apparently, the leaders of the revolt had arranged transport from the Italian mainland to Sicily for the slave army to ignite the uprising there. However, the Cilicians reneged on the agreement, and Spartacus' rebellion was defeated shortly thereafter. The Cilician pirates were also a major threat to Rome's shipping lines, particularly its grain supply. Thus, the Senate ordered the general to 'clean up' what the Romans called the *Mare Nostro*, which is Latin for 'Our Sea.' With some 500 ships and 120,000 troops, Pompey swept the Mediterranean Sea from west to east in a mere three months. The Romans destroyed hundreds of pirate ships, killed ten thousand Cilicians, and took some twenty thousand prisoners. Even so, the Romans' success was largely due to the fact that they managed to catch the pirates off guard and pick them off in small groups. Pompey was likely fortunate that he did not have to face the combined pirate fleet in a naval engagement (Plutarch n.d. The Internet Classics Archive; Clough n. d.: 376–382; Pleticha 1997: 10–11; Defoe 1999: 29). Still, the number of ships and troops was considerable compared to other Roman campaigns. Caesar commanded less than half the number of legionaries during the height of the Gallic Wars in 52 and 53 BC (Bruce 1986: 9, 29). The extent of the operation not only tells the reader of the threat piracy posed to Roman trade, but also hints at the importance of this practice to the Cilicians' economy.

In *The Life of Charlemagne*, written between 817 and 837 AD, the Frankish chronicler Einhard mentioned the appearance of large fleets of Norman, or Viking pirate ships. The Normans raided the coasts of Britain, Ireland, France, and Germany. Many coastal cities, such as Hamburg on Germany's northern shore, in 845 fell victim to them. Even larger cities situated further inland were not safe from attack. The small and maneuverable ships of the Vikings allowed them to enter shallow waters and move up rivers. Sailing up the Seine river, the Normans conquered and plundered Paris three times between 845 and 861. Charlemagne's old capital city, Aix-la-Chapelle — today the German city of Aachen — was also pillaged. The Vikings even navigated their ships down river from the Baltic to the Black Sea, and laid siege to Constantinople, the capital of the Byzantine Empire. However, this particular venture failed (Gosse 1946: 88–90; Einhard 1969: 39–40; Stein 1974: 402–406; Franke 1974: 85–88).

The activities of sea robbers in the Caribbean were certainly dwarfed by the so-called *Ladrone* pirates in the Far East, led by the Chinese female pirate Cheng I Sao, which means 'wife of Cheng I,' although she is also referred to as a "Dragon Lady" (Murray 1987: 71; Ellms 1996: 171–190). She commanded a fleet of some two hundred ocean-going vessels, each armed with twenty to thirty cannons and carrying crews up to four hundred strong, operating along the Chinese coastline in the early nineteenth century. Cheng I Sao's career began in 1801, after marrying the pirate Cheng I. By 1805, his ships were in complete control of the coastal waters of southern China. After Cheng I's death in 1807, his wife assumed command of the fleet. Every attempt by the Chinese imperial navy to dislodge her proved futile. The Chinese lost sixty-three ships in 1808 and were helpless against her pirate fleet. Still, following a government amnesty, in which Cheng I Sao secured the best of terms for herself and her pirates, she and most of her forces surrendered in 1810. In fact, her lieutenants entered government service and hunted down those of her captains who had refused to submit (Murray 1987: 144; Cordingly 1997: 75–78).

The decline of piracy in the nineteenth century had a number of causes. One important factor has been technological progress. Steam ships proved superior to the pirates still relying on sails. Those who switched their mode of transportation did not survive for long because of the necessity to enter harbors to load coal. Furthermore, the introduction of wireless communications made it possible to call for immediate relief. The efforts of the United States and British navies to protect their countries' trade played an important role in the almost complete eradication of piracy. Recently, the practice has had a comeback, particularly along the sea lanes in the coastal regions of Southeast Asia (Schreiber 1983: 11; Vagg 1994; *Der Spiegel.* June 7, 1999: 173; Gottschalk and Flanagan 2000).

The Political Economy of Violence

In the drama *Faust II* by the German playwright Johann Wolfgang von Goethe, the main character Mephisto observed that war, trade and piracy could not be separated from one another (Von Goethe 1972: 329). For the Cilicians and the Vikings, few differences existed between these activities. These pirates came from societies whose economies depended on this practice, and whose leaders led the raids, contributed to the gear, and shared in the loot. Thucydides also wrote that pirate leaders of Greek antiquity undertook their raids out of "self-interest and in order to support the weak among their own people . . . . and by plundering . . . . they would gain their livelihood. At this time such a profession, so far from being regarded disgraceful, was considered quite honorable" (Thucydides 1985: 37).

Piracy as an economic activity required access to a market where plundered goods could be traded. The same is also a necessity for an individual drug trafficker and his or her wares. However, a criminal practice, piracy included, takes on different dimensions when it becomes an economic activity in which large segments of a country's or region's population participate for their livelihood and which is organized by a political leadership. Ormerod (1924) described piracy in antiquity as "a means of production," which was certainly not confined to that time and place (1924: 67–69). For example, Senior (1976) claimed that England was a "nation which had grown accustomed to living by plunder at sea," while its sailors "had already gained a reputation as arch-pirates by 1600" (1976: 7–8).

Gosse (1946) viewed the emergence and decline of pirate organizations as cyclical progressions which displayed some likeness to Naylor's (1993) evolutionary perspectives on organized crime (1993: 20–22). In his view, first came the stage of "outlaws," when "a few individuals would band together . . . . owning one or . . . . few vessels and attack only the weakest of merchantmen" (Gosse 1946: 1–2). This corresponds to Naylor's "predatory" stage (1993: 20–22).

The second step involved "organization," as the larger groups either assimilated the smaller ones or simply eliminated them (Gosse 1946: 1–2). While Naylor (1993) termed this stage "parasitical," his own explanation included a reference to the growth of organized crime groups who, for example, increase their reach from the local to the regional if not national level (1993: 20–22). Such a process would also include the assimilation of smaller groups or their physical destruction as a result of gang warfare.

During the next phase of its evolution, the "pirate organization" attained the "status of an independent state" which possessed the capacity to make alliances with other states against common foes (Gosse 1946: 1–2). This again compares to Naylor's (1993) "symbiotic" phase, in which an organized crime group blends with society and economy, while its reach extends to the international level (1993: 20–22). Gosse (1946) observed further: "What had been piracy became war, and in that war the vessels of both sides were pirates to the other and subject to the same treatment" (1946: 1–2). Finally, the cycle closed with "the victory of one side" which resulted in the "breakup of the naval organization of the other"(*ibid.*). Its components "would be reduced to the position of outlaw bands," and returned to the first stage of their evolution (*ibid.*).[3]

The merger of these dimensions of crime, political leadership (state), economy, and society generates a phenomenon of a different quality. Depending on the degree to which they converge, and on the perspective of the observer, piracy is either a criminal act or a form of warfare, that, oddly enough, is no longer criminal. The issues require a discussion of the notions of so-called letters of marque, privateering, and piracy on the Spanish main between the sixteenth to eighteenth century.

Letters of marque "are authority formerly given to private persons [namely the privateers] to fit out an armed ship and use it to attack, capture, and plunder enemy merchant ships in time of war" (Hornby, Gateby, and Wakefield 1970: 529). Originally, such letters of marque had been used to correct a private transgression committed in peacetime. Let's say a French trader had his or her goods stolen in the Netherlands, and would not gain compensation for the loss through legal or diplomatic means. This person could then be granted a letter of marque by his or her government which permitted the capture of a Dutch merchant ship by a privateer as a reimbursement for the loss. The privateer might be the trader who had suffered the offense or somebody designated by him or her. Privateers acted on a commission recognized under international law. Still, the practice also reflected the absence of international law as it initially arose due to the lack of permanent diplomatic representations to settle such conflicts (Thomson 1994: 22). It was standard procedure that a letter of marque specifically named the country whose vessels one was permitted to capture legally, while stiff penalties could be exacted if the property of other nations was taken (Reinhardt 1997: 22–29, 167, 186; also see Andrews 1964: 5; Hoppé 1972: 36; Preston and Wise 1979: 214; Cordingly 1997: 219–220).

While letters of marque were initially used to right a private wrong in times of peace, governments also came to rely on the practice during periods of official hostilities. The granting of letters of marque created an auxiliary navy designed for the sole purpose of "damaging the enemy nation's war effort by cutting into its trade and thus its ability to raise and supply armies and navies" (*Ibid.*, 22). The practice represented the privatization of warfare and degenerated into the legalization of piracy. Ormerod (1924) observed that the equivalent of letters of marque and privateering already existed in antiquity: "Buccaneering enterprises . . . . were the natural outcome of the exclusive commercial policy pursued by . . . . [Greek city] states, as the Spaniards also found to their cost in the seventeenth century" (1924: 156).

The first English letters of marque were issued to attack French and Portuguese shipping in the thirteenth century. The late-fourteenth-century Hanseatic pirates, also called the *Victual Brothers*, led by Klaus Störtebeker, who became the scourge of the Baltic and North seas, represent another early example. Hanseatic League merchants and aristocrats were initially allied with the pirates in a war against Denmark. They supplied the *Victual Brothers*, took part in their expeditions, and shared in their profits. After the end of the conflict, the pirates turned against their former sponsors and attacked all shipping in the Baltic and in the North Sea later on (Gosse 1946: 90–92; Burbach 1973: 27–29; Thomson 1994: 22; Pleticha 1997: 15–18). The alliance between the *Victual Brothers* and the Hanseatic League and the subsequent shift describes a pattern that can be observed elsewhere.

Still, the difference between pirates and privateers was largely marginal and a question of perspective. The main distinction between the two was that privateers had a government which protected and harbored them. In times of war, pirates could find lawful employment under this semilegal blanket and make out well. A captured privateer was often executed for piracy. Between wars, the same men, in need of work, took to the illegal side because of the promise of wealth (Reinhardt 1997: 22; Galvin 2000: 5). The practice evolved further and also became an instrument of informal warfare and nonstate violence against former, future, or potential enemies during times of peace. For example, England's Elizabeth I ordered her privateers, the *Sea Hawks*, against Spain's treasure fleets, although the two countries were not engaged in official hostilities. King James I of England, who succeeded Elizabeth to the throne, considered privateering immoral and unsuccessfully tried to stop the practice (Senior 1976: 8).

From the sixteenth to the early nineteenth century, this shifting pattern of legal and illegal employment opportunities was repeated quite a few times as England, France, the Netherlands, Spain, the Hapsburg Empire, and various smaller European powers fought several wars amongst each other. After the outbreak of the War of the League of Augsburg (1688–1697), in which Britain was allied with the Hapsburg Empire, the Netherlands and Spain against France, King William III pardoned pirates and turned them into hired privateers. The end of the conflict resulted in an increase in piracy as the privateers again turned to the illegal side of the profession. Similarly, after the end of the Spanish War of Succession (1701–1713), which pitted France, under Louis XIV, against most European powers including Britain, many unemployed privateers became pirates once again. They set up bases in the Bahamas and raided the North American coast (Defoe 1999: xxi–xxii).[4] Rankin (1969) commented on the former privateers put out of business by peace: "Poverty drove them to crime and experience drove them to piracy" (1969: 82).

The impact of the 'private navies' on warfare was considerable. For example, during the Napoleonic Wars, French privateers apparently captured some eleven thousand British ships. The British themselves issued some ten thousand letters of marque to their own privateers. During the War of 1812, American privateers captured over 1,300 British ships. In fact, it was the havoc wreaked on international trade during this period, by privateers of all colors on shipping of all countries, that led to an international agreement to end the practice during the next major European conflict. In 1856, during the Crimean War, the Great Powers met in Paris and established an international regime of conduct on seizures of goods during wartime. Of the major powers at the time, only the United States failed to sign, and with the outbreak of the American Civil War in 1861, both North and South issued letters of marque against each other (Hoppé 1972: 36; McIntyre 1975: 184–189; Preston and Wise 1979: 214; Pleticha 1997: 41; Cordingly 1997: xvii).[5]

Piracy as State-Organized Crime

Analogous to the cases of modern organized crime already discussed, sixteenth to eighteenth century piracy could flourish only because of the collaboration of states, in particular, the governments of Britain, France, and the Netherlands, and because of the mercantilist economic policies they pursued. These policies were designed to build up the wealth of a country and pay for standing armies and navies. While early mercantilist economists believed that state power derived from access to precious metals, others realized that gold and silver could be amassed by maintaining a trade surplus with other countries. For that purpose, the state guarded a country's commerce, industry, and agriculture; regulated the flow of trade; exploited colonies; and promoted merchant shipping (Winslow 1948: 13; Crane and Amavi 1991: 5–6; Short 1993: 9).[6]

After 1492, Spain and Portugal found immense new sources of wealth in the Americas, from which they excluded other European nations. The Dutch, English, and French could watch the power shift toward Spain and Portugal or find means to share in the wealth. One option open to them was going to war. However, the Hapsburg Empire was the dominant military and naval power in Europe, and this course of action was a perilous one. Indeed, Preston and Wise (1979) pointed out that the Spanish infantry soldiers of the time were renowned for their training and discipline. Moreover, a Spanish-led naval force had imposed a decisive defeat on the Turks in the battle of Lepanto in 1571. They noted further: "Spain dominated the sixteenth century because she was enormously wealthy and could maintain during war time a great professional army" (1979: 106, 123).

A less precarious alternative, that would generate a similarly desirable outcome, involved forming alliances with pirates. Although at peace, the governments of England, France, and the Netherlands issued letters of marque to 'their' pirates directing them to engage the Spanish treasure fleets. In return, the pirates had to share their plunder with the governments protecting them (Chambliss 1989: 185–186; also see Pleticha 1997: 20; Galvin 2000: 21–49).

The English pirate-privateer, Francis Drake, received financial and material support from Elizabeth I. From one excursion Drake made a profit of 4,700 percent and handed over sufficient booty to allow his sovereign to finance the English government and all its expenditures for some seven years. Officially, and in the presence of the envoy presenting the diplomatic protests of the government of his Catholic Majesty, King Phillip II of Spain, the Queen distanced herself from the pirates. Yet unofficially, she contributed financially to the fitting of their vessels, profited from these ventures herself, and welcomed the contributions to the English treasury made by the likes of John Hawkins and his nephew Francis Drake. The latter also received a knighthood for his efforts (*Ibid.*; also see Schulz 1971: 27; Hampden 1997: 332). Undoubtedly, the continued English privateer-pirate attacks against Spanish ships crossing the Atlantic figured highly in the reasoning of Philip II when he ordered the Great Armada against England in 1588.

In order to minimize the damage done by pirates the Spanish adopted the convoy system for their treasure fleets in 1561. However, pirates responded by attacking in large formations themselves. Indeed, in 1628, Dutch Admiral Piet Heyn, in command of some thirty ships and two thousand sailors and troops, captured the entire Spanish treasure fleet off the coast of Cuba and made off with "nearly 15 million guilders worth of booty" (Galvin 2000: 37, 47–49).

English privateer-pirate leader Henry Morgan worked similarly. Alexander Olivier Exquemelin, who sailed with Morgan, recorded the pirate's exploits in a volume published in 1678. Like Drake a century earlier, although on a larger scale involving far more ships and 'troops,' the buccaneer leader, supplied with letters of marque from the governor of Jamaica, attacked Spanish shipping and plundered cities on the Caribbean coast, although England and Spain were not at war. Morgan's most famous raid in 1673 targeted the city of Panama, which he sacked (Exquemelin 1983: 235–241).[7]

As with Drake, the government in London officially disowned Morgan, claiming that his actions were beyond its control and not representative of official policy. Even so, Morgan not only was knighted for his efforts, but was appointed Lieutenant-Governor of Jamaica and put in charge of suppressing piracy in the Caribbean. (*Ibid.*, 117; Reinhardt 1997: 48). This is reminiscent of Horkheimer's (1985b) observation that "the circumstances of domestic and foreign policy" determine whether a "bandit leader, condottiere, guerilla, [or] racketeer" is categorized as "warrior" or "criminal" (1985b: 269). Cordingly (1997) wrote of the pirates-privateers Henry Morgan and Francis Drake:

> Whether Morgan was a pirate, a corsair, or a privateer is a matter of debate. The Spanish regarded him as a corsair, and since some of the most spectacular raids were carried out when England was at peace with Spain, those actions, like those of Francis Drake, were acts of piracy. But Morgan always carried a commission from the governor of Jamaica so that technically he was a privateer. He no doubt simply regarded himself as a soldier fighting the enemies . . . of England. The one label we can give him is that of buccaneer . . . . which applied to several generations of fortune hunters who roamed the Caribbean for plunder (1997: 41).

The Caribbean of Henry Morgan was also home to what Gosse (1946) would describe as pirate organizations that had attained statelike qualities. Morgan's Jamaica differed little from the French island colony of Tortuga, a 'pirate state' from which the buccaneers of various nations raided Spanish shipping and coastal cities in the Americas. New Providence in the Bahamas was another pirate haven (Exquemelin 1983: 117–121; Reinhardt 1997: 75–83; Galvin 2000: 75–108). The nineteenth-century Chinese pirates led by Cheng I, and later on his widow — whose military strength turned them into an organization with statelike qualities — also operated from a stronghold that was not easily accessible, situated south of Guangzhou (Canton) on the Chinese coastline (Murray 1987: 68–69).

Conclusion

Piracy-privateering added a unique dimension to the international conflicts that took place from the sixteenth to the nineteenth century, which remained relatively unexplored in the literature on European state making. Tilly (1993) among others, discussed the role of violence and war in that process. As noted previously, he referred to European state making during the sixteenth century as "organized violence" and "organized crime" (1993: 169–191). Schwartz (1994) also explored the relationship between the monopoly of violence and military conquest during the rise of the Western state (1994: 10–42). However, neither greatly discusses the role of piracy. Conversely, Galvin (2000) and Thomson (1994) provided excellent examinations of this issue. Still, few scholars are as succinct and clear-cut as critical criminologist William J. Chambliss (1989), who described Caribbean piracy as a form of "state-organized crime" because "the state specifically instructed selected individuals to engage in criminal acts," even though in England, France, and Holland piracy was a crime punishable by death (1989: 185–186). Chambliss also compared the practice to the activities of US intelligence agencies who collaborated with criminal organizations during the Cold War (*ibid.*).

Regardless, the transfer of war-making powers to private individuals, and the reliance on and sanction of private nonstate violence during conflict or peace implied that European states like Britain or France lacked important resources and overcame this shortcoming through temporary alliances with criminals. Pirates not only came to defend existing elites but frequently merged with them or had derived from them. However, once pirates-privateers were no longer required or even deemed dangerous, they were treated as criminals by nation-states. This is explicit in the case of Britain: Once its hegemonic status had been secured, the Royal Navy went after pirates to protect the empire's trade. For example, during the 1720s, after the War of the Spanish Succession, British warships hunted down most of the pirates in the Caribbean within a few years. The merchant protests in British North America helped to end the practices of their corrupt colonial governors, who harbored pirates in return for spoils. The hegemonic status implied the decline of mercantilism and the rise of free trade under the British flag (Reinhardt 1997: 30, 72, 125). The decline of piracy holds some important insights for the struggle against modern organized crime which will be discussed next.

Endnotes

1. For information on Hollywood pirate films, see Parish (1995). The following anecdote about Klaus Störtebeker, the leader of the *Victual Brothers*, who raided shipping in the Baltic and North Seas during the late fourteenth century, is typical pirate lore. In 1402, this German pirate was captured and condemned to death by beheading in the city of Hamburg. Störtebeker allegedly made the following bargain with the court. He requested to be executed first, but those of his companions standing in line behind him awaiting their turn, whom he would manage to walk by without his head in place, were to go free. After decapitation, Störtebeker allegedly stood up and passed by four of his comrades before the executioner tripped him (Burbach 1973: 28).

2. An analysis of piracy must rely on a few primary sources and on official naval annals. Some of these sources, which I also employed, include: *Sir Francis Drake: Pirat im Dienst der Queen*, which originally appeared in English, is a collection of reports, documents, and accounts by Drake and his contemporaries (Hampden 1997). Alexandre Olivier

Exquemelin's book, *The Buccaneers of America*, originally published in Amsterdam, Holland, by Jan ten Hoorn in 1678 under the title *De Americaenschen Zee-Roovers*, is also one of the few reports by an actual pirate who sailed with the buccaneer Henry Morgan. I am working with the edited German translation (Exquemelin 1983). William Dampier who wrote *New Voyage around the World*, published in 1697, was also a pirate, albeit an unsuccessful one. His account is of particular interest because of his descriptions of the geography, foods, wildlife, and different peoples he met during his journey. Besides, Dampier's work contains references to marooning, a common punishment among pirates, which is said to have inspired Daniel Defoe's novel *Robinson Crusoe* (Dampier 1977; Cordingly 1997: 137–138). *The General History of the Pyrates*, published in London, England, in 1724, contains the bibliographies of the best-known pirate captains who sailed the Spanish main. Originally, one Charles Johnson was named as the writer of the work. However, in 1932, the authorship of Johnson was challenged by scholars claiming that Daniel Defoe was the originator of *The General History of the Pyrates*. Cordingly maintained in his book, which appeared in 1997, that the dispute was over and that Johnson had again been confirmed as the writer of the work (*ibid.*). However, I purchased a 1999 reprint which featured Defoe as the author. Charles Elm's, *The Pirates' Own Book*, which was printed in Boston, Massachusetts, in 1837, draws considerably on *The General History of the Pyrates* (Ellms 1996). Its value lies mostly in the description of non-Western pirates. The book describes, for example, the *Jossamee* pirates in the Persian Gulf, who preyed on the shipping of the British East India Company in the late eighteenth century, or the *Ladrone* pirates who virtually controlled the shipping along the southern Chinese coast in the early nineteenth century (Ellms 1996: 17–34, 171–190). Other period sources are provided by the reports of the Hakluyt Society, which focus on the travels of English privateers during the late sixteenth century (Andrews 1959). As far as more recent research is concerned, I was fortunate to be situated in Halifax, Nova Scotia, Canada, a city with historical links to piracy and privateering, whose university libraries contain a considerable number of volumes on the subject. To name a few recent works, Galvin (2000) produced an excellent study of the politics behind Caribbean piracy in his work *Patterns of Pillage*. Thomson (1994) also provided a first-rate analysis of this issue. Her work, titled *Mercenaries, Pirates, and Sovereigns*, studied the activities of nonstate agents, such as pirates, who used private violence in the name of the state and for their own gain (Thomson 1994). Other recent publications include Reinhardt's (1997) *Pirates and Piracy* or *Under The Black Flag* by Cordingly (1997). While these works are informative, they are largely descriptive and tend to rely on the old sources discussed above.

3. Pirates and organized crime groups differ here. While Gosse's pirates fight each other on the international level, it should be maintained that organized crime groups are at least as likely to cooperate at that stage. For example, as noted earlier, the February 1993 confiscation of one ton of cocaine with a street value estimated by Russian authorities of US$200 million hints at the cooperation between Colombian and post-Soviet criminal groups. There have also been reports of 'summits' between different national organized crime groups to establish a division of labor and "international hierarchies of crime" (Handelman 1994: 180, 239). Conversely, while organized crime groups tend to be made up of members of the same ethnic background, pirate crews, in the Caribbean, at least, were often multinational and multi-ethnic. For example, those who served under Henry Morgan were English, Dutch, French, Italian, Portuguese, mulatto, and Black (Cordingly 1997: 15).

4. There has been a criminal continuum in geographic terms in the case of the Bahamas, which was initially a hideout for pirates during the seventeenth and eighteenth centuries. The islands then became a base for blockade runners supplying the Confederacy during the American Civil War. The Bahamas were subsequently used by rum smugglers during the prohibition era of the 1920s in the United States. More recently, the islands have been a base for cocaine traffickers from South America (Schreiber 1983: 54; Bullington 1991; Domínguez 1998).

5. Conversely, Crowhurst (1989) observed that the eleven thousand ships captured by the French "between 1793 and 1814" represented "no more than about two and a half percent of all British shipping" (1989: 31).

6. Much of the silver produced in the Spanish silver mines in the Americas ended up across Western Europe, including Holland, France, the Northern Italian city of Genoa, England, and Germany, while only about five percent remained in Spain. The seventeenth-century French Navy Minister Colbert believed that "the more trade a country has with Spain, the more silver it has" (Galeano 1982: 34–36).

7. According to Exquemelin, the raiders displayed the utmost brutality during these ventures. He wrote: "Now they began to extort the prisoners with the most cruel tortures. A sixty-year-old Portuguese . . . . was whipped for a long time, then tied to four stakes by his thumbs and big toes. Then they flogged him with ropes, so that his whole body trembled. Finally, they placed a large stone on his mid section and lit palm leaves under, so that his face was completely scorched . . . . Some were hung by their genitals, until they fell down by their own weight, then somebody stabbed them with a cutlass and left them lying until God released them through death. Others were tied, and their feet covered with oil, placed in front of a fire, so that they were practically grilled" (Exquemelin 1983: 198). The buccaneer William Dampier, who also sailed the Spanish main for spoils a decade later, noted that Panama had been completely destroyed by Morgan and that the Spanish had not rebuilt the city on the same site but moved it further inland (Dampier 1977: 45).

Chapter 8

The Racket and New World Disorder: Control and Domination in the Age of Globalization

There is also the rift . . . . between the people in the privileged nations and those who in this shrinking world are not only ruled by their own traditional elites but also by the leading groups in the industrially developed countries. The [racket] principle has not changed.

(Horkheimer 1985: 89)

Not only does the process of globalization enhance the possibilities of nonstate actors like organized crime groups, it also greatly contributes to the anomic conditions on which criminal societies feed and which simultaneously may generate authoritarian government as citizens call for law and order. Conversely, internationalized organized crime groups may themselves become partners in repressive regimes anywhere on the globe, making arrangements with local, regional, or national elites.

Introduction

Globalization is a buzzword that means many things to many people. Robertson (1993) argues that the concept "refers both to the compression of the world and the intensification of consciousness of the world as a whole" (1993: 8). Globalizing practices, according to Sklair (1991), represent "a sociological totality" whose three dimensions are "economic, political, and cultural-ideological" (1991: 6). In the context of the present analysis, it refers to "the integration of the global economy" and its consequences (Ellwood 2002: 12). Globalization is a historical process that started centuries ago with the European colonial conquests. It gathered momentum after the Industrial Revolution in Europe and North America during the second half of the nineteenth century. The process quickened again since the 1970s with the arrival of modern communication technologies, the removal of obstacles to trade and finance, and the increasing political and economic clout of multinational companies (*ibid.*; Khor 2001: 7–10; Petras and Veltmeyer 2001: 13). As noted, European colonialism also produced a global narcotics economy which greatly contributed to the illegal drug trafficking of today.

This latest stage of globalization has generated many contradictions, such as the informal, shadow, and criminal economies, especially in the developing world and the former Soviet Bloc. Participants in these economies are those left out who suffer from the massive displacements caused by globalization in its present accelerated stage. As well, there are those who take advantage of the gaps, loopholes, and opportunities provided by the transformation of the global economy, such as the confederates of international crime groups. For example, in developing countries, peasants create the first stage of the illicit global narcotics industry by cultivating the plants, such as coca leaves and opium poppies, destined to be turned into drugs, as licit crops do not allow for sufficient incomes. Similarly, the deregulation of financial markets since the 1970s has allowed organized crime to participate in elaborate money-laundering schemes (Naylor 1994: 434; Chossudowsky 1997; Smith, Lyons, and Moore 1998: 127–146; Mittelman and Johnston 1999: 110–113; Portocarrero 2004: 283).[1]

Globalization and Anomie

The critical European International Relations (IR) scholars Krippendorff (1972), and Hein and Simonis (1973), among others, already warned decades ago that the process of globalization was out of control and would set free enormous conflict potentials resulting in anomic conditions on many parts of the globe. Globalization not only refers to "global economic integration" but equally implies processes of "political and social disintegration" (Barnet and Cavanagh 1995: 13). Sunkel (1995), for example, points to the "uneven globalization" within "peripheral countries" which "may . . . . generate conditions of social segregation, fragmentation, and disintegration" (1995: 55). The deteriorating conditions in many parts of the developing world had already been noted by the late 1980s. Not only did developing nations experience a drop of almost 20 percent in their exports between 1980 and 1988, by 1989, their accumulated debt had risen to US$1.3 trillion. Because of debt repayment and capital flight, more money left than entered the South in the form of aid and investment. Development was, in fact, reversed in many countries. In sub-Saharan Africa and Latin America, the 1980s were referred to as the "lost decade" (Head 1991: 60–61). Still, the developed countries significantly reduced aid payments after the end of the Cold War (Mason 1997: 436). By the turn of the millennium some two billion people existed on less than two dollars daily, while 1.3 billion made due with less than one dollar (Passas 2000: 25).

The deteriorating situation in many parts of the developing world was bound to have repercussions. Following the decline of the socialist alternative model, new political forces have emerged to challenge Western capitalism and globalization. These forces feed on tribalism, nationalism, and religious fundamentalism, generating social upheaval and civil unrest and anomic conditions in many parts of the South. Conversely, in Venezuela in 2000, and in Brazil and Ecuador in 2002, populist left-wing governments have been elected with the votes from the poorest sectors of their respective societies. As the Colombian case indicates, left-wing rebel movements have also received a boost from the negative consequences of globalization (Barber 1996; Passas 2000; BBC Aug. 1, 2000; BBC Nov. 25, 2002a; BBC Jan. 2, 2003; BBC Jan. 15, 2003; Chua 2004).

The Global Racket ?

Horkheimer (1982; 1988c) had viewed the racket as the "archetype of domination," while he also regarded the nation-state as its pre-eminent manifestation (1982: 35; 1988c: 334). Still, as noted earlier, the Frankfurt School scholar pointed to a multinational racket of developed countries already during the early 1940s (Horkheimer 1985: 89). While he did not write elsewhere on the multinational racket, it is nonetheless befitting to enquire how such structures have developed, how they manifest themselves, and how criminal organizations may participate within them, while keeping in mind the Frankfurt School scholar's thoughts on this subject.

Ross and Trachte (1990) refer to global capitalism as the "new Leviathan." They write:

> The multinational conglomerate symbolizes, crudely, the power of the new Leviathan. Yet the irony of the New Leviathan is that its individual agents, global firms, and financial institutions are not sovereigns but severely constrained competitors committed to the economic war of each against all. The only Sovereign is indirect, fluid, acting upon states as well as embodied in them. The new Leviathan is the system of global capitalism itself, not any of its powerful parts (1990: 2).

Neoliberal globalization has called into question the role of the state with the emergence of transnational companies (TNCs) operating in a borderless economy. As Barnet and Müller (1974) observed during the 1970s:

> The global corporation is the most powerful human organization . . . . devised for colonizing the future. By scanning the entire planet for opportunities, by shifting . . . . resources from industry to industry . . . . country to country, and by keeping its overriding goal simple — world-wide profit maximation — it has become an institution of unique power. The World Managers are the first to [develop] a model for the future that is global. They exploit the advantages of mobility while . . . . governments are still tied to particular territories. For this reason, the corporate visionaries are far ahead of the rest of the world in making claims on the

future . . . . [and] are creating a politics for the next generation (1974: 363; also
see Barnet and Cavanagh 1995).

In 1973, approximately ten thousand companies were considered to be transnational
firms with "at least one foreign affiliate" (Mirow and Maurer 1982: 34). In 1971,
transnational firms were responsible for 20 percent of global economic output
(*ibid.*). By 1995, the United Nations Conference of Trade and Development
(UNCTAD) had identified nearly forty thousand companies which maintained
production locations in more than three countries. By 2000, some sixty thousand
such companies had been registered. These corporations were responsible for over
60 percent of global trade, half of which transpired as intra-firm transfers. The bulk
of this trade was conducted by a few hundred of the largest of these
conglomerations. Moreover, in 1995, thirty-three thousand of these enterprises had
their headquarters in Canada, the European Union, Japan, and the United States
(White 1995: 40; Martin and Schumann 1996: 157; Raghavan 1996: 31; Petras and
Veltmeyer 2001: 12–15; Robinson 2004: 55).

Beck (1997) explains the power of transnational corporations with their "access
to the material veins of modern nation-states" because they force countries, and
even regions within them, into competition with each other in order to create better
opportunities for themselves (1997: 16). Such corporations can export jobs to
wherever costs are the lowest; they can partition as well as subcontract production,
and manufacture components in different locations. Transnational firms may
produce and invest in one location and pay taxes in another. As their mobility
allows large corporations to relocate almost anywhere on the globe where taxes are
low and environmental and labor regulations are scarce, governments the world
over have been forced to reduce such levies resulting, among other, in diminished
incomes for public coffers (*ibid.*, 17). Cox (1987) calls this process the
"internationalizing of the state" as "national policies and practices" are made to
conform to the vagaries of the global economy (1987: 253).

For example, corporate taxes in the Federal Republic of Germany (FRG) in
1965 amounted to 35 percent of annual tax income by the state. By the mid-1990s,
corporate taxes provided only 13 percent (Beck 1997: 20). In the United States,
during the 1950s, corporations contributed 30 percent annually to government
coffers. Today, US corporations pay "less than 12 percent" (Ellwood 2002: 63). The
decline of the state ultimately results from its shrinking tax base, which in turn has
consequences for its ability to fulfill its functions. In turn, governments, including
those in the developed world, introduce cutbacks in social welfare and health care
and other public services like swimming pools, museums, libraries, schools, and
universities.

Martin and Schumann (1996) described the impact of corporate tax reductions
on the community level in Frankfurt, the richest and simultaneously the most
indebted city in Germany. Although the city's economy had grown over 20 percent
between the mid-1980s to the mid-1990s, city council was forced to close thirty out
of forty-six community centers. Many of the public swimming pools were either
sold or closed off. The city lacked the funds to implement badly needed social

initiatives. The theater and opera seasons were cut short. A member of city council warned that if this trend continued, "the peaceful cohabitation of classes, nations, and lifestyles in Frankfurt . . . . [would] explode" (1996: 284). If this is the impact in one of the richest countries in the world, the consequences for developing nations are even more devastating.

Conversely, instead of paying taxes, transnational firms often receive hundreds of billions in subsidies. Moreover, they still ship their goods on the public transportation systems, hire graduates educated with state funds, and generally rely on the infrastructure to whose upkeep they no longer contribute. Indeed, transnational firms have become parasites who feed on their public hosts (Martin and Schumann 1996: 282–284). Van der Pijl (1995) observed that the wealth of globalizing elites from countries such as Brazil derived from the privatization of public property. He concluded: "'Growth' figures celebrated the world over as a sign of economic health should therefore be interpreted first of all as a sign of the capacity of . . . . [such elites] to appropriate public goods" (1995: 117).[2]

Furthermore, Horkheimer (1988) noted that racket formation in National Socialist Germany and Fascist Italy was closely linked to the emergence of economic monopolies (1988: 319). He wrote: "The economy no longer has its own dynamic. It lost its power to the economically powerful" (*ibid.*, 316). Similar observations can be made in the age of globalization as the process of monopolization has accelerated considerably since the 1970s. Mirow and Maurer (1982) write:

> Just as the great trusts were formed in the late nineteenth century in order to
> fortify and extend their member firms' hold on their respective national industries,
> so a few hundred corporations today are extending their sway over world markets
> (1982: 207).

Thus, by the new millennium, "the ten largest corporations in their fields" dominated "86 percent of the telecommunications sector, 85 percent of the pesticides industry, 70 percent of the computer industry, and 35 percent of the pharmaceutical industry" (Ellwood 2002: 56). Khor (2001) maintains that the increased "concentration and monopolization" of wealth and influence in the hands of transnational companies and international financial institutions is an important characteristic of globalization (2001: 10). As a consequence of fusions and buyouts, a decreasing number of multinational corporations have control over a growing share of international markets. Indeed, as Khor points out: "Where a multinational company used to dominate the market of a single product, a big transnational company now typically produces or trades in an increasing multitude of products, services and sectors" (*ibid.*; also see Clairmont 1995).

Barber (1996) observed that the number of global media companies, as a result of mergers and buyouts, dropped from forty-three in 1981 to twenty-three in 1991 (1996: 138). He noted further:

Not only is the corporate proprietor of a conglomerate likely to own a stable of
publishers, one which will publish a given book, but it can also own the agency
that sells the book, the magazine that serializes it, the movie studio that buys and
films it, the distributor that purveys it, the cinema chain that screens it, the video
export firm that brings it to the global market, and perhaps even the satellite pods
or wires through which it is broadcast and the television set and VCR on which
it is finally screened somewhere in, say, Indonesia or Nigeria. This is not synergy:
This is commercial totalitarianism — a single value (profit) and a single owner
(the monopoly holder) submerging all distinctions and rendering all choice
tenuous and all diversity sham (*ibid.*, 138–139).

The governance of the global corporation is hierarchical; authority lies in the
hands of a small number of decision makers on the board of directors and,
indirectly, with the share holders. Hence, if several hundred large concerns control
the global economy, the traditional pattern of domination by the few continues
(Mirow and Maurer 1982: 207; Beck 1997: 102).[3] Indeed, Pearce's and Tombs'
(1999) portrayal of the internal politics of the corporation as "some kind of
aristocratic or oligopolistic republic" that is home "to bloody struggles between its
elites" is reminiscent of Horkheimer's observations on the racket (1999: 117).
Multinational corporations may be referred to as *pragmatic totalities* that are neither
universal nor individual but particularistic in character, while such organizations
also symbolize the rise of the group over individual and society (Horkheimer
1985a: 290; Stirk 1992: 143).

Horkheimer (1988c) had described the racket as "a conspiring group who push
for their collective interests against the interests of the whole" (1988c: 334).
Various scholars have described a phenomenon, which Horkheimer would likely
classify as a global racket in embryonic form. Sklair (1991; 2000), for example,
refers to the members of a "transnational capitalist class" (TCC) whose power base
is increasingly global (1991: 6, 62, 117–118; 2000: 70). This category describes
those who run and control transnational companies and their local subsidiaries,
bureaucrats and politicians who further the globalizing process, and global
professionals and academics. The members of the TCC view their interests as being
"best served by an identification with the interest of the capitalist global system"
(1991: 62; 2000: 69–71). The neo-Gramscian political economist Robert Cox
(1987) describes a "transnational managerial class" comprising of those who
control global corporations, and also "public officials in national and international
agencies," as well as "experts and specialists" who offer services that contribute to
"the maintenance of the world economy" (1987: 358–360). His colleague Stephen
Gill (1995) refers to a "transnational historic bloc," incorporating "internationally
oriented elements of the states and civil societies of many nations," including
"transnational firms and banks and international organizations," with its main
power bases located among the major industrial powers (1995: 86). Robinson
(2004) uses the term more sparingly and merely includes "the owners of
transnational capital," those who control "the leading worldwide means of
production . . . . and private financial institutions" (2004: 47).

The potential racket character of this global elite is well illustrated by the notion of the "20:80 Society," a neoliberal nightmare scenario for the twenty-first century. The term apparently originated at a 1995 gathering of world's business elites in San Francisco, California, held to discuss the trends of the future global society. The 20:80 figures are based on the assumption that if globalization continues unabated on its present path, only one-fifth of the world's population would be required to make, provide, buy, and consume all the goods and services needed to run the global economy of the future. The fortunate 20 percent of the global population with access to formal employment and consumption will reside in high-security communities guarded from the other 80 percent who exist on the margins of society, making a living by delivering services to the privileged or by participating in informal or criminal economies. Neoliberal globalization, it is feared, may transform humanity into two sectors consisting of a small sophisticated high-tech globalized elite surrounded by large socially and economically marginalized populations who produce criminal and/or militant antigovernment subcultures. The excluded are to be kept amused and passive through a twenty-first century version of 'Bread and Games' (Martin and Schumann 1996: 12–14; also see Ekins 1992: 4–13; Rifkin 1995: 215–217; Beck 1997: 166; Robinson 2004: 105–106).

In addition, a previous chapter made reference to the past contributions of international drug companies to the growth of the global narcotics economies in existence today. Similarly, neoliberal globalization is inherently criminogenic because it generates unethical behavior on the part of fiercely competitive global corporations engaged in an "economic war of each against all" (Ross and Trachte 1990: 2). In such an environment "legitimate opportunities" for profit may be "limited and constrained" (Box 1983: 35). This in turn causes "executives [to] investigate alternative means, including law avoidance, evasion, and violation and pursue them if they are evaluated as superior to other available strictly legitimate alternatives" (*ibid.*).

Passas (2000: 36) emphasizes that the global power differentials make it possible for the majority of multinational companies to implement a new form of colonialism. He termed these practices "crimes without law violations" as many countries in the South do indeed lack the necessary legislation which classifies such acts as unlawful (*ibid.*). He writes:

> Such asymmetries of power make for legal norms that allow overseas that which is, for good reason, criminalized in the base country (e.g., toxic-waste dumping, testing drugs on humans, bribery, tax evasion, as well as the patenting of life forms by biotechnology companies . . . .) (*ibid.*).

The imbalance of power between North and South becomes evident when one considers the consequences of the corporate control of the global food system. Although the world possesses the capacity to feed the present population and more, hundreds of millions go hungry as a result of the organization of the planetary food supply by transnational agribusiness corporations (George 1985). As noted by Norberge-Hodge, Merrifield, and Gorelick (2002), this dilemma results from the

> global economy's perverse logic in which it makes economic sense that luxury foods are grown on the best land in countries where people are starving and then exported to countries where food is so abundant that obesity is a problem. The profit of this trade goes not to the landless and starving poor but to the wealthiest business people in these nations (2002: 95).

Susan George (1992) discusses another important criminal dimension in the relationship between North and South, namely the international debts owed and paid by developing countries. Indeed, she described the role of the debt as a form of "warfare" against the South that manifested itself in the reduction of budgets on "education, housing, transport, health, and the environment" as well as an "increase" in "hunger, illiteracy, and disease" (1992: 15–18).[4] Vega Vega (1987) refers to the debt as the "international crime of usury" (1987: 46). In his perspective the exorbitant rates of interest paid to Northern lenders do represent a form of criminal plunder taken from defenseless victims. The imposition of Northern policies on the South has had catastrophic repercussions because they prevented developing societies from modernizing and are the cause of massive social problems. As Vega Vega describes:

> Overcrowding, ... lack of access to clean water, lack of sanitary services, and increases in violence, prostitution, and drugs — all provoke an incessant increase in crime in general which, with its known social and economic roots, constitutes a serious problem (*ibid.*).

Conversely, Braithwaite (1979) views the corruption of officials in developing countries by TNCs as a most destructive practice because it takes away from those who need it most and gives to those who already have plenty. Moreover, corruption brings into position of power politicians and officials "who in general will put self-interest ahead of public interest and transnational corporation interest ahead of national interest" (1979: 126). A study published in 2000 estimated that TNCs pay some US$80 billion worldwide annually in bribes to win trade deals or concessions. These practices weaken efforts toward development and contribute to higher rates of poverty and inequality, increase debt burdens, sidestep local democracy and existing legislation, and encourage armament sales (Singh 2000: 38–39).

In the Peru of the 1990s, the corruption of traditional elites merged with that generated by transnational corporations creating a new combination that culminated during the Fujimori era, which has deeply affected Peruvian society and will continue to do so for many years to come (Ugarteche 2005: 99–127). Quiroz (2005) referred to the regime as one of the worst in the country's history since independence in the 1820s. Accordingly,

> the generalized and systemic corruption reached the most important institutions and personalities of the country: bureaucrats, judges, heads of national and

international corporations, military officials, members of congress, ministers, and the highest echelons of the government. . . . [What came into existence] was a combination of bureaucratic corruption and capture of the state by a corrupt clique who aimed to illegally enrich themselves, . . . (2005: 79).

Corruption is also likely at the root of much of the corporate crime that takes place in the developing world. While a comprehensive study of the extent and impact of corporate crime on developing societies still has to be written, it is possible to extrapolate from existing works which usually focus on specific events that the amount of unethical practices on the part of TNCs is considerable and may manifest itself in numerous ways (*ibid.*). For example, in December 1984, an explosion at the Union Carbide plant in Bhopal, India, had killed thousands and maimed tens of thousands. Pearce and Tombs (1998: 194–219) included a thorough investigation of the Bhopal disaster into their study of corporate crime in the chemical industry. They concluded that while the dimensions of the disaster were unequaled, "its causes were all too common" (*ibid.*, 217). Not unlike drug-producing countries such as Bolivia or Peru who ignored the drug trade because it generated desperately needed hard currency, many underdeveloped nations, in the hope of attracting foreign investment and access to technological and scientific know-how, have provided business climates with few regulations on hazardous materials or emissions from plants (*ibid.*).

The activities of pharmaceutical companies qualify as an another dimension of corporate crime in the South. Included among these practices are the use of citizens from Southern nations as guinea pigs for newly developed medicines, or the promotion and sale of dangerous drugs (Braithwaite 1984: 245–278; Chetley 1991). Even so, few practices make evident the criminal covetousness of this particular industry like the frivolous lawsuit by thirty-nine transnational pharmaceutical companies against South Africa over patent laws for drugs to combat the Acquired Immune Deficiency Syndrome (AIDS). In 1997, while the country was in the grip of a major health crisis with close to five million infected, the South African parliament made changes to the so-called Medicines and Related Substances Control Act. The amendment permitted the generic manufacture of anti-AIDS drugs by local companies as well as their import from generic producers abroad. For example, the Indian company Cipla offered anti-AIDS drugs at prices ten to fifteen times lower than those of international drug manufacturers. The lawsuit was ultimately withdrawn in early 2001 following an international outcry ('T Hoen 2000: 12–17; Singh 2001: 11–15).

The legal action taken against the South African government, which named Nelson Mandela as a co-defendant, also demonstrates the racket character of the industry. The changes made by the South African government affected only the four pharmaceutical corporations in the business of producing anti-AIDS drugs, namely Merck, Glaxo-SmithKline, Bristol-Myers Squibb, and Boehringer Ingelheim. Furthermore, the combined African pharmaceutical market accounts for less than 2 percent of global sales and is of little value to multinational corporations.

Nonetheless, the lawsuit was not merely launched by the four companies directly affected but by the Pharmaceutical Manufacturer's Association of South Africa, the roof organization representative of the thirty-nine South African subsidiaries of these corporations. While these TNCs normally engage in fierce competition with each other, the move by the South African parliament threatened the interests of all because it could be attempted elsewhere, which caused them to combine efforts (*ibid.*; Oh 2001: 8–10; Sulston 2003: 14–15).

The dumping of hazardous waste embodies another dimension of corporate crime in the South made possible by corruption. According to Clapp (1994), "some 30–45 million tons of toxic waste" were traded internationally per annum by the second half of the 1980s, "with some 20 percent going to Third World countries" (1994: 506). Growing international trade connections make it possible to move such material with little costs, while "poverty and international debt patterns have encouraged its movement to less industrialized countries in need of foreign exchange" (*ibid.*, 509). Moreover, the practice, even if stopped today, will have negative repercussions on future economic development, increase impoverishment, and cause ecological harm to societies who have the least resources to address the dilemmas produced by short-sighted and corrupt governments. Finally, the practice was severely restricted due an international agreement that came into effect in December 1997, which banned the export of toxic waste from the industrialized countries (Raghavan 1995: 31). Still, it is reasonable to assume that corporations may hire criminal organizations to dispose of such materials. Naylor (1993), after all, observed that "illegal waste-disposal" was part of criminal organizations operating at the "symbiotic" stage when it was the most integrated with formal society (1993: 20).

Money laundering, as already noted, also represents an important dimension of criminal behavior on the part of global financial institutions and serves as an example of the banking world's links to criminal organizations. According to well-known Italian Mafia researcher Umberto Santino (1988), one of the principal figures in the Centro Siciliano di Documentazione (CSD) in Palermo, Sicily, possibly the leading research center on organized crime in the world, the *Sicilian Mafia* reinvested its criminal profits into international concerns who dominate the global financial and corporate system. Indeed, Santino argues that global organized crime is part of a "financial-industrial complex" (1988: 203; see also Werner 1994; Chossudowsky 1997). Justin Vitiello (1992), another scholar at the Palermo Institute observed, "as substantiated by CSD research, the primary reasons for the success of multinational mafias are their transnational connections culminating in their drug-money laundering and recycling contacts" (1992: 263).

A lawsuit filed in US District Court in Florida on July 20, 2001, may also be indicative of the relationship between criminal organizations and global corporations. Coca-Cola Company, its Colombian subsidiary, and business affiliates were accused of employing death squads to slay, torture, kidnap, and intimidate union leaders at the soft drink manufacturer's Colombian bottling plants. It was filed by the United Steelworkers of America and the International Labor Rights Fund on behalf of SINALTRAINAL, the Colombian union that speaks for workers at Coca-Cola's Colombian bottling plants, the relatives of a murdered union leader, and several other union activists who worked for the company and who had been bullied, abducted, or tortured by death squads (*Colombia Report.* 2001; *The Guardian.* 2001).

In short, the criminal activities of corporations and financial institutions which constitute forms of corporate crime provide an additional dimension to the global disorder in the new millennium. Moreover, many of these activities are made possible by corruption. Global concerns operate in an arena with no social contract, engaged in an "economic war of each against all" (Ross and Trachte 1990: 2). This state of affairs not only grants considerable leeway to corporate actors, it also contributes to what Beck (1997: 195) calls "disorganized capitalism" and turns them into potential bedfellows of international criminal organizations who take advantage of the same environment.

The futuristic 20:80 scenario referred to earlier is one possible outcome. If it were to come true, Horkheimer's comparison of the means of production with the weapon of a "robber," or observations made by Petras and Veltmeyer, who equated the activities of transnational corporations with a "gun pointed at the heads of workers and legislators" which forestalls "democratic politics" are certainly descriptive of the more disagreeable aspects of this world order (Horkheimer 1985: 102; Petras and Veltmeyer 2001: 70).

Carroll (2004) also observes that "corporate power grows at the expense of workers, communities, and the ecosystem itself" (2004: 218). In fact, while Horkheimer viewed the racket's social function as safeguarding and restraining the lower orders, which still implied a limited responsibility to provide for the excluded, the globalizing elites of today moved beyond such restrictions. The global arena is to today's corporations what the American West was to the robber barons of the nineteenth century, or the Americas to the Spanish conquistadors of the sixteenth century. Sakamoto (1995) observed that "the logic of capitalist development" does not entail the "economic necessity" to improve the living conditions of the world's poorest and starving (1995: 134). Indeed, he noted that "those people" represented surplus whose demise from starvation would have "no adverse effect" on the global economic system (*ibid.*). McMurtry (2001) argues alike that human rights have been turned into consumer rights. Only those with the necessary purchasing power have access to any goods and services deemed essential human rights ranging "from food and water to housing, health care and whatever else can be privatized for profit" (2001: 15). Regardless, Gray (1998) observes that "the utopia of the global free market has not incurred a human cost in the way that Communism did . . . . [however], over time it may come to rival it in the suffering it inflicts" (1998: 30).

Yet, if elites have no more commitments to the excluded, then the latter will reciprocate in like manner. Carroll (2004) likened the negative consequences of neoliberal globalization to a "ticking time bomb" (2004: 218). Still, as Beck (1997) points out, those left behind by globalization, "unlike the proletariat of the nineteenth and early twentieth centuries, have lost all their power because they are no longer needed. What is left to them is only naked violence to scandalize their situation" (1997: 166). The excluded, therefore, require policing. Policing and keeping the peace are functions commonly associated with the agencies of the state and its "monopoly of legitimate use of physical force within a given territory," to quote German sociologist Max Weber (Gerth and Mills 1958: 78–79). In the era of globalization the states' ability to impose such force has been severely hampered. In turn, when states are incapable of imposing their monopolies, other actors may take over this and other practices associated with government. Such parties may not possess the legitimacy of state agencies. Likewise, these actors may not govern by what Antonio Gramsci called a hegemonic process but rely on coercion instead. For this reason, the notion of "monopoly of violence" which an organization practices in a territory where it exercises control is more applicable than Weber's "monopoly of the legitimate use of physical force" (*ibid*).[5]

Weberian-based views of the state are unsuitable for countries like Colombia, Peru, or Bolivia, which historically have been incapable of monopolizing the legitimate use of armed force on their respective territories. Bonilla (1993), for example, maintains that the governments of the producer countries of cocaine are not able to control their own territories and concludes that "the premise that the state exercises the monopoly of the legitimate use of force simply does not exist" (1993: 162). He states further:

> Aside from states, the production, distribution, and consumption of psychotropic drugs involves a series of different actors which range from domestic North American Mafias to drug trafficking organizations . . . . [as well as] financial institutes, banks and industries which participate in the business of money laundering, or sub-national groups such as South American guerrillas (*ibid*).

Due to the impact of globalization, the state agencies of such countries are even less capable of stopping the production and export of drugs, while the law enforcement agencies in Europe and North America fail to control their importation and distribution. Thus, it is required to reinterpret some of Weber's basic notions of the state or view them as so-called Weberian ideals because, strictly speaking, even a totalitarian regime may not possess a complete monopoly of violence.

In the developed world, most states may be still be capable of imposing an albeit limited monopoly of legitimate armed force. However, numerous localities on the globe lack a state presence, such as in Latin America or in some of the republics of the Commonwealth of Independent States (CIS). Hence, other actors impose their monopolies of violence that may change from one province to the next or even one city district to the next. One ought to conceive, therefore, of the existence of various actors imposing multiple and even overlapping monopolies of violence in the territories under control, whereby these areas where power is effectively exercised may be fluid and subject to change. In addition, several actors, including criminal ones, may join forces to thwart the ambitions of others whom they consider a threat, as discussed, for example, in the case of the "mafia republics" in Colombia (Mayer 1990: 199).[6] Multiple monopolies, or *oligopolies* of violence, may emerge and interconnect at various levels from the local to the global.

As noted, the militarily weak nation-states of sixteenth-century Western Europe, particularly Britain, France, and the Netherlands, lacked the means to go to war with Spain and relied on private actors, namely, pirates, to gain their share of the gold and silver the Spanish had looted in their American possessions (Chambliss 1989; Thomson 1994). History has come full circle as globalization has resulted in a decline of state power. Neoliberal globalization has disproved the notion of the relative autonomy of the state by demonstrating that economic elites, albeit internationalizing ones, have come to exercise great influence over state policies. Ross and Trachte (1990), for example, refer to the "relative decline in the relative authority of the state" (1990: 67).

It is too simplistic to argue that globalization has merely weakened the state. Rather, the state shifted away from its role of economic regulator, while strengthening its traditional function of social control (*ibid.*, 67–68). According to Biersteker (1993: 108), neoliberal economic policies resulted in "a reduction and transformation" of the state's economic role. This conversion was already under way during the 1970s in many developing societies because the implementation of neoliberal policies required the repressive capacity of the state to deal with the consequences (Kay 1993: 693). These may be the spontaneous food riots that erupt after the imposition of neoliberal belt-tightening programs or the protests of organized labor groups against job losses or of organizations of indigenous peoples whose environment is being ruined. Another consequence is the growing strength of rebel movements, such as the Colombian *Fuerzas Armadas Revolucionarias de Colombia* (FARC).

A number of actors aside from the state are capable of maintaining limited monopolies of violence or participate in *oligopolies* of violence with others. In addition to government security agencies, parts of a country's national territory may be controlled and 'policed' by national and international private security companies, criminal organizations, paramilitaries, rebel forces, local self-protection groups, or various combinations of these. Hence, it is important not only who controls the state, but also who replaces it, when it is not in control. Policing, even in the strictest sense of keeping the peace, takes very different forms depending on the ideological preferences and/or economic priorities of actors imposing their respective monopolies, or *oligopolies* of violence, within a given territory. By implication, after territorial changes, the new masters will introduce different norms in the manner policing is conducted. The policing done by a private security company likely differs considerably from the practices of a left-wing rebel organization, or those of a right-wing paramilitary unit financed by an OC group.

Colombia's FARC rebels do indeed police the territory they control. Those living under guerrilla law do not necessarily consider themselves unfortunate about the imposition of 'revolutionary justice.' For example, the town of San Vincente in southern Colombia was part of the territory ceded to the FARC rebels as a safe area during the peace talks with the Pastrana government during the late 1990s. The rebels have since evacuated the territory following the breakdown of the negotiations. Prior to the arrival of the FARC in 1999, its inhabitants regarded San Vincente as "a lawless frontier town" (*The Globe and Mail.* July 19, 1999: A11). The killings which the community suffered on a daily basis while the Colombian military was present stopped almost completely once the heavily armed rebels began patrolling the streets. The FARC also drove out the official local judges, replacing the country's judicial system with their own. As long as the rebels were in control of the territory, most criminal cases involved domestic disputes, 90 percent of which were resolved by the rebel courts. In cases of domestic violence and wife abuse, the perpetrator would be "locked in the town jail for a few days or set to work sweeping streets or building roads" (*ibid.*). Conversely, the Peruvian Maoist rebel movement *Sendero Luminoso* practiced the same sort of social cleansing as did Colombian right-wing paramilitaries, namely, persecuting homosexuals and prostitutes whom both viewed as deviants (Pearce 1990: 22; González 1994: 129; Isbell 1994: 79).[7]

Recent years have seen not only an enormous increase in private policing but also the emergence of a global private security industry (Rifkin 1995: 213; Harding 1997; Davis 2002; Rigakos 2002). As states are losing their monopoly on legitimate armed force, private security companies are providing military services and protection for governments, nongovernmental organizations, and private businesses. The threat of political and social turmoil and the increase in crime in many parts of the world are challenges not only to the security organs of states but also impede the activities of multinational corporations or international aid organizations.[8] The private protection industry, as well as the participation of criminal organizations within it, have been briefly discussed in the chapter on Soviet and post-Soviet organized crime. As rates of political and criminal violence shot up during the 1980s, Peru also experienced a considerable increase in the number of companies offering private protection, from 64 in 1980 to 430 in 1991 (Arana Soto 1991). Still, it should be noted that the 1990s saw the emergence of an "international security industry . . . . worth close to US$60 billion annually in 1998 and . . . . expected to be worth $200 billion" by 2008 (Davis 2002: 28; also see Johnson 2004: 140–149).

Private security companies are very sensitive about being characterized as mercenary outfits and cautiously pick their employees from large numbers of available ex-military personnel no longer needed after the Cold War. While most such companies offer experts in logistics, communications, private protection, intelligence, advising, and training, a few private security firms provide combat soldiers who are indeed difficult to distinguish from mercenaries. Firms providing military combat services may constitute a threat to international stability and security because they do not have to account to anyone except their employer. As such, they may come to act as agents of repression to 'pacify' certain regions, allowing multinational companies to operate and profit. Yet such organizations may have little interest in ending a conflict from which they benefit. Executive Outcomes, the now defunct mercenary company from South Africa, was one such private military company in the business of protecting the interests of multinational corporations in zones of conflict. Made up largely of former members of the South African Defense Force (SADF) of the apartheid era, the company was involved in several civil wars in Africa during the 1990s, including Sierra Leone and Angola. Since 2003, some thirty thousand private 'soldiers' are operating in Iraq as part of the US occupation force. The proliferation of such services, and the fact that they operate in a legal gray zone, has led to calls that the international community should establish regulations to ensure that these companies assist global security rather than obstruct it (Harding 1997; Burrows 2002: 96–99; Davis 2002: 182–186; Macomber 2004). Canadian political scientist Peter McKenna (2004) observed that the privatization of warfare has become a "growth industry" and warned of the danger such organizations represented. He noted that private military companies "have already offered their security services" to terrorist and criminal organizations, while they also "would have no compunction about selling their expertise to rebels bent on toppling a democratic government or to greedy corporations intent on plundering resource-rich countries" (2004: A 25). O'Brien (1999) maintained that the privatization of violence resulted in a situation whereby a private military company would be "either . . . . exploiter or peacemaker" and occasionally both at the same time (1999: 54). Mehlum, Moene, and Torvik (2002: 447–448) argue that "violent enterprises" such as criminal organizations take advantage of the failure of the state to provide basic policing and peace keeping. Conversely, other "violent entrepreneurs" such as private military companies take advantage of the very same situation by offering protection against criminal plunder (*ibid.*).

Military scholar Martin van Crefeld (1991) noted that, as a result of the state's loss of "the legal monopoly of armed force . . . . existing distinctions between war and crime will break down . . . ." and "crime will be disguised as war, whereas in other cases war itself will be treated as if waging it were a crime" (*ibid.*, 204). He assumed further that conflict "will not be waged by armies but by groups whom we today call terrorists, guerrillas, bandits, and robbers" (*ibid.*, 197). If the globalization process continues on its present course, its consequences may very well include the integration of internationalized criminal organizations into local, regional, and national power structures anywhere on the globe as well as their participation in the establishment and maintenance of repressive social orders in these societies.

The US *Mafia's* involvement in Batista's Cuba prior to the 1959 Castro Revolution qualifies as an early example of an internationalized OC group supporting a foreign repressive regime (Cirules 1993). A modern crime group, like the now defunct *Medellín Cartel*, is a criminal organization but also a multinational firm with considerable international reach. Indeed, the groups composing the *Medellín Cartel* were active in some two dozen countries and cooperated with other international criminal organizations in a specific division of illegal labor and profit. In addition, the cartel possessed quasi-military capabilities, as its leaders controlled a paramilitary force armed with Galil, Heckler and Koch, Kalashnikov, M-16, and

Styer assault rifles as well as Uzi machine pistols. The arsenal of Medellín traffickers also included grenade and rocket launchers, ground-to-ground missiles, and possibly ground-to-air-missiles (Gómez Ordoñez 1991: 162; Lee III 1991: 6; Handelman 1994: 180–181, 239–240).

As noted, leading members of the *Medellín Cartel* had helped set up so-called "mafia republics" where local police, military, and agrarian elites directly collaborated with OC groups in jointly financing and organizing right-wing paramilitaries responsible for serious human rights abuses (Mayer 1990: 199). Given the economic, political, and military capacities of the *Medellín Cartel*, it certainly possessed the ability to impose a monopoly of violence of its own or participate in an *oligopoly* of violence with other partners, inside or outside of Colombia.

Shelley (1999) writes that in the age of globalization and declining state power "[t]ransnational organized crime represents a new form of nonstate-based authoritarianism" (1999: 25). Studies presented at the 1994 UN Conference on Organized Crime alluded to the actual takeover of power by internationalizing crime groups who join forces in various parts of the world by 2020 (Raith 1995: 113–114; also see Freemantle 1995: 23–35; Williams and Savona 1995; Dammert Ego Aguirre 2001: 12–13).

One may ask with Max Horkheimer (1982: 34) whether "social domination" does indeed "lead to gangster rule by virtue of its own economic principle?" Globalization, if it continues on its present course, may bring about the *Colombianization* of world order by engendering the repressive regime structures into which criminal groups will be able to integrate with few impediments as global elites become increasingly criminalized themselves, while confronting the challenges posed by counter-hegemonic movements.

A world order based on such foundations is not likely to be a stable one. As noted, Block (1987) commented in his analysis of the elites in state and economy of capitalist societies that "those who accumulate capital are not conscious of what is necessary to reproduce the social order" (1987: 54–55). Conversely, "[t]hose who manage the state apparatus" are preoccupied "with the reproduction of the social order" on which their own power is grounded (*ibid.*).

In the Union of Soviet Socialist Republics (USSR), those managing the economy and the state, not only were one and the same, neither demonstrated sufficient interest in maintaining the very foundations of the Soviet system, which greatly contributed to the 1991 collapse. Global economic elites who are primarily interested in accumulating wealth and power appear to be equally unconscious of the need "to reproduce the social order" (*ibid.*). Meanwhile, the "relative decline in the relative authority of the state" has curtailed the ability of political elites to do so (Ross and Trachte 1990: 68). Indeed, instead of reproducing it, state elites in many countries around the globe often practice corruption as the social order. Globalization, therefore, not only weakens the state but in the medium and long term also undermines the foundations of the neoliberal global order itself, particularly when globalized elites do not govern by means of a hegemonic process.

Endnotes

1. According to a 1987 study by the International Monetary Fund (IMF), the *Esteva Report*, the global economy has been running a deficit with itself, whose origin can be traced back to the late 1960s. This deficit was the result of the sum of national surpluses and deficits, which, mathematically speaking, should cancel each other out. By 1983, the deficit had grown to an estimated US$600 billion. Couvrat and Pless (1993) estimated that this "black hole" in the global economy, which averaged some US$63 billion annually between 1979–1983, increased to US$1 trillion by 1988, an amount that corresponded then to the total debts of developing countries (1993: 19, 207–212; also see IMF 1987: 92–95; Motala 1997: 24–25). It stands to reason not only that the size of this global deficit has increased since but that considerable portions of the funds, which disappear into this black hole derive from criminal activities.

2. The transformation of public into private property that van der Pijl (1995) observed in the case of Brazilian globalizing elites differs little from the privatization practices in the post-Soviet republics.

3. Moreover, as knowledge is mobilized on a global scale, its control is in the hands of technocrats, who constitute a new bureaucratic subclass that will act in support of the global elite, confirming Horkheimer's (1988a) suspicion that power is increasingly concentrated in the hands of specialists (1988a: 309–310; also see McLuhan and Powers 1989).

4. A 1991 report by the World Health Organization (WHO) blamed the outbreak of the cholera epidemic which swept South America on the failure of health infrastructures across the continent. In the case of Peru, the WHO's Director-General Hiroshi Nakajima told the press that the country was unable to deal with the health crisis because it lacked the funds after making its debt payments. Indeed, had Peru committed some US$60 million dollars to fix its sanitary infrastructure, the impact of the health crisis could have been greatly reduced (*Third World Resurgence*. 1991: 7).

5. Upon closer inspection Weber's definition may not need many modifications. According to the German sociologist, "a state is a human community that (successfully) claims the monopoly of the legitimate use of physical force within a given territory" (Gerth and Mills 1958: 78–79). What about those human communities that are not successful in claiming such a monopoly, or movements who have not yet successfully claimed it but may do so in the future? Giddens (1985) also relies on a modified version of Weber's original. He refers to the state "as a political organization whose rule is territorially ordered and which is able to mobilize the means of violence to sustain that rule" (1985: 20). This definition acknowledges both the likely existence of other actors and the possible lack of legitimacy of state agencies (*ibid.*). The definition by political geographer Joe Painter (1995) is even further removed from the Weberian original. He defines states as "spatialized social practices which are to a greater or lesser extent institutionalized (in a 'state apparatus') and which involve claims to authority which are general in social scope and which secure at least partial compliance through either consent, or coercion, or both" (1995: 34).

6. While I did not come across direct examples of paramilitary policing in the literature, I can provide some personal observations. In November 1992, while traveling in Colombia, I attended a native music festival in the Andes. As it turned out, the area where the event took place was controlled by an alliance of local police, military, and drug lords. I noticed this after midnight, when many people were intoxicated from consuming wine and hard liquor at the festival. A Colombian soldier, recognizable by his uniform with rank and insignia, and carrying an M-16 rife, patrolled the streets of the city accompanied by a member of the local paramilitary outfit. The paramilitary was as heavily armed and wore camouflage clothing. However, his uniform resembled the fantasy mercenary apparel one would see in a *Rambo* movie. Their job at the time was to keep the peace, although their primary task was the maintenance of the social order, namely, to keep out Marxist guerrillas. The mere appearance of the two calmed things down considerably. They sent people home, checked identification cards, and stopped fights using the butts of their M-16 rifles on those who had been too drunk to notice their arrival.

7. As noted by González (1994), *Sendero Luminoso's* revolutionary law prescribed the death penalty for many offences. Accordingly, *Sendero* law "has two parts: cardinal rules and commandments. The three cardinal rules are: (1) Obey orders; (2) Take from the masses neither a single needle nor a piece of string; (3) Turn over everything which is captured. The eight commandments are: (1) Speak courteously; (2) Pay an honest price for everything; (3) Return everything borrowed; (4) Give compensation for anything broken or destroyed; (5) Do not hit or injure people; (6) Do not take farm produce; (7) Do not abuse women; (8) Do not mistreat prisoners" (1994: 128). González further writes: "Rules were enforced with iron-handed discipline: There were no second chances, with offenses punishable by either exile or summary execution" (*ibid.*).

8. For a discussion of security issues in the developing world, see Acharya 1997.

Chapter 9

Conclusion (Part I)

Peace . . . .
Has ceased to be a dream. Today it is
Unvarnished reality. And to secure
This peace I have put in an order
For more machine-guns, rubber truncheons
Etcetera. . . .

(Bertolt Brecht. 1987. *The Resistible Rise of Arturo Ui.* Scene 15)

The main argument of this work has been that criminal groups, or rather their leaderships, under certain conditions develop ideological or ideology-like preferences during their evolution. As a result, they may participate in and even come to the defense of the elites of the regimes which allow them to flourish. These groups become ideological by default as they adapt to the preferences of those in power. However, the varieties of organized crime discussed in this work, namely mercantile piracy, Soviet and post-Soviet organized crime, criminal organizations spawned in various modern capitalist societies and globalizing crime groups, display important similarities and differences.

The manifestations of organized crime discussed in this work were created and fostered by the dilemmas generated within their respective socioeconomic formations. The legal practice of privateering during military conflict in the age of mercantilism generated peacetime piracy. The necessity to fill the gaps of the command economy in the USSR resulted in the shadow economy and the rise of criminal groups supplying and managing it. Similarly, in capitalist countries, the prohibition of certain goods and services, such as alcohol, narcotics, or prostitution, engendered the groups who deliver them to willing customers. The emergence of global criminal infrastructures was furthered by the removal of trade barriers, the subsequent increase in trade, and the deregulation of financial markets. These developments allow criminal groups to move their illegal products without fear of detection as well as launder and hide their illicit profits with ease.

Furthermore, piracy-state collaboration ranged from the corruption of single individuals in positions of power, such as colonial governors in British North America, who protected and harbored pirates in return for a share of their profits, to an actual alliance between states and pirates' organizations. Similarly, organized crime–elite collaboration may range from individual cases of corruption to the complicity of entire regimes. In fact, irrespective of time and place, the emergence of strong criminal societies is made possible by weak states whose elites not only tolerate such groups but may collaborate with them. The mercantile state relied on privateering but was unable and unwilling to control piracy, which allowed the emergence of strong pirate organizations. Similarly, OC groups in capitalist countries and in the former Soviet Union emerged in spaces free of the state while providing services that the latter failed or refused to render. As far as global organized crime is concerned, few examples exist, such as the dealings between the US *Mafia* in Cuba during the Batista years (Cirules 1993). Still, authors of high reputation, such as US scholar Louise I. Shelley (1999), have warned of the threat posed by "[t]ransnational organized crime" as "a new form of nonstate-based authoritarianism," while others foresee the possibility that internationalizing OC groups join forces and actually take control in various parts of the world by 2020 (1999: 25; Raith 1995: 113–114; also see Freemantle 1995: 23–35; Williams and Savona 1995).

In addition, members of criminal organizations have historically contributed to the preservation of elites and even merged with them in a process not unlike what Gramsci (1973) styled *trasformismo*, namely, the integration of hostile elites into the existing structures of domination for the purpose of maintaining them (1973: 243). Notwithstanding, there are important differences in the case of the Soviet *Mafiya* as well as mercantile piracy. While this work has examined instances of close links between organized crime and elites in state and economy, especially the pirates-privateers and Soviet criminal groups managed to integrate into the power structures to a far greater extent. In fact, it is difficult to distinguish amongst criminal, semicriminal, and legal structures and activities because these are simultaneously criminal, semicriminal, and legal. Given these precedents discussed, it is likely that in the age of globalization, criminals will support beleaguered elites under certain conditions, the more so as the process goes hand in hand with a decline of the state that in turn is no longer capable of providing such assistance.

Moreover, as with modern organized crime, pirates required access to markets — if only to convert their loot into money, edibles, arms, munitions, and other supplies. Like piracy, the participation in a criminal economy, such as the production and distribution of illegal drugs, functions as a means of production and may involve large segments of the population within a geographically confined space. However, while most of the criminal organizations examined here have contributed to their respective national economies, Soviet crime groups have generally pillaged theirs — as do their post-Soviet successors. As far as globalizing organized crime in general is concerned, the trend seems to follow the example set by post-Soviet groups as well as multinational corporations. Investments, whether from criminal sources or not, will take place in locations where the best conditions are offered. Similar to the elites with whom they collaborate, the investments by mafia groups are likely to be guided not by patriotic sentiments but profit motives, unless the two happen to coincide.

Finally, piracy-privateering faded away only once the socioeconomic structures that maintained the practice had developed beyond the need to make alliances with criminals. A decline in modern organized crime strongly depends on transformations to the socioeconomic structures that rely on criminal groups to sustain them. Such changes, however, which will be briefly discussed next, need be far-reaching and are unlikely to be realized in the near future.

Conclusion (Part II)

The 'theory' of the society of rackets was left fragmented and incomplete, while Horkheimer (1985a) offered little advice on how to overcome its repressive structures. He noted that it was the purpose of progressive politics to "transform the world" by breaking down "the boundary between inside and outside" (1985a: 291). The concept of the racket, Horkheimer (1985) observed elsewhere, required further study that "could help define the goal of political practice: A society whose designs differ from those of the racket, a racket-less society. Such a true sociology could contribute to define the idea of democracy . . . ." (1985: 103). The Frankfurt School scholar himself had given up on grand solutions to the problems of humanity. Instead, he proposed that people try to improve conditions within their own communities (*ibid.*, 104).[1] All the same, given the multiple linkages between the global and the local, important issues cannot be ignored. Or as described by International Relations (IR) scholar Mark Hoffman (1994), even "if single, objective, ... answers are not possible, this does not mean that we should abandon the attempt to clarify our understanding of dilemmas in the effort to develop practical guidelines for action" (1994: 39).

Reliance on repression, such as the measures implemented at home and abroad by successive US governments as part of the War on Drugs, neither had much impact on the cultivation and output of narcotics in producer countries like Afghanistan or Colombia, nor did it greatly reduce their consumption in Europe and North America. These failures are also direct consequences of the unwillingness or inability to initiate workable international solutions to deal with organized crime.

The management of the growing interdependence, according to Haas (1975), is based either on an effective single-state foreign policy or on an expansion of international cooperation. Sakamoto (1995) observed that "the state and the state system" had been seriously weakened by the process of globalization, while "international organizations" were not sufficiently evolved to take over the burden (1995:131). One of the fundamental dilemmas is the gap between states' aspirations for autonomy of action and the need for voluntary limitations as a precondition for a mutually beneficial international cooperation. Beck (1997) warns of single-state responses to regulate the impact of globalization. Such policies, which presumably would include the export of one country's law enforcement practices, such as the US Drug War to Latin America, are destructive and cost intensive, whereby the sacrifices are not simply economic but also social. Conversely, Beck states that governments would benefit from "transnational cooperation" (1997: 188; also see Passas 2000).[2]

All the same, a necessary response to global organized crime is the creation and implementation of some form of international law enforcement based on an "international criminal code" (Anderson 1989: 186–194; Moore 1996: 193–195). Successful international cooperation presupposes the creation of institutions at the global level that are truly under multilateral control, such as an International Criminal Court not just for war criminals and the regimes they served but also for international crime bosses and their organizations. The international community will also need to create a global law enforcement agency that has the cooperation of national police forces. The basic structures of such an agency already exist in Interpol, the International Police Organization, which presently functions as an office that merely "coordinates international police activity" (Bresler 1993: 1; also see Strange 1996: 120–121).

The deregulation of financial markets, which has occurred since the 1970s, has allowed OC groups to participate in elaborate money-laundering schemes. Hence, mechanisms set in place to control international finances would be useful tools against money laundering by criminal organizations. This predicament also argues for the implementation of a strict code of conduct for corporations and financial institutions. Yet, a United Nations Center on transnational corporations to research their activities and impact, created in 1975, was shut down in 1992 (Mirow and Maurer 1982: 216–219; Naylor 1994: 434; Chossudowsky 1997; Mittelman and Johnston 1999: 110–113; Capedevilla 2000: 55; Passas 2000: 38–39; Robinson 2004). However, because of the hostility to such measures in the international banking community, law enforcement agencies fail to seriously interrupt the illicit flows of money. In turn, it is not possible to dismantle the economic structures of organized crime, and domestic law makers "the world over respond with strengthening their police apparatuses" (Martin and Schumann 1996: 291; also see Flynn 1995). As noted, though, most of the laundering of global drug profits and subsequent investments transpire in the developed countries (Castillo 1991: 147; Cabieses 1994: 51; 1996: 2).

Still, the availability of information technologies not only increases the capacities of criminal organizations to move illegal funds but simultaneously augments the capabilities of law enforcement agencies to track financial movements. Helleiner (1999) claims that "electronic fund transfers, unlike transactions in cash, leave an electronic trace that can be monitored" (1999: 78). One would merely have to supervise the few existing electronic payment services running the industry. Moreover, electronic money transfers are easily distinguished from other types of electronic information (*ibid.*).

An international police force, which should rely on brain rather than brawn, would have a strong financial division that has the collaboration of international financial organizations, such as a reformed International Monetary Fund (IMF), to curb money laundering and tax evasion. Given that these practices are largely possible due to the complicity of the international banking community and of governments in dire need of currency, the introduction of such a regime seems illusory at present (Andreas 1993; Flynn 1995; Sakamoto 1995: 131; Martin and Schumann 1996: 291).[3]

Anderson (1989) observed that sensible "improvements [in international policing] are possible although they require imaginative thinking and political support; both are in short supply" (1989: 194). Similarly, Passas (2000) maintained that despite the visible need for the creation of institutions of global governance "nationalist insistence on sovereignty" prevents the "introduction of common principles and law enforcement mechanisms" (2000: 39).

An international police agency capable of monitoring financial transfers would be a useful tool to combat money laundering, which represents the financial base of OC power. At the same time, given such authority, such an agency would also expose the illegal activities of legal businesses and of private individuals, who shelter their riches from taxation or from their ex-spouses in offshore banks.

The establishment of a better functioning global anti-money laundering regime is therefore also a question of political will because of the great resistance to such measures in the international banking sector. In turn, law enforcement agencies are unable to take down the economic power bases of organized crime, and governments continue to react by implementing repressive legislation at home (Flynn 1995; Martin and Schumann 1996: 291). The failure to come up with multilateral answers to global problems ensues in national solutions such as the US War on Drugs, which increases repression at home as well as abroad. Repressive solutions, in turn, keep drug prices and criminal profits high, thereby contributing to the economic structures that are the bases of OC's political power.

When engaged in the fight against organized crime, it is also worthwhile to consider Roberts' (1972) observations on the myth of secret societies in Western Europe during the eighteenth and early nineteenth centuries. He wrote that "their main importance was what people believed about them," which "always mattered more than what they did," while "their numbers and practical effectiveness were in no way proportionate to the myth's power" (1991: 347). The notion of secretiveness is an important component in the creation and implementation of measures against criminal organizations. The sociologist Georg Simmel (1906) wrote in this context: "The folly which treats the unknown as the non-existent, and the anxious imaginativeness which inflates the unknown at once into gigantic dangers and horrors, are wont to take turns in guiding human actions" (1906: 497). The public believes what it does about organized crime or terrorism because of what it is told. Given the secrecy of those involved in such activities, many claims can be made about the threats posed, which may or may not be reflected in reality but serve the goals of agencies eager to increase their budgets, or may have other more sinister purposes.[4]

Policies designed to combat organized crime or terrorist organizations can easily lead to abuses against individuals and groups engaged in legal opposition politics. The introduction of the so-called faceless courts in Colombia, a practice that leaves everybody but the defendant unidentified and allows hearsay as evidence, was initially designed to stop the drug traffickers from killing judges. However, it deteriorated into an instrument of repression of legitimate political organizations, such as labor unions and community groups (Weiner 1996: 31–36). In the United States, the Drug War not only failed to achieve the desired effects, but the increased powers handed to police resulted in corruption and grave dangers to the state of civil liberties, law, and democracy itself (Elias 1991: 45–54).[5] According to Canadian economist R.T. Naylor, "emergency legislation" that gives the police special powers may endanger individual rights. In an interview to a Canadian daily, he referred to the seizure laws in the United States that are "turning police forces into looters, into self-financed bounty hunters," because law enforcement agencies are permitted to retain what they confiscate in property and cash (*Toronto Star*. June 11, 1998: A15). This development is particularly worrisome when law enforcement not only is concerned with "breaches of the law" but becomes a political police turning officers into "moral censors of private beliefs" (Chapman 1970: 138; also see Giddens 1985: 302–304). Finally, the danger to civil liberties following the anti-terrorist legislation in the United States after the 9/11 attacks is demonstrated by the abuses documented in the Abu Graibh prison camp in Irak or in Camp X-Ray in Guantanamo, Cuba.

It is worthwhile recalling that the only states which successfully controlled organized crime were Fascist Italy, National Socialist Germany, and the Soviet Union under Stalin. These regimes did not put up with any organization capable of challenging their authority and used the violence at their disposal to eliminate any potential opposition. The *Sicilian Mafia*, for example, lost out to the totalitarian state, which itself was criminal and used comparable methods to suppress organized crime. Notwithstanding, the knowledge that only the most repugnant regimes in modern history have managed to hold down large criminal organizations ought to make lawmakers reflect on whether organized crime or repressive legislation represents the greater threat to their societies. Given some of the unfortunate realities of US Drug War policies; or of recent antiterrorist measures, it is useful to consider "whether, in the process of extending the ambit of threats requiring a military response, one is not further militarizing society rather than dealing more directly with political difficulties" (Dalby 1997: 5).

Even the militarization of society may not have the desired results. Farrel (1995), for example, believes that drug trafficking would remain profitable with an interdiction rate of 75 percent (1995: 145). Given that present rates are far lower despite the measures already introduced, it is certainly arguable whether the sort of society whose law enforcement agencies intercept 75 percent of illegal narcotics would be one its citizens find enjoyable to live in, due to the large numbers of uniformed and undercover police personnel necessary to accomplish the task. The maintenance of such a repressive apparatus is likely to be very costly, even for a wealthy nation like the United States. It could be financed only through cutbacks in other areas. Such a regime is remindful of Kornbluth's (1982) reflections on government in his novel *The Syndic*. He described it as a "dawn-age monster, specialized all to teeth and claws and muscles to drive them with. The Government was now, whatever it had been, a graceless, humorless incarnate ferocity" (1982: 99–100). Given the problems and dilemmas of the War on Drugs, it seems certain that the renowned late US historian Barbara Tuchman (1984) would have included this conflict in her well-known work on folly in history, had she lived to see the day. The preceding observations also apply to the measures taken by some countries, such as the United States, in the more recent War on Terrorism.

Most important, however, it is necessary to reorganize the global economic system in such ways that substantial segments of the populations in many countries around the globe do not need to participate in criminal economies to secure their livelihoods. This is a call not for the violent overthrow of a particular regime but for a fairer and better regulated global economic order. Without such fundamental changes violence will likely become a permanent feature of this new world disorder until its final demise. As noted, despite the fact that the 1980s had been a 'lost decade' for many countries in the South, development aid declined during the 1990s. Moreover, only a few developed countries have actually contributed 1 percent of their Gross Domestic Product (GDP) to international development, the goal agreed upon by the member states of the United Nations (UN) (Head 1991: 60–61; Mason 1997: 436).

There is literature abound about what may be done to improve the conditions in developing countries. These include, for example, the various UN or World Bank reports, such as the 1969 Pearson Report, the 1983 Brandt Commission Report, or the 1987 Brundtland Report, all of which suggest steps that would lead or would have led to some improvements. These would include items such as fair trade or the transfer of technology from North to South (Nohlen 1989: 105–107, 112–113, 539). These reports on the developing world represent minimalist options as they were written largely by authors from the North or by academics representative of Southern elites. In fact, these reports' suggestions for improvements have been criticized for not properly addressing the problems in these countries. Still, not even these minimalist demands have been met.

Global economic elites are unconscious of the need "to reproduce the social order," while the ability of state power to do so has been curtailed (Block 1987:

54–55; Ross and Trachte 1990: 68). Even so, successful efforts in dealing with international organized crime, drug trafficking, and many other global issues will ultimately require a redefinition as well as reconquest of political power, albeit in a multilateral form. The goal is the furtherance of global governance not the creation of global government, which would be a highly premature.

In conclusion, there are no perfect solutions to the problem of organized crime. Governments ought to pursue those options that are the least damaging to their societies. Thus, the powers and resources given to law enforcement should correspond to the threat actually posed by organized crime, not the perceived internal funding needs of agencies, or political agendas. A society that aims to preserve its democratic institutions and civil liberties may have to accept a certain low level of OC and other criminal activity. The crime-free society is also a totalitarian one.

Given the complexity of issues involved, solutions can be only specific, not general. For example, as observed in a previous chapter, the applications of opium and its derivatives are rather limited as compared to those of coca. In fact, coca is used in over forty products with potential or already established commercial applications. These include coca tea, medications such as *cocabetes* which stimulates the body's insulin production, nutritional preparations such as coca jams or cakes, and beauty and health products such as toothpaste or coca ointments. Other products are coca ice cream, paper, and organic herbicides. However, the criminalization of coca prevents their export, while the potential profits could significantly contribute to long-term stable development in the Andean region (Cabieses 1996: 29–33). The coca-cocaine controversy bears some similarity to the debate on hemp. Its many useful applications, such as paper, clothing, or alternative fuel, are neglected because of the association with marijuana and hashish, and the lobbying efforts of the forestry industry (Conrad 1994). Even so, different settings require different approaches. A similar solution is not an option in Afghanistan because opium poppies have fewer legal commercial uses. In this situation, it would be the most cost-effective approach to either introduce permanently funded alternative cultivation projects, or to create international agricultural boards who set prices that allow farmers an adequate income. Such moves would also improve the conditions of farmers in the developed world, and contribute to a stable global food supply, assuming that these efforts go hand in hand with sound ecological practices.

Finally, as the case of piracy demonstrates, a serious reduction of global organized crime is likely to come about only when state and economic elites cease their collaboration with criminals. This, however, is unlikely to occur during the age of neoliberal globalization because it is inherently criminogenic. While piracy was conquered with help from technological innovations, it could have ended only because the newly predominant nation-states — and the merchant elites running them — came to regard pirates as a threat to trade rather than allies in war, and used their countries' navies to eliminate them.[6]

While the end of piracy is a reflection of growing state power, the process has been reversed in the age of globalization when weakening state agencies are reinforced by private actors. The Soviet example should be a notice of danger for globalizing elites. Organized crime greatly contributed to the decline of the USSR, although the 1991 collapse was possible only due to the simultaneous criminalization of Soviet elites. A similar outcome is conceivable for any socioeconomic system, including the present neoliberal global order, where the criminal economy feeds off the formal one and where felons emerging from below form power structures with criminalized elites submerging from above. As triumphant global economic elites increasingly impair the capacity of states to reproduce the social order, while state elites, corrupt and fearful of further losses of sovereignty, delay and prevent the emergence of global governing structures, such developments are entirely possible.

Globalization should not automatically be associated with neoliberal capitalism. This makes it imperative to contemplate other forms of globalization which might retain some of the positive aspects of capitalism, while surpassing it as a socioeconomic system toward new objectives "which can be defined only as we advance towards them, and the validity of which can be verified only in the process of attaining them" (Carr 1985: 188).

Although the unipolar global order set up in the post–Cold War period is unlikely to be a lasting one, its demise may be long-drawn-out process that will not necessarily usher in a new age of progress. Whether future power structures, on the local or the global level, will be considered protection rackets or not depends on the extent to which the protected come to determine price and conditions of their preservation. Also, the more porous the boundaries, the more included and politically responsible the protected, and the more democratic the decision-making processes, the less likely is the formation of such regimes. Democracy in this context refers not only to formal democratic practices, such as regular elections, but to the ability and willingness of informed individuals to participate in decision-making processes at all levels of society.[7]

Endnotes

1. Horkheimer (1988d) wrote: "It is not the task of the individual to get involved primarily in big politics" which he [or she] cannot change anyway, "but to work for a better society" by improving the conditions at home in the "hospitals, insane asylums, schools, apartments, courts, prisons and only then [help in] the elimination of global hunger" (1988d: 365).

2. A 1994 RAND Corporation study analyzed how much the United States would need to spend on the Drug War abroad to decrease cocaine consumption on its streets by 1 percent. The researchers concluded that such attempts are extremely inefficient, costing twenty-three times more than addict therapy programs (Coffin 1998: 1).

3. Many policymakers may be reluctant to establish an international anti-money-laundering regime. Still, the speed with which the international community of states reacted to shut down the financial networks of alleged or true terrorist organizations following the September 11, 2001, attacks on the United States, demonstrates the inherent capacity of states to create such a mechanism without causing the slowdown, or collapse of the global financial system.

4. In the light of developments since the September 11, 2001, attacks on the United States, future historians may have similar observations about Osama bin-Laden and the *al-Qaeda* terrorist network.

5. Except for homicide rates, which are far higher in the United States than the European Union (EU) given the easy access to guns in the former, crime rates in the two are similar. Still, the total number of inmates in US prisons rose to more than 1.8 million between 1972 and 1998. It continued to climb, reaching 2.1 million in late 2001, which was 5–6 times higher than the EU prison population. In fact, in the year 2000, the United States had 100,000 more individuals imprisoned for drug offenses (458,131) than the European Union kept in its penal institutions for all transgressions (356,626). At that time, the EU's population exceeded that of the United States by approximately 100 million (Doyle 1999; CJCJ 2000; HRW 2003).

6. For example, piracy had existed in the Mediterranean for thousands of years and only ended in the early nineteenth century. France, Britain, the Netherlands, and even the United States sent warships to protect their trade and reduce piracy in the western Mediterranean. In 1816, a combined Dutch-British naval force, in response to kidnapping, hostage taking, and slave trading by the Algerian pirates, attacked and destroyed the pirate ships in the port of Algiers as well as parts of the city itself. While over a thousand mostly southern European slaves were freed during the campaign, the fleet's bombardment also killed several thousand Algiers citizens who had been mistaken for combatants. Although the Algerian pirates were severely beaten, they recovered within a few years and resumed their practices. Piracy in the Mediterranean finally ended with the French invasion and subsequent colonization of Algeria in 1830 (Ormerod 1924: 75; Ellms 1996: 265–287; Pleticha 1997: 9).

7. A racketless society could be described as a society whose members create their "own history under conditions of . . . . [their] own choosing" in a setting where people live "in a productive, crisis-free and nonexploitative set of relations with nature and" each other (Johnston 1983: 78).

Selected Bibliography

Abadinsky, Howard. *Organized Crime.* Belmont, CA: Wadsworth, 1981.
————. *The Mafia in America: An Oral History.* New York: Praeger, 2002.
Abecia Baldivieso, Valentin. *Breve Historia de Bolivia.* Caracas, Venezuela: El Libro Menor, 1985.
Acharya, Amitav. The Periphery as the Core: The Third World and Security Studies. In: *Critical Security Studies.* Edited by Keith Krause and Michael C. Williams. Minneapolis: University of Minnesota Press, 1997.
Adorno, Theodor W. Reflexionen zur Klassentheorie. In: *Gesammelte Schriften*, vol. 8. Frankfurt: Suhrkamp, 1990.
Aguado, Fray Pedro. *Recopilación Historial*, vol.1. Bogotá, Colombia: Biblioteca Presidencia de la República, 1956; as cited in Arango and Child 1987.
Akbar, Syed Imran. Pakistan unter Heroineinfluß. In: *Planet der Drogen.* Edited by Alain Labrousse and Alain Wallon. Frankfurt: Fischer, 1996.
Albert, Michael, Leslie Cagan, Noam Chomsky, Robin Hahnel, Mel King, Lydia Sargent, and Holly Sklar. *Liberating Theory.* Boston, Massachusetts: South End, 1986.
Albini, Joseph. *The American Mafia: The Genesis of a Legend.* New York: Irvington, 1971.
Alexander, Herbert E. Organized Crime and Politics. In: *The Politics and Economics of Organized Crime.* Edited by Herbert E. Alexander and Gerald E. Caiden. Lexington, Massachusetts: Lexington Books, 1985.
Allen, Catherine J. Coca and Cultural Identity in Andean Communities. In: *Drugs in Latin America.* Edited by Edmundo Morales. Williamsburg, Virginia: Studies in Third World Societies, no.37, 1986.
Amboss, Kai. *Drogenkrieg in den Anden.* Munich, Germany: AG-SPAK, 1994.
————. Drogenbekämpfung in den Anden. In: *Der Planet der Drogen.* Edited by Alain Labrousse and Alain Wallon. Frankfurt: Fischer, 1996.
Amnesty International (AI). *The Amnesty International Colombia Briefing.* New York: Amnesty International Publications, 1988.
————. *Kolumbien: Ein Land im Ausnahmezustand.* Bonn, Germany: Amnesty International Publications, 1988a.
Anderson, Jon Lee. *Che Guevara.* New York: Grove, 1997.
Anderson, Malcolm. *Interpol and the Politics of International Police Co-operation.* Oxford: Clarendon, 1989.
Andreas, Peter. Profits, Poverty and Illegality: The Logic of Drug Corruption. In: *NACLA Report on the Americas.* XXVII, 3, 1993.
Andreski, Stanislay. *Parasitism and Subversion.* London: Weidenfeld and Nicholson, 1966.
Andrews, Kenneth R. (Ed.) *English Privateering Voyages to the West Indies 1588–1595:* Documents relating to the English voyages to the West Indies from the defeat of the

218 Selected Bibliography

Armada to the last voyage of Sir Francis Drake, including Spanish documents contributed by Irene Wright. Cambridge: Cambridge University Press, 1959.

———. *Elizabethan Privateering: English Privateering During the Spanish War 1585–1603*. Cambridge: Cambridge University Press, 1964.

Anónimo. *Un narco se confiesa y acusa*. Bogotá: Editorial Colombia Soberana, 1990.

Antezana, Jaime. Interview. Lima, Peru, June 2005. Jaime Antezana is a lawyer, independent investigator, and expert on drug-trafficking in South America. He lives and works in Lima, Peru.

Apuleyo Mendoza, Plinio. La guerra que nunca quisimos ver. In: *El Tiempo*. (Bogotá). Lecturas Dominicales, November 29, 1992: 8.

Arana Soto, Hector V. Manuel. *Las empresas de seguridad: diagnóstico y perspectivas*. Lima: Leyton S.R.L., 1991.

Arango, Mario, and Jorge Child. *Narcotráfico: imperio de la cocaína*. Bogotá: Editorial Percepcíon, 1987.

———. *Impacto del narcotráfico en Antioquia*. Medellín, Colombia: Editorial J.M., 1988.

Arciniega Huby, Alberto. Civil-Military Relations and a Democratic Peru. In: *Orbis*. 38,1, 1994.

Arenas, Jacobo. *La resistencia de Marquetalia*. In: *Las guerras de la paz*. Edited by Olga Behar. Bogotá: Planeta, 1985.

Arlacchi, Pino. *Mafiose Ethik und der Geist des Kapitalismus*. Frankfurt: Cooperative-Verlag, 1989. (Originally published in 1983 in Italy under the title *La mafia imprenditrice: L'etica mafiosa e lo spirito del capitalismo*).

Arnade, Charles. *Bolivian History*. La Paz, Bolivia: Werner Guttentag T., 1984.

Aspiazu, René Bascopé. *Die Weiße Ader: Coca und Kokain in Bolivien*. Zurich: Rotpunktverlag, 1989. (Originally published in 1982 in Bolivia under the title *La veta blanca*).

Avirgan, Tony, and Martha Honey. *John Hull: El finquero de la CIA*. San José, Costa Rica: Varitec, 1989.

Bagley, Bruce Michael. Globalization and Transnational Organized Crime: The Russian Mafia in Latin America and the Caribbean. In: *Mama Coca*. (2001) Available at http://www.mamacoca.org/feb2002/

Barber, Benjamin R. *Jihad vs. McWorld: How Globalism and Tribalism Are Reshaping the World*. New York: Ballantine, 1996.

Barnet, Richard J., and Ronald E. Müller. *Global Reach: The Power of the Multinational Corporations*. New York: Simon and Schuster, 1974.

———, and John Cavanagh. *Global Dreams: Imperial Corporations and the New World Order*. New York: Touchstone, 1995.

Barraclough, Solon. The Legacy of Latin American Land Reform. In: *NACLA Report on the Americas*. XXVIII, 3, 1994.

Bascone, G. Economic and Social Aspects of Cocaine in the Andean Region. In: *Cocaine Today: Its Effects on the Individual and Society*. Edited by Francesco Bruno. Publication no. 44. Rome: United Nations Interregional Crime and Justice Institute, 1991.

Bauer, Richard. Alle sprechen von Koka, niemand von Kokain. In: *Neue Züricher Zeitung*. NZZ-Folio. June 1995: 28.

Beck, Ulrich. *Was ist Globalisierung?* Frankfurt: Suhrkamp, 1997.

Bedürftig, Friedemann (Ed). *Lexikon Drittes Reich*. Munich: Piper, 1997.

Beerman, R. The Parasites Law. In: *Soviet Studies*. XIII, 2, 1962.

Béjar, Héctor. *Peru 1965: Notes on a Guerilla Experience.* Monthly Review Press, 1970.
Bejarano, Jesus Antonio. Mas diferencias que parecidos. In: *El Tiempo.* Lecturas Dominicales. January 24, 1993: 7.
Bell, Daniel. Crime as an American Way of Life. In: *The Antioch Review.* 13, 1953.
Bellers, Juergen, and Wichard Woyke (Eds). *Analyse Internationaler Beziehungen.* Opladen, Germany: Leske und Budrich, 1989.
Bergamini, David. *Japan's Imperial Conspiracy.* New York: Pocket, 1972.
Bergére, Marie-Claire. The Other China: Shanghai from 1919 to 1949. In: *Shanghai: Revolution and Development in an Asian Metropolis.* Edited by Christopher Howe. Cambridge: Cambridge University Press, 1981.
Bergquist, Charles. *Coffee and Conflict in Colombia, 1886–1910.* Durham, North Carolina: Duke University Press, 1986.
Berkov, Robert. *Strong Man of China.* Freeport, New York: Books for Libraries, 1970. (Originally published in 1938).
Bernard, Jean-Pierre. Bolivia. In: *Guide to the Political Parties of South America.* Edited by Richard Gott. Middlesex, England: Penguin, 1966.
Berrios, Ruben. Transideological Collaboration and East-West-South Economic Relations. In: *World Development.* 18, 12, 1990.
Bertram, Eva, Morris Blachmann, Kenneth Sharpe, and Peter Andreas. *Drug War Politics.* Berkeley: University of California Press, 1996.
Bewley-Taylor, David R. *The United States and International Drug Control, 1909–1997.* New York: Pinter, 1999.
Biersteker, Thomas. The 'Triumph' of Neoclassical Economics in the Developing World: Policy Convergence and Bases of Governance in the International Economic Order. In: *Government Without Government: Order and Change in World Politics.* Edited by James N. Rosenau and Ernst-Otto Czempiel. Cambridge: Cambridge University Press, 1993.
Birman, Igor. The Financial Crisis in the USSR. In: *Soviet Studies.* 1, 1980.
Block, Alan. The Snowman Cometh: Coke in Progressive New York. In: *Criminology.* 17, 1979.
——, and William Chambliss. *Organizing Crime.* New York: Elsevier, 1981.
——. A Modern Marriage of Convenience: A Collaboration between Organized Crime and US Intelligence. In: *Organized Crime: A Global Perspective.* Edited by Robert J. Kelly. Totowa, New Jersey: Rowman and Littlefield, 1986.
——. *Space, Time & Organized Crime.* New Brunswick, New Jersey: Transaction Publishers, 1994.
Block, Fred. The Ruling Class Does Not Rule: Notes on the Marxist Theory of the State. In: *Revising State Theory.* Edited by Fred Block. Philadelphia: Temple University Press, 1987.
Blok, Anton. *The Mafia of a Sicilian Village: A Study of Violent Peasant Entrepreneurs.* Prospect Heights, Illinois: Waveland, 1988.
Blomström, Magnus, and Björn Hettne. *Development Theory in Transition.* London: Zed, 1988.
Böhme, Waltraud, Siegrid Dominik, Andrée Fischer, Felicitas Klotsch, Renate Polit, Hans-Jochen von Treskow, Karen Schachtschneider, Ilse Scholz, Gertrud Schütz, Martina Weigt (Eds). *Kleines Politisches Wörterbuch.* East Berlin, German Democratic Republic (GDR): Dietz, 1988.
Bonilla, Adrián. Dimensiones internacionales del narcotráfico y el caso de Ecuador. In:

Economía política de las drogas. Edited by Roberto Laserna. Cochabamba, Bolivia: CERES–CLACSO, 1993.

Booth, Martin. *The Triads: The Chinese Criminal Fraternity*. London: Grafton, 1990.

———. *Opium: A History*. New York: St. Martin's, 1999.

———. *The Dragon Syndicates*. London: Bantam, 2000.

Box, Steven. *Power, Crime and Mystification*. New York: Tavistock Publications, 1983.

Boyer, Jean-Francois. *La guerra perdida contra las drogas*. Mexico City: Editorial Grijalbo, 2001.

Braithwaite, John. Transnational Corporations and Corruption: Toward Some International Solutions. In: *International Journal of Sociology and Law*, 7, 1979.

———. *Corporate Crime in the Pharmaceutical Industry*. London: Routledge, 1984.

Brecht, Bertolt. *Der aufhaltsame Aufstieg des Arturo Ui*. Berlin: Suhrkamp, 1965.

———. *The Resistible Rise of Arturo Ui*. London: Methuen, 1987.

Bremmer, Ian, and Raymond Taras. The Black Marketers under Perestroika. In: *Soviet Social Reality in the Mirror of Glasnost*. Edited by Jim Riordan. New York: St. Martin's, 1992.

Bresler, Fenton. *Interpol*. Middlesex, England: Penguin, 1993.

Brockhaus Enzyklopädie, vol. 4 . Wiesbaden, Germany: Brockhaus, 1968.

Brockhaus Enzyklopädie, vol. 14. Wiesbaden, Germany: Brockhaus, 1972.

Broszat, Martin. *The Hitler State*. New York: Longman, 1981.

Browder, George C. *Foundations of the Nazi Police State*. Lexington, Kentucky: The University of Kentucky Press, 1990.

Bruce, George (Ed). *The Paladin Dictionary of Battles*. London: Paladin, 1986.

Bruun, Kettil, Lynn Pan, and Ingemar Rexed. *The Gentlemen's Club: International Control of Drugs and Alcohol*. Chicago: The University of Chicago Press, 1975.

Buci-Glucksmann, Christine. *Gramsci and the State*. London: Lawrence and Wishart, 1980.

Bullington, Bruce. A Smugglers' Paradise: Cocaine Trafficking through the Bahamas. In: *Crime, Law and Social Change*. 16, 1991.

Bullock, Alan. *Hitler: A Study in Tyranny*. New York: Bantam, 1961.

Burbach, Karl Heinz (Ed). *Das Spätmittelalter*. Frankfurt: Diesterweg, 1973.

Burrows, Gideon. *The No-Nonsense Guide to the Arms Trade*. Toronto: New Internationalist Publications, 2002.

Burt, Jo-Marie. Unsettled Accounts. In: *NACLA Report on the Americas*. XXXII, 2, 1998.

Bushnell, David. *The Making of Modern Colombia: A Nation in Spite of Itself*. Berkeley: University of California Press, 1993.

Cabieses, Hugo. *About Coca, Coca Tea, Development and Football*. La Paz, Bolivia: Andean Action, 1994.

———. *Commercialising Coca: Possibilities and Proposals*. London: The Catholic Institute for International Relations, 1996.

Caldwell, Oliver J. *A Secret War: Americans in China, 1944–1945*. Carbondale, Illinois: Southern Illinois University Press, 1972.

Camacho, Alvaro. *Droga y sociedad en Colombia*. Bogotá: CIDSE–CEREC, 1988.

Cameron, Maxwell A. The Eighteenth Brumaire of Alberto Fujimori. In: *The Peruvian Labyrinth*. Edited by Maxwell A. Cameron and Philip Mauceri. University Park, Pennsylvania: Pennsylvania State University Press, 1997.

Campodónico, Humberto. Importancia económica del narcotráfico y su relación con las reformas neo-liberales del gobierno de Fujimori. In: *Drogas y control penal en los Andes*. Lima: Comisión Andina de Juristas, 1994.

Capedevilla, Gustavo. NGOs Demand Firm Regulation of Transnationals. In: *Third World Resurgence.* 120/121, August– September 2000.

Caretas Dossier. Montesinos: Toda la historia. In: *Caretas*, Lima, Peru: 2000.

Carr, Edward H. *What is History?* Middlesex, England: Penguin, 1985.

Carrigan, Ana. A Chronicle of Death Foretold: State-Sponsored Violence in Colombia. In: *NACLA Report on the Americas.* XXVIII, 5, 1995.

Carroll, William K., *Corporate Power in a Globalizing World.* Don Mills, Ontario: Oxford University Press, 2004.

Casas, Ulises. *De la guerrilla liberal a la guerrilla comunista.* Bogotá: Escuela Ideologica, 1987.

Castillo, Fabio. *Los jinetes de la cocaína.* Bogotá: Editorial Documentos Periodisticos, 1987.

——. *La coca nostra.* Bogotá: Editorial Documentos Periodisticos, 1991.

Castillo III, Celerino and Dave Harmon. *Powderburns: Cocaine, Contras & the Drug War.* Oakville, Ontario: Mosaic, 1994.

Castro Caycedo, Germán. *Con las manos en alto.* Bogotá: Planeta, 2001.

Center on Juvenile and Criminal Justice (CJCJ). Poor Prescription: The Costs of Imprisoning Drug Offenders in the United States. (July 2000). Available at http://www.cjcj.org/pubs/poor/pp.html

Chalidze, Valery. *Criminal Russia.* New York: Random House, 1977.

Chambliss, William J. *On The Take: From Petty Crooks to Presidents.* Bloomington, Indiana: Indiana University Press, 1988.

——. State-Organized Crime — The American Society of Criminology, 1988 Presidential Address. In: *Criminology.* 27, 2, 1989.

Chanamé. Drugs, Soldiers, and Guerrillas. In: *The Peru Reader: History, Culture, Politics.* Edited by Orin Starn. Durham, North Carolina: Duke University Press, 1998.

Chang, Iris. *The Rape of Nanking.* New York: Penguin Books, 1998.

Chang, Maria Hsia. *The Chinese Blueshirt Society.* Berkeley, California: Institute of East Asian Studies, 1985.

Chapman, Brian. *Police State.* New York: Praeger, 1970.

Chernick, Marc W. The Drug War. In: *NACLA Report on the Americas.* XXIII, 6, 1990.

——. The Paramilitarization of the War in Colombia. In: *NACLA Report on the Americas.* XXXI, 4, 1998.

Chesneaux, Jean. *Secret Societies in China in the 19ᵗʰ & 20ᵗʰ Centuries.* Hong Kong: Heinemann Educational Books (Asia) Ltd, 1971.

——. Secret Societies in Historical China's Evolution. In: *Popular Movements and Secret Societies in China 1840–1950.* Edited by J. Chesneaux. Stanford, California: Stanford University Press, 1972.

——, Francoise Le Barbier, and Marie-Claire Bergère. *China: From the 1911 Revolution to Liberation.* New York: Pantheon, 1977.

Chetley, Andrew. Dumped on the Third World. In: *Third World Resurgence.* 10, June 1991.

Chieh-ju, Ch'en. *Chiang Kai-shek's Secret Past.* Boulder, Colorado: Westview, 1993.

Chin, Ko-lin. Triad Societies in Hong Kong. In: *Transnational Organized Crime.* 1, 1, 1995.

Chossudowsky, Michel. Crime Goes Global: The Criminalization of the World Economy. In: *Third World Resurgence.* 80, December 1997.

Chua, Amy. *World on Fire.* New York: Anchor Books, 2004.

Chubb, Judith. *The Mafia and Politics: The Italian State under Siege.* Western Societies Program Occasional Paper No. 23. Center for International Studies, Ithaca, New York:

Cornell University, 1989.

Cieza de Leon, Pedro. *La chronica del Perú*, part I. Lima: Ediciones Peisa, 1973. (Originally published in Spain in 1550).

Cintron, Myrna. Coca: Its History and Contemporary Parallels. In: *Drugs in Latin America.* Edited by Edmundo Morales. Williamsburg, Virginia: Studies in Third World Societies, 37, 1986.

Cirules, Enrique. *El imperio de la Habana.* Havana, Cuba: Casa de las Americas, 1993.

Clairmont, Frederic. The Unstoppable Behemoths. In: *Third World Resurgence.* 63, November 1995.

Clapp, Jennifer. The Toxic Waste Trade with Less-Industrialized Countries: Economic Linkages and Political Alliances. In: *Third World Quarterly.* 15, 3, 1994.

Clark, William. Crime and Punishment in Soviet Officialdom. In: *Europe-Asia Studies.* 45, 2, 1993.

Cleaves, Peter S., and Henry Pease García. State Autonomy and Military Policy Making. In: *The Peruvian Experiment Reconsidered.* Princeton, New Jersey: Princeton University Press, 1983.

Clough, Arthur H. (Ed). *Plutarch's Lives*, vol. 3. Philadelphia: John D. Morris and Co, n.d.

Coble, Jr. Parks M. *The Shanghai Capitalists and the National Government, 1927–1937.* Cambridge, Massachusetts: Harvard University Press, 1980.

Cockburn, Claud. An Interview with Al Capone, Chicago, 1930. In: *The Mammoth Book of How it Happened: Eye-Witness Accounts of Great Historical Moments.* Edited by Jon E. Lewis. London: Robinson, 1998.

Coffin, Phillip. Coca Eradication. In: *Foreign Policy in Focus.* 3, 29, 1998.
   Available at http://www.foreignpolicy-infocus.org/briefs/vol3/v3n29coca.html

Collett, Merrill. El fantasma de la narco-guerrilla. In: *Nueva Sociedad.* (Caracas, Venezuela). 102, 1989.

Colombia Alert. 1. September 1997: 1–3.

Colombia Report. Information Network of the Americas (INOTA). July 23, 2001.
   Available at http://www.colombiareport.org/colombia73.htm

Comisión Andina de Juristas (CAJ). *Violencia en Colombia.* Lima: Comisión Andina de Juristas, 1990.

———. *La sombra de la corrupción.* Lima: Comisión Andina de Juristas, 2002.

Conrad, Chris. *Hemp: Lifeline to the Future.* Los Angeles: Creative Xpressions, 1994.

Cook, David N. *Demographic Collapse: Indian Peru 1520–1620.* Cambridge: Cambridge University Press, 1981.

Cordingly, David. *Under The Black Flag.* Orlando, Florida: Harcourt, 1997.

Cotler, Julio. *Drogas y Política en el Perú.* Lima: Instituto de Estudios Peruanos, 1999.

Council of Hemispheric Affairs (COHA). Drugs Replace Communism as the Point of Entry for US Policy on Latin America. (August 1999). Available at http://www.coha.org/

Couvrat, Jean-Francois, and Nicolas Pless. *Das Verborgene Gesicht der Weltwirtschaft.* Münster, Germany: Westfälisches Dampfboot, 1993.

Cox, Robert W. Forces, States and World Orders: Beyond International Relations Theory. In: *Millennium.* 10, 2, 1981.

———. *Production, Power, and World Order.* New York: Colombia University Press, 1987.

Crane, George T., and Abla Amavi (Eds). *The Theoretical Evolution of International Political Economy.* New York: Oxford University Press, 1991.

Cressey, Donald. Organized Crime: The Code and its Functions. In: *The Sociology of Crime and Delinquency.* Edited by Marvin E. Wolfgang, Leonard Zavitz, and Norman Johnston. New York: Wiley, 1970.

Crowhurst, Patrick. *The French War on Trade: Privateering 1793–1815.* Aldershot, United Kingdom: Scolar, 1989.

Dahl, Robert. *A Preface to Democratic Theory.* Chicago: University of Chicago Press, 1956.

Dalby, Simon. Contesting an Essential Concept: Reading the Dilemmas in Contemporary Security Discourse. In: *Critical Security Studies.* Edited by Keith Krause and Michael C. Williams, Minneapolis, Minnesota: University of Minnesota Press, 1997.

Dammert Ego Aguirre, Manuel. *Fujimori-Montesinos: El Estado Mafioso.* Lima: Ediciones El Virrey, 2001.

Dampier, William. *Freibeuter: 1683–1691: Das abenteuerliche Tagebuch eines Weltumseglers und Piraten.* Stuttgart: Thienemans, 1977. (Originally published in England in 1697 under the title *A New Voyage Round the World*).

Daraul, Arkon. *A History of Secret Societies.* New York: Pocket, 1969.

Davies, James C. Toward a Theory of Revolution. In: *American Sociological Review.* 27, 1962.

Davis, James R. *Fortune's Warriors: Private Armies and the New World Order.* Vancouver: Douglas and McIntyre, 2002.

Deacon, Richard. *The Chinese Secret Service.* New York: Ballantine, 1976.

Debray, Régis. *Revolution in the Revolution?* New York: Grove, 1967.

Dederichs, Mario R. Gemeinsame Geschichte: Deutsche und Russen. In: *Der Neue Flirt.* Edited by Klaus Liedtke. Hamburg: Gruner und Jahr, 1989.

Defoe, Daniel.*A General History of the Pyrates.* Mineola, New York: Dover, 1999.

Degregori, Carlos Iván, and José Coronel, Ponciano del Pino, and Orin Starn. (Eds.) *Las rondas campesinas y la derrota de Sendero Luminoso.* Lima: Instituto de Estudios Peruanos, 1996.

———. After the Fall of Abimael Guzmán. In: *The Peruvian Labyrinth.* Edited by Maxwell A. Cameron and Philip Mauceri, University Park, Pennsylvania: Pennsylvania State University Press, 1997.

De la Vega, Garcilaso, *El Inca. The Royal Commentaries of the Incas*, Part I. Austin, Texas: University of Texas Press, 1966. (Originally published in 1609 in Spain).

Del Olmo, Rosa. *¿Prohibir o domesticar?* Caracas: Editorial Nueva Sociedad, 1992.

Del Pino, Ponciano. Tiempos de guerra y de dioses: Ronderos, evangélicos y senderistas en el valle del río Apurímac. In: *Las rondas campesinas y la derrota de Sendero Luminoso.* Edited by Carlos Iván Degregori, José Coronel, Ponciano del Pino, and Orin Starn. Lima: Instituto de Estudios Peruanos, 1996.

Della Porta, Donatella, and Alberto Vannucci. *Corrupt Exchanges.* New York: De Gruyter, 1999.

De Rementería, Ibán. La crisis agrícola y los cultivos ilícitos de drogas naturales. In: *Debate Agrario.* (Lima). 22, 1995.

———. *La elección de las drogas.* Lima: Fundación Friedrich Ebert, 1995a.

Deschner, Karl-Heinz. *Der gefälschte Glaube.* Munich: Heyne, 1980.

Deutscher, Isaac. *Stalin.* Middlesex, England: Penguin, 1970.

Diáz, Pedro. Interview. Lima. August 2003. Pedro Diáz is a human rights lawyer who works for the Interamerican Commission of Human Rights, which is associated with the Organization of American States (OAS).

Djilas, Milovan. *The New Class.* New York: Praeger, 1959.

Domich Ruiz, Marcos. *Ideología y mito: Los origenes del fascismo boliviano.* La Paz,

Bolivia: Editorial Los Amigos Del Libro, 1978.

Domínguez, Jorge I. The Powers, the Pirates, and International Norms and Institutions in the American Mediterranean. In: *From Pirates to Drug Lords.* Edited by Michael C. Desch. Albany, New York: State University of New York Press, 1998.

Doyle, Sir Arthur C. The Sign of Four. In: *Sherlock Holmes: The Long Stories.* Leicester, England: Galley, 1987.

Doyle, Roger. Behind Bars in the US and Europe. *Scientific American.* August 19, 1999. Available at http://www.sciam.com/article.cfm

Drug Enforcement Administration (DEA). Congressional Testimony by Thomas A. Constantine, Administrator, Drug Enforcement Administration before the Senate Foreign Relations Committee, Subcommittee on the Western Hemisphere, Peace Corps, Narcotics, and Terrorism regarding "International Organized Crime Syndicates and their Impact on the United States." February 26, 1998. Available at http://www. usdoj.gov/dea/pubs/cngrtest/ct980226.htm#FARC

———. Congressional Testimony by Donnie R. Marshall, Administrator, DEA, before the Senate Caucus on International Narcotics Control. February 28, 2001. Available at http://www.dea.gov/pubs/cngrtest/ct022801p.htm

———. Congressional Testimony. Drugs, Money and Terror. April 24, 2002. Available at http://www.usdoj.gov/dea/pubs/cngrtest/ct042402.html

———. Congressional Testimony by Asa Hutchinson, Administrator, DEA, before the Senate Caucus on International Narcotics Control. September 17, 2002a. Available at http://www.usdoj.gov/dea/pubs/cngrtest/ct091702.html

Duggan, Christopher. *Fascism and the Mafia.* New Haven, Connecticut: Yale University Press, 1989.

Dunkerley, James. *Rebellion in the Veins.* London: Verso, 1985.

———. Bolivia at the Crossroads. In: *Third World Quarterly.* 8, 1, 1986.

Duque Gómez, Diana. *Una guerra irregular entre dos ideologías.* Bogotá: Intermedio Editores, 1991.

Durand, Francisco. The Growth and the Limitations of the Peruvian Right. In: *The Peruvian Labyrinth.* Edited by Maxwell A. Cameron and Philip Mauceri, University Park, Pennsylvania: Pennsylvania State University Press, 1997.

Eastman, Lloyd E. *The Abortive Revolution: China under Nationalist Rule, 1927–1937.* Cambridge, Massachusetts: Harvard University Press, 1974.

Eckstein, Susan. Revolution and Redistribution. In: *The Peruvian Experiment Reconsidered.* Edited by Cynthia McClintock and Abraham Lowenthal. Princeton, New Jersey: Princeton University Press, 1983.

Ekins, Paul. *A New World Order: Grassroots Movements For Global Change.* New York: Routledge, 1992.

Einhard. *The Life of Charlemagne.* Ann Arbor, Michigan: University of Michigan Press, 1969.

Elias, Robert. Drug Wars as Victimization and Social Control. In: *New Political Science.* 20, 1991.

Ellms, Charles. *The Pirates.* Avenel, New Jersey: Gramercy, 1996.

Elton, G. R. (Ed.) *Problems of Empire: Britain and India, 1757–1813.* London: Allen and Unwin, 1968.

Ellwood, Wayne. *The No-Nonsense Guide to Globalization.* Toronto: New Internationalist Publications, 2002.

Engelbrecht, Ernst and Leo Heller. Night Figures of the City (1926). In: *The Weimar*

Republic Source Book. Edited by Anton Kaes, Martin Jay, and Edward Dimendberg. Berkeley: University of California Press, 1994.

Engelbrecht, Ernst, and Leo Heller. Opium Dens (1926). In: *The Weimar Republic Source Book.* Edited by Anton Kaes et al. Berkeley: University of California Press, 1994a.

Exquemelin, Alexandre Olivier. *Das Piratenbuch von 1678.* Stuttgart: Thienemans, 1983. (Originally published in the Netherlands under the title *De Americaenschen Zee-Roovers* in 1678).

FARC-EP. *Historical Outline.* Toronto: International Commission, 1999.

Farrel, Graham. The Global Rate of Interception of Illicit Opiates and Cocaine, 1980–1994. In: *Transnational Organized Crime.* 1, 4, 1995.

Fay, Peter Ward. *The Opium War.* Chapel Hill, North Carolina: University of North Carolina Press, 1997.

Femia, Joseph. *Gramsci's Political Thought: Hegemony, Consciousness and the Revolutionary Process.* London: Clarendon, 1981.

Ferenczi, Caspar. Der Stalinismus und seine Folgen. In: *Aufbruch mit Gorbatschow.* Edited by Caspar Ferenczi and Brigitte Löhr. Frankfurt: Fischer, 1987.

Feyerabend, Paul. *Against Method.* London: Verso, 1993.

Fields, Jeffrey. A Global Affairs Commentary: Small Arms Trafficking in the Americas. In: *Foreign Policy Focus.* 2001. Available at http://www. foreignpolicy-infocus.org/commentary/2001/0108arms.html

Filippone, Robert. The Medellín Cartel: Why We Can't Win The Drug War. In: *Studies in Conflict and Terrorism.* 17, 4, 1994.

Financial Action Task Force on Money Laundering (FATF). Basic Facts about Money Laundering, 2002. Available at http://www1.oecd.org/fatf/MLaundering_en.htm

Finckenauer, James O., and Elin J. Waring. *The Russian Mafia in America.* Boston, Massachusetts: Northeastern University Press, 1998.

Fischer Weltalmanach 1993. Frankfurt: Fischer, 1992.

Flynn, E. Lieutenant, Ph.D., Commander US Coast Guard. The Erosion of Sovereignty and the Emerging Global Drug Trade. A paper presented to the Annual Conference of the International Studies Association (ISA), Chicago, 1995.

Fontana, Benedeto. *Hegemony and Power.* Minneapolis: University of Minnesota Press, 1993.

Franke, Franz R. *Vom Römischen Reich zum Reich der Franken.* Munich: Diesterweg, 1974.

Freemantle, Brian. *Importeure des Verbrechens.* Munich: List, 1996. (Originally published in 1995 under the title *The Octopus: Europe in the Grip of Organized Crime* by Orion in London, England).

Freiberg, Konrad, and Berndt Georg Thamm. *Das Mafia-Syndrom.* Hilden, Germany: VDP, 1992.

Freud, Siegmund. *Schriften über Kokain.* Frankfurt: Fischer, 1999.

Frisby, Tanya. The Rise of Organized Crime in Russia: Its Roots and Social Significance. In: *Europe-Asia Studies.* 50, 1, 1998.

Fuhr, Harald, and Marion Hörmann. Peru. In: *Handbuch der Dritten Welt: Südamerika.* Edited by Dieter Nohlen and Franz Nuscheler. Bonn: Dietz, 1992.

Gagliano, Joseph A. The Coca Debate in Colonial Peru. In: *The Americas.* XX, 1, 1963.

Galeano, Eduardo. *Las venas abiertas de América Latina.* Mexico City: Siglo Veintiuno, 1982.

Galleotti, Mark. Perestroika, Perestrelka, Pereborka: Policing Russia in a Time of Change. In: *Europe-Asia Studies.* 45, 5, 1993.

Galvin, Peter R. *Patterns of Pillage*. New York: Lang, 2000.
Gareau, Frederick. The Anglophone 'Science' of International Relations: The Failure of a Noble and Painful Experiment. In: *The Indian Political Science Journal*. XVI, 1, 1982.
George, Susan. *How the Other Half Dies*. Middlesex, England: Penguin, 1985.
———. Debt as Warfare: An Overview of the Debt Crisis. In: *Third World Resurgence*. 28, December 1992.
Gerassi, John. *The Great Fear in Latin America*. New York: Collier, 1973.
Gerth, H. H., and C. Wright Mills. *From Max Weber: Essays in Sociology*. New York: Oxford University Press, 1958.
Giddens, Anthony. *The Nation-State and Violence*. Cambridge, England: Polity Press, 1985.
Gill, Stephen. Theorizing the Interregnum: The Double Movement and Global Politics in the 1990s. In: *International Political Economy: Understanding Global Disorder*. Edited by Björn Hettne. Halifax, Nova Scotia: Fernwood, 1995.
Girling, John. *Corruption, Capitalism and Democracy*. London: Routledge, 1997.
Gleason, Gregory. Nationalism or Organized Crime? The Case of the 'Cotton Scandal' in the USSR. In: *Corruption and Reform*. 5, 1990.
Gómez Ordoñez, Leonidas. *Cártel: Historia de la Droga*. Bogotá: Grupo Editorial, 1991.
González, José E. Guerrillas and Coca in the Upper Huallaga Valley. In: *Shining Path of Peru*. Edited by Scott Palmer. New York: St. Martin's Press, 1992.
Gonzáles, Raúl. Coca y subversión en el Huallaga. In: *Quehacer*. (Lima) 48, 1987.
———. El Huallaga: Todos los conflictos, In: *Quehacer*. 71, 1991.
Gosch, Martin A., and Richard Hammer. *The Last Testament of Lucky Luciano*. New York: Dell, 1976.
Gosse, Philip. *The History of Piracy*. New York: Tudor, 1946.
Gott, Richard. *Guerrilla Movements in Latin America*. Bungay, England: Chaucer, 1970.
Gottschalk Jack A., and Brian P. Flanagan. *Jolly Roger with an Uzi: The Rise and Threat of Modern Piracy*. Annapolis, Maryland: Naval Institute, 2000.
Gramsci, Antonio. *Selections From the Prison Notebooks*. Edited by Quentin Hoare and Geoffrey N. Smith. New York: International Publishers, 1971.
———. *Letters from Prison*. Edited by Lynne Lawner. New York: Harper and Row, 1973.
Gray, John. *False Dawn: The Delusions of Global Capitalism*. New York: New Press, 1998.
Gregory, Paul R., and Robert C. Stuart. *Soviet Economic Structure and Performance*. New York: Harper and Row, 1986.
Grinspoon, Lester, and James B. Bakalar. *Cocaine: A Drug and its Social Evolution*. New York: Basic, 1976.
Grinspoon, Lester, and James B. Bakalar. Coca and Cocaine as Medicines: An Historical Review. In: *Journal of Ethnopharmacology*. 3, 3, 1981.
Grosse, Robert. The Economic Impact of Andean Cocaine Traffic on Florida. In: *Journal of Interamerican Studies and World Affairs*. 32, 4, 1990.
Grossman, Gregory. *Economic Systems*. Englewood Cliffs, New Jersey: Prentice-Hall, 1977.
———. The Second Economy of the USSR. In: *Problems of Communism*. XXVI, 1977a.
Guerrero Paz, Manuel J. *Memoria al Congreso Nacional 1988–89*. Bogotá: Imprenta y Publicaciones de las Fuerzas Militares; as cited in Duque Gómez 1991: 212.
Gumucio Dagron, Alfonso. *La mascara del gorila*. Mexico City: Editorial Oasis, 1982.
Gutiérrez, Miguel. A la caza de un sobreviviente. In: *La República*. Sunday Supplement. June 1, 1997: 6–7. (Miguel Gutiérrez is an investigative journalist working for the daily *La República* with whom I have collaborated in the past. He lives and works in Lima, Peru).

————. Personal communication electronic mail. September 19, 2002.

Guzman, German, Orlando Borda, and Eduardo Umana Luna. *La Violencia en Colombia: Estudio de un proceso social.* Bogotá: Ediciones Tercer Mundo, 1963.

Haas, E. B. Is There a Hole in the Whole? Knowledge, Technology, Interdependence, and the Construction of International Regimes. In: *International Organization.* 29, 1975.

Haffner, Sebastian (Ed). *Der Vertrag von Versailles.* Frankfurt: Ullstein, 1988.

Hampden, John (Ed). *Sir Francis Drake: Pirat im Dienst der Queen.* Stuttgart: Thienemans, 1997.

Handelman, Stephen. *Comrade Criminal.* Middlesex, England: Penguin, 1994.

————. The Russian 'Mafiya.' In: *Foreign Affairs.* 73, 2, 1994a.

————. Interview. Canadian Broadcasting Corporation. CBC-Radio. Sunday Morning. October 23, 1994b.

Harasymiw, Bohdan. Die sowjetische Nomenklatur: I. Organisation und Mechanismen. In: *Osteuropa.* 27, 7, 1977.

Harding, Jeremy. The Mercenary Business: 'Executive Outcomes.' In: *Review of African Political Economy.* 24, 71, 1997.

Hardinghaus, Nicolas. Droga y crecimiento económico. In: *Nueva Sociedad.* 102, 1989.

Hargreaves, Clare. *Bitterer Schnee.* Munich: Beck, 1993. (Originally published in 1992 by Zed, London, under the title *Snowfields: The War on Cocaine in the Andes*).

Harris, Peter. Socialist Graft: The Soviet Union and the People's Republic of China — A Preliminary Survey. In: *Corruption and Reform.* 1, 1986.

Havel, Václav. *Versuch in der Wahrheit zu leben.* Hamburg: Rowohlt, 1980.

Head, Ivan L. *On A Hinge of History.* Toronto: University of Toronto Press, 1991.

Healy, Kevin. The Boom Within the Crisis: Some Recent Effects of Foreign Cocaine Markets on Bolivian Rural Society and Economy. In: *Coca and Cocaine: Effects on People and Policy in Latin America.* Edited by Deborah Pacini and Christine Franquemont. Boston, Massachusetts: Cultural Survival, 1986.

Heckethorn, Charles William. *The Secret Societies*, vol. I. New York: University Books, 1966. (Originally published in 1900).

Hein, Wolfgang, and Georg Simonis. Theoretische und methodische Probleme einer kritischen Theorie internationaler Politik. In: *Politische Vierteljahresschrift.* Wiesbaden, Germany. XIV, 1, 1973.

Helleiner, Eric. State Power and the Regulation of Illicit Activity in Global Finance. In: *The Illicit Global Economy and State Power.* Edited by H. Richard Friman and Peter Andreas. New York: Rowman and Littlefield, 1999.

Hendley, Kathryn, Barry W. Ickes, Peter Murrell, and Randi Ryterman. Observations on the Use of Law by Russian Enterprises. In: *Post-Soviet Affairs.* 13, 1, 1997.

Henman, Anthony. *Mama Koka.* Bremen, Germany: Verlag Roter Funke, 1981.

Hennessy, Alistair. Bolivia. In: *Latin America and the Caribbean.* Edited by Claudio Vélez. New York: Praeger, 1968.

Hensler, Al. National Security: A Changing View. *Carleton University Magazine.* Carleton University, Ottawa, Fall 1994.

Hess, Henner. The Traditional Sicilian Mafia: Organized Crime and Repressive Crime. In: *Organized Crime: A Global Perspective.* Edited by Robert J. Kelly. Totowa, New Jersey: Rowman and Littlefield, 1986.

————. *Mafia: Zentrale Herrschaft und Lokale Gegenmacht.* Tübingen, Germany: Mohr, 1988.

Hoffman, Mark. Normative International Relations Theory: Approaches and Issues. In:

Contemporary International Relations Theory. Edited by Margot Light and A. J. R. Groom. London: Pinter, 1994.

Holmstedt, Bo. Sundry Episodes in the History of Coca and Cocaine. In: *Journal of Ethnopharmacology.* 3, 3, 1981.

Holsti, K.J. *International Politics.* Englewood Cliffs, New Jersey: Prentice-Hall, 1977.

———. *The Dividing Discipline: Hegemony and Diversity in International Theory.* Boston, Massachusetts: Allen and Unwin, 1985.

Holtbrügge, Dirk. Ursachen, Ausmasse und Ausprägungen der Schattenwirtschaft in der UDSSR. In: *Osteuropa.* 41, 1, 1991.

Hoppé, E.O. *Pirates, Buccaneers, and Gentlemen Adventurers.* New York: A. S. Barnes, 1972.

Horkheimer, Max. The End of Reason. In: *The Essential Frankfurt School Reader.* Edited by Andrew Arato and Eike Gebhardt. New York: Continuum, 1982.

———. Zur Soziologie der Klassenverhältnisse. In: *Gesammelte Werke,* vol.12. Edited by Gunzelin Schmid Noerr. Frankfurt: Fischer, 1985.

———. Die Rackets und der Geist. In: *Gesammelte Werke,* vol.12, 1985a.

———. Theorie des Verbrechers. In: *Gesammelte Werke,* vol.12, 1985b.

———. Editorische Vorbemerkung. In: *Gesammelte Werke,* vol.12, 1985c.

———. Die Juden und Europa. In: Max Horkheimer. *Gesammelte Werke,* vol.4: Schriften 1936–1941. Edited by Gunzelin Schmid Noerr. Frankfurt: Fischer, 1988.

———. Fachmann, Führer und die Vernunft. In: Max Horkheimer. *Gesammelte Werke,* vol.14: Nachgelassene Schriften 1949–1972. Edited by Gunzelin Schmid Noerr. Frankfurt: Fischer, 1988a.

———. Clique als zentraler soziologischer Begriff für die heutige Gesellschaft. In: Max Horkheimer. *Gesammelte Werke,* vol.14, 1988b.

———. Herrschende Klasse, die von Rackets beherrschte Klasse und die Rolle der Fachleute. In: Max Horkheimer. *Gesammelte Werke,* vol.14, 1988c.

———. Eine neue Politik der Linken? In: Max Horkheimer. *Gesammelte Werke,* vol.14, 1988d.

———. Die Utopie vom Reich der Freiheit. In: Max Horkheimer. *Gesammelte Werke,* vol. 14, 1988e.

———. Das Racket der Ärzte I. In: Max Horkheimer, *Gesammelte Werke* Vol.14, 1988f.

———. Vernunft und Selbsterhaltung. In: Max Horkheimer. *Gesammelte, Schriften,* vol. 5: "Dialektik der Aufklärung" und Schriften 1940–1950. Edited by Gunzelin Schmid Noerr. Frankfurt: Fischer, 1997.

———. Aus einer Theorie des Verbrechers. In: Max Horkheimer. *Gesammelte Schriften,* vol. 5, 1997a.

Hornby, A. S., E. V. Gatenby, and H. Wakefield (Eds). *The Advanced Learner's Dictionary of Current English.* London: Oxford University Press, 1976.

Human Rights Watch (HRW) *World Report 2003: United States.* 2003. Available at http://www.hrw.org/wr2k3/us.html#incarceration

Hunter, Holland. *The Future of the Soviet Economy: 1978–1985.* Boulder, Colorado: Westview, 1978.

Hyams, Edward, and George Ordish. *The Last of the Incas.* New York: Dorset, 1963.

Ianni, Francis A. *Family Business: Kinship and Social Control in Organized Crime.* New York: Russel Sage, 1972.

Inca, Gerónimo. *El ABC de Sendero Luminoso y del MRTA.* Lima: GEGISA, 1994.

Informationen zur Politischen Bildung. Die Sowjetunion. 182. (Bonn, Germany), 1979.

International Monetary Fund (IMF). *Report on the World Current Account Discrepancy.* Final Report of the Working Party on the Statistical Discrepancies in World Current Account Balances. Washington, DC: International Monetary Fund, 1987.

Isaacs, Harold. *The Tragedy of the Chinese Revolution.* Stanford, California: Stanford University Press, 1962.

Isbell, Billie Jean. Shining Path and Peasant Responses in Rural Ayacucho. In: *Shining Path of Peru.* Edited by Scott Palmer, New York: St. Martin's Press, 1992.

Jackson, W.A. Douglas. *Russo-Chinese Borderlands.* New York: Van Nostrand, 1962.

Jancar, Barbara. Reform and Continuity in the USSR. In: *Public Bureaucracies between Reform and Resistance.* Edited by J. Piekalkiewicz and Christopher Hamilton. New York: Berg Publishers, 1991.

Jary, David, and Julia Jary (Eds). *The HarperCollins Dictionary of Sociology.* New York: Harper Collins, 1991.

Jenkins, Philip. Narcotics Trafficking and the American Mafia: The Myth of Internal Prohibition. In: *Crime, Law and Social Change.* 18, 1992.

Jennings, John. *The Opium Empire: Japanese Imperialism and Drug Trafficking in Asia 1895–1945.* Westport, Connecticut: Praeger, 1997.

Jochamowitz, Luis. *Ciudano Fujimori: La construción de un político.* Lima: Peisa, 1994.

Johnson, Chalmers. *The Sorrows of Empire: Militarism, Secrecy, and the End of the Republic.* New York: Holt, 2004.

Johnston, R. J. (Ed). *The Dictionary of Human Geography.* Oxford: Blackwell, 1983.

Jordan, Donald A. *The Northern Expedition.* Honolulu: The University of Hawaii Press, 1976.

Kaplan, David E., and Alec Dubro. *Yakuza.* Reading, Massachusetts: Addison-Wesley, 1986.

Karnow, Stanley. *Vietnam: A History.* New York: Penguin Books, 1984.

Katsenelinboigen, Aron. Colored Markets in the Soviet Union. In: *Soviet Studies.* XXXIX, 1, 1977.

Kawamura, Gabrielle. *Yakuza.* Pfaffenweiler, Germany: Centaurus Verlagsgesellschaft, 1994.

Kay, Cristóbal. For a Renewal of Development Studies: Latin American Theories and Neoliberalism in the Era of Structural Adjustment. In: *Third World Quarterly.* 14, 4, 1993.

Kay, Bruce H. Violent Opportunities: The Rise and Fall of 'King Coca' and Shining Path. *Journal of Interamerican Studies and World Affairs.* 41, 3, 1999.

Keen, Benjamin. *Latin American Civilization: The Colonial Origins.* Boston, Massachusetts: Houghton-Mifflin, 1974.

Kelly, Robert J. Criminal Underworlds: Looking Down on Society from Below. In: *Organized Crime: A Global Perspective.* Edited by Robert J. Kelly. Totowa, New Jersey: Rowman and Littlefield, 1986.

———, Rufus Schatzberg, and Patrick Ryan. Primitive Capitalist Accumulation: Russia as a Racket. In: *Understanding Organized Crime in Global Perspective.* Edited by Patrick Ryan and George E. Rush. Thousand Oaks, California: Sage, 1997.

Kenney, Dennis J. and James O. Finckenauer. *Organized Crime in America.* Belmont, California: Wadsworth, 1995.

Khor, Martin. *Rethinking Globalization.* Halifax, Nova Scotia: Fernwood, 2001.

Khryshtanovskaya, Olga, and Stephen White. From Soviet *Nomenklatura* to Russian Élite. In: *Europe-Asia Studies.* 48, 5, 1996.

Kidron, Michael. *Die Aufrüstung der Welt.* Hamburg: Rowohlt, 1983.

Kinder, Hermann, and Werner Hilgemann (Eds). *DTV-Atlas für Weltgeschichte*, vol.1. Munich: DTV, 1977.

Kinder, Hermann, and Werner Hilgermann (Eds). *DTV-Atlas zur Weltgeschichte*, vol.2. Munich: DTV, 1977a.

Klaus, Georg, and Manfred Buhr (Eds). *Marxistisch-Leninistisches Wörterbuch der Philosophie*, vol.1. Hamburg: Rowohlt, 1983.

Klein, Herbert S. *Bolivia: The Evolution of a Multi-Ethnic Society.* New York: Oxford University Press, 1992.

Knaur's Weltspiegel 1989. Munich: Droemer, 1988.

Kneen, Peter. Political Corruption in Russia and the Soviet Legacy. In: *Crime, Law and Social Change.* 34, 2000.

Knoester, Mark. War in Colombia. In: *Social Justice.* 25, 2, 1998.

Koestler, Arthur. *The Yogi and the Commissar.* New York: Macmillan, 1945.

Kolesnikow, Wadim, and Sergej Sidorow. Reformen in Rußland: Auf dem Weg zum Korrumpierten Markt? In: *Osteuropa.* 44, 4, 1994.

Kornbluth, Cyril M. *The Syndic.* New York: TOR Books, 1982.

Kraushaar, Beat and Emilie Lieberherr. *Drogenland in Mafiahand.* Zurich: Werd Verlag, 1996.

Krausnick, Helmut, and Martin Broszat. *Anatomy of the SS State.* London: Paladin, 1970.

Krauthausen, Ciro. *Moderne Gewalten: Organisierte Kriminalität in Kolumbien und Italien.* Frankfurt: Campus, 1997.

Kremer, Edward, and George Urdang. *History of Pharmacy.* Philadelphia: Lippincott, 1963.

Krippendorff, Ekkehart. Internationale Beziehungen—Versuch einer polit-ökomischen Rahmenanalyse. In: *Politische Vierteljahresschrift.* XIII, 3, 1972.

———. *International Relations as a Social Science.* New Delhi, India: Radiant Publishers, 1982.

Krumwiede, Heinrich W., and Reinhard Stockmann, *Kolumbien.* In: *Handbuch der Dritten Welt: Südamerika.* Edited by Dieter Nohlen and Franz Nuscheler. Bonn: Dietz, 1992.

Kuhn, Philip A. *Rebellion and its Enemies.* Cambridge, Massachusetts: Harvard University Press, 1980.

Kühnl, Reinhard (Ed). *Texte zur Faschismusdiskussion*, vol. I. Edited by Reinhard Kühnl. Hamburg: Rowohlt, 1974.

———. (Ed). *Texte zur Faschismusdiskussion*, vol. II. Hamburg: Rowohlt, 1979.

———. *Formen bürgerlicher Herrschaft*, vol. I. Hamburg: Rowohlt, 1983.

Ladman, Jeremy. The Political Economy of the Economic Miracle of the Banzer Regime. In: *Modern-Day Bolivia: Legacy of the Revolution and Prospects for the Future.* Edited by Jeremy Ladman. Tempe, Arizona: Center for Latin American Studies, Arizona State University, 1982.

Landsberger, Artur. The Berlin Underworld (1929). In: *The Weimar Republic Source Book.* Edited by Anton Kaes et al. Berkeley: University of California Press, 1994.

Laszlo, Ervin. *The Age of Bifurcation.* Philadelphia: Gordon and Breach, 1991.

Lee, Martin, and Norman Solomon. *Unreliable Sources.* New York: Carol, 1990.

Lee III, Rensselaer W. The Latin American Drug Connection. In: *Foreign Policy.* 61, 1985-1986.

———. *The White Labyrinth: Cocaine and Political Power.* New Brunswick, New Jersey: Transaction, 1988.

———. Colombia's Cocaine Syndicates. In: *Crime, Law and Social Change.* 16, 1991.

————, and Scott B. Macdonald. Drugs in the East. In: *Foreign Affairs.* 72, 2, 1993.

Lehmbruch, Gerhard. Liberal Corporatism and Party Government. In: *Comparative Political Studies.* 10, 1977.

Leichtmann, Ellen. Bolivia, Coca and US Foreign Policy. In: *Critical Criminology: An International Journal.* 9. 1 / 2, 2000.

Lennhoff, Eugen. *Politische Geheimbünde.* Munich: Amathea Verlag, 1966.

Leóns, Madeline B. Cocaine in the Bolivian Yungas. In: *Journal of Latin American Studies.* 25, 1, 1993.

————, and Harry Sanabria. Coca and Cocaine in Bolivia. In: *Coca, Cocaine, and the Bolivian Reality.* Edited by Madeline B. Leóns and Harry Sanabria. Albany, New York: State University of New York Press, 1997.

Lessmann, Robert. *Drogenökonomie und internationale Politik. Die Auswirkungen der Antidrogen-Politik der USA auf Bolivien und Kolumbien.* Frankfurt: Vervuert, 1996.

Levine, Michael, and Laura Kavanau-Levine. *The Big White Lie.* New York: Thunder's Mouth, 1994.

Lilly, J. Robert, Francis T. Cullen and Richard A Ball. *Criminological Theory.* Thousand Oaks, California: Sage, 1995.

Lindblom, Charles E. *Politics and Markets.* New York: Basic, 1977.

Linklater, Andrew. The Question of the Next Stage in International Relations Theory: A Critical-Theoretical Point of View. In: *Millennium.* 21, 1, 1992.

Linklater, Magnus. *The Fourth Reich.* London: Hodder and Stoughton, 1984.

Lipset, Seymour M. *Political Man.* New York: Doubleday, 1963.

Luke, Timothy W., and Carl Boggs. Soviet Subimperialism and the Crisis of Bureaucratic Centralism. In: *Studies in Comparative Communism.* XV, 1982.

Lunev, Stanislav. *Through the Eyes of the Enemy.* Washington, DC: Regnery, 1998.

Lupsha, Peter A. Organized Crime in the United States. In: *Organized Crime: A Global Perspective.* Edited by Robert Kelly. Totowa, New Jersey: Rowman and Littlefield, 1986.

————. Transnational Organized Crime versus the Nation-State. In: *Transnational Organized Crime.* 2, 1, 1996.

Lusane, Clarence. *Pipe Dream Blues: Racism and the War on Drugs.* Boston, Massachusetts: South End, 1991.

Lyman, Michael D., and Gary W. Potter. *Organized Crime.* Upper Saddle River, New Jersey: Prentice Hall, 2000.

Lyonette, Kevin J. Colombia. In: *Latin America and the Caribbean: A Handbook.* Edited by Claudio Velíz. New York: Praeger, 1968.

Maas, Peter. *The Valachi Papers.* New York: Bantam, 1972.

MacDonald, Scott B. *Mountain High, White Avalanche: Cocaine and Power in the Andean States and Panama.* New York: Praeger, 1989.

Mach, Holger. Exclusion and Extinction — The Fight Against Narcotics in the Third Reich. In: *Journal of Drug Issues.* 32, 2, 2002.

MacIntyre, Donald. *The Privateers.* London: Paul Elek Ltd, 1975.

MacKenzie, Norman. *Secret Societies.* New York: Collier, 1971.

Macomber, Shawn. You're Not in the Army Now. In: *The American Spectator.* 37, 9, November 2004.

Maier. Hans W. *Cocaine Addiction.* Toronto: Alcoholism and Drug Addiction Research Foundation, 1987. (Originally published as *Der Kokainismus— Geschichte/Pathologische/Medizinische und behördliche Bekämpfung.* Leipzig,

Germany: Georg Thieme Verlag, 1926).

Maingot, Anthony P. Offshore Secrecy Centers and the Necessary Role of States: Bucking the Trend. In: *Journal of Interamerican and World Affairs*. 37, 4, 1995.

Malloy, James, and Eduardo Gamarra. *Revolution and Reaction: Bolivia 1964–1985*. New Brunswick, New Jersey: Transaction, 1988.

Mann, Michael. *The Sources of Social Power*, vol.1. Cambridge: Cambridge University Press, 1986.

Manrique, Nelson. Time of Fear. In: *NACLA Report on the Americas*. XXIV, 4, 1991.

———. The Two Faces of Fujimori's Rural Policy. In: *NACLA Report on the Americas*. XXX, 1, 1996.

———. The War for the Central Sierra. In: *Shining And Other Paths*. Edited by Steve Stern. Durham, North Carolina: Duke University Press, 1998.

Mappes-Niedik, Norbert. *Balkan-Mafia: Staaten in der Hand des Verbrechens*. Berlin: Ch. Links, 2003.

Marcuse, Herbert. *Soviet Marxism: A Critical Analysis*. New York: Random House, 1961.

Martin, Brian G. *The Shanghai Green Gang*. Berkeley: University of California Press, 1996.

Martin, Hanns-Peter, and Harald Schumann. *Die Globalisierungsfalle*. Hamburg: Rowohlt, 1996.

Marx, Carlos. *El dieciocho Brumario de Luis Bonaparte*. Barcelona, Spain: Ariel, 1971. (Originally published as *Der Achtzehnte Brumaire des Louis Bonaparte* in Germany in 1869).

Mariátegui, José Carlos. *7 ensayos de interpretación de la realidad peruana*. Lima: Empresa Editora Amauta, 2002.

Mason, Mike. *Development and Disorder: A History of the Third World since 1945*. Toronto: Between The Lines, 1997.

Maximenkov, Leonid, and C. Namiesniowski. Organized Crime in Post-Communist Russia —A Criminal Revolution? In: *Commentary*. (A Canadian Security Intelligence Service publication), 48, 1994.

Mayer, Enrique. Coca Use in the Andes. In: *Drugs in Latin America*. Edited by Edmundo Morales. Williamsburg, Virginia: Studies in Third World Societies, no.37, 1986.

Mayer, Heinz. *Kolumbien: Der Schmutzige Krieg*. Hamburg: Rowohlt, 1990.

McCauley, Martin. *Bandits, Gangsters and the Mafia: Russia, the Baltic States and the Mafia*. London: Pearson, 2001.

McClintock, Cynthia. Velasco, Officers, and Citizens. In: *The Peruvian Experiment Reconsidered*. Edited by Cynthia McClintock and Abraham Lowenthal. Princeton, New Jersey: Princeton University Press, 1983.

McCoy, Alfred W. *The Politics of Heroin*. New York: Lawrence Hill, 1991.

———. Coercion and its Unintended Consequences: A Study of Heroin Trafficking in Southeast and South West Asia. In: *Crime, Law and Social Change*. 33, 3, 2000.

McKenna, Peter. Private Warriors are the New Face of Warfare. In: *The Globe and Mail*. (Canada) December 11, 2004: A25.

McIllwain, Scott. Organized Crime: A Social Network Approach. In: *Crime, Law and Social Change*. 32, 4, 1999.

McLuhan, Marshall, and Bruce Powers. *The Global Village*. New York: Oxford University Press, 1989.

McMurtry, John. The FTAA and the WTO: The Meta-Programme For Global Corporate Rule. In: *Third World Resurgence*. 129/130. May–June 2001.

Medina Gallego, Carlos. *Autodefensas, paramilitares y narcotráfico*. Bogotá: Editorial

Documentos Periodisticos, 1990.

Mehlum, Halvor, Karl Ove Moene, and Ragnar Torvik. Plunder & Protection Inc. In: *Journal of Peace Research.* 39, 4, 2002.

Merry, Uri. *Coping With Uncertainty.* Westport, Connecticut: Praeger, 1995.

Merton, Robert K. *Social Theory and Structure.* Glencoe, Illinois: Free Press, 1957.

―――. Social Structure and Anomie. In: *The Sociology of Crime and Delinquency.* Edited by Marvin E. Wolfgang, Leonard Zavitz, and Norman Johnston. New York: Wiley and Sons, 1970.

Meschkat, Klaus, Petra Rohde, and Barbara Töpper. *Kolumbien: Geschichte und Gegenwart eines Landes im Ausnahmezustand.* Berlin: Wagenbach, 1983.

Meyers, Reinhard. *Die Lehre von den Internationalen Beziehungen.* Düsseldorf, Germany: Droste, 1977.

Michels, Robert. *Political Parties: A Sociological Study of the Oligarchical Tendencies of Modern Democracy.* New York: Free Press, 1966. (Originally published in Germany in 1911 as *Zur Soziologie des Parteiwesens in der Modernen Demokratie: Untersuchungen über die Oligarchischen Tendenzen des Gruppenlebens*).

Midlarsky, Manus, and Kenneth Roberts. Class, State and Revolution in Central America. In: *Journal of Conflict Resolution.* 29, 2, 1985.

Miliband, Ralph. *The State in Capitalist Society.* London: Quartet, 1973.

Millar, James R. The Little Deal: Brezhnev's Contribution to Acquisitive Socialism. In: *Slavic Studies.* 44, 4, 1984.

Miller, Andrew. Colombia in Crisis. In: *Foreign Policy in Focus.* 6, 20, 2001.Available at http://www.foreignpolicy-infocus.org/briefs/vol6/v6n20colombia.html

Mirow, Kurt R., and Harry Maurer. *Webs of Power: International Cartels and the World Economy.* Boston, Massachusetts: Houghton-Mifflin, 1982.

Mitchell, Christopher, Michael Stohl, D. Carleton, and George A. Lopez. State Terrorism: Issues of Concept and Measurement. In: *Government Violence and Repression.* Edited by Michael Stohl and George A. Lopez. New York: Greenwood, 1986.

Mittelman, James H., and Robert Johnston. The Globalization of Organized Crime, the Courtesan State, and the Corruption of Civil Society. In: *Global Governance.* 5, 1, 1999.

Mols, Manfred. Politikwissenschaft. In: *Wörterbuch Staat und Politik.* Edited by Dieter Nohlen. Munich: Piper, 1995.

Mommsen, Hans. Zur Verschränkung traditioneller und faschistischer Führungsgruppen in Deutschland beim Übergang von der Bewegungs — zur System-phase. In: *Faschismus als soziale Bewegung: Deutschland und Italien im Vergleich.* Edited by Wolfgang Schieder. Hamburg: Hoffmann, 1976.

Moore, Barrington. *Social Origins of Dictatorships and Democracy.* Boston: Massachusetts: Beacon, 1966.

Moore Jr., Richter H. Twenty-First Century Law to Meet the Challenge of Twenty-First Century Organized Crime. In: *Technological Forecasting and Social Change.* 52, 1996.

Morales, Edmundo. The Political Economy of Cocaine Production: An Analysis of the Peruvian Case. In: *Latin American Perspectives.* 17, 4, 1990.

―――. The Andean Cocaine Dilemma. In: *Drug Trafficking in the Americas.* Edited by Bruce M. Bagley and William O. Walker III. Miami, Florida: North-South Center Press, 1996.

Mori, Cesare. *The Last Struggle With The Mafia.* London: Putnam, 1933.

Mortimer, W. Golden. *History of Coca.* San Francisco: Fitz Hugh Ludlow, 1974.

Morton, James. *Gangland International.* London, England: Warner, 1999.

Mosca, Gaetano. *The Ruling Class.* London: Mcgraw-Hill, 1939.

———. *¿Qué es la mafia?* Buenos Aires, Argentina: Fondo de Cultura Económica, 2003. (Originally published in Italy in *Giornale degli Economisti.* 20, 1900)

Motala, John. Statistical Discrepancies in the World Currency Account. In: *Finance & Development.* 34, 1, 1997. Available at http://www.worldbank.org/fandd/ english/ abstract/0397/015a0397.htm

Murray, Dian H. *Pirates of the South China Coast.* Stanford, California: Stanford University Press, 1987.

Murrell, Peter, and Mancur Olson. The Evolution of Centrally Planned Economies. In: *Journal of Comparative Economics.* XV, 2, 1991.

Musto David. *The American Disease.* New Haven, Connecticut: Yale University Press, 1973.

Naranjo, Plutarco. Social Function of Coca in Pre-Columbian America. In: *Journal of Ethnopharmacology.* 3, 1981.

Naylor, R.T. The Insurgent Economy: Black Market Operations of Guerilla Organizations. In: *Crime, Law and Social Change.* 20, 1, 1993.

———. *Hot Money and the Politics of Debt.* Montreal: Black Rose, 1994 .

Neira, Hugo. Peru. In: *Guide to the Political Parties of South America.* Edited by Richard Gott. Middlesex, England: Penguin, 1973.

Nelli, Humberto S. Overview. In: *Organized Crime: A Global Perspective.* Edited by Robert J. Kelly. Totowa, New Jersey: Rowman and Littlefield, 1986.

Nicholson, Michael. Conceptual Problems of Studying State Terrorism. In: *Government Violence and Repression.* Edited by Michael Stohl and George A. Lopez. New York: Greenwood, 1986.

No Author. *Movimientos revolucionarios de America Latina*, vol. 1. Caracas: Indal, 1972.

No Author. *Case 1/1989: End of the Cuban Connection.* Havana, Cuba: Jose Marti Publishing, 1989.

No Author. *Nueva Constitución: Política de Colombia.* Bogotá: Asamblea Nacional Constituyente, 1991.

Nohlen, Dieter, and René Antonio Mayorga. Bolivien. In: *Handbuch der Dritten Welt: Südamerika.* Edited by Dieter Nohlen and Franz Nuscheler. Bonn: Dietz, 1992.

Nolte, Ernst. Die 'herrschenden Klassen' und der Faschismus in Italien. In: *Faschismus als soziale Bewegung: Deutschland und Italien im Vergleich.* Edited by Wolfgang Schieder, Hamburg: Hoffmann, 1976.

Norberg-Hodge, Helena, Todd Merrifield, and Steven Gorelick. *Bringing the Food Economy Home.* Halifax: Fernwood, 2002.

North, Liisa L. Ideologial Orientations of Peru's Military Rulers. In: *The Peruvian Experiment Reconsidered.* Edited by Cynthia McClintock and Abraham Lowenthal. Princeton, New Jersey: Princeton University Press, 1983.

Nove, Alec. Is there a Ruling Class in the USSR? In: *Soviet Studies.* XXVII, 4, 1976.

Obando, Enrique. Civil-Military Relations in Peru, 1980–1996: How to Control and Coopt the Military (and the consequences of doing so). In: *Shining And Other Paths.* Edited by Steve Stern. Durham, North Carolina: Duke University Press, 1998.

O'Brien, Kevin A. Privatizing Security, Privatizing War? The New Warrior Class and Regional Security. In: *Warlords in International Relations.* Edited by Paul B. Rich. London: St. Martin's Press, 1999.

Observatoire Géopolitique des Drogues (OGD). *Der Welt-Drogen-Bericht.* Munich: DTV, 1993.

Oh, Cecilia. The Health Crisis in Developing Countries. In: *Third World Resurgence.* 131/132. July–August 2001.

Ormerod. Henry A. *Piracy in the Ancient World.* Liverpool: University of Liverpool Press, 1924.

Ortega y Gasset, José. *The Revolt of the Masses.* New York: Norton and Co, 1960. (Originally published in Spain as *La rebelión de las masas* in 1930).

Oschliess, Wolf. 'Oekokriege' in Osteuropa. In: *Bericht des Bundesinstitutes für Ostwissenschaftliche Fragen.* 29. (Bonn, Germany), 1990.

Painter, James. *Bolivia and Coca: A Study in Dependency.* Boulder, Colorado: Lynne Rienner, 1994.

Painter, Joe. *Politics, Geography and 'Political Geography': A Critical Perspective.* London: Arnold, 1995.

Pakulski, Jan. Bureaucracy and the Soviet System. In: *Studies in Comparative Communism.* XIX, 1986.

Palmer, David S. Peru, the Drug Business and Shining Path: Between Scylla and Charybdis? In: *Journal of Interamerican Studies and World Affairs.* 34, 3, 1992.

———. Peru, Drugs, and Shining Path. In: *Drug Trafficking in the Americas.* Edited by Bruce M. Bagley and William O. Walker III. Miami, Florida: North-South Center Press, 1996.

Paloczi-Horvath, Georg. *Mao Tse-tung.* Frankfurt: Ullstein, 1967.

Pantaleone, Michele. *The Mafia and Politics.* London: Chatto and Windus, 1966.

Paoli, Letizia. Drug Trafficking in Russia: A Form of Organized Crime? In: *Journal of Drug Issues.* 31. 4 , 2001.

Pareto, Vilfredo. *The Rise and Fall of the Elites: An Application of Theoretical Sociology.* Totowa, New Jersey: Bedminster, 1968.

Parish, James Robert. *Pirates and Seafaring Swashbucklers on the Hollywood Screen.* Jefferson, North Carolina: McFarland, 1995.

Pascal, Nina. East European-Soviet Relations in a Changing Economic Environment. In: *East European Quarterly.* XXIII, 1, 1989.

Parssinen, Terry M. *Secret Passions, Secret Remedies: Narcotic Drugs in British Society 1820–1930.* Philadelphia: Institute for the Study of Human Issues, 1983.

Passas, Nikos. Global Anomie, Dysnomie, and Economic Crime: Hidden Consequences of Neoliberalism and Globalization in Russia and Around the World. In: *Social Justice.* 27, 2, 2000.

Payne, Robert. *The Life and Death of Lenin.* New York: Avon, 1964.

Pearce, Frank. *Crimes of the Powerful.* London: Pluto, 1976.

———. Organized Crime and Class Politics. In: *Crime and Capitalism: Readings in Marxist Criminology.* Edited by David F. Greenberg. Palo Alto, California: Mayfield, 1981.

———, and Steve Tombs. *Toxic Capitalism.* Toronto: Canadian Scholarly Press, 1999.

Pearce, Jenny. *Colombia: Inside the Labyrinth.* London: Latin American Bureau, 1990.

———. The Dirty War. In: *NACLA Report on the Americas.* XXIII, 6, 1990a.

Petras, James, and Henry Veltmeyer. *Globalization Unmasked.* Halifax, Nova Scotia: Fernwood, 2001.

Philip, George D. F. *The Rise and Fall of the Peruvian Military Radicals 1968–1976.* London: Athlone, 1978.

Picasso, Connie, and Gonzalo Martin. *Itinerario de mil desaciertos políticos 1990–2001.* Lima: Editorial Don Augustin, 2001.

Pizarro, Eduardo. Revolutionary Guerrilla Groups in Colombia. In: *Violence in Colombia.* Edited by Charles Bergquist, Ricardo Peñaranda, and Gonzalo Sánchez. Wilmington, Delaware: SR Books, 1992.

Pleticha, Heinrich. *Freibeuter, Piraten, und Korsaren.* Stuttgart: Thienemans, 1997.

Plowman, Timothy. Coca Chewing and the Botanical Origins of Coca (*Erythroxlon Spp.*) in South America. In: *Coca and Cocaine* (Proceedings of the conference "The Coca Leaf and Its Derivatives — Biology, Society and Policy." Edited by Deborah Pacini and Christine Franquemont. Published with the Latin American Studies Program, Cornell University, 1986.

Plutarch. *Crassus.* Translated by John Dryden. The Classics Archive, n. d. Available at http://classics.mit.edu/Plutarch/crassus.1b.txt

Pohrt, Wolfgang. *Brothers in Crime.* Berlin: Verlag Klaus Bittermann, 2000.

Poole, Deborah, and Gerardo Rénique. *Peru: Time of Fear.* London: Latin America Bureau, 1992.

Porch, Douglas. *The French Secret Services.* New York: Farrar, Straus and Giroux, 1995.

Portes, Alejandro, and József Böröcz. The Informal Sector under Capitalism and State Socialism. In: *Social Justice.* 15, 3–4, 1988.

Portocarrero, Gonzalo. *Rostros criollos del mal.* Lima: Red para el desarollo de las ciencias sociales en el Peru, 2004.

Pott, Marcel. *Allahs Falsche Propheten.* Bergisch Gladbach, Germany: Bastei Lübbe, 2001.

Poulantzas, Nicos. *Political Power and Social Classes.* London: New Left, 1969.

Prescott, William H. *History of the Conquest of Peru.* London: Dent and Sons, 1963.

Preston, Richard and Sydney Wise. *Men in Arms.* New York: Holt, Rinehart and Winston, 1979.

Prybyla, Jan. *Issues in Socialist Economic Modernization.* New York: Praeger, 1980.

Pütter, Norbert. *Der OK-Komplex.* Münster, Germany: Westfälisches Dampfboot, 1998.

Putzger, F. W. (Ed). *Historischer Weltatlas.* Bielefeld, Germany: Cornelsen-Velhagen and Klasing, 1970.

Quiroz, Alfonso W. Costos históricos de la corrupción en el Perú Republicano. In: *El pacto infame: estudios sobre la corrupción en el Perú.* Edited by Felipe Portocarrero S. Lima: Red para el desarrollo de las ciencias sociales en el Perú, 2005.

Raghavan, Chakravarthi. OECD Toxic Waste Exports Banned Under New Agreement. In: *Third World Resurgence.* 63, November 1995.

———. TNCs Control Two-Thirds of the World Economy. In: *Third World Resurgence.* 65/66, January–February 1996.

Raith, Werner. *Das Neue Mafia-Kartel.* Berlin: Rowohlt, 1994.

———. *Organisierte Kriminalität.* Hamburg: Rowohlt, 1995.

Rangel, Carlos. *Del buen salvaje al buen revolucionario.* Caracas: Monte Avila Editores, 1982.

Rangel Suárez, Alfredo. Colombia: la guerra irregular en el fin de siglo. In: *Análisis Político.* 28, 1996.

Rankin, Hugh F. *The Golden Age of Piracy.* Williamsburg, Virginia: Colonial Williamsburg, 1969.

Reid, Michael. Una región amenazada por el narcotráfico. In: *Coca, cocaína y narcotráfico.* Edited by Diego García-Sayán. Lima: Comisión Andina de Juristas, 1989.

Reinhardt, David. *Pirates and Piracy.* New York: Konecky and Konecky, 1997.

Renborg, Bertil. *International Drug Control: A Study of International Administration By and Through the League of Nations.* New York: Kraus Reprint Co, 1972. (Originally published in 1947).

Rey, Romeo. *Zehn Jahre Grausamkeit oder die Erdrosselung Lateinamerikas.* Hamburg: Rowohlt, 1983.

Reyes, Alejandro. Drug Trafficking and the Guerrilla Movements in Colombia. In: *Drug Trafficking in the Americas.* Edited by Bruce M. Bagley and William O. Walker III. Miami, Florida: North-South Center Press, 1996.

Reyna Izaguirre, Carlos. Hard-Learned Lessons: Plan Colombia and Democracy in Peru. In: *Foreign Policy in Focus.* 2001. Available at http:// www.foreignpolicy-infocus. org/commentary/2001/0105peru.html

Richani, Nazih. The Political Economy of Violence: The War-System in Colombia. In: *Journal of Interamerican Studies and World Affairs.* 39, 2, 1997.

———. Colombia at the Crossroads: The Future of the Peace Accords. In: *NACLA Report on the Americas.* XXXV, 4, 2002.

Rifkin, Jeremy. *The End of Work: The Decline of the Global Labour Force and the Dawn of the Post-Market Era.* New York: Putnam, 1995.

Rigakos, George S. *The New Parapolice: Risk Markets and Commodified Social Control.* Toronto: University of Toronto Press, 2002.

Roberts, J. M. *The Mythology of Secret Societies.* London: Secker and Warburg, 1972.

Roberts, Kenneth, and Mark Peceny. Human Rights and United States Policy Toward Peru. In: *The Peruvian Labyrinth.* Edited by Maxwell A. Cameron and Phillip Mauceri, University Park, Pennsylvania: Pennsylvania State University Press, 1997.

Robertson, Roland. *Globalization: Social Theory and Global Culture.* London: Sage, 1993.

Robinson, William I. *A Theory of Global Capitalism: Production, Class, and State in a Transnational World.* Baltimore, Maryland: John Hopkins University Press, 2004.

Robles, Rodolfo. General (ret). Peruvian Armed Forces. Interview. Lima, August 1996.

Rosner, Lydia S. *The Soviet Way of Crime.* South Hadley, Massachusetts: Bergin and Garvey, 1986.

Rospiglioso, Fernando. El poder del narcotráfico. In: *El poder en el Perú.* Edited by Augusto Alvarez Rodrich. Lima: Editorial Apoyo, 1993.

———. *Montesinos y las fuerzas armadas.* Lima: IEP Ediciones, 2000.

Ross, Robert J. S., and Kent C. Trachte. *Global Capitalism: The New Leviathan.* New York: New York State University Press, 1990.

Rostow, Walt W. *The World Economy.* Austin, Texas: University of Texas Press, 1979.

Rostow, Walt W. and Alfred Levin. *The Dynamics of Soviet Society.* New York: Mentor, 1960.

Roth, Jürgen. *Die Russen-Mafia.* Hamburg: Rasch und Röhring, 1996.

———. *Schmutzige Hände: Wie die westlichen Staaten mit der Drogenmafia kooperieren.* Munich: Goldmann, 2001.

Ruiz, Bert. *The Colombian Civil War.* Jefferson, North Carolina: McFarland, 2001.

Rumrill, Roger. Piden ampliar diálogo con todos los gremios cocaleros. In: *La República.* (Lima) July 8, 1991: 16.

———. The Highs and Lows of a Cocaine Economy. In: *Why People Grow Drugs: Narcotics and Development in the Third World.* Edited by Michael Smith, Charunjee Normita Thongtham, Najma Sadeque, Alfredo Molano Bravo, Roger Rumrill, and Amanda Dávila. London: Panos, 1992.

———. Interview. August 1996. Lima. Roger Rumrill is a Peruvian environmental activist.

At the time of the interview, he was the president of *Oro Verde*, a nonprofit organization which aims to preserve the cultures and traditions of the peoples of Amazonia.

Ryan, Kevin F. Globalizing the Problem: The United States and International Drug Control. In: *The New War on Drugs: Symbolic Politics and Criminal Justice Policy.* Edited by Eric E. Jensen and Jurg Gerber. Cincinnati, Ohio: Anderson, 1998.

Sakamoto, Yoshikazu. Democratization, Social Movements and World Order. In: *International Political Economy: Understanding Global Disorder.* Edited by Björn Hettne. Halifax, Nova Scotia: Fernwood, 1995.

Salisbury, Harrison. *Russia.* New York: Athenaeum, 1965.

Salvemini, Gaetano. *Under the Axe of Fascism.* New York: Citadel Press, 1971.

Santino, Umberto. The Financial Mafia: The Illegal Accumulation of Wealth and the Financial-Industrial Complex. In: *Contemporary Crises.* 12, 1988.

————. Die sizilianische Mafia und die neuen Drogenmärkte. In: *Der Planet der Drogen.* Edited by Alain Labrousse and Alain Wallon. Frankfurt: Fischer, 1996.

————. Mafia and Mafia-type Organizations in Italy. Centro Siciliano di Documentazione 'Guiseppe Impastato' (CSD), 2001. Available athttp://www.centroimpastato.it/ publ/ online/mafia-in-italy.htm (Accessed February 19, 2001.)

Schacher, Gerhard. *Germany Pushes South-East.* London: Hurst and Blackett, 1937.

Schelling, Thomas C. Economics and Criminal Enterprise. In: *The Public Interest.* 7, 1967.

Scherrer, Christoph. Critical International Relations: Kritik am neo-realistischen Paradigma der Internationalen Beziehungen. In: *PROKLA: Zeitschrift für kritische Sozialwissenschaft.* (Berlin) 24, 2, 1994.

Schieder, Wolfgang. Thesenpapier zur Tagung bei der Katholischen Akademie in Schwerte. April 29, 1972. As cited in: *Texte zur Faschismusdiskussion*, vol.II. Edited by Reinhard Kühnl. Hamburg: Rowohlt. 1979.

Schleich, Carl Ludwig. Cocaineism. (1921) In: *The Weimar Republic Source Book.* Edited by Anton Kaes et al. Berkeley: University of California Press, 1994.

Schmidt-Häuser, Christian. Die Macht schlägt zurück. In: *Die Zeit.* (Bonn) November 4, 1994: 6.

Schneider, Arnd, and Oscar Zarate. *Mafia For Beginners.* Cambridge, England: Icon, 1994.

Scholl-Latour, Peter. *Der Tod im Reisfeld: Dreißig Jahre Krieg in Indochina.* Stuttgart: Deutsche Verlags-Anstalt, 1979.

Schreiber, Hermann. Foreword to *Das Piratenbuch von 1678*, by Alexandre Olivier Exquemelin. Stuttgart: Thienemans, 1983.

Schulte-Bockholt, A. A Neo-Marxist Explanation of Organized Crime. In: *Critical Criminology: An International Journal.* 10, 3, 2002.

Schulz, Paul. *Piraten Ihrer Majestät.* Würzburg, Germany: Arena, 1971.

Schultze-Kraft, Peter. *Der Tag an dem wir die Waffen vergruben.* Frankfurt: Goldmann, 1982.

Schwartz, Herman M. *States versus Markets.* New York: St. Martin's Press, 1994.

Scott, Peter Dale, and Jonathan Marshall. *Cocaine Politics.* Berkeley: University of California Press, 1991.

————. Cocaine, the Contras, and the United States: How the US Government has Augmented America's Drug Crisis. In: *Crime, Law and Social Change.* 16, 1991.

Seagrave, Sterling. *The Soong Dynasty.* New York: HarperCollins, 1985.

————. Dragon Lady. New York: Vintage Books, 1992.

Seefelder, Matthias. *Opium: Eine Kulturgeschichte.* Hamburg: Nikol, 1996.

Senghaas, Dieter. *Von Europa Lernen.* Frankfurt: Suhrkamp, 1982.

Senior, C. M. *A Nation of Pirates.* Vancouver: Douglas David and Charles, 1976.

Serio, Joseph, (Ed.) *USSR Crime Statistics and Summaries: 1989 and 1990.* Chicago, Illinois: University of Illinois Press, 1992.

Servadio, Gaia. *Mafioso.* London: Secker and Warburg, 1976.

Shannon, Elaine. *Desperados.* New York: Penguin, 1989.

Shelley, Louise I. Crime in the Soviet Union. In: *Soviet Social Problems.* Edited by Anthony Jones, Walter D. Connor, and David E. Powell. Boulder, Colorado: Westview, 1991.

————. Transnational Organized Crime: The New Authoritarianism. In: *The Illicit Global Economy and State Power.* Edited by H. Richard Friman and Peter Andreas. New York: Rowman and Littlefield, 1999.

Shevchenko, Arkady N. *Breaking with Moscow.* New York: Ballantine, 1985.

Short, John Rennie. *An Introduction to Political Geography.* London: Routledge, 1993.

Short, Martin. *Crime Inc.* London: Mandarin, 1996.

Sifakis, Carl. *The Encyclopedia of American Crime.* New York: Smithmark, 1982.

Silvermann, Bertram, and Murray Yanowitch. *New Rich, New Poor, New Russia: Winners and Losers on the Russian Road to Capitalism.* New York: M.E. Sharpe, 1997.

Simis, Konstantin. *The Corrupt Society.* New York: Simon and Schuster, 1982.

Simmel, Georg. The Sociology of Secrecy and of Secret Societies. In: *The American Journal of Sociology.* XI, 4, 1906.

Singh, Someshwar. Privatization and 'Reforms' Spread Corruption. In: *Third World Resurgence.* 120/121, August–September 2000.

Singh, Kavaljit. Patents vs. Patients: AIDS, TNCs and Drug Price Wars. In: *Third World Resurgence.* 131/132, July–August 2001.

Sinha, Jay. The History and Development of the Leading International Drug Control Conventions. Law and Government Division. Prepared for the Senate Special Committee For Illegal Drugs. Library of Parliament. Ottawa, Canada, 2001.

Skidmore, Thomas, and Peter H. Smith. *Modern Latin America.* New York: Oxford University Press, 1984.

Sklair, Leslie. *Sociology of the Global System.* Baltimore, Maryland: The John Hopkins University Press, 1991.

————. *The Transnational Capitalist Class.* Oxford: Blackwell, 2000.

Smith, Dwight. *The Mafia Mystique.* New York: Basic, 1975.

Smith, Joseph W., Graham Lyons, and Evonne Moore. *Global Meltdown.* Westport, Connecticut: Praeger, 1998.

Smith, Michael. The Gordian Knot: The Connection between Narcotics and Development. In: *Why People Grow Drugs: Narcotics and Development in the Third World.* Edited by Michael Smith, Charunjee Normita Thongtham, Najma Sadeque, Alfredo Molano Bravo, Roger Rumrill, Amanda Dávila. London: Panos, 1992.

Smith, Peter H. Semi-organized International Crime: Drug Trafficking in Mexico. In: *Transnational Crime in the Americas.* Edited by Tom Farrer. New York: Routledge, 1999.

Smyth, Frank. Colombia's Blowback: Formerly CIA-Backed Paramilitaries are Major Drug Traffickers Now. In: *Crime in Uniform: Corruption and Impunity in Latin America.* La Paz, Bolivia: Transnational Institute (TNI) and Acción Andina, 1997. Available at http://www.tni.org/drugs/folder3/smyth.htm

Snow, Edgar. *Roter Stern über China.* Frankfurt: Fischer, 1974. (Originally published in 1938 under the title *Red Star Over China*).

Soberón, Ricardo G. ¿Sueños de Opio en los Andes? In: *Quehacer.* 75, 1992.

———. El fracaso de la legislacíon represiva del narcotráfico. In: *Debate Agrario.* (Lima) 22, 1995.

Sörensen, Georg. A Revised Paradigm for International Relations. In: *Cooperation and Conflict.* XXVI, 1991.

Space and Tech. STRELA — Summary, 2003. Available at http://www.spaceandtech.com/ spacedata/elvs/strela_sum.shtml

Spedding, Alison L. The Coca Field as a Total Social Fact. In: *Coca, Cocaine, and the Bolivian Reality.* Edited by Madeline Léons, Barbara and Harry Sanabria. Albany, New York: State University of New York Press, 2000.

Stalin, Joseph V. *Fragen des Leninismus.* Moscow: Verlag für Fremdsprachige Literatur, 1947.

Stanley, William. *The Protection Racket State: Elite Politics, Military Extortion, and Civil War in El Salvador.* Philadelphia: Temple University Press, 1996.

Staples, Steven. The Relationship Between Globalization and Militarism. In: *Social Justice.* 27, 4, 2000.

Starn, Orin. Villagers at Arms: War and Counterrevolution in the Central-South Andes. In: *Shining And Other Paths.* Edited by Steve Stern. Durham, North Carolina: Duke University Press, 1998.

Stein, Werner. *Kulturfahrplan.* Vienna: Herbig, 1974.

Stepan, Alfred. *The State and Society: Peru in Comparative Perspective.* Princeton, New Jersey: Princeton University Press, 1978.

Stiglitz, Joseph E. *Globalization and its Discontents.* New York: Norton and Company, 2002.

Stille, Alexander. *Die Richter: Der Tod, die Mafia und die Italienische Republik.* Frankfurt: Fischer, 1999.

Stirk, Peter M. R. *Max Horkheimer: A New Interpretation.* Hempel Hempstead, England: Harvester Wheatsheaf, 1992.

Stokes, Doug. Better Lead than Bread? A Critical Analysis of the US's Plan Colombia. In: *Civil Wars.* 4, 2, 2001.

Strange, Susan. *The Retreat of the State.* Cambridge: Cambridge University Press, 1996.

Strong, Simon. *Shining Path: The World's Deadliest Revolutionary Force.* London: Harper Collins, 1992.

———. *Whitewash: Pablo Escobar and the Cocaine Wars.* London: Pan, 1996.

Sukup, Viktor. *Zeitbombe Südamerika.* Cologne, Germany: Pahl-Rugenstein, 1988.

Sully, Francois. *Age of the Guerrilla.* New York: Avon, 1968.

Sulston, John. The Rich World's Patents Abandon the Poor to Die. In: *Third World Resurgence.* 149/150, January–February 2003.

Sunkel, Osvaldo. Uneven Globalization, Economic Reform, and Democracy. In: *Whose World Order?: Uneven Globalization and the End of the Cold War.* Edited by Hans-Henrik Holm and Georg Sorensen. Boulder, Colorado: Westview, 1995.

Szulc, Tad. *Fidel: A Critical Portrait.* New York: Avon, 1987.

Tai Hsün-chih. *The Red Spears.* Ann Arbor, Michigan: University of Michigan: Centre for Chinese Studies, 1985.

Tanaka, Martín. *La situación de la democracía en Colombia, Perú y Venezuela a inicios de siglo.* Lima: Comisión Andina de Juristas, 2002.

Tapia, Carlos. La Subersión. In: *El Poder en el Perú.* Edited by Augusto Alvarez Rodrich. Lima: Editorial Apoyo, 1993. (Carlos Tapia is an author and expert on *Sendero*

Luminoso. He lives in Lima, Peru).

―――. Interview. Lima, August 1996.

Tarazona-Sevillano, Gabriela. *Sendero Luminoso and the Threat of Narcoterrorism*. New York: Praeger, 1990.

Tasca, Angelo. *The Rise of Italian Fascism 1918-1922*. New York: Howard Fertig, 1966.

Taxa Cuadros, Manuel. *Cocaína y narcotráfico*. Lima: Dieselpesa, 1987.

Taylor, Lewis. Patterns of Electoral Corruption in Peru: The April 2000 General Election. In: *Crime, Law and Social Change*. 34, 2000.

Tefft, Stanton K. *The Dialectics of Secret Society Power in States*. London: Humanities Press, 1992.

Tenbrock, Robert H., and Kurt Kluxen (Eds). *Zeiten und Menschen*, vol.1. Paderborn, Germany: Schöningh, 1976.

Ter Haar, Barend J. *Ritual and Mythology of the Chinese Triads: Creating an Identity*. Leiden, The Netherlands: Sinica Leidensia, 1998.

Thalheimer, August. *Über den Faschismus*. Berlin: Press of the German Communist Party, 1930. Reprinted in *Texte zur Faschismusdiskussion*, vol. I. Edited by Reinhard Kühnl. Hamburg: Rowohlt, 1974.

Thamm, Berndt Georg. *Stichwort Drogen*. Munich: Heyne, 1994.

―――. Drogenbekämpfung im 20. Jahrhundert. In: *HI*. 11. (Germany), 1994a.

―――. *Drachen bedrohen die Welt*. Hilden, Germany: VDP, 1996.

The Economist Intelligence Unit. *Quarterly Economic Review of Peru, Bolivia*. 1, 1983.

―――. *Country Profile: Russia*. 1996–1997.

The Transnational Institute (TNI). Coca, Cocaine and the International Conventions. *Drug Policy Briefing*. No. 5. April 2003. Available at http://www.tni.org/drugs/reports/brief5.htm

Thiess, Frank. *Tsushima*. Hamburg: Rowohlt, 1987.

'T Hoen, Ellen. Globalization and Equitable Access to Essential Drugs. In: *Third World Resurgence*. 120/121, August–September 2000.

Thomson, Janice E. *Mercenaries, Pirates, and Sovereigns*. Princeton, New Jersey: Princeton University Press, 1994.

Thoumi, Francisco E. *Political Economy and Illegal Drugs in Colombia*. Boulder, Colorado: Lynne Rienner, 1995.

Thucydides. *History of the Peloponnesian War*. Middlesex, England: Penguin, 1985.

Tilly, Charles. *Coercion, Capital, and European States, AD 990–1990*. Oxford: Blackwell, 1990.

―――. War Making and State Making as Organized Crime. In: *Bringing the State Back In*. Edited by Peter B. Evans, Dietrich Rueschemeyer, and Theda Skocpol. Cambridge, England: Cambridge University Press, 1993.

Timofeyev, Lev. *Russia's Secret Rulers*. New York: Alfred Knopf, 1992.

Toche, Eduardo. La izquierda que murió de melancolía. In: *Quehacer*. 153, 2005.

―――. Interview. Lima, June 2005.

Tuchman, Barbara. *Stilwell and the American Experience in China 1911–45*. New York: Bantam, 1972.

―――. *The March of Folly: From Troy to Vietnam*. New York: Alfred Knopf, 1984.

Turbiville, Graham H. Organized Crime and the Russian Armed Forces. In: *Transnational Organized Crime*. 1, 4, 1995.

Ugarteche, Oscar. Notas sobre la nueva corrupción económica en el Perú finisecular: desde la mafia, el mercantilismo y la teoría económica. In: *El pacto infame: estudios sobre la corrupción en el Perú*. Edited by Felipe Portocarrero S. Lima: Red para el desarrollo de las Ciencias Sociales en el Perú, 2005.

Ulfkotte, Udo. *Verschlußsache BND*. Munich: Koehler and Amelang, 1997.

Unanue, Hipolitó. *Sobre el aspecto, cultivo, comercio y virtudes de la famosa planta de Perú nombrada coca*. Dissertation. Lima: Mercurio Peruano, 1794. (I purchased a direct copy of the 1794 original. The copy itself has no date).

United Nations (UN) Commission for Europe. East-West Trade in Investment Goods, 1970–1987. In: *Economic Bulletin of Europe*. 41, 1989.

United Nations Office for Drug Control and Crime Prevention (UNODCCP). Global Illicit Drug Trends. ODCCP Studies on Drugs and Crime, 2002. Available at http:// www. odccp.org/

United Nations Office for Drug Control and Crime Prevention (UNODCCP). *Afghanistan Opium Survey 2002*. 2002a. Available at http://www.undcp.org/pdf/afg/afg_opium_survey_2002.pdf

United Nations Office for Drug Control and Crime Prevention (UNODCCP). *Annual Coca Cultivation Survey 2001*. 2002b. Available at http://www.undcp.org/pdf/peru/peru_cocasurvey_2001.pdf

United Nations Office on Drugs and Crime (UNODC). *Bolivia: Coca Survey in the Yungas of La Paz in 2002*. 2003. Available at http://www.undcp.org/pdf/bolivia/bolivia_coca-survey_2002.pdf

United States Department of Justice, Drug trafficking: A Report to the President of the United States. Washington, DC: US Government Printing Office, 1989.

United States (US) Senate Committee on Foreign Relations, Drugs, Law Enforcement and Foreign Policy. A Report Prepared by the Subcommittee on Terrorism, Narcotics and International Operations. Washington, DC: US Government Printing Office, 1989.

Vagg, Jon. Rough Seas: Contemporary Piracy in South East-Asia. In: *British Journal of Criminology*. 35, 1, 1994.

Van Crefeld, Martin. *The Transformation of War*. New York: Free Press, 1991.

Van der Pijl, Kees. The Second Glorious Revolution: Globalizing Elites and Historical Change. In: *International Political Economy: Understanding Global Disorder*. Edited by Björn Hettne. Halifax, Nova Scotia: Fernwood, 1995.

Vargas Meza, Ricardo. The FARC, the War and the Crisis of the State. In: *NACLA Report on the Americas*. XXXI, 5, 1998.

———. A Military-Paramilitary Alliance Besieges Colombia. In: *NACLA Report on the Americas*. XXXII, 3, 1998a.

Varese, Federico. *The Russian Mafia: Private Protection in a New Market Economy*. Oxford: Oxford University Press, 2001.

Vazquez Carrizosa, Alfredo. *El poder presidencial en Colombia*. Bogotá: Ediciones Suramerica, 1986.

Vega Vega, Juan. The International Crime of Usury: The Third World's Usurious Foreign Debt. In: *Crime and Social Justice*. 30, 1987.

Vitiello, Justin. The New World Order — From Fraud and Force to Business as Usual in the Global Free Market: The Up-to-Date Evidence. In: *Crime, Law and Social Change*. 17, 1992.

Volkov, Vadim. Violent Entrepreneurship in Post-Communist Russia. In: *Europe-Asia Studies*. 51, 5, 1999.

Von Bülow, Andreas. *Im Namen des Staates*. Munich: Piper, 1998.

Von Goethe, Johann Wolfgang. *Faust II*, Act V, in *Werke*, vol. 2. Munich: Winkler, 1972.

Von Hagen, Victor W. *Realm of the Incas.* New York: Mentor, 1957.

Von Lampe, Klaus. *Organized Crime: Begriff und Theorie Organisierter Kriminalität in den USA.* Frankfurt: Lang, 1999.

Wagenlehner, Günther. Ideologie und Macht in der Sowjetunion. In: *Osteuropa.* 28, 9, 1978.

Wagner, Patrick. *Volksgemeinschaft ohne Verbrecher: Konzeptionen und Praxis der Kriminalpolizei in der Zeit der Weimarer Republik und des Nationalsozialismus.* Hamburg: Christians Verlag, 1996.

Wakeman, Frederic E. *Policing Shanghai 1927–1937.* Berkeley: University of California Press, 1995.

———. *The Shanghai Badlands: Wartime Terrorism and Urban Crime, 1937–1941.* Cambridge: Cambridge University Press, 1996.

Waksberg, Arkadi. *Die Sowjetische Mafia.* Munich: Piper, 1992.

Waldmann, Peter, and Ulrich Zelinsky (Eds). *Politisches Lexikon Lateinamerika.* Munich: Beck, 1982.

Watson, Cynthia A. Political Violence in Colombia: Another Argentina? In: *Third World Quarterly.* 12, 3, 1991.

Wehrling, Thomas. Berlin is becoming a Whore (1920). In: *The Weimar Republic Source Book.* Edited by Anton Kaes et al. Berkeley: University of California Press, 1994.

Weiner, Robert. War by Other Means: Colombia's Faceless Courts. In: *NACLA Report on the Americas.* XXX, 2, 1996.

Weir, Carol. Costa Rica and the Drug Trade. In: *Drug Trafficking in the Americas.* Edited by Bruce M. Bagley and William O. Walker. Miami, Florida: North-South Center Press, 1996.

Wellard, James. *The French Foreign Legion.* Boston, Massachusetts: Little, Brown and Company, 1974.

Werner, David. Pushing Drugs in Free Market Economy. In: *Third World Resurgence.* 46, June 1994.

Wheatley, Margaret J. *Leadership and the New Science.* San Francisco: Berret-Kohler, 1992.

White, Randall. *Global Spin: Probing the Globalization Debate.* Toronto: Dundurn, 1995.

Wilber, Charles K., and Kenneth P. Jameson. Paradigms of Economic Development and Beyond. In: *The Political Economy of Development.* Edited by in C. K. Wilber. New York: Random House, 1988.

Williams, Phil, and Ernesto U. Savona. Problems and Dangers Posed by Organized Transnational Crime in the Various Regions of the World. In: *Transnational Organized Crime.* 1, 3, 1995.

Williamson, Peter J. *Corporatism in Perspective: An Introduction to Corporatist Theory.* London: Sage, 1989.

Wilson, Robert. The Confessions of Klaus Barbie. Vancouver: Pulp Press Book Publishers, 1984.

Winslow, E. M. *The Pattern of Imperialism.* New York: Columbia University Press, 1948.

Wisotsky, Steven. *Beyond the War on Drugs.* Buffalo, New York: Prometheus, 1990.

Wolkow, Wladimir. Ethnokratie — Ein verhängnisvolles Erbe in der post-kommunistischen Welt. In: *Aus Politik und Zeitgeschichte.* (Bonn), December 1991.

Wu, Tien-Wei. Chiang Kai-shek's April 12th Coup of 1927. In: *China in the 1920s.* Edited by F. Gilbert Chan and Thomas H. Etzold. New York: New Viewpoints, 1976.

Young, T. R. Paradigm Theory: Foundations of Postmodern Science, 1994. Available at http://www.tryoung.com/chaos/parad.htm 004

Zambrano Perez, Jesus. Del azadón al fusil. In: *El Tiempo*. Lecturas Dominicales. January 24, 1993: 8.

Zapata, Antonio. La corrupción bajo el fujimorismo. In: *El pacto infame: estudios sobre la corrupción en el Perú*. Edited by Felipe Portocarrero S. Lima: Red para el desarrollo de las ciencias sociales en el Perú, 2005.

Zelik, Raul, and Dario Azzelini. *Kolumbien: Große Geschäfte, Staatlicher Terror und Aufstandsbewegung*. Cologne, Germany: Neuer ISP Verlag, 2000.

Zile, Zigurds. Amnesty and Pardon in the Soviet Union. In: *Soviet Union/Union Soviétique*. 3, 1, 1976.

Dailies, Weeklies, and Internet Sources

British Broadcasting Corporation (BBC)

ELN says it wants new Colombian government to control paramilitary, June 5, 1998. Available at http://news.bbc.co.uk/2/hi/americas/130147.stm

Colombian troops 'withdrawn,' November 7, 1998. Available at http://news.bbc.co.uk/ 2/hi/americas/209521.stm

Colombian peace negotiations to start Saturday, January 8, 1999. Available at http://news.bbc.co.uk/2/hi/americas/250904.stm

Violence overshadows Colombian peace talks, January 8, 1999a. Available at http://news.bbc.co.uk/2/hi/americas/250672.stm

Bias accusation in Colombia peace bid, January 19, 1999. Available at http://news.bbc.co.uk/2/hi/americas/258502.stm

Colombia unveils elite anti-drugs unit, September 13, 1999. Available at http://news.bbc.co.uk/2/hi/americas/446504.stm

Colombia unveils elite anti-rebel force, December 8, 1999. Available at http://news.bbc.co.uk/2/hi/americas/554990.stm

Military-paramilitary links persist in Colombia, February 23, 2000. Available at http://news.bbc.uk./2/hi/americas/653989.stm

Colombian paramilitary chief defends massacres, March 2, 2000. Available at http://news.bbc.uk./2/hi/americas/663386.stm

Colombian rebels refuse to meet paramilitaries, March 3, 2000. Available at http://news.bbc.uk./2/hi/americas/662133.stm

Colombian rebels to get safe haven, April 25, 2000. Available at http://news.bbc.uk./2/hi/americas/725154.stm

Chavez promises revolutionary change, August 1, 2000. Available at http://news.bbc.co.uk/2/hi/americas/860623.stm

Colombia changes tactics in drugs war, August 31, 2000. Available at http://news.bbc.co.uk/2/hi/americas/891289.stm

Two former Popes beatified, September 3, 2000. Available from http://news.bbc.co.uk/2/hi/europe/908433.stm

Peru set to be drug leader, February 17, 2001. Available from http://news.bbc.co.uk/2/hi/world/americas/1176452.stm

Colombian general's 'cartel' bombshell, April 5, 2001. Available at http://news.bbc.co.uk/2/hi/americas/1261443.stm

Twenty reported dead in Colombian clashes, April 30, 2001. Available at http://news.bbc.co.uk/2/hi/americas/1304587.stm

Colombian rebels 'stronger than ever,' May 28, 2001. Available at http://news.

bc.uk./2/hi/americas/1355513.stm

Colombians puzzled by IRA 'bomb theory,' August 19, 2001. Available at http://news.
bc.uk./2/hi/americas/1498935.stm

Q&A: Why is Colombia so violent?, January 4, 2002. Available at http://news.
bc.co.uk/2/hi/americas/1738963.stm

Colombia's peace process collapses, January 13, 2002. Available at http://news.
bc.uk./2/hi/americas/1757634.stm

Peace talks collapse in Colombia, June 1, 2002. Available at http://news.
bbc.uk./2/hi/americas/2019808.stm

Peru makes huge drugs haul, June 11, 2002. Available from http://news.
bbc.co.uk/2/hi/world/americas/2039043.stm

Colombian president declares emergency, August 12, 2002. Available at http://news.
bbc.co.uk/2/hi/americas/2187654.stm

Coffee slump fuels Peru's coca bonanza, September 18, 2002. Available at http://news.
bbc.co.uk/2/hi/americas/2266657.stm

Colombia creates security zones, September 22, 2002. Available at http://news.
bbc.co.uk/2/hi/americas/2273680.stm

Colombia in talks with paramilitaries, November 25, 2002. Available at http://news.
bbc.co.uk/2/hi/americas/2510051.stm

Analysis: Latin America's left shift, November 25, 2002a. Available at http://news.
bbc.co.uk/2/hi/americas/2510285.stm

Colombian rebel attack kills 60, December 28, 2002. Available at http://news.
bbc.co.uk/2/hi/americas/2610701.stm

Brazilians hail new president, January 2, 2003. Available at http://news.
bbc.co.uk/2/hi/americas/2618783.stm

Leftist takes office in Ecuador, January 15, 2003. Available at http://news.
bbc.co.uk/2/hi/americas/2662009.stm

Diplomat testifies in Colombia, April 10, 2003. Available at http://news.
bbc.co.uk/2/hi/uk_news/northern_ireland/2937837.stm

Colombia tapes to be examined, April 12, 2003. Available at http://news.
bbc.co.uk/2/hi/uk_news/northern_ireland/2941795.stm

Peru's coca farmers stage protest, April 22, 2003. Available at http://news.
bbc.co.uk/2/hi/business/2965423.stm

Colombia murder rate soars, April 24, 2003. Available at http://news.
bbc.co.uk/2/hi/americas/2971779.stm

Cable News Network CNN (United States)

Colombian paramilitary chief admits getting backing from businessmen, September 6, 2000.
Available at http://www.cnn.com/2000/WORLD/americas/09/06/colombia.
paramilitary.reut/

Cambio 16 (Latin American edition)

Año nuevo bajo las balas, December 18, 1993: 6–10.
Apoyaremos las autodefensas, December 23, 1996: 14–15.

Canadian Broadcasting Corporation (CBC)

Go-pills, bombs & friendly fire, March 19, 2003. Available at http://www.cbc.ca/
news/indepth/cdn_casualties/

Caretas (Lima, Peru)
Hablando a calzón quitado, October 29, 1990: 13.
Señal de guerra, July 8, 1991: 28–29.
Dedo en la llaga, November 28, 1996: 10–14.

Correo (Lima)
Las FARC y ejército colombiano usan civilies como escudos humanos, April 30, 2005: 17.

Der Spiegel (Hamburg, Germany)
Dreckiges Geld, Saubere Helfer, February 24, 1992: 141–142.
Revolver in der Hand, June 19, 1995: 128–129.
Piraterie: Angst vor Ölpest, June 7, 1999: 173.

Die Woche (Hamburg)
Die Moskau-Connection, July 15, 1993: 16.
Der Mob, der aus der Kälte kam, May 11, 1994: 22.

El Caribe (Dominican Republic)
Uribe insiste en negociar el canje de prisioneros, December 20, 2004: 52.

El Comercio (Lima)
Muy extraños muertes . . . . , November 24, 1994: A16.
Narco afirma que puede ubicar la casa de San Borja, August 21, 1996: A14.
Hasta ahora no me explicó las razones de mi cambio, August 29, 1996: A21.
Aislado en el Real Felipe, October 14, 1996: A16.
Testigo dice que entregó dos toneladas de droga a Zevallos, May 18, 1997: A17.
Narcos de Perú operan en México desde 1980, July 13, 1997: A1.
La meta del Plan Patriota es traer a las guerrillas de las FARC a la mesa, June 26, 2004: A22.
Patrullas de Satipo arrinconan a los senderistas en Vizcatán. May 10, 2005: A11.
Ex ministro implicado en asesinato. May 14, 2005: A20.
Traficantes del Perú implicados en caso de gigantesco alijo de cocaína, May 24, 2005: A13.
Las Farc siguen atacando con violencia a los poblados indígenas, May 29, 2005: A32.

El Espectador (Bogotá)
450 investigaciones por auxilio a la guerrilla, November 10, 1992: 11A.
Las arcas de la narcoguerrilla, December 13, 1992: 6A.

El País (Cali, Colombia)
La vida no vale nada, November 22, 1992: C10.

El País (Madrid, Spain)
Pastrana, obligado a dar un giro al proceso de paz de Colombia, May 30, 1999: 8.

El Peruano (Lima)
Confirman orden de captura a ex general Eduardo Bellido Mora, January 4, 2003.
Available at http://www.editoraperu.com.pe/edc/03/01/04/soc6.asp

El Siglo (Bogotá)
El Siglo. August 18, 1989: 1; as cited in Duque Gómez 1991: 208.

El Sol (Lima)
Democracia significa mejores oportunidades de vida, June 15, 1997: 11. (Speech by
    former Peruvian President Alberto Fujimori–Sunday Supplement)
¡Liberados! June 16, 1997: C1.
Sólo les falta aviación y tanques, June 16, 1997a: C1.
En barcos mercantes iba la droga hacia Europa, August 2, 1997: 8A.
Ríos Araico dice que lo accusan por venganza politíca, September 28, 1996: A6.

El Tiempo (Bogotá)
Dinamitados dos oleoductos, October 24, 1992: 10A.
Dictadura en estados de excepción, November 7, 1992: 5A.
La otra estrategia contra la subversión, November 15, 1992: 3A.
Capturado en Cali el Pablo Escobar de Perú, January 14, 1994: 3A.

Focus (Munich, Germany)
Deutschland im Visier, January 25, 1993: 44.
Alptraum Mafia-City, May 6, 1996: 52–64.

Frankfurter Rundschau (Frankfurt a. M., Germany)
Plutonium vom Schwarzen Markt, July 14, 1993: 1.
Der Drogenzar ist tot, das Geschäft blüht, December 4, 1993: 3.
Koka-Plantagen verdoppelt, April 13, 1994: 30.

Gestión (Lima)
Los galones del narcotráfico, August 25, 1996: 15.

Houston Chronicle (Houston, Texas)
Is the FARC a drug cartel? August 3, 2001. Available at http://www.chron.com/cs/ CDA/
    printstory.hts/special/rebelheld/986501

La Nación (Bogotá)
January 1, 1886: 1, as cited in Arango and Child 1987: 102–103.

La República (Lima)
Utilizaron mil kilos de dinamita, December 11, 1989: 21.
Matan a dirigente de cocaleros que respaldó a convenio antidroga, July 7, 1991: 3.
Vaticano y Colocho Juan se reparten la selva, January 27, 1992: 14–15.
Hernando de Soto renuncia como asesor del Presidente Fujimori, January 29, 1992: 8.
Droga corrompe a soldados y subversivos, January 31, 1992: 13–14.
Identifican a militares corrompidos por narcos, February 29, 1992: 14–15.
Hernando de Soto asegura que la subversión puede triunfar, March 21, 1992: 2.
Declararon en emergencia los aeropuertos de zona cocalera, April 10, 1992: 4.
Si, hay militares en caso Vaticano, June 27, 1994: 17–19.
Amenazan asesinar a la esposa de General Robles, July 27, 1994: 2.
Piden 15 años de carcel para 10 oficiales y dos subalternos del ejército, June 24, 1995: 4.

25 mil ronderos armados defienden cocales en valles de Apurímac y Ene, August 13, 1995: 2.

Vaticano niega todo y dice que combatió a terroristas, June 26, 1996: 3.

Suzy Díaz defiende a narco Vaticano y plantea que revisan su sentencia, August 6, 1996: 10.

Oposición pide al congreso se investigue a Montesinos, August 20, 1996: 6.

Colaboradores del SIN ligados al narcotráfico, August 23, 1996: 17.

Lavado de dinero se extiende a toda la economía Peruana, August 25, 1996: 24A.

Vaticano y militares mataron a periodista por revelar a mafia, August 30, 1996: 16–17.

Todo traficante debía negociar con el Ejército, August 31, 1996: 16–17.

El juicio del descaro, September 22, 1996: 20–22.

Los lazos de la conexión, September 22, 1996a: 2.

Solicitan a la Interpol búsqueda de empresario Zevallo, May 14, 1997: 7A.

General Saucedo niega que haya el Plan Narval, June 25, 1997: 15.

Autoridades corruptas liberaron dos veces a 'El Ministro' en Peru, August 12, 1997: 8.

Revocan fallo en favor de ex agente La Rosa y defensor acudirá al TC, August 12, 1997a: 13.

Muertos documentados: 24,692 no documentados: más de 60 mil, August 26, 2003: 8.

La verdad es el principio de la justicia, August 29, 2003: 9.

Revelan que tropas colombianas han ingresado al Perú desde enero pasado. June 13, 2004: 10.

Afirman que 'Tirofijo' ya no es jefe de las FARC, June 13, 2004: 33.

Coca ilegal produjo US$ 112 millones, June 18, 2004: 10.

SL reaparece con nuevas armas, June 25, 2004: 2.

Visita de Rice a Colombia coincide con 'razzia' militar, April 28, 2005: 24.

Alemania no entrega al piloto que descargó las armas para las FARC, May 1, 2005: 10.

Marines proveían de armas a paramilitares, May 5, 2005: 27.

Aumentan las críticas en EEUU por los gastos del Plan Colombia, May 5, 2005: 37.

Capturan a ex senador por crimen de candidato liberal Carlos Galán, May 13, 2005: 27.

Cocaleros y papers se unirían en paro nacional, May 14, 2005: 8.

"Pablo, mátalo. Si Galán es presidente te extradita," May 15, 2005: 36.

Cinco afghanos muertos tras emboscada en Kabul, May 19, 2005: 26.

Se disparan los cultivos de amapola a 2 mil hectáreas, May 20, 2005: 8.

Mafia colombiana distribuye semillas de amapola en Perú, May 21, 2005: 21.

El repunte de la coca en el Monzón, May 23, 2005: 8.

Latin American Weekly Report

International outcry against military seizure of power in Bolivia, July 25, 1980: 1–2.

MAS report raises storm, February 11, 1983: 5.

Two victories for Betancur, April 6, 1984: 4–5.

Holdouts threaten guerrilla peace, September 7, 1984: 5.

Congress to vote on formal amnesty, May 24, 1985: 8.

Tirofijo's debut is obstructed, July 19, 1985: 4.

Siege report queried by attorney-general, July 3, 1986: 3.

Colombian Self-Defense: Legal Basis, August 13, 1987: 6.

Death squads total 140, says report, October 15, 1987: 8.

Drug money in real estate, December 8, 1988: 12.

Rural property is targeted by narcos, December 15, 1988: 10–11.

Talks get started with M-19, January 19, 1989: 8.
Guerrillas extend their influence, March 2, 1989: 4.
MRTA: A group riven by dissent, March 2, 1989a: 4.
M-19 peace deal enters Phase II, August 3, 1989: 4.
New party for the extreme right, August 24, 1989: 9.
Castro publishes the Ochoa story, September 21, 1989: 3.
It may be premature to bury bipartisan politics in Colombia, December 20, 1990: 1.
Two steps forward, one step back, February 21, 1991: 3.
Going public on defense spending, March 7, 1991: 2.
Fujimori gives way on agreements, March 28, 1991: 4.
Fujimori to 'privatize' war by arming urban self-defense groups, March 5, 1992: 1.
Major successes in counterinsurgency, June 25, 1992: 2.
ELN dissidents sue again for peace, April 1, 1993: 146.
General denounces army 'hit squad,' May 30, 1993: 22.
Urabá killings raise election fears, February 3, 1994: 38.
Two-party system remains on top, March 24, 1994: 13.

Moscow News (Moscow)
Rußland ohne Ikonen. (German-language edition), September 1992: 12.
Is there a Nuclear Mafia? (English-language edition), October. 21–27, 1994: 3.
Murdered journalist speaks out, October 21–27, 1994: 2.
Who's Behind Kholodov's Assassination? October 28–November 3, 1994: 1.

Oiga (Lima)
Fujimori no tenía programa, May 28, 1990: 30–34.
¿Donde está la coca de Java? April 22, 1991: 43–45.
Revolución en el Huallaga, September 16, 1991: 39–42.
El show de Vaticano, January 24, 1994: 18–22.
En el país de la inmoralidad, February 14, 1994: 35.
Narcotráfico en salsa 'china,' May 30, 1994: 14–16.
Porque somos narcoestado, May 30, 1994: 16–17.
Creciente malestar en el ejército, May 30, 1994: 22.

Resistencia (Colombia)
Conflicto interno y narcotráfico. *Resistencia.* 18, 1998. Available at the FARC-EP
    website: http://burn.ucsd.edu/~farc-ep/RevistaR/ Resistencia18/ frames. html
    (Visited January 15, 2000)

RTÉ News (Ireland)
Video casts doubt on Colombia prosecution, February 17, 2003. Available at http://
    eurovision.ie/news/2003/0217/colombia.html

Semana (Bogotá)
January 30–February 6, 1990: 30 No. 404. as cited in Duque Gómez 1991: 214.
El madrugón del gobierno, January 9–16, 1996: 18–21.
El dedo en la llaga, January 14–21, 1997: 24–25.
Esto fue un circo con muchos payasos reunidos. Interview with Colombian General
    Harold Bedoya, June 16–23, 1997. Available at http://www.semana.com.co/

users/semana/ jun16/entrevista.htm

Sí (Lima)

Del campo a la ciudad, June 12, 1989: 30–34.
Foco terrorista, July 12, 1989: 18–21.
Estos son los capos, November 21, 1994: 26.

The Economist (London, England)

Guerrilla Economics, January 13, 1996: 40.
A crop that refuses to die, March 4, 2000: 25.

The Globe and Mail (Canada)

Former elite prospers in Russia, September 17, 1994: A1.
Moscow Police play catch-up with criminals, October 3, 1994: A6.
Free trade benefitting Colombian drug cartels, January 16, 1996: A9.
Drug trade infiltrates all Latin America, February 10, 1996: D4.
Latin America rate of killing rising in Colombia, May 5, 1998: A12.
Colombians lose farms to paramilitary, May 30, 1998: A12.
Warring Colombian groups say they're ready to make peace, August 1, 1998: A8.
Crime permeates far reaches of society, November 28, 1998: A12.
The mysterious 'family' that keeps Yeltsin in power, June 15, 1999: A1.
Peru captures Shining Path leader in Andes, July 15, 1999: A11.
Colombian rebels impose law of the gun, July 19, 1999: A11.
Falun Gong challenging Beijing's rule again, October 28, 1999: A11.
Chinese officials declare Falun Gong dangerous cult, November 1, 1999: A13.
China cocks the trigger of rebellion, November 3, 1999: A19.
Pastrana and rebels wrangle over peace, January 17, 2002: A14.
Trial begins for Peru's "most corrupt public official," February 19, 2003: A23.

The Guardian (Manchester, England)

Coca-Cola sued over bottling plant 'terror campaign,' July 21, 2001. Available at http:// www.guardian.co.uk/Archive/Article/0,4273,4225809,00.html

The Irish Times (Dublin, Ireland)

'Necklace bomb' nearly closed down peace process, May 22, 2000. Available at http:// www.colombiasupport.net/200005/irishtimes-carrigan-0522.html

The Miami Herald (Miami, Florida)

Private armies control much of rural Colombia, July 18, 1990: 4A.

The New Internationalist NI (London, England)

Humpty Dumpty, the Scriptwriter and the Little Bean, July 1989: 24–25.

The New York Times (United States)

Plight. . . . is pitiable, May 4, 1927; as cited in Seagrave 1985: 234–235.

Third World Resurgence (Penang, Malaysia)

Poverty linked to cholera epidemic, says WHO, June 1991: 7.

Time Magazine (United States)
Heat on the Mob, June 3, 1996: 21–23.

The Toronto Star (Toronto, Canada)
$37-Billion-a-year cash crop brings killings, corruption, March 22, 1997: A1.
Canadian warns against 'hysteria' in war on drugs, June 11, 1998: A15.

Index

About the Author

Alfredo Schulte-Bockholt (Ph.D., Carleton University, Ottawa, Canada, 2000) is Associate Professor at the Department of Criminology and Sociology at St. Mary's University in Halifax, Nova Scotia. He teaches courses on organized and state crime as well as crime in developing countries. His present research focuses on the linkages between criminal organizations and elite structures in Latin America in the age of globalization.